COLLECTED WHEEL PUBLICATIONS

VOLUME 6

NUMBERS 76 – 89

BPE

BPS Pariyatti Editions

BPS Pariyatti Editions
An imprint of Pariyatti Publishing
www.pariyatti.org

Although this is an American edition, we have left any British spelling of words unchanged.

First BPS Pariyatti Edition, 2020
ISBN: 978-1-68172-144-6 (Print)
ISBN: 978-1-68172-145-3 (PDF)
ISBN: 978-1-68172-146-0 (ePub)
ISBN: 978-1-68172-147-7 (Mobi)
LCCN: 2018940050

Contents

WH 76 The Threefold Refuge
Nyanaponika Thera 1

WH 77 & 78 Essays and Poems
Dr. Paul Dahlke 23

WH 79 The Kandaraka and Potaliya Suttas
Nārada Thera, Mahinda Bhikkhu 75

WH 80 & 81 Dialogues on the Dhamma
Francis Story 101

WH 82 The Discourse Collection
John D. Ireland 171

WH 83 & 84 With Robes and Bowl
Bhikkhu Khantipālo 201

WH 85 & 86 Buddhism in Thailand
Karuna Kusalasaya 261

WH 87 The Greater Discourse on Voidness
Ñāṇamoli Thera 287

WH 88 & 89 Buddhist Meditation and Depth Psychology
Douglas M. Burns 313

Key to Abbreviations

A	Aṅguttara Nikāya	Paṭis	Paṭisambhidamagga
Ap	Apadāna	Peṭ	Peṭakopadesa
Bv	Buddhavaṃsa	S	Saṃyutta Nikāya
Cp	Cariyāpiṭaka	Sn	Suttanipāta
D	Dīgha Nikāya	Th	Theragātha
Dhp	Dhammapada	Thī	Therigātha
Dhs	Dhammasaṅgaṇī	Ud	Udāna
It	Itivuttaka	Vibh	Vibhaṅga
Ja	Jātaka verses and commentary	Vin	Vinaya-piṭaka
Khp	Khuddakapāṭha	Vism	Visuddhimagga
M	Majjhima Nikāya	Vism-mhṭ	Visuddhimagga Sub-commentary
Mil	Milindapañha	Vv	Vimānavatthu
Nett	Nettipakaraṇa	Nidd	Niddesa

The above is the abbreviation scheme of the Pali Text Society (PTS) as given in the *Dictionary of Pali* by Margaret Cone.

The commentaries, *aṭṭhakathā*, are abbreviated by using a hyphen and an "a" ("-a") following the abbreviation of the text, e.g., *Dīgha Nikāya Aṭṭhakathā* = D-a. Likewise the sub-commentaries are abbreviated by a "ṭ" ("-ṭ") following the abbreviation of the text.

The sutta reference abbreviation system for the four Nikāyas, as is used in Bhikkhu Bodhi's translations is:

AN	Aṅguttara Nikāya	DN	Dīgha Nikāya
MN	Majjhima Nikāya	Sn	Saṃyutta Nikāya
J	Jātaka story	Mv	Mahāvagga (Vinaya Piṭaka)
Cv	Cullavagga (Vinaya Piṭaka)	SVibh	Suttavibhaṅga (Vinaya Piṭaka)

The Threefold Refuge

by

Nyanaponika Thera

WHEEL PUBLICATION NO. 76

I. Buddhaghosa's Exposition

Translated from the Commentary to the "Middle Collection" (Commentary on the Bhayabherava Sutta, MN 4).

After listening to the Buddha's Discourse called "Fear and Dread," the Brahman Jānussoni becomes a lay follower of the Buddha by taking the Threefold Refuge. The words used by him differ slightly from the usual formula in so far as in the latter the words "the Lord Gotama" are replaced by "the Buddha." Buddhaghosa's comment, here slightly abridged, runs as follows:

"I go for refuge to the Lord Gotama" (*Bhavantaṃ Gotamaṃ saraṇaṃ gacchāmi*). This means: The Lord Gotama is my refuge and my guiding ideal.[1] I am going for refuge to the Lord Gotama. I resort to him, follow and honor him, in the sense of his being the Destroyer of Affliction and the Provider of Weal. Or: I know and understand him to be of such a nature.

This last explanation is based upon the fact that in the Pali language the verbal roots denoting "going" (*gati*) may also have the meaning of "knowing" (*buddhi*). Therefore the words "I go for refuge to the Buddha" may also be taken to express the idea: "I know and understand him to be the refuge."

"I go for refuge to the Dhamma." The word *dhamma*, i.e., the Doctrine or the Law, is derived from the verb *dhāreti* (from the root dhar), to keep or to bear. In accordance with that derivation, the Dhamma may be regarded as refuge, because it keeps, upholds and supports the beings by way of preventing their fall into the states of woe[2] by way of enabling a life according to instruction (as given by the Dhamma), by way of attainment of the Path, and by realisation of the extinction (of suffering). Accordingly, the Dhamma (meant in the formula of refuge) is the (supramundane) Noble Path as well as Nibbāna. Besides, it is the attainment of the noble fruitions (of the stream-enterer, the once-returner, the non-returner, and the saint), and also the Dhamma of Learning (laid down in the Scriptures: *pariyatti-dhamma*).

---

1. See note 6.
2. I.e., rebirth as animal, ghost, Titan, or in hell.

"I go for refuge to the Sangha." The Sangha is (here) the community of (holy) monks which is united by the communion of right view and virtue (*diṭṭhi-sīla-saṅghāṭena saṃhato' ti saṅgho*).

That is to say: the Sangha (meant in the formula of refuge) is the group of the eight noble beings (*ariya-puggala*: those in possession of 1) the path of stream-entry, 2) the fruition thereof, etc.).

In order to gain proficiency with regard to this subject of "refuge," one should be acquainted with the following method of exposition, dealing with 1) the word *saraṇa*; 2) the going for refuge (*saraṇāgamana*); 3) Who is going for refuge?; 4) the divisions; 5) the results; 6) the defilements; 7) the breach.

(1) As to the meaning of the word *saraṇa*, the commentator relates it, not in the sense of a linguistic derivation, but for the purpose of exposition, to the verb *sarati*, "to crush," having the same meaning as *hiṃsati*, "to kill." The refuge is explained in that way, because, for those who are taking that refuge, it kills and destroys danger and fear, suffering, and the defilements leading to evil destiny. The refuge is a name of the Triple Gem. Another explanation: The Buddha destroys fear in beings by promoting their happiness and by removing harm from them. The Dhamma does it by making the beings cross the wilderness of existence and by giving them solace. The Sangha does it by (enabling devotees) to obtain rich results even from small religious acts (like homage, offerings, etc.).

(2) The going for (or taking) refuge is a state of mind in which defilements are destroyed owing to the faith in and veneration for the Triple Gem; a state of mind which, without relying on others (*apara-paccayo*[3]), *proceeds by way of taking the Triple Gem as its guiding ideal* (*parāyaṇa*).

(3) Who is going for refuge? It is a being endowed with a state of mind as described above.

(4) The going for refuge has two main divisions: it may be mundane or supramundane.

The supramundane refuge is taken by those who have a (true) vision of the Noble Truth (*diṭṭha-sacca*; i.e., by the eight noble beings). In the path-moment (of stream-entry, where any trace of the fetter of doubt has been removed), the supramundane refuge

3. Addition in the *Paramatthajotika*, the commentary to Khuddakapāṭha.

succeeds in exterminating any blemish that may still attach to the going for refuge. It has Nibbāna as its object, and in its function it comprises the entire Triple Gem (in that object of Nibbāna).

The mundane refuge is taken by worldlings (*puthujjanas*; i.e., all those, monks or laymen, who are still outside of the four stages of sanctity). It succeeds in effecting a temporary repression of the blemishes attaching to their going for refuge. Its objects are the noble qualities of the Buddha, Dhamma and Sangha. It consists in the acquisition of faith (*saddhā*) in these three objects. It is this faith in the Triple Gem that is referred to when, among the ten meritorious acts (*puññakiriyavatthu*), the "straightening of views" (*diṭṭhujjukamma*) is defined as Right Understanding rooted in faith (*saddhāmūlika-sammā-diṭṭhi*).

This mundane refuge is of four kinds: (a) the surrender of self (*atta-sanniyyātana*); (b) the acceptance (of the Triple Gem) as one's guiding ideal (*tapparāyaṇatā*); (c) the acceptance of discipleship (*sissabhāvūpāgamana*); (d) homage by prostration (*paṇipāta*).[4]

a. The surrender of self [5] is expressed as follows:

"From today onward I surrender myself to the Buddha ... to the Dhamma ... to the Sangha."

Ajja ādiṃ katvā ahaṃ attānaṃ Buddhassa niyyādemi Dhammassa Saṅghassā 'ti.

This is the giving over of one's self to the Triple Gem. It may also be done in this way:

"To the Exalted One I am giving my self, to the Dhamma I am giving my self, to the Sangha I am giving my self. I am giving them my life! Given is my self, given my life! Until my life ends, I am taking refuge in the Buddha! The Buddha is my refuge, my shelter, and my protection."

Bhagavato attānaṃ pariccajāmi. Dhammassa Saṅghassa attānaṃ pariccajāmi, jīvitañca pariccajāmi. Pariccatto yeva me attā, pariccattaṃ yeva me jīvitaṃ. Jīvita-pariyantikaṃ Buddhaṃ saraṇaṃ gacchāmi. Buddho me saraṇaṃ leṇaṃ tānan'ti.

---

4. In the following passage the sequence of the text has been partly changed.

5. "Performed, e.g., by those devoting themselves to a subject of meditation" (addition in *Paramatthajotika*).

b. The acceptance of the guiding ideal.[6]

"From today onward the Buddha is my Guiding Ideal, the Dhamma, and the Sangha. Thus may you know me!"

Ajja ādiṃ katvā ahaṃ Buddhaparāyaṇo Dhammaparāyaṇo Saṅghaparāyaṇo. Iti maṃ dhāretha.

It is illustrated by the following verse spoken by Āỳavaka:

"From village to village, from town to town I'll wend my way, lauding the Enlightened One and the perfection of His Law" (Sn 1.10 [v. 192]).

Thus the acceptance of the guiding ideal by Āỳavaka and others has to be understood as equaling their going for refuge.

c. The acceptance of discipleship:

"From today onward I am the Disciple of the Buddha, the Dhamma and the Sangha. Thus may you know me!"

Ajja ādiṃ katvā ahaṃ Buddhassa antevāsiko Dhammassa Saṅghassa. Iti maṃ dhāretha.

This is illustrated by the following passage expressing Kassapa's acceptance of discipleship that has to be understood as equaling his going for refuge:

"Fain would I see the Master, the Exalted One, him I would wish to see! Fain would I see the Blessed One! The Exalted One, him would I wish to see! Fain would I see the Enlightened One! The Exalted One, him I would wish to see!

"Then I prostrated myself before the Exalted One and addressed him thus: The Exalted One, O Lord, is my Master, and I am his disciple!" (SN 16:11/S II 220)

d. Homage by prostration:[7]

"From today onward I shall give respectful greeting, devoted attendance, the *añjali*-salutation (by joining the palms and raising

---

6. *Parāyaṇa* is, in ordinary usage, a synonym of *saraṇa*, having the meaning of resort, support, etc. Here when denoting a particularly distinguished way of taking refuge, it is probably intended to be taken in a strict sense, as often used in religious literature, Pali as well as Sanskrit: the going to the highest, the way to the beyond, the chief or best aim; the essence. We have therefore ventured upon the above free rendering by "guiding ideal."

7. In the *Paramatthajotika* this mode of refuge is called *tappoṇatā*, the proclivity, inclination, or devotion to it, i.e., to the Triple Gem.

the hands) and homage only to those three: the Buddha, the Dhamma and the Sangha. Thus may you know me!"

Ajja ādiṃ katvā ahaṃ abhivādana-paccuṭṭhāna-añjalikamma-sāmīcikammaṃ Buddhādīnaṃ yeva tiṇṇaṃ vatthūnaṃ karomi. Itī maṃ dhāretha.

This way of going for refuge consists in showing deep humility towards the Buddha, the Dhamma and the Sangha. (It is illustrated by the Brahman Brahmāyu's homage after his being deeply stirred by a stanza spoken by the Buddha. See the Discourse "*Brahmāyu*," MN 91.)

Homage by prostration may be of four kinds: being paid towards (senior) relatives, out of fear, towards one's teacher, and towards those deserving highest veneration. Only the latter case—i.e., the prostration before those worthy of highest veneration—is to be regarded as "going for refuge"; the three other cases do not count as such. Only if referring to the highest (in one's scale of values), refuge is taken or broken, respectively.

Therefore if a member of the Sakya or Koliya clan worships the Buddha, thinking: "He is our relative," no refuge is taken in that case. Or, one may think: "The recluse Gotama is honored by kings and has great influence. If he is not worshipped, he might do me harm." If, thinking thus, one worships out of fear, no refuge is taken in that case. Furthermore, a person remembers to have learned something from the Blessed One while he was a Bodhisatta, an aspirant to Buddhahood; or, after his attaining Buddhahood, one has received from the Master advice relating to worldly knowledge. If for these reasons, one regards the Buddha as one's teacher and worships him, no refuge is taken in that case too. But if one pays worship to the Buddha in the conviction "This is the most venerable being in the world," only by such a one is refuge taken.

On the other hand, the going for refuge remains unbroken in the following situations. A male or female lay devotee who has taken refuge in the Triple Gem, worships a (senior) relative, thinking: "He is my kinsman." Even if that relative is a recluse of another faith, the refuge in the Triple Gem is unbroken; still less can it be said to be broken if it is not a recluse or a priest. When prostrating before a king, out of fear: "If he who is honored by the whole country is not worshipped, he will do me harm!"—in that case too the refuge is unbroken. If one has learned any science, art, or craft even from a non-Buddhist, and one worships him in his capacity as one's teacher, in that case too the refuge remains unbroken.

(5) **Results.** The fruit of the supramundane refuge, in the sense of being its karmic result (*vipāka-phala*), is the four fruitions of monkhood (*sāmañña-phala*), viz. the fruition of stream-entry, etc. The fruit in the sense of advantage or blessing (*ānisaṃsa-phala*) is the destruction of suffering; further, the blessings mentioned in the following scriptural passage:

"It is impossible, O monks, that a person endowed with insight (*diṭṭhi-sampanno*—i.e., stream-enterer, etc.) should regard any conditioned thing as permanent, enjoyable, or an ego; that he should take the life of his mother, his father, or a saint; that, with a thought of hate, he should shed the blood of the Blessed One; that he should cause a split in the community of monks; that he should choose another teacher. There is no possibility of that." (A I 26)

But the fruit of the mundane refuge is only the attainment of favorable rebirth and the attainment of property and enjoyment.

(6) **Defilements.** In three cases the mundane refuge is defiled and without great brightness and radiating influence: if connected with ignorance, doubt and wrong views. The supramundane refuge is free from any defilements.

(7) A **breach** of the mundane refuge might be blameable or blameless. It is blameable when occurring as a going for refuge by self-surrender, etc., to other religious masters: in that case the breach will have undesirable results. The breach is blameless at the time of death, as it will not cause any karmic result. The supramundane refuge is without breach. Even in another existence a holy disciple will not turn to another master.

The Threefold Refuge

In all Buddhist lands the followers of the Buddha profess their allegiance to him and his liberating doctrine by the ancient, simple, and yet so touching formula of *going for refuge* to the Triple Gem: the Buddha, the Dhamma and the Sangha.

The "going for refuge," as this figurative expression itself suggests, should be a conscious act, not the mere profession of a theoretical belief or a habitual rite of traditional piety. The protecting refuge *exists,* but we have to go to it by our own effort. It will not come to us by itself, while we stay put. The Buddha, as he repeatedly declared, is only the teacher, "pointing out the way." Therefore, the going for refuge, expressive of Buddhist faith (*saddhā*), is in the first place a conscious act of *will* and determination directed towards the goal of liberation. Hereby the conception of faith as a mere passive waiting for "saving grace" is rejected.

In the Pali commentaries there is a remarkable statement that the expression "going for refuge" is meant to convey, in addition, the idea of "knowing" and "understanding." This points to the second aspect of going for refuge—namely as a conscious act of *understanding*. Hereby unthinking credulity and blind faith based on external authority are rejected.

The commentator emphasises this aspect by describing the going for refuge as a state of mind that does not rely on others (*aparapaccaya*). On many occasions the Master warned his disciples not to accept teachings out of mere trust in him, but only after personal experience, practise, and reflection. Here it may suffice to recall the famous sermon to the Kālāmas: "Do not go by hearsay, nor by tradition, nor by people's tales, nor by the authority of scriptures. Do not go by reasoning, nor by logic and methodical investigations, nor by approval of speculative views, nor moved by reverence, nor by the thought: 'The recluse is my teacher!'" (AN 3:65).

It is a threefold knowledge that is implied in the act of going for refuge. It is a knowledge answering the following questions: Is this world of ours really such a place of danger and misery that there is a need for taking refuge? Does such a refuge actually exist? And what is its nature?

There are many who do not see any need for a refuge. Being well pleased with themselves and with the petty, momentary happiness of their lives, they are fully convinced that "all is well with the world." They do not wish, or are not able, to look beyond their narrow horizons. For them neither the Buddha nor any other great religious teacher has yet appeared. But the majority of human beings know very well, by their own bitter experience, the hard and cruel face of the world which is only temporarily hidden by a friendly mask. There are others who, sufficiently aware of a fellow being's actual existence, add to that personal experience by observation of other lives. And there is a still smaller number of people who are able to reflect wisely on both experience and observation. Particularly to those latter ones "whose eyes are less covered by dust," life will appear as a vast ocean of suffering of unfathomable depth, on the surface of which beings swim about for a little while, or navigate in their fragile nutshells of which they are very proud.

True, there are spells of calm on the waters when it is pleasant to float upon a smooth sea, or to prove and to enjoy the strength of one's body by a long swim. But those with open eyes and minds are not deceived by these short moments of respite: they know the overpowering fierceness of a storm-swept sea, its dangerous currents and whirlpools, the demons and monsters of the deep. They know that, even under the most favourable conditions, the feeble strength of man will soon be exhausted by the impact of life's elemental forces. The vicissitudes of life give no chance of maintaining permanently, during the unlimited sequence of transformations, even the lowest degree of happiness, even the lowest standard of moral worth. There is nothing to gain by traversing ever anew the infinite expanse of life's ocean, in any of its regions. There is only the same senseless repetition of the ups and downs, of ebb and tide. Faced by the ever-present perils of life and by its essential monotony, there will be only the one cry for refuge in a heart and mind that has truly grasped its situation within the world. A refuge is the one great need of all life and "going to it" the one sane act demanded by that situation.

But, granting its necessity, does a refuge from the world's ills actually exist? The Buddhist affirms it and proves by that affirmation to be anything but a pessimist. The refuge to which he turns his steps is the triad of the Buddha, his doctrine and the Order of noble disciples. Being what is most precious and most pure, it has been called "the Triple Gem." But the fact that it provides the final refuge and not only a temporary shelter, those who take refuge can prove only to themselves, by actually attaining to the refuge through their own inner realisation.

The Triple Gem has objective existence as an impersonal idea or ideal as long as it is known and cherished. Even in that mode it is doubtlessly a persisting and active source of benefit for the world. But it is transformed from an impersonal idea to a personal refuge only to the extent that it is realized in one's own mind and manifested in one's own life. Therefore, the existence of the Triple Gem in its characteristic nature as a refuge cannot be proved to others. Each must find this refuge in himself by his own efforts. The refuge becomes and grows by the process of going to it.

By effort, earnestness and self-control
Let the wise man make for himself an island
Which no flood can overwhelm.

(Dhp 25)

The refuge exists for us only so far as something within ourselves responds and corresponds to it. Therefore the Sixth Zen Patriarch said:

Let each of us take refuge in the Three Gems within our mind!

With regard to the first refuge, in the Buddha, the Master himself said, shortly after his Enlightenment:

Like me they will be conquerors
Who have attained to the defilements' end.

(MN 26)

Concerning the second refuge, in the Dhamma, the Buddha said shortly before his decease:

Be islands for yourselves, be refuges for yourselves! Take no other refuge! Let the Dhamma be your island, let the Dhamma be your refuge! Take no other refuge!

(DN 16, *Mahāparinibbāna Sutta*)

In the commentarial literature it is said, in reference to another passage, but applicable to the one just quoted:

The Dhamma is called "self" (*attā*), because, in the case of a wise one, the Dhamma is not different from himself and because it pertains to his personal existence.

Ṭīkā to the Mahāsatipaṭṭhāna Sutta

The third refuge, the Sangha, being the Order of noble disciples, is the great and inspiring model for emulation. The actual foundation of that refuge is the capacity inherent in all beings to become one of the purified noble beings who form the Sangha of the refuge.

We turn now to the third subject of the knowledge implied in taking refuge, the ultimate nature of the Threefold Refuge.

We have seen that the refuge becomes attainable only by way of the living roots, by the actual foundations it has within the average mind. Like the lotus it arises within the waters of worldly existence; there it develops and from there it takes its nourishment. But what is still immersed in the ocean of worldliness and suffering cannot be the ultimate refuge, the place of safety and bliss. It must not only assuage, but must also ultimately transcend the world of danger, fear and ill, like the lotus that rises above the surface of the water and remains unsullied by it. Therefore, the consummate refuge meant in the traditional formula is of supramundane nature—*lokuttara*, world-transcending.

Thus the first refuge is not the Recluse Gotama, but the Buddha as the personification of world-transcending Enlightenment. In the *Vīmaṃsaka Sutta* it is said of the noble disciple: "He believes in the Enlightenment of the Exalted One" (MN 47).

The Dhamma of the second refuge is not the faint, fragmentary, or even distorted picture of the doctrine as mirrored in the mind of an unliberated worldling. It is the supramundane path and its consummation in Nibbāna. The commentator underlines the supramundane nature of the second refuge by saying that the Dhamma, as an object of learning, is included in the refuge only in so far as it is a formulation of the consummate knowledge acquired on the path to liberation.

The Sangha of the third refuge is not the all-inclusive congregation of monks, having all the weaknesses of its single members and sharing in the shortcomings attached to any human institution. It is rather the Order of noble disciples who are united by the invisible tie of common attainment to the four stages of liberation. In other words, it too is of supramundane nature: the assurance of possible progress to the world-transcending heights of a mind made holy and pure.

By this threefold knowledge about the need, existence and nature of the refuge, the going for refuge becomes a conscious act of *understanding*.

This knowledge and understanding form the firm basis of the third, the emotional aspect of taking refuge, which has three facets: confidence, devotion and love. The knowledge of the existence of a refuge provides the basis for a firm and justified confidence, for the calmness of inner assurance and the strength of conviction. The knowledge of the need for a refuge instills unswerving devotion to it. And the understanding of its sublime nature fills the heart with love towards the highest that can be conceived. Confidence is the firmness in faith; devotion is the patient endurance in loyal service and effort; and love adds the element of ardour, warmth and joy. In the sense of these three constituents, the going for refuge is also a conscious act of wise *faith*.

We may now define the going for refuge as a conscious act of will directed towards liberation, based upon knowledge and inspired by faith; or briefly: a conscious act of determination, understanding and devotion.

These three aspects of taking refuge have their counterparts in the volitional, rational and emotional sides of the human mind. Thus for a harmonious development of character the cultivation of all three is required.

Will, understanding and faith support each other in their common task. Will, transformed into purposive action, frees faith from the barrenness and dangers of emotional self-indulgence; it prevents intellectual understanding from stopping short at mere theoretical appreciation. Will harnesses the energies of both emotion and intellect to actual application.

Understanding gives direction and method to will; it provides a check to the exuberance of faith and gives to it its true content.

Faith keeps will from slackening, and is the vitalising and purposive factor in intellectual understanding.

The presence of these three aspects is the distinguishing feature of true Buddhist faith. In the conception of faith, as found in other world religions, the emotional aspect tends to be over-stressed at the expense of will and understanding. Against such an overemphasis on emotional faith, Buddhism moves from the very beginning of its spiritual training towards wholeness and completeness, towards a harmonious development of mental faculties. Therefore, the act of going for refuge in its true sense is accomplished only if there is connected with it at least a minimal degree of purposeful will and genuine understanding. Only in that case will faith have the quality of a "seed" attributed to it by the Buddha, a seed productive of further growth. The element of will in that seed of faith will grow until maturing into the irrepressible desire for liberation (*muñcitukamyatā-ñāṇa*), one of the advanced stages of insight (*vipassanā*). The element of initial understanding in true faith will grow into the penetrative wisdom that finally transforms the assurance of faith into the inner certitude conferred by realisation.

Taking refuge by way of thoughtless recital of the formula is a degradation of that venerable ancient practise. It deprives it of its true significance and efficacy. "Going for refuge" should be the expression of a genuine inner urge, in the same way as, in ordinary life, one may be urged by the awareness of a great danger to seek without delay the refuge of a place of safety.

When taking refuge, one should always keep in mind the implications of this act, as outlined above. This will be, at the same time, a beneficial training in right mindfulness. One should always ask oneself how the presently undertaken act of going for refuge can be translated into terms of will and understanding. Seeing that the house of our life is ablaze, it will not do merely to worship the safety and freedom that beckons outside, without making an actual move to reach it. The first step in that direction of safety and freedom is taking refuge in the right way, as a conscious act of determination, understanding and devotion.

The commentarial literature preserves a precious document of ancient Buddhist practise showing the thoughtful and discriminating way in which the devotees of old took refuge in the Triple Gem. The document mentions four different methods of going for refuge, each represented by the utterance of its own specific formula, each entailing a different degree of commitment. Ranked in ascending order, the four begin with homage by prostration, evolve through the acceptance of discipleship and the acceptance of the Triple Gem as the guiding ideal and culminate in complete self-surrender. The formulas all commence with the words "From today onwards ...," which mark the day of the first utterance as initiating a new period in the life of the devotee and stress that the act is a definite and personal dedication as distinguished from an impersonal ritual. The three lower formulas conclude with the words "Thus may you know me!"—a call to witness, giving to those declarations the strong emphasis and solemnity of a vow. Both the beginning and end of these modes of refuge echo the earliest expression of commitment reported in the suttas: "I go for refuge to the Lord Gotama, the Dhamma and the Order of monks! May the Lord Gotama know me as a lay follower! From today onwards, as long as life lasts, I have taken refuge!"

From the formulas it is clear that the ancient devotees who coined and used them were highly sensitive to the deep significance of going for refuge. They perceived this apparently simple act as a most momentous step decisive for life, entailing sacred responsibilities. By means of their fourfold distinction demanding a definite personal choice, they safeguard the process of taking refuge from degenerating into a routine habit and enable it to accommodate a growing intensity and earnestness of dedication. The structure of the gradation shows that the ancients were aware that the going for refuge is actually consummated only by complete self-surrender to the Triple Gem, without any reservations. In the lesser modes of the act, there is still something of the presumed self that is kept back; it is a going for refuge with reservations. Nevertheless, these lesser modes are definite steps towards the highest, and should be consciously cultivated. As in any harmonious mental development, here too the higher level does not exclude the lower but absorbs it into its wider compass. In trying to obtain a clearer picture of those four modes, we shall therefore start from the lowest level and work up to the highest.

I. The first mode of going for refuge is *homage by prostration* (*paṇipāta*), expressed by the formula: "From today onwards I shall give respectful greeting, devoted attendance and salutation only to the Buddha, the Dhamma and the Sangha. Thus may you know me!" Homage is the mental attitude, and the bodily and verbal expression, of reverence, resulting from the recognition and appreciation of something higher than oneself. It breaks through the first and hardest shell of pride and self-contented ignorance that knows of nothing better than one's own petty self. When encountering something higher, animals and undeveloped people, whether "primitive" or "civilized," usually react by distrust, fear, flight, attack, resentment, hostility or persecution; for they can view that higher form of life only as something different, alien and therefore suspect. It is the sign of a truly developed human mind that it meets the higher with due respect, with admiration and with the wish to emulate. Recognition and appreciation of something higher are therefore the preliminary condition of spiritual growth, and the true respect resulting from it forms the basis of moral education as well.

For this reason, in man's relation to the highest, the Triple Gem, true homage comes first. As a way of taking refuge, homage is the spontaneous expression of the deep veneration felt when becoming aware of the existence and significance of the supreme refuge. It is the emotional reaction in gratitude, devotion and joy when feeling the full weight of the tremendous fact that there is actually a refuge from this universe of suffering. Thus, in the commentary this mode of taking refuge is illustrated not by the habitual act of worship by confirmed devotees, but by the highly emotional conversion of an aged brahmin who, deeply stirred, prostrates himself before the Exalted One, embracing and kissing his feet.

Homage represents the emotional side of taking refuge, being its aspect as a conscious act of faith. Through its single-heartedness and humility, the act of doing homage by body, speech and mind prepares the disciple emotionally for complete self-surrender. It is an indispensable step to it, but, being deficient with regard to understanding and determination, it requires supplementation by the following two stages.

II. While homage is still a distant and one-sided relationship to the Supreme, the devotee still being in the outer court of the sanctuary, the next step—*the acceptance of discipleship* (*sissa-bhāv' ūpagamana*)—ushers him through the door. The disciple declares: "From today onwards I am a disciple of the Buddha, the Dhamma and the Sangha. Thus may you know me!" and through that declaration goes for refuge to supreme wisdom, opening himself to its permeating influence.

The respect and humility acquired earlier by true homage has earned for the disciple the right of entry into the sanctuary of wisdom. Only if approached in that reverential attitude will the guru, the spiritual teacher of the East, impart his knowledge, as these qualities are the first indication that the disciple is ready to receive.

If refuge is taken in the sense of discipleship, life becomes a constant act of learning, of adapting the mind to the standards set by the Buddha, the Dhamma and the Sangha. It is the character of the wise man that he is always willing and anxious to learn. The process of learning establishes a mutual relationship between teacher, teaching and pupil, such that a gradual and partial identification takes place and the pupil can absorb the teacher's wisdom and make it his own.

The acceptance of discipleship represents the rational side of taking refuge, which is here a conscious act of understanding. It supplies the full and satisfying reasons for the act of homage, and in that way adds to the strength and loyalty of devotion. But man is not always a devotee or learner. There remains much in life that cannot be mastered easily by faith and understanding alone. It requires a strong will and determination, as well as the skill of long experience, to change the course of the manifold habitual activities of life into the direction of the refuge. This task of gradually making the refuge the centre of one's life is performed by the third mode of taking refuge.

III. At the third level, the disciple accepts *the Triple Gem as his guiding ideal* (*tapparāyaṇatā*), avowing: "From today onwards the Buddha is my guiding ideal, and so too the Dhamma and the Sangha. Thus may you know me!" In taking this form of refuge, the disciple pledges himself to subordinate, step by step, all the essential activities of his life to the ideals embodied in the Triple Gem. He vows to apply his strength to the task of impressing this sacred threefold seal upon his personal life and upon his environment, too, as far as he can overcome its resistance. The Threefold Refuge in its aspect as the guiding ideal, the determining factor of life, calls for complete dedication in the sphere of external activities.

But this dedication to the service of the Triple Gem is not yet the highest form of taking refuge. There still exists in the disciple's mind a difference between the noble objective and the person working for it. The delusive ego has been retained: it rejoices at the success of the work and grieves when it fails. In a subtle way, instead of the Triple Gem, the work itself becomes the refuge. If identification of self and work is not complete, the ego, as it were, hides in the work and evades the call for full surrender to the true refuge. Progress beyond this step is possible only if the service of the guiding ideal is done in a highly detached way, without looking for any reward.

IV. This detached attitude towards work will be one of the many fruits of the last step: complete *self-surrender* to the Triple Gem (*attasanniyyatanā*). This form of refuge taken by the worldling leaves no room for reservations. Yet also, in a sense, it demands nothing; for if true understanding has told us before that nothing can be gained in *saṃsāra*, which is the objective aspect of self, then nothing can be lost by the surrender of self, which is the subjective aspect of *saṃsāra*. However, though this surrender of self is only the surrender of a delusion, it is a very hard sacrifice, as all of us know. But if we ever wish to be free of the bonds of *saṃsāra*, at one time or another this self-surrender must be done, and thus it may as well be done today as tomorrow.

The highest prize is won only by the highest stake, by the sacrifice of that illusive self that has assumed so much power that it requires the highest effort to break it. In taking refuge by way of self-surrender, the disciple will follow in his own modest way the example of the Exalted One, who, in the last great struggle before his Enlightenment, addressed his inner opponent, personified as Māra, with the following words: "It's muñja grass I wear! Shame on life! I would rather die in battle than live on as a vanquished one!" (Sn v. 440). Muñja grass was the crest of those ancient Indian warriors who entered battle with the vow "to do or die." It should be the symbol of the spiritual warrior too. If any reservations, regrets or reluctance are retained, there will be merely a half-hearted attempt instead of that single-minded effort which alone can bring victory.

If the grave step of taking refuge by self-surrender has once been taken, a feeling of lightness, unconcernedness and fearlessness will enter the heart of the disciple. A self that has been renounced cannot and need not have any fear for a life that has been surrendered and that is now kept only on trust for the definite purpose of being used for the highest realihtion. Therefore, in the early days of the Dhamma, when those of determined mind entered the "field of spiritual action," taking up a subject of meditation to be cultivated up to Arahatship, they would start their work by taking the vow of self-surrender, as advised in the following passage of the *Visuddhimagga* (III, 123-27):

> Having approached his Noble Friend (i.e., the meditation master), the meditator should first surrender himself to the Buddha, the Exalted One, or to his teacher, and then, possessed of a strong desire and a high resolve, he should ask for the subject of meditation. His surrender of self to the Buddha should be as follows: "This personal existence of mine, I offer to thee, O Exalted One!" For one who, without such a surrender of self, lives in lonely places will be unable to stand firm against fearful objects that approach him. He may return to the village, and, associated with lay folk, might take up a search that is wrongful and come to distress. But to one who has surrendered his self, no fear arises even when approached by fearful objects. Only gladness will arise in him when he reflects: "Hast thou not, O wise man, on that earlier day surrendered thyself to the Buddha?"
>
> And again, in surrendering himself to his teacher, he should say, "This personal existence of mine, Revered Sir, I offer to thee!" For without such a surrender of self, he will be unruly, stubborn, unwilling to accept advice; he will go about at his own will without asking the teacher's leave. And the teacher will favour him neither with material nor with spiritual help and will not instruct him in difficult books. Not receiving this twofold favour, he will become unvirtuous, or return to lay life.

This way of taking refuge by self-surrender is, of course, still far from the complete abolition of egotism and self-delusion, but it is a powerful means to that end. It may mark the transition from the worldly or mundane refuge to which it still belongs, to the supramundane refuge at which it aims.

The refuge by self-surrender is given in the commentarial text by the following formula:

> From today onwards I surrender my self to the Buddha, the Dhamma and the Sangha. To the Exalted One I am giving my self, to the Dhamma I am giving my self, to the Sangha I am giving my self. I am giving them my life. Until my life ends, I take refuge in the Buddha. The Buddha is my refuge, my shelter, my protection, and so too the Dhamma and the Sangha.

Even in its external form, this mode of refuge differs from the preceding three in that it lacks the concluding call to witness, "Thus may you know me!" From this we may conclude that this gravest of all vows was to be taken in the secrecy of one's heart, as befits the sacredness of the resolve. Here the presence of a witness as a kind of moral support for keeping the vow should no more be required; such a requirement would only prove that it is premature to take this step. Any public avowal would only detract from the supreme dignity of the vow, and would render its observance more difficult by making the disciple too self-conscious or even proud. Needless to say, a deliberate parading of the vow would defeat its very purpose, by reinstating the self that was to be surrendered.

The longer formula of self-surrender enlarging upon the short sentence in the *Visuddhimagga* has been rendered here into a Western language for the first time. Its Pali original also seems to have evoked little attention in our day. If we reproduce that formula here, we do so in the hope that it will be received with the reverence due to that precious document of ancient devotion, hallowed by the efforts and achievements of those who may have practised in accordance with it. We add the earnest request that it not be made use of lightly for the purpose of ordinary devotion, and that the vow not be taken rashly on the spur of a moment's enthusiasm. This solemn pledge should be taken only after having tested one's strength and perseverance for a long time by minor observances and renunciations. We should beware of making those highest things of the spirit cheap and common by approaching them in too facile a way, by talking too glibly about them, or by taking them into our hands and dropping them again when interest fades or our feeble fingers get tired. Therefore, if we are not sure of our strength, we should not take upon ourselves the severe demands of self-surrender, but take our refuge by way of those lesser modes. For these will likewise prove to be powerful helpers to high spiritual achievements.

In making an intelligent use of that fourfold devotional road of the ancients, we shall preserve the most popular religious practise in the Buddhist world, the going for refuge, from becoming stale and ineffective. We shall be able to turn it into a strong, life-giving current of devotion that will carry us one day to the Isle of Final Peace, to Nibbāna, where refugee and refuge are merged into one.

Essays and Poems

by

Dr. Paul Dahlke

WHEEL PUBLICATION NO. 77/78

Foreword

This selection of essays by that great Buddhist thinker of Germany, Dr. Paul Dahlke, is issued in commemoration of the centenary of his birth: from 25th January 1865 to 1965.

The articles presented here have been taken from the two periodicals, *Neu-Buddhistische Zeitschrift* (*New-Buddhist Journal*) and *Die Brockensammlung* (*Shard Collection*), edited by Dr. Dahlke and entirely written by himself. From these two periodicals, which contain a very large number of articles and other writings, only a small selection can be offered here, and larger essays had to be excluded for reason of space. Earlier translations of the articles selected, as published in *The British Buddhist* and other magazines, have been compared with the German original and some major changes have been made in them.

The author of the biographical sketch that introduces this selection, the late Kurt Fischer, was for many years a friend and secretary of Dr. Dahlke. After the latter's death he ably edited the bi-monthly magazine *Buddhistisches Leben und Denken* (*Buddhist Life and Thought*), which, for many years presented to German readers the teachings of the Buddha, according to Dr. Dahlke's interpretation.

Two tributes to Dr. Dahlke, by Bhikkhu Sīlācāra and Anāgārika Dhammapāla, have been included here.

Other essays by Dr. Dahlke have appeared in this series, in *The Five Precepts* (Wheel No. 55) and *German Buddhist Writers* (Wheel No. 74/75).

We are well aware that the present selection of short essays will be insufficient to give an idea of the range and significance of Dr. Dahlke's contribution to Buddhist literature, which can only be gathered from his larger works. Not all of them have appeared in English versions, and even these have been out of print for many years. We hope that the present publication will be found stimulating by our readers and create a demand for a reprint of the larger works.

The Editor

Foreword

Dr. Paul Dahlke: His Life and Work

Kurt Fischer

Dr. Paul Dahlke was born on 25th January 1865 at Osterode in East Prussia. While still a child, he experienced some of the hardships of life. His father was a civil servant and a large family had to be brought up on a very modest income, so that privation and self-denial were part of the daily life at his home.

After some years at a preparatory school, Paul Dahlke attended the secondary school at Frankfort-on-Main. On the completion of his education there, he took up medical studies; and after his examinations applied himself to homeopathy, perceiving instinctively that this method of healing was most suited to his talent.

Dr. Dahlke was one of those physicians who are not mere routine practitioners. He was a real healer, as expressed by the German word "*Arzt*" (a doctor), which is derived from the Greek word *archiatros*, "supreme healer." So it came that this young doctor met with exceptional success and soon his reputation extended far beyond his place of work in Berlin.

But Dr. Dahlke's genius was far too active for confining itself to medical practise alone. It drove him beyond the boundaries of the commonplace into realms of thought which lay quite outside his professional work. Even in his remarkable achievements as a physician, he displayed a keen sense of actuality (*Wirklichkeit*), i.e., of "things as they really are," a mental quality with which only few people are generously endowed. It was, moreover, through that sense of the width and depth of actuality that Dr. Dahlke was drawn to fields outside medicine, to the religious ideas of the East and finally to the teachings of the Buddha. Schopenhauer's writings had made the first impact on him, but soon he outgrew them in his untiring research and inquiry.

We cannot do better than repeat here the words by which Dahlke himself described his first contact with Buddhism and its effect on him.

"It was not in the shape of an emotional shock or of some decisive event that Buddhism entered my life. Slowly, imperceptibly, like the seed in the ground, did it take root and grew, when, in 1898, I started on my first long voyage. I had already known Buddhism for some time, but in spite of this, at that time, not India but the South Seas were the goal of my desire. Tahiti and Oweihi, as described in Chamisso's writings, attracted me more than all the wisdom of India; and when, on June 1898, I landed at Apia on the island of Sama, it appeared to me as the perfect fulfilment of my life.

"After about a year I returned home again, and the Buddha's teaching must have been developing silently in me, unperceived; for already when, in the following year, I set out again on my travels, it was with India as my avowed aim: not India alone, but Buddhism.

"In the spring of 1900 I reached Colombo and had the great and good fortune to find at once good teachers who could give me instruction on Buddhism: Sri Sumaṅgala Thera of Maligakanda Vihara, at a suburb of Colombo, was already an old man, but his intellect was still astonishingly keen; and Nyanissara Thera, his first co-worker, who took his place after his death, and who now, unfortunately, has also passed away. Then there was the young Bhikkhu Suriyagoda Sumaṅgala of Sri Vardhanarama (Colpetty) with whom I have ever since kept up a close friendship; and finally, the Pundit Wagiswara (Vācissara), who, at that time, lived at Payagala, on the South Coast of Ceylon. To him I owe most of my first understanding of Buddhism, because it was he who could best adapt himself to the Western view point, and also had a thorough grasp of English.

"It was then, in 1900, that I made my official entry into Buddhism and its teachings. Since that time I have been constantly travelling back and forth between India and my native Germany; and most of the time I was ill, partly due to the climate, partly through my own fault: being dissatisfied with these restless wanderings, and yet ever drawn back to India."

The outcome of this inner awakening to the Dhamma was a number of books, the real value of which lay in the fact that they made Buddhist thought accessible to the outlook of the Westerner.[1] Most of Dahlke's major works have been translated into English, and some have also been rendered into Dutch and Japanese.

1. See the list of Dr. Dahlke's works at the end of this book.

There will always be people who combine energy and purposefulness with an original and creative mind. To their ranks belong all who are called "great men." Such was the mind of Dr. Paul Dahlke, who occupies quite an exceptional place in the history of Western thought. He possessed not only an incredible store of energy, combined with a keen intellect and an artist's sensitivity and creativity; but—and here lies Dahlke's special greatness, he also had a keen sense of actuality which rose above all conventions. As a result of that exceptional combination of qualities, he had a strong urge towards inner purity and honesty which did not allow him to shrink from the most radical consequences of his thought.

Up to the year 1914, Dr. Dahlke undertook several journeys to many of the great countries of the world. He once said jocularly of himself: "I was like a comet, swishing through the world." But the strongest attraction for him were the places of ancient Buddhist culture, chiefly Ceylon. Shortly before the outbreak of the First World War, Dahlke had returned to Germany, and owing to the changed conditions consequent on the outbreak of war, he found himself confined to his home country. The only way by which he could adapt himself to circumstances seemed to him the resumption of his medical practise, given up completely during the latter years; and soon it became known among his avid patients that Dr. Dahlke was again employing his great medical knowledge and skill in the service of the ailing.

But more and more the knowledge grew in Dahlke that there was no greater need for the peoples of the West than a true understanding of Buddhism. His earlier writings had already served to introduce this teaching; and now Dr. Dahlke saw the necessity for producing reliable German translations of the Buddhist scriptures. Though there existed in German language a great many translations from the Pali texts, almost all, and especially the well-known renderings by Karl Eugen Neumann, were more or less tainted with admixtures foreign to the spirit of the pure Teaching. Thus originated Dr. Dahlke's translations of the Dhammapada and parts of the Dīgha-Nikāya and Majjhima-Nikāya. These books were not mere translations; they were at the same time works of doctrinal instruction in which the author, in copious explanatory notes, embodied the results of twenty years' study and personal experience. At that time he also started a quarterly periodical, the *New Buddhist Journal* (*Neu-Buddhistische Zeitschrift*), entirely written by himself. In that magazine, he showed in a unique, and ever fresh and stimulating way, how Buddhism can have a decisive influence on the solution of all great problems of life.

But a spirit so bent on the realisation of what he knew to be the Truth could not for long be satisfied with mere literary work in the cause of Buddhism. Soon arose in him the idea of a "Buddhist House," which was to be a meeting place for those who were no longer in accord with their inherited religion and felt that materialism was not in keeping with true human dignity.

A few years after the end of the first World War, just when the difficulties due to inflation of the German currency were at their peak, a favourable opportunity for acquiring about nine acres of wooded land at Frohnau presented itself, in a suburb of Berlin. Now Dr. Dahlke devoted all his energies to the realisation of this great idea: to establish a home for Buddhism in Germany. The task was completed very slowly, in gradual progress. The difficulties with which he had to contend may be estimated from the fact that the currency inflation in Germany had almost obliterated his financial means for carrying out the project. Thus the money needed for constructing the House had first to be earned, day by day, by hard work, in Dr. Dahlke's consultation room.

Nevertheless he was determined to carry out his plan, and in August 1924 the construction of the Buddhist House was far enough advanced that Dr. Dahlke and a few of his disciples were able to move in. It was his intention that the House should be a monument, a visible expression, of the Teaching; and new plans constantly issued from his fertile brain for expanding the first layout. Besides the House proper, containing the living quarters and a library, a Meeting Hall was built close by, and separate rooms and cells for accommodating guests who wished to stay there for some time, for quiet contemplation and for receiving instruction in the Buddhist teachings.

The Buddhist House was conceived as a place devoted to inner purification, as far as this could be achieved in a life of compromise between the life of a Buddhist monk and Western conditions. It could not well be a monastery since both the material and spiritual requirements were lacking. Therefore it was to be a midway solution between a monastery and a layman's habitation. The Five Precepts were to be the basic rules of conduct for the residents, and their further endeavours for inner purification were to bestow a characteristic atmosphere to the House. The difficulty of doing this under Western conditions can be appreciated only by those who have tried it. In a world where the lusts of life and a brutal struggle for existence were dominant, the courageous attempt of Dr. Dahlke and the small band of his followers was like the struggle of a small boat against the mountainous waves of a stormy sea.

It is, therefore, not surprising that Dr. Dahlke's strength was entirely consumed by his last few years' work in connection with the Buddhist House. Dr. Dahlke had mentioned several times to his friends how weak his heart was; and in fact, without the high degree of inner composure which he owed to Buddhism, he could never have worked as long as he did. For about a year, a severe cold had troubled him, over which he was unable to get control. It was only his constant thought on the Dhamma and his plans connected therewith, which enabled him to withstand for some time the relapses that occurred after a grave crisis in his illness. Also another project, that of founding a House of Retreat on the North Sea island of Sylt, and literary plans occupied him constantly. But death prevented the realisation of these plans. Early in 1928, Dr. Paul Dahlke passed away from the scene of his labours.

Until now hardly an attempt has been made to give an adequate appreciation of Dr. Dahlke's unique personality and of the significant place he held in the mental life of the West and in the forceful and penetrative presentation of the Buddha's Teaching. May the time come soon when his great work is fully understood and utilised for the benefit of humanity.

Dr. Paul Dahlke

by J. F. McKechnie (Bhikkhu Sīlācāra)

In Dr. Paul Dahlke, the Buddhist cause in Europe possessed one of the most efficient and able pens, backed by what was certainly the most able and efficient brain that had so far appeared in Europe to champion and propagate the ideas contained in the Buddha Dhamma. And now that pen is still, that brain has ceased from its endless activity in exploring every promising line of Buddhist thought, and seeking to probe it to the bottom. Dr. Dahlke was a great man, and like all great men, he did not advertise himself. The great do not need to do so. What they are, they are, and all men with eyes to see can see what they are. It is only the would-be great, and the essentially little, who need to call attention to themselves. So Dr. Dahlke never in any way strove to make men look at him. He just went on his way ceaselessly working in his own way for the propagation of the ideas in which he believed, and the result was a body of writing which will long remain as one of the most lucid, and at the same time (most unusually) the most profound exposition, of Buddhism that European Buddhism has thus far obtained.

For Dr. Dahlke was not content just to take what was given him in the Buddhist Scriptures and swallow it whole. He sought to digest it, and incorporate it into his own mental life, as a part of that life: and to do this, turned everything over and over in his mind until he had seen all the implications, full and complete, of every statement in Buddhist books which he deemed worthy of attention. Nay, not only that! When he had seen the truth of any of those statements, he then proceeded to put them into effective embodiment in his own life. As an acute thinker, he early realised the limitations of mere intellectualism. He saw that the intellect is only a limb of life, not life itself; and that an idea is not fully rounded and complete until it is expressed in life, in living; that up till then it is more or less of a toy, an interesting plaything, but not yet brought into real, complete earnest being. It was into full being that he sought to bring his ideas of the Dhamma by giving them actual expression in his life; and it was to this end that he founded, after much difficulty overcome, his Buddhist House.

He felt that if the Buddha produced the effect he had upon human history through the effect the Buddha produced upon the history of Asia, it was not only because he spoke the words he spoke, but because he lived the life he led; and with all reverence Dr. Dahlke felt that the Buddha's European followers who are his followers in more than name, had to do the same— albeit at a great distance behind the Master's great example—in also making their lives a living presentment of the Dhamma, as the only possible effective way of making Buddhist ideas impress themselves upon their fellow-continentals. In short, he felt that we must not only talk "Buddhism," but be Buddhists, be embodiments, to the very best of our ability, of the ideas we believe in, and spare no pains towards making ourselves more and more complete embodiments of these ideas.

When, if ever, the history of Buddhist life in Europe comes to be written, among the names that will stand highest will be that of Paul Dahlke.

Dr. Paul Dahlke and His Buddhist House

Anāgārika Dharmapāla

Dr. Paul Dahlke of Berlin is well known all over the world as a thinker of great originality and as author of *Buddhist Essays,* which was translated into English by Bhikkhu Sīlācāra. The Sinhala Buddhists have every reason to be proud of the achievements of Dr. Dahlke of Germany, for it was in Ceylon that he learned Pali under such well-known scholars as the Thera Sumaṅgala and Pandit Wagiswara. For more than twenty years he has been reading and translating Pali texts, and in Europe there is no more spiritually minded Pali scholar than Dr. Dahlke. He has travelled all over Ceylon, visited the ancient Vihāras, and has been to historic Buddhist places in India and Burma.

It is the personality of Dr. Dahlke that attracts people to him. In his daily life he is a living example to his disciples, strictly observing the Five Precepts, and still attending to his professional duties. It will be hard to find a better Buddhist than Dr. Dahlke. He is a strict vegetarian and takes no alcohol. His literary labours have won him fame in Germany.

His disciples stay with him in the Buddhist House, which he has erected on an elevated and picturesque site near the Kaiser Park in Frohnau, not far from Berlin. The Buddhist House stands on a hillock, calling on the people "to come and see." The architectural features of the building are a surprisingly successful mixture of Sinhalese, Japanese, Chinese and Asokan. The stone pillars of the gate at the entrance are a miniature reproduction of the *Sāñchī torana* of the Asoka period; the portico is of stone with engravings of pictures as found in the great Ruvanweli Dagoba in Ceylon's sacred city of Anuradhapura. The stepping stone with its rows of royal animals and flowers and a fully opened lotus at the centre is a replica of the moon stones found in the Vihāras at Anuradhapura and Polonnaruwa. The lecture hall is in shape similar to a Chinese temple, and at the far end of the hall is an engraving in marble of a Buddha image, and on either side of it is a marble tablet giving stanzas from the Dhammapada and Sutta-Nipāta with a German translation. At a little distance from the hall is an isolated brick hut, with a wall all round, intended for students who wish to devote themselves to *jhāna* contemplation. This is like the *padhāna-ghara* (meditation hut), mentioned in later Pali texts, for the use of Bhikkhus who devote themselves to meditation. There is nothing to disturb the mind of the spiritual student. The grounds are about six acres in extent, and undulating. The atmosphere is exhilarating and the breeze that comes from the pine woods is invigorating. Frescoes of the Sāñchī Stupa and replicas of various sacred figures from Ceylon and Japan are to be seen on the walls of the first and second storeys of the House. All the expenses of building the House were met by Dr. Dahlke himself

Every evening Dr. Dahlke gives Dhamma instruction to his pupils. They read selected verses or passages from the Pali texts, and Dr. Dahlke explains them from the Theravada standpoint. The German pupils practise the *Ānāpānasati Bhāvanā* (Mindfulness on In- and Out-breathing), sitting in the *padmādsana* (*lotus* posture) as required by the *Satipaṭṭhāna Sutta* (the Discourse on the Foundations of Mindfulness). There is a special guest room on the second floor provided with every convenience.

Adapted from "*The Mahā,*" *BMW* (1925)

Essays and Poems

by Dr. Paul Dahlke

Preserve Your Human State!

Very few men are clearly aware of the great boon they possess in the fact that they are born as men, born in a state endowed with thinking and consciousness. Most will say: "Well! How else should it be? I have been born from my parents, and they again from their parents, and so on. Thus I am a man; I belong to the human race."

But that is an idea which, though not factually incorrect, is yet essentially defective and to that extent erroneous. To be sure, man springs from his parents. To be sure, his children spring from him. To be sure, the stream of life where once it manifests itself as a human being, seems to flow on forever as a human being. But this is an illusion. The life-stream of a species, apparently forever restricted to itself, whether it be the human species or any kind of animal species, comprises only what manifests itself in sense experience. According to external experience, men stem only from men; according to external experience, men procreate only men. And exactly the same holds true for all species of animals and plants. But, as we said, this applies only to what presents itself to the senses in ordinary experience. And all this is only the expression, the manifestation of forces which may be emerging from unknown depths.

Let us, for example, take as comparison a rainbow. As a rainbow, it is always the same in colour and shape. But this applies only to what is manifest to the sense: in normal experience. In actual truth, it is made up of single particles of water which are in a state of perpetual change, and flow in from all sides.

Similarly, the Buddha teaches this: What manifests itself through the senses in ordinary experience as the human race, as the animal kingdom—these are not rigid, unchangeable and unalterable facts—they are only processes, phases of development within the field of life's possibilities. Man does not give rise to man in the sense in which it is taught by science. For here, as everywhere, science labours under the disability of an inner contradiction, in as much as one school within the ranks of science teaches the constancy and unchangeability of species, while the other, grouped around Darwin's name, teaches the gradual evolution of species. Hence the dictum, "Man gives rise to man," is no longer entirely correct, since in the course of some billions of years, from some kind of lower animal or other, man at last arose, and thus a change of species occurred.

All this, however, is by the way. Once more it may be stated: Man does not give rise to man. A man is only the means, the tool for helping a certain *kamma*, an individual force, a living destiny that is fit for human birth to appear in the human race to make its breakthrough humanity. The real question is, "Whence springs this *kamma*, this individual force, this dependent process?" It may, likewise, have come from a human source, but may as well have arisen from a life-potential below or above the human level. It is certainly an incontestable fact of experience: a human can only give rise to a human. Man can only be born of man, because his natural possibilities do not permit him anything else. But it should be considered well that the part he plays herein is not an active one, but passive. He is nothing but an instrument and tool for the kammic forces (called by the Buddha *viññāṇa*, consciousness), which want to become actuality in him, seeking to enter into existence and manifestation through him. Parents are not the real begetters and progenitors; they have only the role of a midwife, aiding in the process of birth. They are the biological stage upon which the newly arisen being plays its part. As we have said, these new forces may well have had a human origin; and we may assume that this will be so in by far the majority of the cases of human birth. Human *kamma* most frequently adapts itself to human generative material; but it is not an iron law that this should be so; it may also spring from a source below or above the human state.

In Buddhism, five distinct domains of beings (or realms of animate existence, *sattavacara*) are known, and thereby five possibilities of rebirth: three below the human state, and one above. The three below are the realm of spirits or ghosts (the sporting ground of spiritualism), the animal kingdom, and the world of the hells where only experiences of pain and misery occur, while among animals or ghosts, now and then, *also* pleasurable experiences may occur. The one realm of life above the human one is *sagga-loka,* the lofty worlds of the gods which are, again, divided into the lower ones (of the sense-sphere) and the higher, the Brahma-worlds.

The non-Buddhist may say that these are vain fancies of the mind. But I say: They are not. For understanding it, one must consider what this action (*kamma*) that conditions our rebirth, essentially is. The Buddha himself says: "It is *cetanā* that I call *kamma.*" That is to say: it is directed thought (or as we say today: intentional thinking) that is called *kamma.* It is thinking that decides. From thinking issue words and deeds. Thinking takes the lead. Thinking is a blessing and a curse. It is the quality of our thinking, noble or base, that decides the type of rebirth—noble thinking, noble rebirth or low thinking, low rebirth! The right to rebirth as a human must ever and again be earned anew by thought and action worthy of a human being.

Just as the bird high up in the air must continually keep moving its wings in order to maintain itself at that height; similarly must man constantly practise high thinking and humane action in order to maintain himself in his high position as a man; in order to make sure of another rebirth as man and not to slip back into lower domains of life. Such a task is difficult to carry out in the frenzy and unrest of our times, in this world of brutality and avid search for pleasure. The Buddha exhorts again and again to observe three things that are indispensable for a true human being that deserves this name: guarding the sense doors, moderation in eating, and moderation in sleeping (wakefulness). In the Saṃyutta-Nikāya it is said:

"Endowed with three things, a monk lives happily already in this life, with his insight directed towards the eradication of passion. What three? He guards his sense doors, he observes moderation in eating and trains himself in wakefulness.

"And how, O monks, does a monk keep guard over his sense doors? Seeing a form with the eye, hearing a sound with the ear, smelling an odour with the nose, tasting a flavour with the tongue, feeling a touch with the body, cognising a mind-object with the mind, he does not seize on its general appearance nor on its details. That which might, if he dwells unrestrained as to the eye-faculty (ear-faculty, etc.), give occasion for covetous, sad, evil and unwholesome thoughts to invade him, that he sets himself to restrain. He trains himself in the avoidance of all that, he guards his senses, he practises this restraint.

"Just as if on level ground, at the crossing of four roads, a well-built vehicle stands all ready with driving-whip complete, and a skilled driver who is a well-practised horse-trainer, should mount it, and seizing the reins with the left hand and the whip with the right, should go this way and that, back and forth, wherever he wished; even so does the monk train himself in guarding the six sense doors, he practises the restraint, control and calming of them.

"This, O monks, is called the guarding of the sense doors.

"And how, O monks, does a monk observe moderation in eating? Wisely reflecting does the monk partake of his food, neither for lust, nor for enjoyment, nor for ostentation, nor for comeliness; but only as far as it serves for the continuance and maintenance of the body, for protecting it from harm, so as to be able to lead the holy life, (thinking): 'Thus I shall put a stop to old feelings and shall not arouse new feelings; and I shall be healthy and blameless and live in comfort.'

"Just as a man puts salve on a wound for effecting a speedier cure, or as a man greases the axle of his cart for effecting an easier conveyance of the load, similarly does a monk take food, wisely reflective: neither for lust, nor enjoyment, nor for ostentation, nor for comeliness; but only as far as it serves for the continuance and maintenance of the body... Thus, O monks, does a monk observe moderation in eating.

"And how does a monk practise wakefulness? Walking up and down during daytime, the monk purifies his mind from things that hinder. Also during the first watch of the night, walking up and down, he purifies his mind from things that hinder. In the middle watch of the night, after the manner of the lion he lies down on his right side, one foot placed on the other, mindful and fully aware, thinking of the time of arising. In the last watch of the night, after he has risen, he again, while walking up and down, purifies his mind from things that hinder. Thus does a monk practise wakefulness.

"Endowed with these three things, lives a monk happily already in this life, with his insight directed towards the eradication of passion."

Now you will ask me: "Who can do all that? In the mornings when I wake up, it will be high time to get up. I have to dress in a hurry, eat my breakfast in a hurry, squeeze myself into an over-crowded tram car or subway train to get to my place of work. There I shall rush about hither and thither all day long, and shall hardly have time to eat my midday buns. Coming home in the evening, rather starved, I shall try, at my belated night meal, to make up for the food that I could not eat during the day. Soon after, I shall exhausted fall into sleep, in order to start next day on the same dizzy round—except if some special attraction draws me at night to the cinema, the theatre or a lecture. Leading such a life, how can I cope with those demands you mentioned?"

Quite so. Leading such a life, one cannot cope with such demands. Hence, all depends lastly upon our making up our minds, early and deliberately, and as far as it is in our power, so to shape our lives that we shall not get into such a treadmill, but shall preserve for ourselves some breathing space and some leisure.

True, not all will be able to make this possible; but still, a considerable number of people can do it, and perhaps more than one might think, if only there is the will and determination. There are men to whom the way to a life of self-collectedness is inexorably closed by a bad *kamma*. For them it means to hurry and worry from morning to night, if they wish to keep themselves alive. But there are also those, and they are not few either, who can easily find time and opportunity for self-collectedness if only they have the will.

I may say that the ruling idea in the founding of our "Buddhist House" at Frohnau was to provide a possibility for a life of self-collectedness, or at least to improve the conditions for leading such a life.

From *Die Brockensammlung*, 1929

Buddhism and Pseudo-Buddhism

The fact that everywhere in the universe forces are at work that cannot be comprehended provides a constant incentive to faith. Because one does not comprehend force (energy), one assumes that it is incomprehensible in itself, and hence that it is itself unconditioned and absolute.

Now the trend in modern man clearly moves away from faith towards understanding. Where formerly men were ready and willing to believe, to day they wish to understand. But the preliminary condition is that they understand force, the dynamic nature of life. As long as they are unable to understand, only two choices remain open for them: indifference or the will to believe.

Buddhism, in its essential nature, is based upon the fundamental intuitive insight of the Buddha Gotama into the nature of force (energy). Basically, Buddhism is nothing but a doctrine dealing with force, that is to say, with the process of insight. Everything else in it is derived from that.

In brief, the Buddha's teaching about force (energy) is as follows:

Every living being is a purely flame-like process that keeps burning by virtue of a strictly individual force, peculiar to that being. In the terminology of Buddhism, this force is called *kamma* (Sanskrit: *karma*), which means nothing else but *action*. Wherever processes of conscious life exist, this individual kammic force by which a living being exists manifests itself in a fivefold way: First, as the power to organize a material form peculiar to itself and to preserve it against the impact of the outer world; second, as the power to feel; third, as the power to perceive; fourth, as the power to sort out these perceptions and to discriminate them; fifth, as the power to convert them into conceptions.

These five aggregates (*khandha*), usually called: corporeality, feeling, perception, mental formations and consciousness, comprise the entire living being as far as it is action, that is a dynamic process. The salient point here is that the living being does not *have* all these physical and mental capacities as qualities or functions, but that it *consists of* them and is entirely comprised by that fivefold dynamism, exactly as it is with the flame. I do not *have* my fivefold action as the function of an identical ego, a doer or actor, but I am myself the action, the deed.

The ego-process as experienced by me in its five forma of activity represents—in modern terminology—a particular value of potential energy which, in its friction with the external world, again and again passes over into the living energy of the volitional activities. These latter fully correspond to the new ignition moments of the flame. Just as the flame lives through its ignition moments, which continually spring up anew, so does man live through the recurrent moments of his volitional activities or, in Buddhist terminology: he lives through his thirst for life (*taṇhā*). The Buddha said expressly: "It is thirst (craving) that creates man."

If one has thus comprehended the ego-process, i.e., oneself, then every possibility of foisting upon it a metaphysical substance has disappeared for ever. One understands the whole mechanism, everything that is going on there can be summed up in the one statement: it acts, it burns. In this insight, the totality of experience is comprehended as an infinitely vast sum of individual processes. Each of them exists only by virtue of a strictly individualised force peculiar to itself alone, which manifests itself to the individual as consciousness and volition. These are the individual.

But men feel a need to look beyond this life and get an answer to the questions: "Whence? Whither?" According to whether the answer is derived from actuality or whether it overrides actuality and resorts to metaphysical concepts, one distinguishes between a religion of insight and a religion of faith.

For being able to extract the answer to the questions "Whence?" and "Whither?" from actuality itself, one must have understood force (energy), which is the salient feature of the Buddha's intuitive insight. Briefly put, it consists in the teaching of rebirth according to deeds. Father and mother only furnish the material for a new living being. The force which unfolds the possibilities residing in that material springs from previous forms of existence and lays hold of material wherever, according to its specific affinity, it must lay hold.

In that way, every living being points back to a series of which there is no beginning. Force, whatever it be, can never and nowhere be created anew. Wherever it exists it can never have been non-existent. It only changes the material upon which it works. But this should be well understood: Force, within the constant change of its manifestations, does not persist as a "force" *per se,* i.e., an identical entity, but, in the volitional activities, it springs up again and again, from its own antecedent conditions and in strict accordance with them. It is not a "soul" or any transmigrating entity that connects like a solid strand the several rebirths, but it is the volitional activity that bestows continuity upon that process.

It may be objected: "Is not also this doctrine of rebirth a matter of faith?" I reply: "No. You may take it as a working hypothesis, and very soon you will notice that it is the one working hypothesis which, in face of the puzzling problems set by the life process, saves us from accepting "faith" as a solution. Birth, then, becomes comprehensible. Instead of the two great incomprehensibilities, the "Whence and the Whither," there is here only one great comprehension. For the rest, the Buddha's teaching of a force that makes for continuity of the respective life process, along with a constant change of the material, is nothing but the law of the conservation of energy as known to physics, but applied here to the domain of biology.

After these explanations we come now to our subject proper, the distinction between Buddhism and Pseudo-Buddhism. This distinction is now easy to define. True Buddhism exists wherever there is the understanding that in the world process there is nothing whatsoever of the nature of a metaphysical core; an unconditioned, eternal substance and absolute. The great mystery of force that has provided the ever-fresh incentive to the assumption of something transcendental is solved. Thinking has comprehended itself as force, and henceforth comprehends the entire world process as something that, in all its activities, is the manifestation of a beginningless conformity to law. Dhamma (Skr: *dharma*) means the Buddha's Teaching as well as law, thing, phenomenon., and process. Everything in the world is of a conditioned nature, partly in the passive sense (conditioned through external circumstances), and partly in the reflexive sense (conditioned by itself). Conditionality, in this double sense, is expressed in Pali by the term *saṅkhāra.* There is nothing whatsoever that is unconditioned, a "thing-in-itself."

On the other hand, it is characteristic of Pseudo-Buddhism that, while making use of Buddhist technical terms and ideas, it tries to save some sort of an unconditioned, metaphysical or universal principle.

These attempts generally start from the concepts of Nibbāna or Parinibbāna.

After one has understood oneself as a beginningless process of combustion,[2] there remains as the one goal of life the cessation of this beginningless burning–its extinction. Because man lives, and since time infinite has lived, by reason of the thirst for life (or craving: *taṇhā*), that extinction will only take place when the thirst for life, or craving, ceases through a penetrative insight into the true nature of life. This state of freedom from craving is Nibbāna, and the moment when the body of such an Arahat, breaks up is called Parinibbāna, "complete extinction." What happens is that an ego-process that, from time unfathomable, has lived by power of that thirst for life, has now through insight overcome it finally and, when dying, does no longer assume any new form but becomes extinguished forever, without any trace. That is the meaning of Parinibbāna in the genuine teaching of the Buddha. But if one derived from it a metaphysical principle, a something into which at death the perfect one enters forever, a state of immutability, then we are dealing with Pseudo-Buddhism. In that case, illegitimate use is made of Buddhist terminology, for causing a break in the consistency of the Buddha's thought and for satisfying the yearning of the human mind for something abiding.

Another school of Pseudo-Buddhism makes of the Law (Dhamma or Dharma) a separate entity that directs the world process like a kind of cosmic power. What is erroneous in this idea is evident from the "force doctrine" of the Buddha. The world process conveys the impression of a higher lawfulness because in each of its parts and functions it is the law itself. For the rest, the Buddha himself has said: "Let my Law be a raft to you, for the purpose of escape, not for the purpose of retention."

I can understand a thing only as far as it is conditioned. I understand it wholly if I cognise it as wholly conditioned. Only if one comprehends the world process as through and through conditioned in its nature, as something that carries within itself the conditions of its existence, and extends no roots or feelers into

---

2. In the sense of the Buddha's "Fire Sermon" (the Editor).

a transcendental beyond, then only is a religion of reason possible. As long as one accepts an unconditioned substance, a religion of faith is present; whether one calls this unconditioned entity God or Parinibbāna or Dhamma does not make any difference. It is, therefore, quite understandable that this Pseudo-Buddhism finds it easy to go hand in hand with pantheistic, mystic or theosophical schools. If I here expressly emphasise that Buddhism has absolutely nothing to do with all this, I do not say so with an intention of belittling these schools. I do so only in order to single out Buddhism as that teaching of reason and understanding which stands out as wholly unique among the numerous faith doctrines.

Life has become completely comprehensible because it has completely comprehended itself. Actuality is cognised as what it is. As such a teaching of actuality, Buddhism lays claim to the consideration of modern man.

From *Die Brockensammlung*, 1933

What We Need

When the living body lacks certain substances, it falls prey to illness manifesting itself in pathological symptoms. It is similar with the body of mankind when anything necessary for its health is lacking: it falls sick and this sickness shows its presence by pathological conditions. The pathological conditions under which the body of mankind suffers today, stand clearly out before all eyes: love of pleasure, love of gain, lying, dishonesty, violence, distrust, oppression of peoples, sexual immorality, lack of respect for elders, and many other social ills.

What is lacking in the body of mankind that so many symptoms of disease reveal themselves? We answer in one word: morality. What the world needs is morality. But from where can mankind get it?

Up to the time of the First World War one could still in a manner say that the fount from which the world's morality sprung was "godly fear," taking these words in their proper significance of "fear of God." But this already rather turbid and scanty spring of morality was as good as cut off by the First World War. The various religious denominations allowed themselves to get entangled with national interests and thereby compromised themselves too much to still dare to recommend themselves as sources of morality. Moreover, thinking men had already come to their own conclusions. They perceived that the religions which during the World War boasted, in tragicomical fashion, of their God and his special assistance to their own nation, have all contributed not to the stability and improvement of moral standards, but to an undeniable deterioration of them. The leaders of nations during the first World War could not have committed so many infamies if they had not been backed up by their religions. Religion provided them with the easy conscience required for doing wrong. Hence as the latest solution appeared the slogan: "Away from religion! The amalgamation of morality with religion is an evil! Complete separation of the two is what is needed!"

The outcome in practise of this view was the nonreligious school in which, in place of religion, purely moral instruction was given.

One must certainly take cognisance of the facts on the basis of which this result has been arrived at. Men would be better if the God-belief would not so often prove an assistance to being bad. But are the conclusions here drawn quite correct? Firstly: will purely moral instruction, without a religious background, be in a position to foster morality? And secondly: is it really religion that is to blame for this decline of morality?

To be able to answer this question, we must first ask: "What is morality?" And to this question I answer: Morality is selflessness, or at the very least, the deliberate, serious struggle against self-seeking. There is, after all, only one immorality out of which the thousandfold forms of evil-doing flow—and this is self-seeking. Man, however, does not have self-seeking as a mere quality which he can lay aside or slough off: but he is embodied self-seeking. Hence if he wages war against self-seeking, this means that he wages war against himself, against his very own being. For doing this, however, he must have a very strong motive, otherwise this combat against himself will become a mere sport, as it were, which will be pursued as long as it can be carried on without too much inconvenience, but will be thrown aside the moment the struggle for existence makes such a step necessary.

Morality is getting into this bad predicament where bare

moral instruction is given in modern schools. It then becomes a mere sport, a matter of good taste, of personal decency, of common sense: but the compelling force of necessity is wholly lacking. When the hour of trial arrives, when it is a question of "to be or not to be," then one breaks through all restraints, breaks one's pledged word, commits perjury, attacks others violently. It may happen on a large scale what is done in small matters: when, for instance, we wish to get at night into the last tramcar: if there is room enough for all, then, politely and considerately, we allow others to pass in before us. But if there are not enough seats for all, then everybody makes a wild rush to secure a seat and uses his elbows with utter disregard of others.

What is actual is what acts. If a morality is to be actual (that is genuine), it must act; that means, it must assist in the combat against self-seeking. This service bare moral instruction in schools can never perform. The "morality" which such instruction yields is not genuine morality.

That is one of the defects of an abstract moral instruction in school. Another is that it underrates, nay, completely misunderstands the nature and meaning of religion.

There are many, many definitions of religion, and none of them entirely covers the meaning of that term. What, however, genuine religion is, of that there is one sure, distinguishing mark: tolerance. A religion that does not make men tolerant is not true religion. Tolerance, however, is nothing but tolerance in demonstration. Hence, religion, if it is to be actual and genuine, must produce selflessness.

Here we come face to face with that function of religion which for mankind as a social phenomenon is the most important of all. Man needs religion; for it is that irreplaceable value which produces morality out of itself. To push religion to one side and try to run morality by itself means to begin to build a house by starting with the roof. Hence men ought not to begin by hunting religion out of the schools, but by introducing into them actual religion, genuine religion, which can demonstrate its actuality, its genuineness precisely by teaching how to wage successful war against self-seeking. But, as said before, there must be a strong motive for morality; and it must be powerful enough to act with compelling force.

In the last analysis, man can only be compelled to what he

compels himself. That is to say, he can only be compelled by his own thinking. The compulsion which the faith-religions exercise as begetters of morality proceeds from emotion; to be precise, from fear of God. Fear is an emotion. Emotions, however, are liable to radical change: they can turn into their very opposite; they can also entirely disappear. Hence, if the religions of faith no longer perform the function of instilling morality, the reason for this lies not in the mere fact that they are religions, but in the fact that they are religions based on emotion. The most intimate, the most important thing by far about a man is his thinking. If a religious structure is to have any soundness, any solidity, it must be erected upon a foundation of clear thinking. Man's indisputable and firm possession is only what he has laid hold of by his own thinking. If on the basis of any kind of thought-process he once has comprehended that he must be moral, such morality will never permit itself to be shaken. It well may happen that the man may be too weak to carry it out in its entirety; but it will never permit him to tell lies to himself.

Hence everything depends upon finding a religion which begets morality as a *necessity of thinking;* and that religion is Buddhism. Because from the insight into egolessness follows that a man does not *have* his words, thoughts and deeds as functions of an "I" or self, or any independent and separate agent; but that he is action itself, through and through, nothing but action. But if he is action itself, the reward of good, that is, of selfless action; the punishment of evil, that is, of self-seeking action, does not need to be searched for and found somewhere else; for he himself precisely *becomes* his own action, as the blossom becomes the fruit, an "I" or self as a "doer" who "has" deeds just like any other "alienable property" of his, but in the core of his being remains unaffected by them—such a thing there is not. There is nothing but this action, running its self-actuated course in the fivefold play of the physical and mental aggregates (*khandha*) constituting the so-called personality. *"Suddha-dhammā pavattanti,"* "bare processes roll on." His good and evil actions may or may not affect others; they will always affect himself and, that, inescapably.

This idea, thought out and lived accordingly, produces morality as a necessity of thinking, as a logical inevitability. I *must* be selfless. My thinking compels me to it. If I am not, I shall hurt myself. And if I cannot act as I ought, at least I shall carry with me the awareness that this is so; and this will be a seed of renewed efforts towards a good and selfless life.

To sum up: What mankind needs before everything else is actual morality. In order to arrive at this, however, there is need of right understanding, that is to say, of Buddhism. Only from this soil grows an *actual* morality, which is realistic and effective. And so, let it be each man's care to see to it that he actualises that understanding within himself, in tolerance, in readiness to renounce, in compassion; and that he helps in spreading it to the best of his ability by pointing it out to others and by gifts given in its service.

Homage to Him, the Teacher

Is the Buddhist Selfish?

One of the objections, that is to say reproaches, most frequently met with, when presenting Buddhism, is this:

"The Buddhist criticises the Christian for living a moral life only because of his hope of eternal life with God. To do good for this reason is selfishness. But the Buddhist himself acts just as selfishly when he does what is right in order to secure a good rebirth. That is to say, he acts rightly not for the sake of the good, but for the sake of self."

At first sight, this objection seems justified; and for one who is only half-informed about Buddhism, it is sufficient to reject Buddhism altogether. But actually this objection is quite unjustified, and only shows a complete misunderstanding of the nature of Buddhism. Selfishness means, of course, what the word itself suggests: it is a craving, longing, planning and grasping in the service of self, in the service of self-preservation. Selfishness is necessarily bound up with the idea of self-preservation. But good action in the Buddhist sense, is not meant for preserving the self, but for getting free from self. The Buddhist is not concerned with a self that has to be purified and ennobled, but with a self that has to be worked off, worn away, got rid of. Selfishness is, here, not a property that man has, a sort of taint, a stain on the splendour of a shining "self," but from the point of view of Buddhist insight, man is selfishness itself. And to get rid of selfishness, does not mean in Buddhism that a self should get cured of selfishness and arrive at an "ego" pure and free from selfishness; but it means in the most serious and strictest sense: to rid oneself of one's self, to be free of self.

Doing good is an external symptom. Every symptom has aspects of different significance. It is quite a different thing whether one does good, as in the case of the Christian, in order to become a purified self (a blessed soul), or with the object of doing away with self as does the Buddhist. To speak of the latter attitude as selfishness has no sense.

Besides, if one has understood Buddhism correctly, one will understand that there is no room for an external purpose, for any "in order to." The Buddhist does not act rightly in order to gain something better, to recover himself in an everlasting form, but he discards self because he knows that "to be rid of self" is a definite possibility and hence it becomes a necessity. He knows that this "rid of self" is the fulfilment of the innermost conditions of man's existence, the fulfilment of his ultimate possibilities. Existence is such that it does not allow for the attainment of any (worldly) goal for the sake of which one feels that one exists. Existence is such that, if rightly understood, it tends towards "the ending," the ceasing of existence. Hence an "in order to" would be as much out of place here as in the case of a dying flame. The flame does not burn in order to go out; but it becomes extinct because this, too, is included in the condition of its existence. For a soul as assumed by the faith religions, being-in-existence is natural because it is a necessity; and to live so as to reach a higher level of life is a logical consequence. In the case of a flame, or in the case of life pictured as a flame, existence is not natural because it is not necessary. Here existence is something artificial and it is *maintained* artificially: and ceasing of existence is the ultimate and highest, the deepest and innermost fulfilment of the conditions of existence. The Buddhist does not give up "in order to" give up. By doing so he would, as it were, stumble over his own legs; he would forge for himself a new chain that is more subtle than any other. To give up for the sake of giving up would mean non-willing for the sake of non-willing, whereby one would succumb to, "willing," worse than before. For "willing" is of such a nature that non-willing is also a form of willing. Willing has no opposite; either it is present or it is not.

The Buddhist does not practise non-willing because he does not wish to will (or to desire), but because he no longer can will (or desire). His way of thinking, his new attitude of mind, his new sense of reality make any willing (as a desire) impossible for him, whether in the form of willing or of non-willing.

Thereby it becomes likewise impossible for him to take up an optimistic or pessimistic attitude towards actuality. The Buddhist is neither an optimist nor a pessimist; he is an "actualist," a realist. That is to say, he himself is actuality, and by intuitively responding to it, that is to himself, he exhausts the ultimate possibility inherent in actuality, the possibility of cessation; and this, not because he deliberately wills it, but because he has recognised it as the ultimate possibility.

What is true of the goal is also true of the way leading to it. If the Buddhist really is a Buddhist, he will act rightly not for the sake of a favourable rebirth—ever and again does the Buddha warn against this—but simply because his new insight compels him to act rightly; and the favourable rebirth follows as a natural consequence, just as blue sky will appear when the clouds disperse, or like the feeling of comfort after a satisfying meal. Just as one does not eat for the sake of having that comfortable feeling, but in complying to natural conditions of life, so also the right action of a Buddhist is not meant to bring about future comfort, but it is in pursuance of the natural conditions of existence, which, of course, demand a good measure of keen insight to be recognised as such.

Thus the right action of the Buddhist is of a nature that serves, not for the *affirmation of self*, but for the giving up of self. For the Buddhist who does not rely on belief but on experience, and for whom in his experience all possibility of belief in an eternal soul has disappeared, there is neither truth in *itself*, nor goodness *in itself*, as absolutes. *Truth is*, for him, nothing but the ceasing of ignorance, and *goodness is* nothing but the relinquishing of evil. And that relinquishment of evil is nothing but the relinquishment of self, bit by bit, thread by thread, until finally all is unravelled, crumbling away, extinguished.

If one has once understood thus the right action of a Buddhist and his motive for it, there is no further room, no possibility, for selfishness.

From *Die Brockensammlung*, 1932

Buddhist Propaganda

A very great difference can be noticed between the propagation of Buddhism and that of Christianity; and from this difference again a conclusion can be drawn as to the basic difference between these two religions.

Buddhism, like Christianity, is a world religion. Like Judaism, neither of them is restricted to a limited area of our world; nor, unlike Hinduism, are they restricted to a limited cultural zone; instead, both claim to have a message for the whole world, for all humanity. But the means used by these two religions for spreading their message are as different as their essential nature.

When, years ago, I was at Point Pedro, the northernmost place of the island of Ceylon, the tree was shown to me—as far as I can recollect, it was a giant fig-tree—under which Francis Xavier, the Jesuit apostle, had preached his first sermon. Ill and exhausted by a long and trying sea voyage, he nevertheless did not delay to preach his gospel, no sooner he had set foot on the island.

It is well known that Buddhist Ceylon did not much care for Christianity, and Francis Xavier did not preach there with any great success. But here we are not so much concerned with the question of success as with the path that is pursued. Xavier's first step on land is symptomatic for the way of offering the Christian gospel and for its teaching of salvation. Thus does a man act whose heart is full of the gift that he has to impart to others, and who, therefore, makes use of every possible opportunity to share this gift. Whether there is a demand or desire for it is a matter of indifference. Irrespective of that it is offered, not to say forced upon, others. In the very nature of every faith-religion there is a craving for making converts. To propagate means here trying to proselytise and thus to increase the numbers of believers. The basic nature of Buddhism precludes this sort of propaganda. Attempts at conversion have as little sense in Buddhism as if one would try converting someone to the correct solution of a mathematical problem. The person concerned must himself make the calculations for finding the mistakes hidden in the problem set to him; then he himself will know when he has come to a correct solution. If he does not act like that, then all attempts at his conversion will be useless, even if the correct solution is presented to him ready-made.

There are many who call themselves Buddhists. They talk about Buddhism and may even talk quite correctly about it. But they themselves have not accomplished the task laid before them. And thus they resemble a man who has come across the right solution only by good luck.

What then is the way by which Buddhism can be propagated. It is a way that is in conformity with a teaching of actuality. It is not enough that one talks about it and spreads its praises abroad. It must become a personal experience and must be actualised, put into practise, in life. In the Suttas, the Discourses of the Buddha, we are told about a certain venerable monk, Puṇṇa by name, who wanted to carry the Buddha's message to others. But we must not think that he did it by preaching at street corners. He quietly, earnestly, resolutely *lived* the Teaching; and so, slowly but irresistibly, he drew to himself those who felt attracted by the Word of the Buddha.

For it must be recognised that not all and every one will be attracted by the Buddha's Teaching. The Buddha himself, in the *Saccaka Sutta*, gives the following three similes.

"Suppose a piece of wood is lying in the water, soaked through with water. Do you think that, by rubbing it, anyone could produce fire out of it?—Certainly not—Again, there is another piece of wood, lying on dry ground, but it is wet itself, soaked through with moisture. Do you think it possible to kindle fire with it?—Certainly not—And finally, there is a piece of wood that is dry itself and lies on dry ground. Do you think that out of it, fire may be kindled?—Certainly." It is similar with men's receptivity for the Teaching, with their "inflammability" by the Teaching. There is a man who is similar to the wet wood immersed in water; he lives in unfavourable circumstances and is himself unfavourably disposed. To him the Buddha speaks in vain. Or there is a man who is like the wet wood lying on dry ground: he is in favourable circumstances, but himself is unfavourably disposed. And finally, there is a man who is similar to the dry wood lying on dry ground: he lives in favourable circumstances and is himself favourably disposed. When such a one hears the Teaching of renunciation, of relinquishment and cessation, his understanding is set aflame, his mind's vibration is in harmony with the Teaching; he is elated, gladdened and he knows well: "There is an escape from this Saṃsāra, for ever! Indeed, there is!" For him his whole attitude towards life takes shape in a great threefold chord: lust after the world, in the beginning; suffering, in the middle; and escape from all this, in the end!

Of course, if one is to be gripped by the Word of the Buddha, it must be there. And for being there, a Buddha, an Enlightened One, must have arisen in the present aeon (*kalpa*), must have blossomed in this era, like the rarest of flowers. But not in every aeon does a Buddha blossom forth. There are many eras without Buddhas, without Enlightened Ones. These are the dark world periods, while our present era, in which we have the good fortune to live, is illumined by the Buddha-light. Our world period is a fortunate one, a *Bhadda-kappa,* because in its immeasurably long intervals of time Buddhas have arisen no less than three times before the Enlightened One of our own age.

People speak so much of the misery of our present days. Certainly, there is misery enough. But all this weighs but little against the advantage our age enjoys in being shone upon by the Teaching.

May everyone see clearly what an advantage this is! May everyone, in the measure of his strength, try to make the best use of it, lest he lose precious time which can never be brought back again. "*Of all gifts, the best is the gift of the Dhamma.*"

From *Die Brockensammlung*, 1929

Saving Knowledge

Men may be divided according to their attitude towards life: there are those who look upon this life here as a given, positive value in itself; and there are others who look upon it, not as a positive, but as a provisional value, and therefore as something from which one must and can become free. In other words, men divide into those who feel they belong to life and long for it and those who feel themselves alien to it and long to be out of it.

Bearing in mind this fundamental division, let us try to arrive at some clear idea as to the nature of religion. Religion must be something that embraces both aforementioned attitudes towards life. That a person who is not concerned with any idea of salvation may, at the very outset, be excluded from all religion and religious feeling is in conflict with historical facts. The whole of China would then have to be placed outside of religion; for the Chinese mind, in its original modes of thought, is not concerned with ideas of salvation. For the Chinese mind, world and life are something to which man finally and for ever belongs. The world is a well-ordered system where the inner relations correspond to the outer. It is a cosmos, a genuinely human world, a world for men, a world that carries its meaning (the Tao) within itself, a world that has meaning because it is "meaning" in itself.

The idea of a God existing outside this human world, through whom alone it acquires sense and significance, is here excluded. But on that account one is not entitled to deny the term "religion" to Chinese thought. The only thing we can deduce from that fact is that religion is by no means identical with belief in a god: and people will do well to keep this firmly in mind.

Religion in its purest sense is the question as to the meaning of life. It thus stands quite apart from a *Weltanschauung*, that is a theory of the universe, which is only concerned with data of life and an orderly arrangement of these data. And if to the question about life's meaning, the Chinese mind gives the answer: "Life is just itself, it is meaning-in-itself," while the faith-religions say that "Life receives meaning only from some metaphysical entity, from a Beyond; in other words, from God," then both teachings, despite their internal differences, agree in that they are answers to the question about the meaning of life, and hence, both of them are religions.

Thus do these two views of life compare with each other, that of the Chinese mind and that of the religions of faith. And the former is obviously a unique phenomenon in the mental life of mankind, endowed with all the allurement of the singular, before which all others, especially we Europeans, stand perplexed, asking the question: "But how is it possible to get along without God?" Well, this is possible, because one can be religious even though one has no belief in any god. Belief in a god is not necessarily religion. It is only one of the forms under which the religious question, the religious problem, that is, the question as to the meaning of life, is answered.

Hereby we are immediately faced with the second question: "Which answer now is better; that of the Chinese mind or that of the others?" For being better or worse there is only one standard, and that is, the content of actuality. And in this regard, both answers are inadequate because both are prejudiced.

To answer the question as to the meaning of life, which means, to furnish an actual or realistic religion, this one can only do when one knows what life is. The question as to the what of life takes precedence of all religion, and decides not only as to the justification of the idea of deliverance, but also as to the form in which this idea of deliverance is experienced.

So long as one is not clear as to the what of life, assertion stands against assertion: he who affirms and enjoys life stands opposed to the sufferer in life, the optimist against the pessimist, Nietzsche against Schopenhauer. To one, eternity is "deepest, deepest bliss," as Nietzsche sings in his hymn; to the other it is the deepest torment. The one feels himself called and chosen to eternal life as to a feast; the other feels himself condemned to it as to a martyrdom; and both squander their arguments in vain. For, so long as one does not know what life is, and in consequence judges according to the facts accessible to him, the one has just as much right in what he says as the other, and can also prove his right with equal impressiveness.

And so: What is life? To this question the Buddha answers: Life is a process of grasping which runs its course in the five grasping-groups. In the forty-fourth Discourse of the Majjhima Nikāya, to the question. "What has the Exalted One taught that personality is?" the following reply is given: "The Exalted One has taught that personality is the five grasping-groups, namely, the grasping-group of corporality, the grasping-group of sensation, the grasping-group of perception, the grasping-group of concept, the grasping-group of consciousness." Thus, we have here a grasping which is so fashioned that what we commonly call mental conception belongs to it: we have grasping as nutriment, and thinking, consciousness, as a form of eating.

Correspondingly it is said in the Canon, for example, in the Saṃyutta Nikāya: "There are four kinds of nutriment: first, material nutriment, gross or fine; second, sense-contact; third, volitional thought; fourth, consciousness."

With this insight, Buddhism becomes the "middle teaching," the *majjhima-paṭipadā,* which stands between and above the two extremes of all mental life, faith and science. Faith believes in life as something in its essence metaphysical, purely spiritual. Science seeks to make out that life is something essentially physical, purely corporeal. But both here fall into contradiction with themselves, that is to say, with the fact that there are concepts present. For if life by its essential nature is something purely spiritual, that is, a self-existent spiritual something, how then could we ever arrive at concepts of it? A purely spiritual thing could only be absolutely itself; and could never be present as such, that is to say, as conceptual relation.

On the other hand: If life is a purely corporeal thing, how could the concepts ever issue forth from it? And yet the concepts are there, once for all, and in the facts "faith and science" themselves they experience the impossibility of their own existence; that is to say, they stand in contradiction to the fact of their own existence, in as much as faith believes in something concepts can never reach; while science seeks to prove something which can never reach the concepts. Faith oversteps actuality; it transcendentalises. Science "under-steps" actuality: it "immanentises." And both, despite their apparent opposition, agree with each other in this, that neither is in unison with actuality, an agreement that points to a deeper, common root.

Between and above both stands Buddhism as the Middle Path, the *majjhima-paṭipadā*, in as much as it teaches that life is neither a purely corporeal, physical thing: but a conceptual thing, a mental conceiving, taken in that actual sense in which it comprises in itself grasping and conceiving, mental as well as physical grasping; "grasping" taken here in the strictest, most actual sense, in as much as this insight that it is so, the knowledge of myself as a conceptual process, is not something outside this process, self-existent and cognising, but is itself a conceptual process. In other words, the knowledge of the fact that I am a purely conceptual process implies no act of cognition, directed towards myself, from the standpoint of a self-existent ego (*attā*). But what occurs here is just another instance of processes rolling on, a continued growth of conceiving and conceptualizing; there is no confrontation with myself, but an ever-repeated remembrance within myself; I am writing this down here and express it in these short sentences, not because I think that my readers will now understand it at once without difficulty. I myself have spent long years in patient and persistent thought in order to arrive at this insight; and I place it before my readers only for stirring and rousing them to equally patient reflection.

In my essential nature I am neither something metaphysical (pure spirituality) as faith tries to make out, nor something physical (pure corporeality) as science would have us believe. In my essential nature I am certainly "mentality," but not self-existent mentality, mind-in-itself, that is something metaphysical. Rather I am a mental *process*, a conceptual *process*, that is, something which, just because it is a process, requires the corporeal for its existence. Hence I am, in my essential nature *a-metaphysical* or, as the Buddha puts it, *an-attā* (not self), which is the Pali word exactly corresponding to our word *a-metaphysical*.

Also the nature of the mutual relationship that obtains here between the corporeal and the mental was stated by the Buddha, namely in the formula of the mutual conditionality of mind-and-matter and consciousness (*viññāṇa-paccayā nāma-rūpa*, and the reverse), which can here be mentioned only in passing.

Hence, I am a process of grasping, a process of conceiving, a conceptual process; and the knowledge that this is so is likewise a form of conceiving. But whence does this conceptual and conceiving process spring? What is the line of descent of the ego?

In the act-of-faith I am (as *attā*, "soul") a self-existent entity, eternal, absolutely beginningless, absolutely endless; condemned to eternal existence. In the attempted act-of-experience of science, I am a biological phenomenon that descends from other biological phenomena, from "my parents." These again descend from their parents, and so forth, in an endless series that leaves the question as to a first beginning completely unanswered, by showing it ahead and along, again and again.

Here, too, the Buddha-word shows itself as a Middle Path between, and above, both faith and science: As a conceiving and conceptual process, as a nutritional process, I am a self-sustaining process, and hence not a mere reaction of other life-processes, not a mere offshoot of my parents. Force (energy) exists, but it is not a force in an absolute force, absolutely beginningless and endless, but it is a process, just this process of conceiving; so therefore, it is something which, for being present at all, must always and only spring from its own antecedent conditions. And the starting-point where it springs up is ignorance about itself. Thus, in place of the absolute beginninglessness of faith and the relative beginninglessness of science, we get at a reflexive beginninglessness, that is the beginninglessness of reference to itself, as in the Buddha's Teaching.

The role which ignorance (*avijjā*) plays as an ever new starting-point of the conceiving-process called "I" is given in the twelve-linked series of the simultaneously Dependent Origination (*paṭicca samuppāda*). In the understanding of that formula: the ego can experience itself as a process in the strictest sense, that is to say, as being capable of arising and hence also of stopping—in short, as a beginningless process so constituted that it includes the possibility of stopping. The ego, i.e., "life as experiencing itself," is a possibility of stopping, a "ceasability."

Here, we have pronounced the key-word to which all life hearkens and to which all life is subject: the possibility of stopping. What am I? What is life? A possibility of stopping! Herewith we have arrived at our subject proper; and at the same time, at the answer to it. Saving knowledge is the knowledge that it is possible to be "saved," that is, freed from ever-recurring suffering. Here "salvation" has no longer the meaning of a divine act of grace, nor the meaning of annihilation in the mechanical, materialistic sense of science. Salvation is here the completion of a task which is possible and therefore necessary to carry out. With the recognised possibility of stopping is also given the actualisation of this possibility of stopping—stopping as the final goal, giving up as the final task.

The saṃsāra, this ever-changing world of ever-new births, of ever-new acts of becoming "world" again, is precisely so constituted that Nibbāna, Deliverance, Salvation, does not lie in any Beyond that can be reached only by a transcendental leap out of the world; but saṃsāra bears Nibbāna within itself as its final fulfilment; a fulfilment that takes place in a process of radical detachment experienced in a progressive inner awareness (*verbewusstung*); this process of detachment starts with Right Understanding as its first link and ends with Right Concentration as the eighth link. Where saṃsāra, this world of ours, has been comprehended as that ever-repeated conceiving which is life itself and creates life, there Nibbāna is no longer something that stands against the conceiving as its object, be it in the form of a scientific conceivability or as a religious inconceivability, but Nibbāna is then seen as the stopping of this conceiving. And salvation is then neither a salvation out of this transient existence into an eternal life, nor is it salvation as a final annihilation, but it is the stopping, the cessation, of that very conceiving which is life itself.

This stopping can be experienced. Salvation, or deliverance, is a process that can be experienced: Nibbāna can be realised. This process of deliverance is not embedded in this existence nor is it external to it; it is neither immanent nor transcendent. It is the fading away, the stopping, the ceasing of this existence itself; it is the last experience: the experience of the cessation of experiencing. Consciousness is there; but it no longer springs up again in a new life-creating act of conceiving. Thus it resembles capital that no longer pays interest but is used up until it is exhausted; or it resembles the flame of a lamp that is not sustained by fresh oil and burns towards its extinction. It is "old *kamma*" (*purāṇaṃ kammaṃ*), the outcome of past thinking, the result of past action; no longer a living flame, but the reaction from former burning, resembling a residual supply of heat that comes to an end because further sustenance is lacking.

Cool and serene rest the senses on their objects, no longer mingling with them, like drops of water on the lotus leaf. Only this one experience reverberates the experience of the cessation of experiencing—an experience, the end of which can be anticipated, just as we can anticipate the end of a flame that does not receive fresh fuel. "In being freed, there is the knowledge of being freed." "Finally extinguished, with consciousness no longer finding a foothold"—this is a standing expression in the Buddhist texts for the Arahant, for him who is finally freed by the ultimate saving knowledge.

In the Udāna the Buddha says: "As the great ocean is permeated by one taste only, that of salt, so the Dhamma is permeated only by the taste of deliverance." In this longing after deliverance rings out the deepest chord of all existence; in that longing the highest opens.

The Chinese mind that feels secure in life and unperturbed, free from doubts and fanaticism, from religious coercion and intolerance, is certainly a surprising and arresting phenomenon. And the life of the Indo-Ariyan nations with the fervour of their ideas of salvation, with the fury of passions that were, and still are, kindled by those ideas, this is surely a terrible and even repugnant phenomenon: and yet, in that fury glow, unconsciously, truth, actuality and final fulfilment. And this final fulfilment is experienced in the saving knowledge, that is, in the Right Understanding bestowed by the Buddha, provided it finds expression in right resolve, and that again is put into practise by right speech, right action, right livelihood, right effort, right mindfulness and right concentration. Here, saving knowledge, first a mere hope, becomes actuality, realisation, because it issues from insight into the "what of life," into the essence of actuality.

Buddhism cannot be proved, and it does not need to be believed. Therefore, the Teaching is called "knowledge and conduct" (*vijjā-caraṇa*). This entails a resolve, just as a resolve is required for taking bitter medicine. Resolve requires confidence in the Buddha; and this confidence, again, requires the staggering suspicion that life may not be all it seems to be, but that it is something questionable, and is through and through vulnerable. It is true, and the Buddha himself had experienced it and given expression to it, that men of understanding are difficult to find. But, well for him who listens and catches a glimpse of what is here set forth.

From *Die Brockensammlung*, 1929

Right Understanding

Often when I read or hear highly emotional speeches, I wish to ask the speakers whether they know what they are excited about, and to tell them that they resemble those who worry about the numerator and take no notice about the denominator of a fraction. However big the numerator may be, the real value will depend on the denominator. You heap up life-values and your claims for life-values, but you take neither time nor trouble to consider what life is, intrinsically; in the service of which you make all your claims, and in the service of which you rave and rage and set up and pull down. Would it not be more reasonable were you to look at the thing for which you reduce existence to a torment and the right of living to an intolerable duty?

A man reflects: Here is this "I," mentality-corporeality, marked off only vaguely from the outer world by a skin, consuming material nutriment (food, drink, air), and mental nutriment (feeling, perception, consciousness), this outer world, in many ways, and drawing in, and nourishing itself on, the world, and excreting. This process of consumption by the "I" is like a flame that is continuously feeding itself to burn on.

The man continues his reflections: In this eating and excreting, in this seizing and letting go, this coming and going, there is no place for what you before called the "I." There is not in this burning a thing-in-itself, something eternal, a soul, which is not burning. To believe in such an "I" or a soul is mere blind belief, error, or ignorance. The destruction of the "I"-delusion, the understanding of the "I" as a delusion, is the great deed of the Buddha that liberates humanity, and because of that deed he calls himself the Buddha, the Awakened One, the Enlightened One, the Teacher, and the Tathāgata, the Perfect One. However far one's thoughts may have strayed, that insight, that leaps into actuality, is enough for reaching the goal at once. However confused a man may be in his dreams, once he awakes he is in actuality: and however far he may have wandered in error, with the destruction of ignorance he is in truth.

So before you eagerly cherish desires for yourself as though you might go on for ever, and before you eagerly cherish desire for wife and child, for friend and fellow countryman, as though these might go on for ever, look at least once at the thing for the sake of which you have become so eager, and for which you make demands, accumulate, heap up, rage and oppress!

There is the "I" with a skin over it, full of unclean matter, subject to decay, disease, corruption, foulness, a thing that is devouring and expelling, attracting and repelling, becoming and vanishing. The only constant thing in it is its continuous grasping of food, drink, air, feeling, perception and consciousness.

Is there nothing besides this grasping in me? Might there not be something eternal, the lord of this play of the flame, a doer who does the deed, a speaker who utters the words, a thinker who thinks the thought? Should there be only a bare process at work?

Man, why do you question thus? Why do you uselessly lose time in doubt and uncertainty? Listen! A man wanted to go to a certain place and came to a signpost on which was written: "To such and such place, one hour." Then the man began to doubt whether he could reach the place in one hour, and while thus doubting a good part of the hour passed away, and he thought, "Much time has gone by and I am not one step nearer the goal. This signpost must be wrong."

The Buddha is such a signpost. He does not want you to argue but to follow him. Do not ask again, "Is it possible that I am nothing but a coming and a going, a grasping and a letting go, a movement due to the wind of the passion for life?" Do not lament that by such an outlook your most beautiful and highest ideals which you and humanity hold, are lost. Do not seek beauty! Seek actuality!

What is actuality?

Contemplate and experience your own self. Then you will know and experience actuality.

Here, in your own self, forms arise, manifest themselves, and pass away; here feelings, perceptions, mental formations and consciousness arise, manifest themselves, and pass away. As a flame burns, so burn these five aggregates because of an inner force. That force is craving. What is craving? Mere craving and nothing more. From where does it come? From the last craving. And that craving? From the one before that. From where do all cravings come? From ignorance. From where does ignorance come? It is not possible to find a beginning of beings obstructed by ignorance. What is the source of the next craving? The present craving. How is craving nourished? With the attraction of forms, sounds, odours, flavours, contacts and concepts. What is the end of craving? Craving ends when ignorance ends, that is, the ignorance of the "I" as not-self, not-personality, not-soul, and as a working without a worker. How can ignorance cease? Through right instruction. When ignorance ceases, what ceases? The craving for forms, sounds, odours, flavours, contacts and concepts ceases. When craving ceases what ceases? World-grasping ceases. And when world-grasping ceases, what ceases? Violence and bloodshed cease; quarrels and intolerance cease; anguish, fear, the will to possess they will not let go, all these bad things cease. Now all these things are external to me. What ceases in me? The flame of the "I," the craving to continue through ignorance ceases when ignorance ceases. When that ceases what happens? Just as a flame that does not get oil goes out, so the "I" flame that is not fed by ignorance goes out, too. The play of phenomena comes to an end when the formations (*kamma*) cease. Of what were phenomena the expression? Of craving, which comes to end without remainder, with the ending of ignorance.

So, if I want to act without ignorance, must I generally give up all bodily and mental nutriment? The fault is not in taking nutriment. All beings live because of nutriment, teaches the Buddha. There is no existence without food.

But all depends on the way you take food. You should take food without craving for it, without greed, continually ready to give it up. Truly, life becomes worth living when one no longer clings to it, as a ring becomes easy to wear when it does not chafe the finger. How free and happy all could live, were each person to find contentment in himself and were not to trouble others! A person will be contented within himself and will not trouble others if he knows what he wants for himself; and he will know what he wants for himself if he knows what he is. He will know what he is when he receives right instruction. That is the value of Right Understanding. Tolerance, peace, happiness, and all blessings of mankind have their roots in Right Understanding.

From *Neu-Buddhistische Zeitschrift*, 1918/19

Dr. Dahlke's Last Lecture

This lecture, here slightly abridged, was to be given through the Berlin Radio; but illness prevented Dr. Dahlke from delivering it in person. It was read on his behalf on 22 February 1928, just one week before Dr. Dahlke's death.

Buddhism is the Teaching of the Buddhas, that is, the Awakened Ones. There has been not only one but many Buddhas and only the last one of the countless series is the one whom we know as a historical personage.

The name of this last historical Buddha, after whom a countless number of Buddhas will follow, is Gotama. He was born in Kapilavatthu in the extreme north of India and came of a royal family. At the age of 29, having married young and being then the father of a little son, he left his father's gorgeous palace and went forth into homelessness (*pabbajjā*). He became an ascetic (*samaṇa*), a religious mendicant, and, with shorn head and beard, carrying his alms-bowl, he went begging his food from house to house.

There was nothing extraordinary in such a course of conduct in India of these days. People of all stations in life used to do the same. Holy men, alone or in company, used to wander all over the country, and the populace, though not wealthy, considered it a sacred duty to support these mendicants and supply them with the necessities of life.

It was this life that the Ascetic Gotama followed. After many years of extreme self-mortification, a new insight dawned upon him, which made him call himself the Buddha, the Awakened One. In order to understand this new insight he had won, it is necessary to cast a glance at the religious life in India at the time of the Buddha.

The self-contained world of the Indian continent was a land of religions *par excellence.* There is no religious or philosophical possibility that was not thought out here and, as different from the West, radically put into practise. Only one thing never materialized in India as long as it was purely Indian and not influenced by Islam: the formation of churches.

In a certain sense and up to a degree, churches are always a fixation and dogmatisation of the religious spirit, making for rigidity. But in India, religion has always been a living experience, with the changes natural to every living experience. Thus India's entire religious life was a constant process of revision of the God-idea. For it should never be forgotten that man comes first. First man, then his God! The God-idea has meaning only as a function in the mental life of humanity and has a value only in so far as it can help humanity on its road to perfection. To make of the God-idea a value in itself, compared with which man is reduced to nothing, is to misconceive the meaning of man and the universe. Hence, true religion requires from time to time revisions of the God-idea, if its vitality is to be preserved so that it may serve the betterment of mankind.

At the time of the Buddha, India experienced the greatest revision of its God-idea it ever had. Belief in the glittering variety of the polytheistic heaven was "giving way to the idea of a single deity, the monotheistic belief in Brahma, the One, the Glorious and Blessed, before whom the different gods and goddesses who had hitherto satisfied Indian religious thought would fade like stars before the sun.

Into this scene of a tremendous reorientation entered the Buddha and shed the light of his genius upon these problems. What was of limited Indian relevance became now a universal human concern. For the first time in history, a world religion, breaking through the confines of the Indian continent, entered its claim under a seemingly paradoxical motto: *Is the idea of God essential to a religion?*

Buddhism in its entirety may be regarded as an answer to that question, and the answer is: *Man belongs to himself.* The self is the lord of self. The power that created man is not God but man's own deeds. No God sits in judgement upon him but man judges himself through his actions and their outcome. His destiny does not depend upon the will of a God who separates the goats from the sheep; it depends on his own actions.

But Buddhism is not atheism in the ordinary sense of the word. As commonly used, the atheist is conceived as a man whose atheism is an excuse for licence: "Nobody above can see me, none can hear me, I shall do as I like." Buddhism does not fight against the God-idea nor deny it, but it digests that concept fully by virtue of its spirituality, and makes it mean what it really ought to mean: a correlate of humanity, and it is characteristic of this new type of humanity that the individual becomes responsible to himself for every moment of his life.

For the Buddhist there is no God that can absolve him from sin. There is nothing in Buddhism that corresponds to the priest in theistic religions who is the intermediary between God and man. For the Buddhist there are only his own actions and their results. It is the religion of inexorable, unmitigated self-responsibility; hence it is a religion for adults who know that in the realm of reality nothing can be had for nothing.

Buddhism teaches that, as a basic experiential fact, man certainly owes his present existence to his parents. But the parents provide only the material for the new garb of life, the generative substances which, in the act of lust, are, as it were, torn out of their bodies. In those expelled cellular bodies, there vibrate for a while all potentialities and proclivities of life, and only wait for the force that will strike them like lightning and transform these potentialities into the actualities of a new life.

Thus from the mother's womb, there comes forth a new

being whose bodily characteristics are more or less inherited from his parents and ancestors, and in so far as the scientific laws of heredity hold true. But in his directive or motivational faculties or, as the Buddhist will say, in his *kamma*, the new being derives from his own previous existences. This vital kammic force from the past, released when the old form breaks up at death, has now entered this particular mother's womb because it had to enter here in accordance with its inherent merit, its character and moral quality. The new life-long "contract" between the *kamma* of the dissolving past form of life and the generative material in the new womb is a timeless process of direct instantaneous cognisance. All that is "mass" or "matter" in any sense has to wander through the spatial universe in terms of time; and for science with its empirico-physical conception of the universe, space and time are linked inseparably. But *kamma*, the vital force, strikes instantaneously, "not earlier, not later," as the Buddhist texts say; and it strikes where it has to strike owing to kammic affinity. Here there is no physical process following physical laws, but a lawfulness that is independent of all spatial limitations and has the instantaneous impact of lawful occurrence, or what is called fate or destiny. The being that breaks up in death is reborn where it can and must be reborn according to his deeds.

Buddhism, as a teaching of actuality, does not regard man as a creature of God nor of his parents, but as a creature of his own actions (*kamma*). The creative act takes place at birth (or conception) which is always a rebirth. And herein the parents are not "creators," or procreators, but "birth-helpers" (a male and female midwife, as it were); they are instrumental in helping the new being to be born. The new birth occurs in utilisation of the parental generative material, but not through it. Here there is only one true generative force: man's own actions (*kamma*). Good thoughts, words and deeds result in a favourable rebirth in a good environment; bad thoughts, words and deeds result in an unhappy rebirth in a bad environment.

The Buddha teaches that there are four kinds of actions: light, that is, good actions with bright results; dark, that is bad actions with black results; actions that are half and half, that is, partly good and partly bad with results that are a mixture of both; and lastly actions that are neither light nor dark and whose result will be the end of all actions.

The last type of action can issue only from Buddhist insight. While the doctrine of rebirth points to the practical side of Buddhism, the teaching about an "action that leads to the ending of all actions" indicates the profound philosophical aspect of the Dhamma which, in the present context, we can only mention, without elaborating it.

What is now the advantage of the doctrine of rebirth as compared to other religions and philosophies?

Every thinking man will admit that, in considering life, the fact that life exists is of less importance than the question how it exists and comes to be; and this again is dominated by the one question: Why do things happen as they do? The concept of causality governing the physical world becomes the idea of justice inherent in the destinies of living beings. Justice is the ultimate and deepest meaning of the world. Just as the world as far as it is physical, is based on causality so, as far as it acts as destiny in living beings, it rests on justice.

Why are things as they are? Why do they happen in the way they do? Is everything for the best? Are things controlled by order and law, or are they ruled by caprice or blind chance? Why is it that the good suffer and the wicked flourish? Why is it that one is starving and the other lives in luxury? Why is one strong and healthy and the other drags along a sickly body? How is it that one has all the talents and a brilliant mind while the other is as stupid as can be?

Either one *thinks*, and then life poses a problem at every step and throws the question at us "Why is it like this?" or one gives up thinking altogether. But as thinking is natural to man, he demands an answer to the problem: "Justice or Caprice?"

Here Buddhism shows its irreplaceable superiority as a realistic teaching of actuality.

As long as belief in a God and the fear of a God hold sway, that problem offers no intellectual and hence no practical difficulties. All that happens is in accordance with the inscrutable will of God, and who art thou, O man, to argue with Him? The cries of the poor and oppressed, the hunger of the starving multitude, the sufferings of the sick—all that, in the eyes of God, is only one single chord in the harmony of the universe, and man, with all his prying questionings, can only submit and pray!

But when belief in God and fear of God disappear, that summary solution of the problem loses its support and becomes untenable. In fact, belief in God, as everything in the world, has its periods of growth and decline. After a high tide of that belief in the Middle Ages, now a steady ebb of it, just as strong, has set in, and indications are that the low water mark has not yet been reached.

Hence the metaphysical solution of the problem is nowadays no longer adequate. Now, the State, called by Nietzsche "the latest idol," has taken matters in hand with that robust authoritarian arbitrariness that is typical of all institutions which consider only the material and this-worldly aspects of life. The State, itself a stark fact, asks for facts and wants to create facts. Thus, in the State's hands justice also is to become a fact that can be controlled and corrected until it conforms to the concept of justice held by the respective type of State.

But in that kind of approach it is forgotten that justice is not a ready-made fact that can be bodily transferred into life, but it is a process, the very life process. Life as it is experienced in joy and grief, wealth and poverty, in its ups and downs, is justice itself. One must only understand it and go down to the roots from which all this primarily grows. The State wants to realise its notion of justice (which is nothing more than just a notion of it) in this single life, wishing to create hard and ready facts. But this is impossible because it means trying to stop the wheel of life rolling on since times without a beginning. He who tries to put a spoke into that wheel has always brought only misery either for himself or for others. Life is not exhausted during a single spell of existence. Its pendulum swings beyond itself, in both directions, and one has to go along with it if one wants to solve the problem of justice.

Here the Buddha Dhamma steps in as the irreplaceable light bearer. It shows that what happens, and the way how it happens, is only the blossom and the fruit, and the roots of it are in former existences. Actions in thought, words and deeds are the womb from which I was born. I am the architect of my own destiny. It was in former lives that I fitted myself for this life; and it is in this life that I shall lay the foundation for the next.

Thus the Buddhist feels himself as a link in the chain of

inescapable justice against which there is no protest and no rebellion. There is only this one law and nothing else: As you sow, so you will reap.

With the swing of life's pendulum extending beyond present into the past and the future, an element of self-responsibility enters into the life of the individual that elevates Buddhism far above all other forms of religion and makes it a truly human religion, the religion of adult human beings who have actually grown up. Now the answer to the question, "Why are things as they are, and why do they happen in the way they do?" can no longer be that it is due to God's inscrutable will or due to social and economic imperfections that must be removed; but the answer now runs that it is because of my own actions in the past and those of others. Instead of the fear of God and fear of the ruling authority there is now *self-fear,* the fear of the self judgement and self-punishment through our own actions. As much as a religion of self-responsibility, Buddhism has a great mission to fulfil in the life of mankind that cannot be performed by any other religion or philosophy. Irreplaceable for the seeker after Truth, and entirely unique in its mental structure for the thinker, thus the Buddha Dhamma stands secure in the power of its inner Truth, waiting serenely for that recognition of its worth which other religions seek to obtain by eager propagation.

From *Die Brockensammlung, 1929*

Poems

Renunciation

Renunciation is a torment,
So saith one.
I say, No!
Renunciation, if freely done,
Can be the highest happiness.
The renouncing not freely done,
That is torment indeed:
Beggar-like going about,

Seeing others carousing.
That is real agony,
That is the greatest woe.
It is like death on the cross
And rightly called Gethsemane.
Ah, heart? Be no more a beggar,
Become at once a king!
Un-think all thy longings,
So wilt thou be from sorrow freed.
Once more only may I travel
This long pilgrimage alone:
With no other for companion,
Till my latest breath is done.
To the snow-peaks, heaven-high towering,
Dying, let me turn my eyes;
Dying, still look to the Teacher,
And the Lore that never lies.

Transl. by J. F. McKechnie

The End

If I had wings I would fly beyond love,
High to that world from every impulse free;
Where naught approaches—not love nor hate,
Where the only deed is pure abandoning.
Then, become cool, I may look back serene;
None should know me again; alone I walk on,
Walk on calmly, till the Way itself ends,
With him who walks thereon, and all is done.

Transl. by Soma Thera[3]

3. From a letter by Soma Thera: "This poem is a sort of Buddhist reply to the Western mystic who wants to fly to his love. Dahlke's poem shows the translucency of the poet's mind walking to the End of Ill, with full awareness and single-eyed devotion. The verses of the unknown Western mystic to which the poem alludes are called the 'Song of the Bride,' and have these opening lines:

"Had I the wings of Seraphim,
Thus would I fly, high
Upwards, into Eternity,
Unto my Sweet Love."

Bibliography of Dr. Paul Dahlke's Work

Buddhist Books

Aufsätze zum Verstaendnis des Buddhismus (1903) (Transl.: *Buddhist Essays*)

Das Buch vom Genie (1905)

Buddhismus als Weltanschauung (1914) (Transl.: *Buddhism and Science*)

Das Buch Pubbenivasa (1921)

Aus dem Reiche des Buddha. Buddhistische Erzaehlungen (Transl.: *Buddhist Stories*)

Buddhismus als Religion und Moral. Der Buddhismus, seine Stellung innerhalb des geistigen Lebens der Menschheit (1926) (Transl.: *Buddhism and its Place in the Mental Life of Mankind*)

Buddhismus als Wirklichkeitslehre und Lebensweg (1928)

Buddhist Periodicals

Neu-Buddhistische Zeitschrift

Die Brockensammlung

Translations from the Pali

Dhammapada, Dīgha-Nikāya (selection),
Majjhima Nikāya (selection).
Der Buddha (Anthology of Discourses).

Non-Buddhist Books

Englische Skizzen (1914)

Heilkunde und Weltanschauung (1928)

The Kandaraka and Potaliya Suttas

Two Discourses of the Buddha from the Majjhima Nikāya

Translated by

Nārada Thera & Mahinda Bhikkhu

WHEEL PUBLICATION NO. 79

These two discourses first appeared in 1925 in the periodical The Blessing, published by the "Servants of the Buddha" in Colombo. The introductions, and some of the notes, were written by the then-president of that society, Dr. Cassius A. Pereira (the late Venerable Kassapa Thera). In this reprint, a few alterations have been made in the texts and notes.

Introduction to the Kandaraka Sutta
(Majjhima Nikāya No. 51)

The scene of this Sutta is set at Campā, where the Buddha was temporarily residing with his company of bhikkhus on the bank of the Gaggarā tank.[1]

Campā, the capital of Aṅga, was on the east bank of the river of the same name, which formed the eastern boundary of Magadha. Prof. Rhys Davids was of the opinion that it was close to the modern Bagalpur.

The Commentary states that the tank was named after a certain Queen Gaggarā, by whose order it was constructed. On the bank was a grove of sweet-scented Campaka trees where the wandering ascetics were accustomed to tarry.

This Sutta may be summarised as follows: Pessa, a Buddhist, and Kandaraka, an ascetic of an alien sect, visit the Buddha. Kandaraka is deeply impressed with the demeanour of the silent disciples. The Master explains to him that there are both *asekhas* and *sekhas* in that company.

Asekhas, it should be noted, are *arahant* saints, who require no further training, having destroyed the fetters (*saṃyojana*) that bound them to existence. *Sekhas*, on the other hand, are those who have attained the first stages of sainthood but have not yet attained to the *arahant* fruit (*phala*) stage. The first seven of the Eight Noble individuals (*aṭṭha ariya puggala*) are *sekhas*.

The term "tank," as used in India and Ceylon, signifies an artificial pond or lake, mostly used as a water reservoir.

---

1. *Bhikkhu* means, literally, a beggar or mendicant. As there is no equivalent in English which exactly corresponds to this word, we prefer to retain the Pali term. A bhikkhu is not a priest who acts as a mediator between God and man. He has no priestly duties to perform. Having renounced worldly pleasure, he lives a life of voluntary poverty and perfect celibacy with the object of attaining deliverance from suffering. Nor is the bhikkhu a "beggar" in the common sense of the word: when collecting his alms food, he does not beg, but stands in front of the house silently, giving opportunity to the pious householder to acquire the merit of supporting a bhikkhu in his noble quest for Deliverance.

The Buddha then proceeds to explain his method of training, i.e., the four foundations of mindfulness (*satipaṭṭhāna*). Readers may refer to the Satipaṭṭhāna Sutta of the Dīgha Nikāya, or the Majjhima Nikāya, for details.[2] Pessa, pleased with the brief discourse, contrasts the openness of the animals with the dissimulation of men. He also expresses his admiration at the conciseness and lucidity with which the Buddha expounds (having understood the real nature of the world) what is truly advantageous and disadvantageous. Continuing, he says that they, laymen as they are, also abide in meditation on these *satipaṭṭhānas*, though not continuously (as monks are expected to), but as time permits.

The Buddha then takes up a new subject, in order to reveal a further contrast between his disciples and others, so that Pessa may appreciate their conduct the better. Unfortunately, soon after the enumeration of the four individuals that are found in this world, Pessa, having expressed his opinion with regard to them, takes leave of the Master.

Thereupon the Buddha draws the attention of the disciples to the fact that, had Pessa remained to hear an exposition of the four kinds of individuals, he would have gone away acquiring a great gain (in other words, having realised the first path of sainthood [*sotāpatti*]). Here is manifest the irresistible force of kamma, with which even a Buddha cannot interfere. The Commentary states that by reason of two conditions one fails to attain to sainthood, even when ripe for it, viz. evil company and lack of effort on one's own part.

Finally, the Buddha, at the request of the disciples, speaks at length on the four individuals.

The description of the first individual enables the reader to understand, to some extent, the austerities of those addicted to self-mortification.

The fourth individual, who neither torments self nor others, is the model of a bhikkhu: one who, as "a youth of a good family," upon seeing a Buddha appear on earth, and hearing him, is compelled to leave his uncongenial home and embrace the independent life of a homeless one. There he lives in strict accordance with the precepts

---

2. The latter version is translated in *The Wheel*, No. 19. See also *The Wheel*, No. 60: *The Satipaṭṭhāna Sutta and Its Application to Modern Life*.

(*sīla*); cultivates one-pointedness of mind (*samādhi*) and insight (*paññā*); and finally attains *arahant*ship, the deliverance of mind.

The Kandaraka Sutta

Thus have I heard. Once the Blessed One, with a large company of bhikkhus, was staying at Campā on the bank of the Gaggarā tank.

Then Pessa, the mahout's son, and Kandaraka, the wandering ascetic,[3] approached the Blessed One. Drawing near, Pessa, the mahout's son, saluted the Blessed One respectfully and sat down on one side. But Kandaraka, the wandering ascetic, exchanged friendly greetings with the Blessed One, and after the customary salutations remained standing aside.

Standing thus, Kandaraka, the wandering ascetic, surveyed the silent company of bhikkhus and addressed the Blessed One as follows: "It is wonderful, friend Gotama! It is marvellous, friend Gotama![4] How well has this company of bhikkhus been trained by you. And those who were exalted Fully Enlightened Ones in the distant past, friend Gotama, did those Blessed Ones also train the company of bhikkhus well, even to this pitch of perfection, as, at the present time, the company of bhikkhus has been well trained by you? And those, friend Gotama, who will be exalted Fully Enlightened Ones in the distant future, will they also train the company of bhikkhus well, even to this pitch of perfection, as at the present time, the company of bhikkhus has been well trained by you?"

"That is so, Kandaraka, that is so. And those, Kandaraka, who were exalted Fully Enlightened Buddhas in the distant past, and those who will be exalted Fully Enlightened Buddhas in the dim future, fulfil this work, even as, at the present time, the company

3. *Paribbājaka*. This term is not applied to Buddhist bhikkhus. The *paribbājakas* were a class of wandering ascetics who generally carried their requisites with them.

4. Being a non-Buddhist, Kandaraka addresses the Buddha as *bho* ("friend"), a term of address used to equals and inferiors, instead of the respectful term *Bhante* (Reverend Sir, Your Reverence, Lord) as used towards one's teacher or senior, and by the Buddhist lay follower in addressing bhikkhus.

of bhikkhus has been well trained by me.

"There are bhikkhus, Kandaraka, in this company, who are *arahant* saints: having extinguished the corruptions, completed the ascetic life, done what was to be done, laid down the burden, attained their goal, utterly destroyed the fetters of existence, and who are delivered by right insight.[5]

"There are also bhikkhus, Kandaraka, in this company, who are undergoing training[6] of virtuous conduct and tranquil deportment, prudent, discreet in their actions, and who live with their minds firmly established in the four foundations of mindfulness. What are the four?

"Here, Kandaraka, a bhikkhu abides in meditation on the body, strenuous, clearly conscious, mindful, having overcome covetousness and despair concerning the world;[7] *abides in meditation on the sensations ... on thoughts ... on the states of mind,*[8] strenuous, clearly conscious, mindful, having overcome covetousness and despair concerning the world."

Upon this being said, Pessa, the mahout's son, addressed the Blessed One as follows: "It is wonderful, Lord! It is marvellous, Lord! How well the Blessed One has expounded the four foundations of mindfulness for the purification of beings, for the overcoming of sorrow and lamentation, for the destruction of

---

5. A stock passage often repeated in the Suttas in order to describe the state of an *Arahant* or saint, who is also called an *asekha*, that is, "one beyond the need of training."

6. Sekha.

7. Concerning the world, *thereanant.* Pali: *loke*, lit., "in the world." Buddhaghosa, in his commentary to the Satipaṭṭhāna Sutta, says, "This body itself is the 'world'; the five aggregates that are clung to [*upādānakkhandha*] also are the world."

8. *Dhammesu dhammānupassi viharati.* Scholars have given various renderings of the enigmatical term "dhamma," such as, "ideas," "mental phenomena," "conditioned nature of existence," etc. We are of opinion that none of them corresponds to the meaning of dhamma as used in this connection. Under dhamma are here considered the five hindrances, the factors of enlightenment, the five aggregates, the six spheres of sense, and the four Noble Truths. Some dhammas are got rid of, some cultivated. As such it would almost be preferable to retain the Pali term. However we venture to give "states of mind" as the closest equivalent.

pain and despair, for the attainment of the path, for the realisation of nibbāna. And we householders also, Lord, dressed in white clothing, from time to time abide with minds firmly established in these four foundations of mindfulness. Here, Lord, we abide in meditation on the body, strenuous, clearly conscious, mindful, having overcome covetousness and despair concerning the world; we abide in meditation on the sensations ... on thoughts ... on the states of mind, strenuous, clearly conscious, mindful, having overcome covetousness and despair concerning the world.

"Wonderful, Lord! Marvellous, Lord! The Blessed One knows what is of advantage and what of disadvantage for beings, despite the fact that among men deceitfulness, vice and treachery are going on. Truly, Lord, men are deceitful,[9] whereas animals, Lord, are open.

"I, Lord, can remember the character of an elephant: whilst going to and returning from Campā, he will display all his treacherous habits, deceitful tricks, cunning practices and crooked ways. But, Lord, our slaves, servants, and workmen behave in one way with the body, another way verbally and, yet, vastly different will be their thoughts.... Truly, Lord, men are deceitful, whereas animals, Lord, are open."

"That is so, Pessa, that is so. Deceitful indeed, Pessa, are men, whereas animals, Pessa, are open.

"These four individuals, Pessa, exist and are found in the world. Who are these four?

"Here, Pessa, a certain individual is a tormentor of self, is addicted to the practice of self-torment; whilst another, Pessa, is a tormentor of others, is addicted to the practice of tormenting others. Again, Pessa, a certain individual is a tormentor of self and others; whilst, Pessa, another is neither a tormentor of self nor of others, is not addicted to the practice of tormenting self or others; he, neither tormenting self nor others, in this life itself, is desireless, quenched [of passions], cool, experiences happiness, lives nobly. Of these four individuals, Pessa, which finds favour with you?"

"That individual, Lord, who torments self and is addicted to

9. *Gahanaṃ*, lit., jungle, impenetrable thicket. Cf. Burlingame, *Buddhist Legends*, Part I, p. 255: "The ways of men are past finding out, but the ways of the beasts are easy to discover."

the practice of self-torment, finds no favour with me. And that individual, Lord, who torments others and is addicted to the practice of tormenting others, he, too, finds no favour with me. And that individual, Lord, who torments self and others and is addicted to the practice of tormenting self and others he, also, finds no favour with me. But that individual, Lord, who neither torments self nor others and is not addicted to the practice of tormenting self or others, who, in this life itself, is desireless, quenched [of passions], cool, experiences happiness, lives nobly: that individual finds favour with me."

"And why, Pessa, do these other three individuals find no favour with you?"

"That individual, Lord, who torments self and is addicted to the practice of self-torment, he torments and mortifies himself who craves happiness and abhors misery; therefore, that individual finds no favour with me.

"And that individual, Lord, who torments others and is addicted to the practice of tormenting others, he torments and mortifies others who crave happiness and abhor misery; therefore that individual finds no favour with me.

"And that individual, Lord, who torments self and others and is addicted to the practice of tormenting self and others, he torments and mortifies self and others who crave happiness and abhor misery; therefore that individual finds no favour with me.

"But that individual, Lord, who is neither a tormentor of self nor of others and is not addicted to the practice of tormenting self and others, he, in this life itself, is desireless, quenched [of passions], cool, experiences happiness, lives nobly; therefore that individual finds favour with me.

"And now, Lord, we depart; we have many duties and much to do."

"You, O Pessa, are aware of the hour." Thereupon, Pessa, the mahout's son, pleased with the words of the Blessed One, expressed his thanks, rose from his seat and, having saluted the Blessed One respectfully, passed reverently to the right and departed.[10]

Then the Blessed One, shortly after the departure of Pessa,

10. To pass a person, keeping one's right side to him, is a sign of reverence and respect.

addressed the bhikkhus: "Highly intelligent, O bhikkhus, is Pessa, the mahout's son; a man of great understanding. If, O bhikkhus, Pessa had remained seated for a while until I explained in detail these four individuals, he would have gone away having acquired a great advantage.[11] And even in this short time, O bhikkhus, Pessa did acquire a great advantage."

"This is the opportunity, O Blessed One! Now is the time, O Accomplished One, that the Blessed One should describe in detail these four individuals. The bhikkhus having listened to the Blessed One will bear it in mind."

"Very well, O bhikkhus; listen and bear it well in mind. I shall speak."

"Yes, Lord," responded the bhikkhus. The Blessed One spoke as follows:

"And which individual, O bhikkhus, is a tormentor of self, is addicted to the practice of self-torment?

"Here, O bhikkhus, a certain individual is naked, devoid of social habits,[12] licks his hands [after eating],[13] does not accept alms if called or requested to wait,[14] and neither accepts food brought to him, nor specially prepared for him, nor an invitation [to dine]. Neither does he accept from the brim of a pot, or from the brim of a cooking vessel;[15] nor anything handed across a threshold, over a stick, or over a rice pounder;[16] not from two people eating together,[17] nor from a woman with child,[18] nor from one giving suck,[19] nor from one indulging in courtship with a man.[20] Nor

11. Having attained the *sotāpatti* state, i.e., the first path of sainthood (Comy.).

12. *Muttācāro*, e.g., eating food whilst standing instead of sitting down, as the religious usually do (Comy.).

13. Instead of washing (Comy.).

14. For he would then be obeying others (Comy.).

15. For the vessels may be struck with the spoon (and thereby damaged on account of him) (Comy.).

16. Lest it should have been placed there specially for him (Comy.).

17. That is, if one rises and offers the ascetic food, he may thus be deprived of his just portion by the other individual (Comy.).

18. Lest the child should suffer (Comy.).

19. Lest the child should be deprived of milk (Comy.).

20. Lest their amours be interrupted (Comy.).

does he accept food that has been collected from others,[21] nor from where a dog is waiting for food,[22] nor from where swarms of flies are buzzing round;[23] he neither eats fish nor flesh, nor drinks spirituous liquor, arrack, nor fermented rice.

"He goes to one house only [for alms], or takes but one mouthful; or he goes to two houses, or takes two mouthfuls; ... or he goes to seven houses, or takes seven mouthfuls. He maintains himself on one small plateful, or on two small platefuls, ... or seven small platefuls; he takes food only once a day, or only once in two days ... or only once in seven days; thus, in this manner, even with intervals of half a month, he lives addicted to the practice of taking food only at certain intervals.

"He eats only herbs, or weeds, or wild rice, or waste shreds, or hide, or water plants, or rice dust, or the scum of boiling rice, or the refuse of sesamum seeds, or grass, or cowdung; he lives on roots and fruit found in the forest, or eats only fallen fruit. He wears garments of hemp, or clothing of hemp interwoven with other materials, or cloths taken from corpses, or rags found on dust heaps, or the bark of tiritaka trees, or deer skins with the hoofs attached, or a dress made of kusa grass, or made of strips of bark, or of strips of wood, or garments made of human hair, or of horse hair, or of owls' feathers.

"He is a plucker out of hair and beard and is addicted to the practice of pulling out the hairs of the head and beard; he always stands upright and never accepts a seat; or he constantly squats on the heels, and is addicted to the practice of continually squatting on the haunches; or he uses a thorn bed, always sleeping on a bed of thorns; or he bathes for the third time in the evening, and is addicted to the practice of purification by water. Thus, in this manner, he lives addicted in various ways to the practice of mortifying and tormenting the body.

"This individual, O bhikkhus, is said to be a tormentor of self, addicted to the practice of self-torment. And which individual,

21. In times of drought, the followers of the naked ascetics collect rice from various people and prepare it for the ascetics. The strict naked ascetics do not accept this kind of food (Comy.).

22. Lest the dog should be deprived (Comy.).

23. Lest the flies be driven away and thus be deprived (Comy.).

O bhikkhus, torments others, is addicted to the practice of tormenting others?

"Here, O bhikkhus, a certain individual is a butcher, a pig-killer, a fowler, a deer-stalker, a hunter, a fisherman, a robber, a public executioner, a jailer, or follows any other cruel occupation whatsoever.

"This individual, O bhikkhus, is said to be a tormentor of others, addicted to the practice of tormenting others.

"And which individual, O bhikkhus, is a tormentor of self and others, is addicted to the practice of tormenting self and others?

"Here, O bhikkhus, a certain individual is either an anointed king of warrior caste, or a Brahmin of enormous wealth. On the eastern side of the city he has a new sacrificial hall built, has the head and beard shaved, dons the raw hide of an antelope, rubs the body with clarified butter and oil; and, inflicting wounds[24] on his back with the horns of a deer, goes to the sacrificial hall, accompanied by his chief queen and a Brahmin chaplain. There he sleeps on the bare floor.

"If there be a cow having a calf of similar appearance [to herself], the king maintains himself on the milk in the first teat; the chief queen lives on the milk in the second teat; the Brahmin chaplain on that in the third; with the milk in the fourth teat, they make an offering to fire; and the little calf maintains itself on what is left.

"He speaks thus: 'Let so many bulls, so many steers, so many heifers, so many she-goats, and so many rams be slaughtered for a sacrifice; let so many trees be cut down for sacrificial posts; let so much kusa grass be cut for the enclosure!'

"Then his slaves, servants and workmen, terrified with sticks, driven by fear, with woeful faces and in tears, do the work.

"This individual, O bhikkhus, is said to be a tormentor or self and others, addicted to the practice of tormenting self and others.

"And which individual, O bhikkhus, is neither a tormentor of self nor of others, is not addicted to the practice of tormenting self or others; who, neither tormenting self nor others, in this life itself is desireless, quenched [of passions], cool, experiences happiness, lives nobly?

"Here, O bhikkhus, an Accomplished One appears in the

24. *Kaṇḍuvamāno*, lit., scratching.

world, an Exalted One, a Fully Enlightened One, endowed with perfect knowledge and pure conduct, gone, knower of worlds, an incomparable guide for the training of men, teacher of gods and men, Enlightened and Blessed. He, having by his own wisdom comprehended this world, together with the worlds of the gods, Māras, and Brahmas, including the communities of recluses and Brahmins, gods, and men, makes it known. He expounds the truth, glorious in the beginning, glorious in the middle, and glorious in its consummation, both in the spirit and the letter, making known the holy life of perfect purity.

[Acquisition of confidence] "A householder, or the son of a householder, or one born in some other class, hears that truth. Hearing the truth, he acquires confidence in the Blessed One. Possessing that confidence, he reflects thus: 'Cramped is household life, a den of filth; but the open air is the life of the recluse. Not easy is it for one living the household life to lead the radiant holy life [shining as a polished conch shell] in all its perfection and purity. How if I should shave head and beard, put on the yellow robes, and go forth from home to homelessness!'

[Renunciation] "Subsequently, abandoning his possessions, whether few or many; forsaking his circle of relatives, be it small or large; he shaves head and beard, dons the yellow robes, and goes forth from home to homelessness.

[Practice of the precepts] "And now, as a recluse, he observes the rules regulating the life of the bhikkhus. Renouncing killing, he abstains from taking the life of any living creature; laying aside stick and sword, modest and merciful, he lives kind and compassionate to all living creatures. Renouncing theft, he abstains from taking what is not given; only what is given to him he takes, waiting till it is given; and he lives with a heart honest and pure. Renouncing incontinence, he lives the celibate life, aloof [from sensuality], abstaining from the vulgar practices of sexuality. Renouncing lying, he abstains from false speech; speaking the truth and never deviating from it, he is reliable, trustworthy, and no deceiver of people. Renouncing slander, he abstains from tale-bearing; what he hears here he does not relate elsewhere, to create discord with these people; nor does he repeat to these what he heard elsewhere, to create dissension with those people. Thus he reconciles those who are divided and encourages those who are united; concord gladdens him, he delights and rejoices in concord, and he utters words conducive to concord. Renouncing harsh speech, he abstains from unkind words; those words that are blameless, pleasant to the ear, affectionate, going to the heart, courteous, agreeable and giving pleasure to many, such are the words he utters. Renouncing frivolous talk, he abstains from idle chatter; speaking at the right time, in accordance with the facts, to the purpose, in accord with the doctrine and discipline, he utters words worthy of remembrance, seasonable, appropriate, concise, and to the point.

"He refrains from injuring seeds and all forms of vegetation. Taking but one meal daily,[25] and abstaining from food at night, he refrains from eating at unseasonable hours. He refrains from dancing, singing, music and horn, and watching theatrical exhibitions. He abstains from wearing garlands, perfumes, ointments, ornaments, and personal decorations. He refrains from the use of high and luxurious beds. He refrains from accepting gold and silver, uncooked corn, raw meat, women and girls, male and female slaves, goats and sheep, fowls and pigs, elephants, cattle, horses and mares, land and buildings. He refrains from the practice of going on errands like a messenger. He abstains from trading, from false balances, unjust weights and fraudulent measures. He refrains from bribery, deception, fraud and crooked practices; from wounding, killing, chaining, highway robbery, plundering and violence.

"He contents himself with the robe that protects his body, and with [the almsfood gathered in] the almsbowl which stills his hunger.[26] Wherever he goes, he takes with himself [these two things]. Just as a bird carries its wings wherever it flies, even so the bhikkhu is contented with the robe protecting his body and with the almsbowl for satisfying his stomach, taking these with him wherever he goes. Possessing this noble code of morality, he

25. *Eka-bhattiko*, lit., he who takes one meal a day. This does not mean that the bhikkhu is allowed to take only one meal a day. Buddhaghosa says that it may mean any number of meals taken before midday. The usual practice is to take a light meal, generally rice-porridge, in the morning, and a more substantial meal at about 11 a.m.

26. Literally, "which protects his stomach."

experiences within himself the bliss of blameless conduct.

[Sense control] "Perceiving a form with the eye, he is neither arrested by its general appearance nor by its details; in as much as the evil, de-meritorious states of covetousness and grief would result from living with the organ of vision unrestrained, he practises the control of it; guarding the organ of sight, he brings it under subjection. Hearing a sound with the ear, smelling an odour with the nose, tasting a flavour with the tongue, feeling a touch with the body, or cognising an idea with the mind, he is neither arrested by its general appearance nor by its details; in as much as the evil de-meritorious states of mind would result from living with the organs of sense unrestrained, he practises the control of them; guarding the organs of sense, he brings them under subjection. Possessing this noble control of the senses, he experiences within himself an unblemished bliss.

[Mindfulness] "Whether going or coming, looking straight ahead or looking aside, bending or extending the limbs, donning his robes, carrying his bowl, eating, drinking, chewing or swallowing, answering calls of nature, walking, standing, sitting, sleeping, walking, speaking or silent, he is fully conscious of what he is doing.

[Inhibition of the Hindrances] "And possessing this noble code of morality, this noble control of the senses, and this noble mindfulness, he seeks a lonely abode: in the forest, at the foot of a tree, on a mountain, in a cleft, in a rocky cave, in a cemetery, in the depths of a jungle, in an open space, or on a heap of straw.

"Having returned from the alms round and taken his meal, he sits down, with legs crossed, the body erect, and his mindfulness alert.[27] Abandoning covetousness, abiding with thoughts free of greed, he purifies his mind of covetousness. Abandoning the taint of ill-will, abiding with thoughts free from ill-will, kind and compassionate to all living creatures, he purifies his mind of the taint of ill-will. Abandoning sloth and torpor, abiding free from sloth and torpor, with a lucid mind,[28] mindful and aware of folly, he purifies his mind of sloth and torpor. Abandoning restlessness and worry, abiding free from restlessness, with mind appeased,

27. *Parimukhaṃ satiṃ ṭhapetvā,* lit., fixing mindfulness in front.

28. *Āloka-saññi,* lit., perceiving light.

he purifies it of restlessness and worry. Abandoning doubt, he abides free from indecision; free from uncertainty with regard to meritorious conditions, he purifies his mind of doubt.

[*Jhānas*] "Abandoning these five hindrances, which are defilements of the mind and which stultify wisdom; remote, indeed, from sense-desires and de-meritorious conditions, he lives abiding in the first *jhāna*,[29] born of seclusion, accompanied by initial and sustained application, conjoined with joy and happiness. Stilling initial and sustained application, by unification of the mind having tranquillity within, he lives abiding in the second *jhāna*, born of concentration, void of initial and sustained application, conjoined with joy and happiness. Detached from delight, he abides serene, mindful and completely conscious, experiencing in his person that bliss of which the Noble Ones say: 'Endowed with equanimity and mindfulness, he abides in bliss.' Thus he lives, abiding in the third *jhāna*. Abandoning pleasure and pain, leaving behind former joy and grief, he lives abiding in the fourth *jhāna*, which is beyond pleasure and pain, and is endowed with equanimity and purified by mindfulness.

[Knowledge of past lives] "Thus with thoughts tranquillised, purified, cleansed, free from defilements, pliable, alert, steady, and unshakable, he directs his mind to the recollection and cognition of former existences. He recalls his varied lot in former existences, as follows: first one life, then two lives, then three, four, five, ten, twenty, up to fifty lives; then a hundred, a thousand, a hundred thousand; then the passing away of many world cycles, then the arising of many world cycles: 'In that place, I was of such a name, such a family, such a caste, such a sustenance, such the pleasure and pain I experienced, such my life's end. Vanishing from there, I

29. *Jhāna*, also translated as "meditative absorption [of mind]," is not a trance, but a fully conscious religious experience attained through strong concentration of mind on specific subjects of meditation (*kammaṭṭhāna*). In other words, it is "one-pointedness of the mind" cultivated as a means to an end, not an end in itself. The word "trance" is indicative of mental passivity. Trance as auto-hypnotism and its resultant phenomena are all subjective. *Jhānas*, on the other hand, are exercises of intense mental activity. For further particulars see the Chapter IV of *The Path of Purification* (*Visuddhimagga*), tr. by Ñāṇamoli Thera.

came into existence elsewhere. Now, such was my name, such my family, such my caste, such my sustenance, such pleasure and pain did I experience, such was that life's end. After dying, I came into existence here.' Thus he recalls the mode and details of his varied lot in former existences.

[Divine Eye] "Thus with thoughts tranquillised, purified, cleansed, free from defilements, pliable, alert, steady, and unshakable, he directs his mind to the perception of the disappearing and reappearing of beings. With clairvoyant vision, purified and super-normal, he perceives beings disappearing from one state of existence and reappearing in another; he beholds the base and the noble, the beautiful and the ugly, the happy and the miserable, and beings in accordance with their deeds. He thinks: 'These beings are given to evil ways in deed, word and thought. They revile the Noble Ones, hold false views, and incur the evil consequences of such views. Upon the dissolution of the body after death they are reborn in states of suffering, of misery, and of torment. But those beings are given to ways of virtue in deed, word, and thought. Not reviling the Noble Ones, they hold right views, and acquire the meritorious results of such views. Upon the dissolution of the body after death they are reborn in realms of divine happiness.'

[Knowledge of the Extinction of the Corruptions] "And he turns his mind to the comprehension of the cessation of the corruptions. He realises in accordance with fact, 'This is sorrow.' ... 'This is the arising of sorrow.' ... 'This is the cessation of sorrow.' ... 'This, the path leading to the cessation of sorrow.' Likewise, in accordance with fact, he realises, 'These are the corruptions.' 'This is the arising of the corruptions'. ... 'This is the cessation of the corruptions.' ... 'This is the path leading to the cessation of the corruptions.' Thus cognising, thus perceiving, his mind is delivered from the corruption of sensual craving; from the corruption of craving for existence; from the corruption of ignorance. Upon being delivered, he knows, 'Delivered am I,'[30] and he realises, 'Rebirth is ended; fulfiled the holy life; done what was to be done; there is none other beyond this life.'

"This individual, O bhikkhus, is said to be neither a tormentor

30. The reference is to the "process of retrospection" (or reviewing, *paccavekkhana-vīthi*). See *Path of Purification*, Ch. XXII, § 19ff.

of self nor of others, addicted neither to the practice of tormenting self nor others; he, neither tormenting himself nor others, in this life itself, is desireless, quenched [of passions], cool, experiences bliss, lives nobly."

Thus spoke the Blessed One. The bhikkhus, delighted, rejoiced at his words.

Introduction to the Potaliya Sutta
(Majjhima Nikāya No. 54)

It appears to have been a common and worthy practice in ancient India for rich men to renounce the world and take to a religious life, just as the modern Croesus decides to "enjoy life" and expend, on his comfort and pleasure, some of his hard-won wealth.

To such an individual we are introduced in this Sutta: one who, formerly wealthy, has renounced all worldly matters, making his sons his heirs and himself their charge.

Potaliya, an ex-merchant and now an ascetic of an abstemious order, the Tirthakas, is annoyed at being addressed by the Master as "householder" (this term being most commonly used to designate a merchant who is yet immersed in trade). The Buddha then explains to Potaliya what renunciation of worldly desires actually signifies in his Dispensation, and Potaliya is not only appeased but becomes a convert.

The Buddha frequently used allegory and parable in his teaching, and this sermon contains many a simile illustrating what the good Buddhist's outlook on material pleasures should be.

That worldly success and wealth are a delusion and a snare is proved by the fact that, out of 120,000 suicides in the United States of America during the year 1922, no fewer than 74 were of the millionaire class. Wealth and temporary well-being might gloss over much of the misery of life, but to one who learns to "see things as they really are," through the veneer of what is today called "civilisation," the awakening can be terrible.

To a seeker, disillusioned with the shallowness of the animistic cults, Buddhism alone offers the sympathy needed by the despondent. Moreover it shows a "way out," an emancipation which, by the law of contraries, can be nothing less than bliss.

The Potaliya Sutta

Potaliya the Householder

Thus have I heard. Once the Blessed One was staying in Aṅguttarāpa,[31] at a market town of the Aṅguttarāpas named Apana. And in the morning, the Blessed One robed himself, took bowl and robe, and entered Apana for alms. Having gone his round for alms in Apana, he returned; and, after the meal, repaired to a certain forest to spend the day. There he entered and sat at the foot of one of the trees.

Now Potaliya, the householder, arrayed in under- and upper-garments, with parasol and sandals, was strolling along taking a walk, and arrived at this wood;[32] entering, he approached the Blessed One. Drawing near, he exchanged friendly greetings with the Blessed One, and having passed the customary compliments, remained standing at a little distance. As he stood there, the Blessed One addressed Potaliya, the householder, as follows:

"Seats are to be found, householder;[33] be seated, if you wish."

When spoken to in this way, Potaliya, the householder, thinking "The ascetic Gotama addresses me as 'householder',"[34] was offended and displeased, and remained silent.

For the second time the Blessed One addressed him thus: "Seats are to be found, householder; be seated, if you wish." A second time also Potaliya, the householder, ... was offended and displeased, and remained silent.

For the third time the Blessed One said, "... householder, be seated." Being spoken to thus, Potaliya, the householder, thinking: "The ascetic Gotama addresses me as 'householder'," was offended and displeased, and spoke to the Blessed One as follows: "It is unseemly,

---

31. *Aṅguttarāpa*: Northern (*uttara*) part of the Aṅga country, drained by the waters (*āpo*) of the river Mahi.

32. *Wood:* a thickly-shaded, beautiful spot on the bank of the river, not far from the township (Comy.).

33. The ground, strewn with fallen leaves, afforded comfortable seats.

34. *Gahapati*, a term invariably applied to laymen.

friend Gotama, it is improper for you to address me as 'householder'."

"It is because, householder, whoever has your bearing, characteristics, and signs must be a householder."

"Indeed! But I, friend Gotama, have given up all occupations and put an end to all worldly affairs."[35]

"In what way then, householder, have you given up all occupations and put an end to all worldly affairs?"

"Whatever wealth I had in this world, friend Gotama, whether corn, silver, or gold, all that have I bestowed on my sons as an inheritance, regarding which I never give advice, not find fault, but live principally supplied with food and clothing. Thus, in this way, friend Gotama, have I given up all occupations and put an end to all worldly affairs."

"In one way, certainly, householder, you speak of putting an end to all worldly affairs; but, truly, another is the total cessation of worldly affairs in the discipline of the ariya.[36]

"In what way then, Lord, are worldly affairs brought to an end in the discipline of the ariyas? It would be well, Lord, if the Blessed One would expound to me the doctrine as to the way in which worldly affairs are brought to an end in the discipline of the ariyas."

"Very well, householder; listen and bear it well in mind; I will speak."

"Very good, Lord," responded Potaliya the householder.

The Blessed One spoke as follows:

"These eight doctrines, householder, in the discipline of the ariyas, are conducive to the breaking off of worldly affairs. Which eight?

"Relying[37] on non-killing, the killing of living beings should be abandoned. Relying on that which is given, stealing should be abandoned. Relying on the truth, lying should be abandoned.

"Relying on words free from malice, slander should be

35. *Vohāra-samucchedo*: In the teaching of the Buddha this refers to the giving up of the eight ignoble (*an-ariya*) practices: killing, stealing, lying, malice, greed and craving, scolding and harshness, hatred and despair, and pride.

36. *Ariya* is a term which frequently appears in the Suttas, meaning a Buddha, an *arahant* and a saint. It signifies those who are "far removed from the state of a worldling." Here the term is applied to the Buddha.

37. *Nissaya*: "relying on" or "because of."

abandoned. Relying on freedom from greed and craving, greed and craving should be abandoned. Relying on freedom from scolding and harshness, scolding and harshness should be abandoned. Relying on freedom from hatred and despair, hatred and despair should be abandoned. Relying on freedom from pride, pride should be abandoned.

"These eight doctrines, householder, briefly stated, not elaborated in detail, in the discipline of the ariyas, are conducive to the breaking off of worldly affairs."

"It would be well, Lord, if the Blessed One, out of compassion, would expound to me in detail these eight doctrines which are briefly stated, not elaborated in detail, by the Blessed One, and are conducive to the breaking off of worldly affairs in the discipline of the ariyas."

"Very well, householder; listen, and bear it well in mind. I will speak."

"Very good, Lord," responded Potaliya the householder.

The Blessed One spoke as follows:

"Truly it was said: 'Relying on non-killing, the killing of living beings should be abandoned.' Concerning what was this said?

"In this world, householder, a noble disciple reflects thus: 'Because of these fetters I may become a killer of living beings; therefore I have set myself to eliminate and eradicate these fetters. Certainly, if I became a destroyer of life, I should reproach myself because of the killing of living beings; the wise, having examined [my fault], would rebuke me; and, upon the dissolution of the body after death, a state of misery is to be expected for having destroyed life. Undoubtedly, this killing of living beings is a fetter, a hindrance; and these corruptions, vexations, and sufferings would arise on account of killing; but he who refrains from destroying life does not have these corruptions, vexations, and sufferings.'

"For this reason was it said, 'Relying on non-killing, the killing of living beings should be abandoned.' Truly it was said, 'Stealing should be abandoned; lying, slander, greed and craving, scolding and harshness, hatred and despair, and pride, should be abandoned.' Concerning what was this said?

"In this world, householder, a noble disciple reflects thus: 'Through these fetters one may become a thief, liar, backbiter, greedy and avaricious, scolding and harsh, hating and despondent, and proud; therefore have I set myself to eliminate and eradicate these fetters. Certainly, if I became any of these, I should reproach myself. The wise, having examined [my faults], would rebuke me; and upon the dissolution of the body, after death, a state of misery is to be expected for having these blemishes. Undoubtedly they constitute fetters and hindrances; and these corruptions, vexations, and sufferings would arise on account of them; but he who is not tainted in this way does not have these corruptions, vexations, and sufferings.'

"Because of this was it said: 'Relying on freedom from these fetters, they should all be abandoned.'

"These eight doctrines, householder, both briefly stated and elaborated in detail, are conducive to the breaking off of worldly affairs in the discipline of the ariyas; yet these alone do not constitute, in the discipline of the ariyas, the breaking off of worldly affairs completely and in every way."

"In what way then, Lord, are worldly affairs broken off completely and in every way in the discipline of the ariyas? It would be well, Lord, if the Blessed One would expound to me the doctrine as to the way in which worldly affairs are broken off completely and in every way, in the discipline of the ariyas."

"Very well, householder; listen and bear it well in mind. I will speak."

"Very good, Lord," responded Potaliya the householder.

The Blessed One spoke as follows:

"It is as if, householder, a dog, overcome with hunger and weakness, was present at a slaughter house; and a skilful butcher or butcher's apprentice were to throw near him a bare bone, closely-cut, scraped, fleshless, but smeared with blood. What do you think, householder? Would that dog, by gnawing such a bare bone, closely-cut, scraped fleshless, but smeared with blood, appease its hunger and weakness?"

"Certainly not, Lord. And for what reason? Because Lord, it is a bare bone, closely cut, scraped, fleshless, and merely smeared with blood; and the dog would only suffer fatigue and vexation."

"In exactly the same way, householder, the noble disciple reflects thus: 'It was said by the Blessed One that sense-desires are like a bare bone, full of pain, full of despair;' thus, thinking

'Here is much danger,' and having, with right wisdom, seen this as it really is, he, rejecting whatsoever equanimity is changeful[38] or bound up with diversity, cultivates whatsoever equanimity is constant,[39] dependent on unity, and where worldly desires and clinging perish utterly and without remainder.

"It is as if, householder, a vulture, or a heron, or a hawk, having taken a small piece of flesh, were flying up, and vultures, or herons, or hawks, were constantly following and snatching at the flesh and tearing it into bits. What do you think, householder? If that vulture, or heron, or hawk did not at once let go of that small piece of flesh, it would in consequence suffer death, or misery comparable to that of death."

"That is so, Lord."

"In exactly the same way, householder, the noble disciple reflects thus: 'It was said by the Blessed One that the sense-desires are like a small piece of flesh, full of pain, full of despair.' Thinking thus: 'Here is much danger,' and having, with right wisdom, seen this as it really is, he, rejecting whatsoever equanimity is changeful or bound up with diversity, cultivates whatsoever equanimity is constant, dependent on unity, and where worldly desires and clinging perish utterly and without remainder.

"It is as if, householder, a person carrying a flaming torch of dry grass were to go against the wind. What do you think, householder? If that person did not get rid of it at once, that flaming torch of dry grass would burn his hand, or arm, or some other part of his body; and, in consequence, he would suffer death, or misery comparable to that of death."

---

38. *Nānatta-upekkhā*: the changeful complacency of the worldling. This refers to the normal equanimity of everyday life, which, varying with the diversity of sense-impressions, arouses sufficient passing interest to lull the intellect. The average man, ever-quenching, or seeking to quench, this thirst and that, is blind to life's innate misery. He never pauses to ask "Whence?" "Why?" "Whither?" But this complacency wilts when its cause, the mist of ignorance, vanishes before the sun of truth.

39. *Ekatta-upekkhā*: this is the unique equanimity of one who has attained the fourth *jhāna* (or absorption). This becomes constant in the hypercosmic equanimity of the *arahant*. But even with the first *jhāna*, the practicer is lifted out of the muck of average, mundane complacency.

"That is so, Lord."

"In exactly the same way, householder, the noble disciple reflects thus: 'It was said by the Blessed One that sense-desires are like a torch of dry grass' ... and he cultivates that constant equanimity, dependent on unity, where worldly desires and clinging perish utterly and without a remainder.

"It is as if, householder, there were a pit of glowing embers, deeper than the height of a man, filled with glowing embers free from flame and smoke; and a person desiring to live and not wishing to die, longing for happiness and loathing pain, were to come, and two strong men were to seize that person by each arm and drag him towards the pit of glowing embers. What do you think, householder? Would that person struggle this way and that?"[40]

"That is so, Lord; and for what reason? Because, Lord, it would be known to that person, 'If I were to drop into this pit of glowing embers, I should, in consequence, suffer death, or misery comparable to that of death'."

"In exactly the same way, householder, the noble disciple reflects thus: 'It was said by the Blessed One that sense-desires are like a pit of glowing embers ...' and he cultivates that constant equanimity, dependent on unity, where worldly desires and clinging perish utterly and without remainder.

"It is as if, householder, a person were to see in a dream a lovely park, grove, landscape, or lotus-pond; upon awakening he would see nothing of it!

"In exactly the same way, householder, the noble disciple reflects thus: 'It was said by the Blessed One that sense-desires are like a dream ...' and he cultivates that constant equanimity, dependent on unity, where worldly desires and clinging perish utterly and without remainder.

"It is as if, householder, a person were to borrow some property obtainable on loan, a chariot suitable for a citizen, or an ear ring of choice gems, and were to resort to the midst of the marketplace, furnished and equipped with those borrowed goods. The people, seeing him, would say: 'What a wealthy man! Just see how the wealthy enjoy their riches!' But should the owners see him anywhere, they would take back their property on the

40. *Kāyaṃ saññāmeyya*, lit., "would bend the body."

spot. What do you think, householder? Is not this truly enough to upset that person?"

"It is, Lord; and for what reason? Because the owners, Lord, take back their property."

"In exactly the same way, householder, the noble disciple reflects thus: 'It was said by the Blessed One that sense-desires are like borrowed goods ...' and he cultivates that constant equanimity, dependent on unity, where worldly desires and cunning perish utterly and without remainder.

"It is as if, householder, not far from a village, or a small markettown, there were a thick forest in which there was a fruittree loaded with fruit, none having fallen to the ground; and a person were to come desiring fruit, looking for, and wandering in search of fruit. He, entering the forest, would see that fruit tree loaded with fruit, and would think thus: 'This, indeed, is a fruit tree loaded with fruit, and none has fallen on the ground; but I know how to climb the tree. What if I were to climb this tree, eat as much as I like, and then fill my pouch?'[41] And, climbing the tree, he would eat as much as he liked, and would then fill his pouch. Meanwhile a second person comes desiring fruit, looking for, and wandering in search of fruit, and carrying a sharp axe. He, entering the forest, would see that fruit tree loaded with fruit, and would think thus: 'This, indeed, is a fruit tree loaded with fruit, and none has fallen on the ground; but I do not know how to climb the tree. What if I were to fell this tree at the root, eat as much as I like, and then fill my pouch?' And he would fell that tree at the root. What do you think, householder? If that person who first climbed the tree did not get down immediately, the tree, in falling, would crush his hand, foot, or some other part of his body; and, in consequence, he would suffer death, or misery comparable to that of death."

"That is so, Lord."

"In exactly the same way, householder, the noble disciple reflects thus: 'It was said by the Blessed One that sense-desires are like a fruit tree, full of pain, full of despair.' Thus, thinking 'Here is much danger,' and having, with right wisdom, seen this

41. *Ucchaṅga*: a pouch or pocket formed by folding the undergarment at the waist.

as it really is, he, rejecting whatsoever equanimity is changeful or bound up with diversity, cultivates whatsoever equanimity is constant, dependent on unity, and where worldly desires and clinging perish utterly and without remainder.

"Now, householder, that noble disciple who has attained the unrivalled purification of mindfulness born of equanimity[42] recalls his varied lot in former existences, namely, first one life, then two lives, then three, and so on... Thus he recalls the mode and details of his varied lot in former existences. Then, householder, that noble disciple who has attained the unrivalled purification of mindfulness born of equanimity, with clairvoyant vision, purified and supernormal, perceives beings disappearing from one state of existence and reappearing in another; he beholds the base and the noble, the beautiful and the ugly, the happy and the wretched, beings passing on in accordance with their deeds. Lastly, householder, that noble disciple who has attained the unrivalled purification of mindfulness born of equanimity, after the extinction of the corruptions, lives corruption-free, having intuitively attained and realised, in this life itself, the mental emancipation and deliverance through wisdom."[43]

"In this way, then, householder, are worldly affairs brought, in every way and definitely, to an end in the discipline of the ariyas.

"What do you think, householder? Such being the breaking off of worldly affairs completely and in every way, according to the discipline of the ariyas, do you actually perceive such a consummation in yourself?"

"What am I, Lord, and what total and definite breaking off of worldly affairs in the discipline of the ariyas! Far am I, Lord, from the complete, entire breaking off of worldly affairs [as understood] in the discipline of the ariyas.

"Formerly, Lord, we were of opinion that the heretical wandering ascetics who really know not [the breaking off of worldly affairs], knew it; and gave them who really know not, the food intended for those who know. On the other hand, Lord,

42. *Upekkhā-sati-parisuddhi*: this is a characteristic of the fourth *jhāna*.

43. The preceding refers to the "threefold-knowledge" (*tevijja*): knowledge of past lives (*pubbenivāsa*), the divine eye (*dibba-cakkhu*), and the knowledge of the extinction of the corruptions (*āsavakkhaya-ñāṇa*).

we thought that the bhikkhus who really know [the breaking off of worldly affairs], knew not; and we gave them who really know, the food intended for those who know not. But now, Lord, we know that the heretical wandering ascetics who really know not, do not know it; and we shall give them who really know not, the food intended for those who know not, and shall put them in the places intended for those who know not. On the other hand, Lord, we now know that the bhikkhus who really know, do know it; and we shall give them who really know the food intended for those who know; and shall put them in the places intended for those who know.

"Truly, Lord, the Blessed One has caused to arise in me pious love[44] towards the ascetics, pious faith in the ascetics, and pious respect for the ascetics.

"Excellent, Lord, excellent! It is as if, Lord, a man were to set upright that which was overturned, or were to reveal that which was hidden, or were to point out the way to one who had gone astray, or were to hold a lamp amidst the darkness, so that those who have eyes may see. Even so has the doctrine been expounded in various ways by the Blessed One.

"So I, too, Lord, take refuge in the Buddha, the Doctrine, and the Order. May the Blessed One receive me as a follower,[45] as one who has taken refuge from this very day to life's end."

44. *Samaṇa-pema*: as distinguished from ordinary worldly affection (*gehasita-pema*).

45. *Upāsaka*: the designation for a male lay-follower of the Buddha. It literally means: "to sit close by." One becomes an *upāsaka* immediately after taking the Three Refuges. A female lay-follower is called *upāsikā*.

Dialogues on the Dhamma

Francis Story

WHEEL PUBLICATION NO. 80/81

Author's Note

Mr. Thompson and the *upāsaka*, the protagonists in these discussions, are imaginary characters. But the questions are real ones, which have been posed at various times by people interested in the Dhamma. It is hoped that the answers given to them here will be helpful to all those to whom the same problems have presented themselves.

"You have come from afar, O Sabhiya," the Blessed One said, "longing to ask questions. I shall put an end to your doubts when I am asked those questions. In regular order, and rightly, I shall explain them to you.

"Ask me then a question, O Sabhiya. Whatsoever is in your mind, that question I will explain and put an end to your doubt."

Then thought Sabhiya, the *Paribbājaka*, "Marvellous it is, and wonderful indeed! This reception, such as I have not from other *samaṇas* and *brāhmaṇas*, has been given me by Gotama!" And gladdened, rejoicing, delighted and highly elated, he asked the Blessed One a question.

Sabhiya Sutta – Sutta Nipāta

> "There are, O monks, four ways of answering questions: there are questions requiring a direct answer, questions requiring an explanation, questions to be answered by counter-questions and questions to be rejected (as being wrongly put)."

Aṅguttara Nikāya II 46

Dialogues on the Dhamma

I

Mr. Thompson: Good evening, sir, I have seen you several times on my visits to this temple, and have been told that you are an *upāsaka*. That means a lay follower of the Buddha, doesn't it?

The Upāsaka: Yes. Is there anything I can do for you?

Mr. T: I was wondering whether you would mind answering a few questions for me. You see, I have been reading some books on Buddhism and find its doctrines very appealing. But there are a number of points that are not quite clear to me, and I should be very grateful for any help you could give.

U: Why, certainly, I hope you will ask me freely about anything you wish to know. I'll try my best to answer your questions.

Mr. T: That is very good of you.

U: Not at all. We consider it a great privilege and a deed of merit to give instruction in the Dhamma when it is asked for. So go right ahead and ask me anything you like. All I ask in return is that you keep an open mind and give serious thought to what I shall say, because the doctrines of Buddhism are not dogmas, to be absorbed without reflection, but universal truths which, to be of benefit, must be understood in all their implications. Buddhism invites, indeed, I would say, insists upon a critical attitude of mind, yet one that is sufficiently flexible to accept a new idea when it is shown to be in accordance with reason, observation and experience.

Mr. T: Yes, that much I have gathered from my reading. So, sir, as you have given me licence to question freely I shall start with a point that has been bothering me. I hope you won't mind if I put it very bluntly?

U: I assure you I shall not mind in the least. But blunt questions sometimes elicit sharp answers, you know! So you must not mind that, either.

Mr. T: Good! I can see by your smile that we shall understand each other very well. Since I want to get at the truth I would rather that we spoke straight to the point—as philosophers rather than as diplomats! Well then, my first question is this: Isn't Buddhism a selfish doctrine since its aim is perfectionist, with *arahantship*[1] *as the goal?*

U: Put like that, your question sounds as though you consider that the aim of making oneself perfect must necessarily be a selfish one, but I don't think that is quite what you mean, surely?

Mr. T: Not exactly. I mean, shouldn't one try to help others to gain perfection, as well as striving for it oneself?

U: There is a twofold answer to that, and you can place the emphasis on whichever aspect of it you like better. To begin with, one who is trying to make oneself perfect *does* help others. Not only by example, which is the strongest influence of all, but also by teaching. Buddhist monks have always had it as one of their functions (although not necessarily a duty) to teach the Dhamma to lay people, especially to children. In the Buddhist countries, formerly, bhikkhus were the chief educators, and they always gave first place to religious instruction, as being that which ultimately is of the greatest benefit to mankind. But as you know, Buddhism does not point to any external means for attaining "salvation." In the end, we all have to strive individually and reach the goal individually. Beyond a certain point no one can help another. Even a Buddha can only show the Way; he cannot tread it for us. Furthermore, one who is himself still sunk in the mire of ignorance cannot lift another person out of it, or even render the same help as can one who is standing on firm ground. A Buddha or an arahant is one who is on firm ground, and it is he who can do most to help others out of the quagmire. So if we want to render the most effective aid it is surely our first task to get out ourselves. Until we have done that, we may be able to extend a little help by way of teaching what we know to those who know less, but that should never be allowed to obstruct our first aim, which must be to liberate ourselves.

Mr. T: Yes, I see your meaning. I suppose to understand Buddhism properly one has to give up thinking in terms of "leading others to God."

---

1. *Arahantship*: the fourth and last stage of purification.

U: Precisely. We can light a lamp for others here and there as we go along the path ourselves, and every conscientious Buddhist will do so, by making use of whatever opportunity comes his way of making the Dhamma known to others. It is then up to the others to take advantage of the light or not, as they wish. Truth cannot be associated with compulsion. It has to be accepted freely and followed freely. We cannot drill others into perfection—only ourselves. But I do want you to realise that to have attained perfection—the complete eradication of ignorance and craving—means to have destroyed selfhood and egotism. So how can it be selfish?

Mr. T: I must confess I hadn't thought about it in that way. It is true, of course. But I was also thinking of social obligations and relationships. Is the doctrine of "withdrawal from the world" and renunciation compatible with social development and "team spirit"?

U: If one were to withdraw from the world out of a spirit of misanthropy, as certain hermits have done and still do, certainly it would be a negative act, a repudiation of society and one's responsibilities towards it. But in a civilisation given over to materialism and competitiveness it is a good thing that some people should point the way to a simpler and healthier way of life, by renunciation. When I say healthier I mean just that—a life that is not dominated by greed for possessions, for sense-gratification or for power over others. It is these things that have brought our present civilisation to the brink of destruction, without giving any real, lasting happiness to anyone in the process. In Buddhism, renunciation of the world is a positive act, not a mere negation. It leads to a life that is sane, balanced and integrated to the highest degree. If people purify their lives, live in accordance with sound ethical principles and exert themselves to get rid of selfishness and the aggressive instincts that arise from it, then social progress follows automatically. Those who practise renunciation introduce new and more wholesome values into life, and their influence is felt permeating society. In fact, this is the only true way to bring about genuine social reform. All improvements in human life must come from within, as an organic growth of human consciousness, out of the developing sensitiveness and refinement of man's nature. It is useless trying to impose reforms of any kind from without, by laws and acts of government. On the contrary, such legal enactments have force and validity only when they are an expression of the real character of the people. The goodness of society is the goodness of the people.

Mr. T: You mean that every society is just an extension of the personality of those composing it? And that the mass personality can be influenced for good by the example and teaching of those who reject the lower values in favour of higher ones?

U: You have put it very well. Our civilisation is primarily a commercial one; it is built up on the intensification and multiplication of "wants." But this encouragement to perpetual *wanting* of one thing after another is nothing but the systematic cultivation of discontent. That in turn breeds conflict—and so we get crime within society and hatred and suspicion among societies. And the more man is integrated with society, the harder it is for him to withstand its pressures. Being forced to accept the prevailing values, he strengthens them by his acceptance, and so there are reciprocal movements, from society inwards and from the individual outwards into society, which accelerate the trends, good or bad, of the age. Now all these mass movements tend to flow along the lower channels of human nature, the grooves worn by greed, hatred and delusion. This is a state of things that can be corrected only by giving the individual opportunity to cultivate detachment, and by setting before him, in place of examples of successful acquisitive competition, examples which prove that our real happiness lies in our capacity for doing without, of being self-sufficient. It is not expected that every man should practise total renunciation, but those who do so help others, by their example, to loosen the bonds of craving and so create a healthier, sounder type of society.

Mr. T: Then what about social service?

U: Well, it is a good thing, of course, and Buddhism encourages it. But even social work may be a failure if it is not grounded on a genuine love for one's fellow-men. If it is not inspired by a real altruism, which stands as the opposite to a desire to win esteem for oneself or to impose one's will on others, it can do more harm than good. And even good intentions are not enough, without sympathy and understanding. That is why we find so much well-meant blundering in the world. But if people improve, social conditions improve—that is the teaching of Buddhism. As for the "team spirit" you mentioned just now, surely it springs up most naturally and strongly where there is least selfishness, least acquisitiveness and individual competition, and most desire to work for a goal beyond that of self. Buddhism maintains that the world should always be guided by men of wisdom and insight, and it has always been from the ranks of those who have renounced the world—the entirely disinterested spirits—that such men have been drawn. They are the guiding lights of humanity, and a world bereft of them would be in spiritual chaos.

Mr. T: But shouldn't the Sangha devote itself explicitly, at least in part, to social service? Why doesn't it do so?

U: Well, you know, making oneself perfect, in the Buddhist sense, is really a full-time job! And that is what a bhikkhu really takes the robes for. Maybe he does not expect to achieve it in this life—few do, in fact—but his main task is to cleanse his mind of the impurities as much as he possibly can, and that, if it is done intensively, leaves little time for anything else. It is not a thing that can be done in the midst of distractions, and no social work can possibly be undertaken without getting oneself involved in distracting situations and becoming burdened with cares—to say nothing of the feelings of aversion that are likely to arise if one is engaged in a battle against man's greed, stupidity and callousness. The bhikkhu's social work consists in teaching the Dhamma, and that is the greatest contribution anyone can make to the welfare of others. If the laymen, who from choice are still in contact with worldly things, take the Dhamma to heart, they will look after its social application. One cannot sincerely practise the meditation on *mettā*, universal benevolence, without feeling the urge to give it some practical form. The bhikkhu plays his part in social service by helping to make good lay Buddhists. If he achieves that, everything else follows.

Mr. T: You said just now that it is not necessarily a bhikkhu's duty to teach the Dhamma.

U: In the strictest sense there are only two duties enjoined on a bhikkhu, the *dve-dhurāni* or twofold charge of the bhikkhu's life. One is *gantha-dhura*, the task of studying the Dhamma as it is written in the texts. The other is *vipassanā-dhura,* the practice of meditation leading to insight. Any instruction that a bhikkhu gives to others, as the outcome of his mastery of either sphere of the monk's endeavour, is something additional, which he takes on out of kindness to his pupils or lay supporters. He is not forced to teach, simply because it is not everyone who is capable of teaching, even though he may know the subject himself. There may be impediments which prevent his preaching. This, incidentally, is one of the distinctions which show that a bhikkhu is not a "priest." But the Buddha did indeed impress certain other obligations on the monks, if they were able to carry them out, and if occasion arose. One was the duty of the bhikkhus to take care of their companions who were sick; another was to give hospitality to visiting bhikkhus and to look after their needs. And he often emphasised, as the Vinaya shows, that the monks were to respect the convenience of their lay supporters in the matter of meals and the other necessities provided for them. For example, the rule of not eating solid food after midday was instituted by the Master, among other reasons, to prevent undue inconvenience to the householders. And of course it is the bhikkhu's duty to observe faithfully the 227 rules of the Sangha. This in itself is no light obligation. It can only be carried out consistently by those who have given up all other duties of a more worldly kind.

Mr. T: Yes, I see the truth of that. Now, I am interested in what you remarked about not being "priests." Can you tell me what other distinction marks the difference between them?

U: A priest is someone who is authorized to act as a mediator between human beings and a god or gods. The bhikkhu is not a functionary of that kind at all. Hence he is not obliged to officiate at any ceremonies, offer up any prayers, give any absolution or perform any sacrificial rites. Buddhism does not recognize any of those offices of a priesthood. All ceremonials, rituals and ecclesiastical performances, designed to awe and impress the multitude, are *sīlabbataparāmāsa*—useless observances. Buddhism has no place for them.

Mr. T: Thank you. You have certainly cleared up for me the matter of the bhikkhu's role in social progress. I have always felt that if the spirit of love and service can be strengthened in the hearts of the people, it must result in the betterment of conditions everywhere. But I wasn't quite sure what part the religious ought to play in translating thought into action. Now I have a question of a different kind—one touching on doctrine.

U: Well, what is it?

Mr. T: It's this: Doesn't the Buddhist conception of heaven and hell as rewards and punishments amount essentially to the same as Christianity teaches?

U: In the sense of moral retribution, yes, there is a similarity. But consider the differences; they are far greater.

Mr. T: In what way?

U: Surely the most obvious difference is that the Christian heaven is an eternal reward, and its hell an eternal punishment, whereas the heavens and hells—or states of purgation would be a better term—taught by Buddhism are impermanent like all other conditioned states. Buddhism does not teach that it is just to inflict an eternity of torment on a being for a wrong action that was limited, both as to its carrying-out and in its effects, by earthly time. Even if a man were to be the worst possible sinner all through his life, it would hardly justify consigning him to hell for all eternity. And it is not in human nature to be so consistently bad. Likewise, no ordinary man during his lifetime could be so free from wrongdoing as to deserve eternal bliss in a heaven, without some further purification. And since moral purification can be achieved only by and through the mind and volitional action and not merely by undergoing a period of physical torture, it can only come about through repeated trial and development in the world of sense-desires—that is to say, through rebirth again and again in this and other worlds. Buddhism teaches that "punishment" is exactly commensurate, in duration and degree, with the wrong action that has brought it about. The same applies to the happy results of good actions. When the results of the good or bad kamma are exhausted, the being leaves the state of reward or punishment and is re-born elsewhere. But we do not really like to use the words "punishment" and "reward," because these results come about as the operation of natural law—a law which is quite impersonal and at the same time inescapable. They are not inflicted or awarded at the whim of a deity who can forgive or increase punishments arbitrarily. The law of moral retribution is an automatic process. That is another very important difference between the Buddhist and the Christian concepts. It is important because it does away with the idea of vengeance in justice. If there were a God who was omnipotent he could forgive and wash out all sins; if he does not, his justice is only another word for revenge. But Buddhism shows that it is the individual himself who passes judgement, in the very act of performing a deed. It is he who sends himself to heaven, or consigns himself to a state of suffering, not a jealous and revengeful God, who is himself impervious to harm from his creatures.

Mr. T: Then do Buddhists really believe in hell? I don't!

U: Whether one believes in it or not has no real bearing on the principle involved, which is that of moral retribution. To believe in "rewards"—that is, heaven—but not in "punishment" is to make good and bad, right and wrong, meaningless words. If you reject hell, you must reject heaven likewise. If you are prepared to do that, well and good—but you are left with nothing more than materialism. That vile and odious crimes against humanity should go unpunished without any evil consequence whatever to their authors is incompatible with any concept of right and wrong. Now it is a fact that many Christians have more or less had to discard the idea of hell, simply because the concept of eternal punishment, no matter how terrible the wrongdoing, is so manifestly unjust, as I have shown. But Buddhists have no need to reshape their Teacher's words to fit more humane modern ideas. Jesus Christ spoke of eternal damnation, of "the everlasting fire."[2] The Buddha spoke of states of suffering in which beings, on account of their evil deeds, may be reborn for periods varying from a day to an aeon. If we do not accept the principle of moral retribution to this extent, we ought logically to close all prisons and abolish all punitive laws on earth. But I do not know of anyone except of a few extremists who advocate that measure.

Mr. T: No doubt that is so. But can one really suppose, in this twentieth century, that there is a place of fiery punishment

2. Math. 25:41, 9:42–48.

situated somewhere in the bowels of the earth? Has not the belief in hell come about because primitive man regarded the craters of volcanoes and seismic fissures in the earth as being the gateways to the supposed infernal regions?

U: Possibly. And it is just possible that the Buddha when he spoke of *niraya* was making use of the current ideas of his time to illustrate an important moral truth. However that may be, we do not have to ascribe a geographical location to either hell or heaven. They are states we can recognize around us and within us. Wherever people are suffering extremes of physical or mental pain, there is a kind of hell. Wherever they are transported by a passing phase of happiness, there is a type of heaven. The man whose mind is darkened by the insanity of hate is in hell, while he who is temporarily lifted outside himself by the ecstasy of religious joy, or even one who is momentarily lost in the contemplation of something beautiful, is in heaven. What are these but states of mind? And what, if it comes to that, is this world of our senses but a state of mind?

Mr. T: You mean that all of it is only a subjective experience?

U: Not quite that, either. The world has an objective reality, of a conditional and relative kind, and so have the heavens and hells. But to the extent to which they correspond to states of mind, this world itself can take on the aspect of either a heaven or a hell. Buddhism avoids both the materialist and the subjectivist or idealist interpretations of the world. But anyone who has seriously thought about the implications of modern physics can scarcely deny the possibility of other planes of existence—spheres of being that are in every respect as "real" on their own level as our present one is for us. That is what most thoughtful Buddhists today believe in, and it is strictly in accordance with the Master's teaching. And, by the way, do you really consider that the theory that the belief in hell arose in the primitive mind from the observation of volcanic fires, and nothing else, is a fully adequate explanation?

Mr. T: Yes, it seems very reasonable.

U: But don't forget that Dante's inferno had its frozen hell, Cocytus, as well as a burning one—just as Buddhism has! In fact, the visions of hells and heavens described by the poets and mystics of all religions bear a surprising likeness to one another, despite all the doctrinal differences that surround them.

Mr. T: Now that you mention it, it does seem rather suggestive. Swedenborg, I remember, claimed to have seen some very gruesome nether worlds in the course of his astral explorations. Would you say that his experiences were genuine ones, not hallucinations?

U: Why not? All kinds of people have had such experiences, and Buddhism does not claim to have the monopoly of knowledge regarding other states of saṃsāric existence. What it does claim is to have the sole means of gaining release from the saṃsāric planes—that is, the Noble Eightfold Path.

Mr. T: Since we are on the subject of doctrine, is *avijjā*, ignorance, the first cause in Buddhism? There must be a first cause, mustn't there?

U: In a consistent system of causality, such as that taught by Buddhism, there cannot be a first cause. There cannot be a something which arises spontaneously out of nothing, for if such causeless arising were possible, the entire system would be invalidated. Furthermore, true causal relationships exist only in a temporal sequence. But we do not consider *avijjā* as being a cause in this temporal relationship sense. It is a conditioning factor. In the formula of dependent origination (*paṭicca-samuppāda*)[3] ignorance is the supporting factor of *taṇhā*, or craving, and these two in combination bring about the other supporting factors, some of which are co-existing auxiliary causes. Nothing can stand by itself as sufficient cause; it must always combine with something else in supportive co-ordinate relationship. When it is said that "dependent upon ignorance arise kamma formations (*saṅkhārā*)" it is implied that the eighth link of the process, craving, is also present. So, when ignorance is eliminated, craving disappears at the same time, and the other factors, grasping (fastening on to life), the process of becoming, rebirth and decay-and-death consequently cease to arise. That is how the entire process can be brought to an end. But as to

3. See The Wheel No. 15, *Dependant Origination* (*Paṭiccasamuppāda*), by Piyadassi Thera and Wheel 394/396, *Fundamentals of Buddhism*, by Nyanatiloka Thera.

a beginning—a first origination in time—there could not have been one, for nothing can spring up uncaused, yet proceed to function as a cause. There could not have been any time when this process of coming-to-be did not exist. *Avijjā* is placed first in the formula only because in explaining the process a start has to be made at some point, and it is convenient to fix on ignorance because it is the nearest approach we can make to define the fundamental and ubiquitous characteristic which makes all the other factors operate. Once we recognize that without ignorance there could be no craving, we are able to appreciate the part that ignorance plays in producing the link that follows it, namely, kamma-formations. In reality, *avijjā* and *taṇhā* are both present along with all the other links that are named subsequently.

Mr. T: Then Buddhism maintains that there was no first cause?

U: Yes, and not only Buddhism. Some outstanding philosophers of our own time are agreed that the belief most people hold, that there must have been a first origin of the cosmos, comes about through an error in thinking. It is largely the result of a misconception regarding the nature of time and causality, our notions of which are limited by the fact that the mind itself functions in time and so is confined to a very narrow view of the relationships that subsist in other dimensions. We tend to think in analogies, and most of these analogies are false. They do not really correspond to things as they are—Do you have a watch?

Mr. T: Why, yes... I'm sorry if I'm taking up your time. It's now—let me see...

U: Never mind the time. That isn't what I meant. I see you have a watch. Well now, from the fact that you have a watch, we can safely infer that the watch had a maker, can't we?

Mr. T: Of course.

U: And from that, people deduce that the world must have had a maker, who is the first cause of all. But it shows nothing of the kind, because the maker of the watch did not exist uncaused. He was the offspring of his parents, and they of theirs. And no matter how many generations back you may go, you cannot find any ultimate origin of the watch. All you find is an ever-increasing number of tributary streams of causality. And that is only one side of the causal process; on the other you find that there is no ultimate origin of the metals that compose the watch. So you see the falseness of the analogy, don't you?

Mr. T: Indeed, yes. It is false in more ways than one, because it assumes also that one cause alone—the watchmaker—could be sufficient to produce the watch, whereas it is obvious that even if the watchmaker existed he could not make a watch without the metals. And if the metals existed, but no watchmaker, there would still be no watch. Also, someone had to make the watchmaker's tools.[4]

U: Now you see the necessity for co-ordinate causal factors, for separate streams of causality converging to the one end. It is precisely this rather complex system of causality that Buddhism teaches. But, you know, this is a very profound philosophical subject, and it is not enough to be given just a brief summary of the conclusions. To understand it properly one must examine the Buddhist doctrine of dependent origination in detail, and also relate it to the supplementary doctrines, such as the doctrine of *paccayā*, which deals with conditionality and relationships, and *niyāmatā*, the order of cosmic necessity. All these things form a part of the analytical knowledge of the Dhamma (*Dhamma-paṭisambhidā*) by which we become able to grasp the true nature of phenomena. Along with these it is a help for modern people to take into account some of the ideas of our contemporary scientific philosophers. If you do that you will find that together they form a perfectly convincing picture of the world we live in, so far as it can be known through the intellect.

Mr. T: Then Buddhism is not simply an intellectualism?

U: Certainly not. So far as the intellect is capable of analysing the elements of the world accurately, it marches with Buddhism. That is why there is no conflict between Buddhism and those ideas which are veridical products of the scientific method. But to confront absolute truth, to comprehend the real order of things in its entirety, one has to transcend the intellect. The intellect selects, narrows the range of cognition and arranges things in its own

---

4. See "Professor Paley's Famous Clock-argument" by Max Ladner (in *The Wheel*, No. 74/75, *German Buddhist Writers*, p. 57).

way, and in so doing imposes the limitations of its nature. We have to break through those conceptual barriers and grasp reality on a different level. That is the great objective of the Buddhist meditation practices—they are to develop the higher consciousness that reaches beyond the intellect. That higher consciousness alone is capable of seeing reality face to face.

Mr. T: Then, if I understand you rightly, Buddhism does not deny the validity of those empirical truths which are capable of being known intellectually, but it definitely asserts that the intellect itself can never come to grips with the final underlying truth of things?

U: Yes, that is just it. And that is precisely what present-day philosophers for the most part believe, also. But since few of them admit the possibility of a higher faculty than the intellect, or of a transcendental order of experience, truth must always appear to be inaccessible. There are some notable exceptions to this, of course. An increasing number of modern thinkers are drawing very close to Buddhism. That is why comparative study of their ideas, along with the ancient teachings of the Buddha, is so rewarding. Some of our present-day scientific philosophers are, all unconsciously, making it easier for the Western mind to understand the concepts of Buddhism. And that is quite natural—they are approaching the same truth by a different, more roundabout route. The Buddha went towards it directly—through the mind itself, which is the basis of all phenomena—instead of trying to get at it through the facts of the physical world alone, as the scientist does.

Mr. T: Yes, I see that the Buddha approached the knowledge of things as they are through the facts of psychology rather than through physics.

U: That is so. And yet we find that his general teaching concerning the physical world is also accurate. It is a true picture in broad outline.[5] Its details, as Western man is interested in them, were of no concern to one who taught only Suffering and the way to its cessation. What the Buddha showed were the fundamental principles of life, its impermanence and "substancelessness", and

5. See *Buddhism and the Scientific Revolution* by K. N. Jayatilleke (*The Wheel*, No. 3, p.3).

consequently its "unsatisfactoriness"—and these principles are found in the physical as well as the mental realm.

Mr. T: You are referring, I suppose, to the three characteristics of phenomena: impermanence, suffering and egolessness.[6] But why should what is impermanent be painful—why suffering? It does not seem to follow at all necessarily. And there is so much good in the world, after all.

U: Surely the joy that slips through our fingers, that fades and dies even as we experience it, is a source of suffering? If we say it is not, that can only be because we expect to experience the same joy, or something similar, again later on. Man can endure the passing of his happiness only through the expectation of gaining it once more. If that expectation is taken from him, he sinks into despair. So it is the renewal of happiness that we are always looking forward to, that keeps us going. And we allow this to compensate us for the knowledge that no individual experience of happiness can be permanent. In fact, man lives alternating between memory and hope. So far as the second part of your question is concerned, Buddhism does not deny that there is good—in whatever way you understand that term—in the world. It simply affirms that on the whole the suffering outweighs the good. And most thinking people who are aware of the condition of the great mass of living beings must and do agree with this. It is only the superficial mind, or the mind that is totally engrossed in its own present felicity, that can resist the conclusion.

Mr. T: Hmm... That's a pretty pessimistic outlook, isn't it?

U: It would be, if Buddhism offered no hope. But as regards the world, it is simply realism. Buddhism offers the cessation of suffering—Nibbāna. That is the sole permanent good—*dhuva* and *parama sukha*—in which suffering can arise no more.

Mr. T: So we are to desire Nibbāna. But isn't desire craving? And isn't craving for Nibbāna a contradiction?

U: Why?

Mr. T: I mean, if Nibbāna is the cessation of craving, it must be a

---

6. See *The Three Signata* by Prof. O. H. de A. Wijesekera (*The Wheel* No. 20).

contradiction to crave for it. But isn't wanting it, or hoping for it, a sort of craving? Does Buddhism make a distinction between that and all other kinds of craving?

U: No distinction of a functional kind can be made between one craving and another. The desire for Nibbāna is an aspiration—a higher form of craving. But it acts in the same way as any other desire when it furnishes the motive for action. All effort is grounded in the wish to gain an objective, and if there were no wish for Nibbāna there could be no striving for it. There is no contradiction in the desire to end desire; for the moment Nibbāna is attained, the desire for it ceases. While the means of gaining the end are being practised, all the other cravings which stand as hindrances are gradually eliminated, until there is only the one desire left. The desire for Nibbāna is therefore the last and highest desire. And since no one goes on desiring what he has already got, it comes to an end the moment its objective is gained. It is the one desire that is not self-regenerating.

Mr. T: I see now that my question was rather unconsidered. How prone we are to verbal entanglements! But isn't the Buddha's teaching of the ending of suffering by the ending of craving, with the consequent ending of existence, rather like a stab in the throat as a cure for a toothache?

U: Well, to make your analogy more fitting you will have to assume that the toothache is *absolutely incurable,* and that any kind of treatment can give only temporary alleviation. Because there is no way of putting an end to suffering in *saṃsāra* except by ending the round of rebirths. Don't you think many people would prefer a stab in the throat to going through eternity with an eternal toothache? But the picture is far too dramatic. It is one of those analogies whose terms do not correspond to the situation at all. The "ending of existence" is nothing more than the ending of a process of "becoming," in which there has never been any true *being.* That is why it is wrong to think of Nibbāna as annihilation. There is no "self" to be annihilated. When the current of causal becoming is brought to an end, the factors of phenomenal personality do not arise anymore. That is all that can be expressed in words. But to imagine Nibbāna as a kind of spiritual suicide is completely wrong.

Mr. T: Forgive my saying so, but that sounds rather like an evasion. For us, life is the phenomenal personality. What alternative can there be to either existing or not existing?

U: When the Buddha was asked that, he replied in effect that the question was wrongly put. Actually, the whole problem hinges on what one means by "existence." The phenomenal personality, by which is meant the five *khandhas*, exists as an aggregate of mutually-supporting factors, one of which, the physical, or *rūpakkhandha,* has a spatial as well as a temporal existence.

The other four, which are mental—that is, sensation, perception, mental formations and consciousness—exist as a continuum in time. Now the existence of each of these is confined to the unitary moments of its arising, persisting and passing away, which are of only infinitesimal duration. These momentary existences are strung, as it were, on the line of causal relationship, "as beads are strung on a cord," forming a progression through time. But the cord is purely imaginary; like the line of the equator, it expresses only an idea; in this case, the idea of cause-effect relationship. There is no absolute identity between the conscious existence of one moment and that of the subsequent one. The only thing that links them is the knowledge we have that one arises because of the prior existence of another. It is from memory that we derive the sense of a persisting personality. But, although we may remember our childhood, we cannot say that we are the same person, in absolute identity, as we were in childhood. If we were the same, we should not be remembering being children—we should be actually *being* children still. The fact that we remember shows that we are not the same. And sometime we experience very vividly the truth of this "otherness," when we think, "Could that really have been I?"

Mr. T: Yes, I know that feeling—the feeling of being a stranger to one's past self. It is rather disturbing when it comes very strongly.

U: Naturally; it is disquieting to the "ego." The process of change precludes any absolute identity of the personality between one phase and another of its progress through time. We have reached our present moment of existence through an infinite series of dead selves. And this present "self" is vanishing even as we think about it. So you see that Buddhism is right in refusing to consider existence as a static quality of some enduring "things," and in refusing to place an imaginary "being" in opposition to an equally imaginary "non-being." The terms of the problem as it is presented in that way simply do not correspond to the reality, with the result that any answer we were to give, affirming existence or non-existence, would be false.

Mr. T: That is a very difficult point to grasp, you know.

U: Indeed, yes. It is so extremely difficult for the average person that the Buddha himself, after he had realized it, at first thought it would be impossible to make anyone else understand it. But as I said before, modern scientific thinkers are independently reaching the same conclusion regarding what we call existence and personality. For the Westerner trying to understand the Dhamma, their approach to it is sometimes very helpful.

Mr. T: In what way?

U: Because they arrive at it by the path that the Western mind has become accustomed to take—via examination and analysis of external phenomena. To that they are now adding the study of the psychological phenomena as well. But because they still continue to treat it as a study of external events in the psychology of others instead of within their own minds, their speculations are often at variance with one another. Many still hold, with Comté, that it is impossible to study the operations of one's own mind. And certainly it is not possible by the methods they use. To take an example, when Freud was making an analysis of his own dreams, he was not making a direct study of his mental processes in dream, but what he remembered of them. Therefore, although he was able to make a very accurate report of what had supplied the content of his dreams, he could make no investigation of the means by which his consciousness registered them. No one can yet say just how the mechanism of consciousness in dreaming differs from that of waking, or even whether it differs at all. But the Buddhist system of mental development proves that the mind can be brought under direct scrutiny, its operations studied at the moment of their occurrence. That is the only way to reach a final understanding of what the personality consists of.

Mr. T: Well, that has certainly given me food for thought. I have just two more questions of this kind. The first stems from what you have just been saying about examining one's own mind. Does not a man know what is right, ultimately, by searching in his own heart, without regard for books or listening to teachers?

U: Do you mean ethically right, or right in the sense of what is ultimately true?

Mr. T: Both.

U: Then let us take your second meaning first. The Buddha was one who discovered absolute truth without a teacher. But to be able to do that, he had previously undergone a process of self-training and spiritual evolution through a long series of lives. Only relatively few beings are able to gain enlightenment for themselves, without a teacher; it is they who become Sammā Sambuddhas or Pacceka Buddhas.[7] It is not that anyone is debarred from attaining Buddhahood—on the contrary, it is open to all; but it is better for most people to take the quicker path to Nibbāna under a guide. Those who take the more arduous path leading to Supreme Buddhahood do so to gain the special powers by which they can make the Dhamma known for the benefit of others. However, during the period in which the *Dispensation* (*Sāsana*) of a supreme Buddha endures, and while the teaching is still extant in the world, those beings who have reached the point at which they can attain Nibbāna do so through the Teaching, not by their own unaided seeking. Obviously it would be a waste of time and effort to search for the truth anew, when the Teaching concerning it is still known to men.

Mr. T: Yes, of course, I see that.

U: Well, now, regarding the knowledge of what is ethically good, I think we can get the answer to your question from common observation. Does it not sometimes happen that men commit all kinds of crimes and atrocities, firmly believing that what they are doing is right and good? Believing, in fact, that they are carrying

---

7. *Sammā Sambuddha*: the Supreme Buddha, qualified to set in motion the Wheel of the Law. *Pacceka Buddha*: a Silent Buddha, one who has attained Enlightenment but is not qualified to teach.

out the "will of God"? Do we find that "conscience" always supplies the right answer to any moral problem? Have not wars, persecutions and all kinds of evils been brought about by people acting, as they were convinced, in accordance with the highest moral principles, through some inner prompting of their own?

Mr. T: Yes, it does seem that conscience, the "inner voice" or the "voice of God," is not always an infallible guide.

U: History shows that it has often been the worst guide possible. Think of the bloodthirsty persecutions of the Middle Ages; think of the unspeakable cruelties inflicted by men who piously believed that they were doing what was right and pleasing to God—the torturing and burning of heretics—to say nothing of the instances of men who have committed crimes of their own accord, under the influence of what they believed to be divine prompting. And if that is not enough, consider the horrible ritual sacrifices of human beings that have been carried out in the name of religion.

Mr. T: Yes, yes, I know. But surely modern civilized man...

U: Please go on.

Mr. T: Well—I mean ... er...

U. Yes...?

Mr. T: Oh, all right... You think that modern civilized man is not any better?

U: Hardly, if at all. And if he were, would it not be the result of past conditioning? The study of behaviour shows that codes of conduct and ideas of right and wrong are not built-in features of man's nature; they have to be learned. And what is so learned is not any universal system of morality, but only the ideas prevailing in one particular place at some given period. So we find that actions which are condemned in one place are blessed with the full approval of society in others, and that at different times totally different standards obtain. Where then is there any innate, infallible guide as to what is right and what is wrong? Where is the standard by which these values are to be measured? All we can say, from observation, is that some people have a more highly-developed moral sense than others, and that sometimes this shows itself at a quite early age. Where it exists it seems to be independent of heredity and, to a surprising degree, of environment as well. That is a fact which the behaviourists cannot explain; but Buddhism accounts for it by past kamma. Yet still it is the outcome of prior conditioning; the ethics and ideals have not come to birth spontaneously, but as the result of learning in previous lives. To that extent Buddhism agrees with the psychology of behaviourism; it maintains that all codes of conduct have to be learned; but by showing causes that are more remote than any operating in a single life, it is able to explain those anomalies which leave the findings of the behaviourists open to question. The sense of right and wrong is not inherent, and it is not of supernatural origin; it has to be acquired; but it is not always acquired in the present life alone. It can be carried over from one life to another, and that is one of the processes which make man's evolution possible. But what we have to remember is that people, besides being differently conditioned as to their ideas of right and wrong by the environment in which their minds develop, are also influenced by the ideas, appearing as instincts, some of which may be true whilst others are false, that they have "inherited" from their past existences. So there can never be any certainty that what a man's "inner voice" tells him is right is really so. It may be most terribly and disastrously wrong. That is why Buddhism holds that intuitive feelings of right and wrong are not a safe guide.

Mr. T: So religious teachings and teachers are always necessary?

U: Yes. But even there one must qualify the statement. We have seen already that much evil has been done in the name of religion and that even today it is still possible for fanaticisms of a religious or pseudo-religious kind to incite men to commit grievous crimes against humanity. There are certain political ideas current in the world which are invested with a kind of religious mystique capable of intoxicating their followers to frenzies of hatred and violence, and they are, unfortunately, extremely contagious. Cults that centre round the personality of some almost deified leader are the modern equivalent of the religious frenzies that drove men to madness in former days. These for the most part have their origin in some supposedly inspired teachings; the leader is given the reverence due to a superman, and even if he fails miserably and comes to a degraded end, there are still weak-minded and fanatical people who are ready to continue idolizing him. The world would be better without "teachers" of that kind.

Mr. T: Very true, indeed.

U: People have a strong tendency, you know, to rationalise their own selfish desires and make them "the will of God." Men have even been known to commit murders at the instigation of some "inner voice" which they devoutly believed was the true voice of their deity. This is an extreme case of pathological delusion, of course, but it points to a fact of the first importance in normal psychology as well. History provides innumerable instances of men finding self-justification for their greed and aggressiveness by dressing their crimes in the trappings of religion. It is the most common device of all for making the baser instincts respectable.

Mr. T: Then how are we to know which teachers are to be followed and which are not?

U: That is the point I was coming to. We can only apply the advice the Buddha gave to the Kālāmas when he said, "In cases where occasion for doubt exists, it is right and proper to doubt. Do not go upon mere report, or tradition or hearsay; neither go upon correspondence with holy writings, upon (unsupported) cogitation or specious reasoning; nor should you go upon the approval of accepted notions, nor upon the authority of one who may appear competent, nor be guided by the instinct of reverence, thinking, 'this ascetic is our teacher.' But, Kālāmas, when you yourselves know (by observation, experience and right judgement), 'Such things are bad, such things are blameworthy, such things are censured by the wise; such things, when undertaken and followed, lead to harm and ill,' then you should abandon such things. But when you yourselves know, 'Such things are good, such things are praiseworthy; such things are commended by the wise, such things, when undertaken and followed, lead to the good and welfare of all beings,' then should you accept, hold to and follow such things."[8] In other words, we have to correct the promptings of the subconscious mind, which too often represents the lower

8. See *Kālāma Sutta*, transl. by Soma Thera, *The Wheel,* No. 8.

nature, by using reason and intelligence. In that way we can form a correct judgement of whatever ideas are offered to us.

Mr. T: But could you give me a summary in brief of the Buddhist criterion of right and wrong?

U: Certainly. It is summed up in the words, "To abstain from all wrongdoing; to develop all good; to purify one's mind—this is the teaching of the Buddhas." And the basic distinction between what is good and what is bad is very simple in Buddhism. All actions that have their roots in greed, hatred and delusion, that spring from selfishness and so foster the harmful delusion of self-hood are demeritorious and bad. All those which are rooted in disinterestedness, friendliness and wisdom are meritorious and good. And this standard applies, irrespective of whether the deeds are of thought, word or physical act. The Pāli word *lobha,* which I have just given as "greed," also includes excessive lust; *dosa* means hatred and anger, while *moha* is equivalent to *avijjā*; it stands for ignorance of the real nature of conditioned existence—ignorance of the fact that all the aggregates of personality are impermanent, liable to suffering and devoid of selfhood, and at the same time ignorance of the Four Noble Truths. *Lobha, dosa* and *moha* are called the three roots of unwholesome action. When we have learned to analyze our thoughts, contemplating them objectively and dispassionately, we become able to know, distinctly and without any shadow of doubt, when any of these three unwholesome factors are present and when they are not. It is only by this intimate self-knowledge that we can develop a true instinct for what is right and wrong.

Mr. T: That is excellent! I really like that very much. Volumes have been written on ethics, from every possible angle, but it seems to me that this Buddhist concept, so simple and direct, gets right to the heart of the matter. It does not depend upon any questionable metaphysical ideas, but on fundamental truths of psychology. It is something that everyone can grasp, and prove for oneself. That much of Buddhism, at least, everyone must accept. But now my other question. It is about rebirth. How can there be rebirth? Isn't it really an impossibility?

U: Well, to that question I usually reply in the words of Voltaire: "It is no more impossible to be born many times than to be born once! Even the old sceptic, Ferney, had to admit that he had been born, and that being so, he could find no reason for supposing the event to be unique in his experience.

Mr. T: That's all very well, but can rebirth be *proved*?

U: That depends on what you are willing to accept as proof. There have been many intelligent people who have believed in rebirth simply because it is the only view that gives any meaning or purpose to life—the only conception that makes any sense of this muddled, apparently futile and inconclusive existence, with all its injustices, its insoluble problems and loose ends of experience. And further, it has seemed to them that if there is any survival beyond the grave, any kind of immortality at all, rebirth is the only form it could take, because the very essence of life is change. They have found these considerations a sufficient ground for accepting it. But there are also others who know it to be true by personal experience. You must surely know that of recent years much has been written on the many cases of people who have actually remembered previous lives, and have given evidence that proves the truth of their statements. And then there are the instances of those who virtually re-live their former existences whilst under hypnosis. Psychologists are now making a special study of these cases. Some of the subjects whilst under hypnosis speak foreign languages that are unknown to them in their normal state—a phenomenon which is known as xenoglossy. In any case we cannot dismiss the belief in reincarnation, which has played so large a part in the religious and philosophical thought of mankind from the earliest times, as mere moonshine, just because we ourselves cannot remember having lived on earth before. How much can any of us remember of our early childhood? Or of the years in between then and now?

Mr. T: Well, regarding what you said first, is it really necessary to assume that life has any meaning or purpose? Granting that one life on its own—whether followed by immortality elsewhere or not—does not make any sense, is there any reason why it should do so? May not the whole of existence be merely a gigantic cosmic accident?

U: It could be, of course, judged only by what our intellect makes of it. But doesn't it strike you as significant that the very people who hold that view themselves behave as though life had meaning, purpose and values? I have in mind one very eminent English mathematician and philosopher who on grounds of strict determinism denies all freewill to man, and believes, apparently, that life is nothing more than a particular function of matter, yet who shows more concern for humanitarian values and the survival of mankind than do many who claim to believe that man's nature and destiny are of paramount and supernatural importance. This same philosopher, who, if he were to conduct himself in accordance with his beliefs, should be sitting quietly in his study awaiting the inevitable outcome of mathematically-determined events, is instead actively engaged in trying to save humanity from a war of nuclear extermination, at great personal inconvenience and not a little real physical danger to himself. And this kind of conduct, from a man who has written, "Some people ... derive comfort from the thought that if God made the world, He may wind it up again when it has completely run down. For my part, I do not see how an unpleasant process can be made less so by the reflection that it is to be infinitely repeated"[9] is somewhat unexpected. One might ask, "Why protest against the possible destruction of humanity if life is merely an unpleasant process that would be better brought to an end rather than infinitely repeated?"

Mr. T: Well, there are certain philosophies that can only be treated as engagements of the intellect. No one could consistently live in accordance with them. But still, neither the fact that people believe in rebirth because it gives meaning to life nor the evidence of those who claim to remember previous lives furnishes real, decisive proof, does it?

U: True. The final and conclusive proof lies only with those who personally remember having lived before. Only to them its truth is beyond dispute. But the weight of evidence, you know, is generally taken as being on the side which can show most facts or inferences in its favour. There are many we "know" to be true

9. Bertrand Russell, *Science and Religion* (*The Scientific Outlook*), 1931.

on this kind of evidence alone. Now in addition to the people who have given proof that they have lived before, we have a great number of philosophical reasons for believing in rebirth. And what is to be set against this? Nothing more than the fact that the enquirer himself cannot remember any previous existence. You must admit that it is scarcely reasonable to set up one's own individual experience against the great mass of evidence that can be brought up on the other side. That would be like refusing to believe that the earth is a sphere, just because one has not seen its rotundity with one's own eyes. In any case there is every reason why we should not all remember our previous births. If we did so, the complications of the present life, which for many of us are already far too weighty, would become insupportable. There has to be "a sleep and a forgetting" but the forgetting is not always complete. We all bring something of our past into our present lives, even if it is only some traits of character.

Mr. T: Well, I must say, that is very reasonable. I can see that whereas one fact in isolation, or even three or four, may not be impressive as evidence, when a great number of facts drawn from different sources all point to one conclusion, we have something like a solid body of evidence. Thank you very much for being so patient with me. I shall give very careful thought to what you have said. May I come and see you again?

U: Of course. I am happy to find that you are interested in the Dhamma sufficiently to ask questions about it. Buddhism welcomes questions, you know. There are no sacred mysteries in our creed; there is nothing that has to be treated with reverential awe as being too holy for human understanding.

Mr. T: Yes, that is what I find so attractive about Buddhism. Thank you once more. I shall come back again when I have digested what you have given me today.

II

Mr. T: What you said to me at the end of our last talk, about the openness of Buddhism to enquiry, prompts me to ask you this: Is Buddhism a form of rationalist atheism or an atheist humanism?

U: Any attempt to label Buddhism, or to fit it into any of the categories of Western thought, which incline to separating the philosophical from the religious, is bound to be misleading. Buddhism is atheistic in the strict sense of rejecting belief in a Creator-god. It is not atheism in the sense of rejecting all belief in a superior order of being or a spiritual purpose in life. It is necessary to mark that distinction, because too often people mistakenly believe that there can be no religious or ethical values without a supreme power, a god in some form or another. In Buddhism the supreme power is the natural law of cause and effect, from which comes the moral order of kamma, or actions, and *vipāka*, or results. The ethical teaching of Buddhism is intrinsically a part of the concept of man's highest purpose, which is to gain his release from the painful conditions of saṃsāra. The goal and the means to it cannot be separated. If there were an omnipotent God, he would be able to release man from his bondage to kamma; and if that God were all-compassionate, he would certainly do so. As I have already explained to you, Buddhism is rationalistic, but it goes beyond rationalism in the scope of its vision of causes unseen. The rationalism which we speak of today is limited to a very small section of the total human experience, and by itself can never encompass the ultimate truth of things. Buddhism, on the other hand, continues where this limited rationalism leaves off; it expands the principles and the frontiers of reason and finally it teaches us how, by developing higher faculties, we may finally transcend the realm of sense-perception and conditionality. In much the same way, Buddhism also has a likeness to humanism. It holds that man is the measure of all things, and can by his own efforts solve the riddle of life; and further it maintains that the human values are the sole standards and arbiters of morality and progress. It does not have to fall back on such theological distinctions as a supposed difference between man's justice and God's. But Buddhism goes beyond mere humanism when it claims that man can become superhuman. The values of humanism, fine as they are, are not enough to form the basis of a progress that aims at lifting man right out of the human situation. The humanist philosophy can only leave man where he is at present, with all his imperfections, his perplexities and his uncertain ethical values fundamentally unchanged.

Mr. T: Why so?

U: Because humanism on its own does not provide any ultimate standard by which man's progress is to be measured. It measures man only by man, and you cannot measure a thing, either quantitatively or qualitatively, by itself. Buddhism provides a standard for normal life and a higher standard for it to measure up to as well—the standard of *Arahantship*. The second, which is the standard of man perfected, is constant and immutable. It serves to mark humanity's highest level, at any time and in any situation. So it gives us a clearly defined goal at which to aim, the state of absolute "desirelessness", dispassion and enlightenment.

Mr. T: I see. But, if enlightenment comes at all, why does it not come all at once, instead of in four stages?

U: You mean the four stages of *Sotāpanna, Sakadāgāmi, Anāgāmi* and *Arahatta*? Well, all progress is made in stages, isn't it? In this case the four stages represent definite psychological changes, each of which occurs at a certain point in consequence of the changes brought about by the preceding stage. You see, there are ten mental obstructions which stand in the path of self-purification, or as fetters (*dasa saṃyojana*) bind us to the wheel of existence. Now all beings have been bound by those ten fetters throughout innumerable cycles of existence, and they are very strong. They cannot be broken all at once. Therefore the Buddha taught a gradual training, a progress by recognizable stages.

Mr. T: Please tell me about the ten fetters.

U: They are (1) delusion of selfhood, (2) doubt or uncertainty, (3) belief in the efficacy of rites and ceremonies; or, in short, superstition, (4) sensual craving, (5) ill-will. These five are called lower fetters, because they bind beings to the planes of sense-gratification. Then come (6) craving for existence in the fine-material worlds, (7) craving for existence in the formless worlds,[10] (8) pride, (9) restlessness, and (10) ignorance. This second group of five is higher fetters, in the sense that they bind beings to the fine-material and formless worlds.

10. Fine-material and formless worlds: planes of the thirty-one abodes of saṃsāra which correspond to highly refined and ethical states of consciousness.

Mr. T: Then how do they separate into four stages?

U: In this way: when the first three fetters are broken one becomes a *Sotāpanna*, which means that one has become confirmed in the knowledge of the truth. One who has reached this stage becomes incapable of committing any of the unwholesome deeds that lead to rebirth in sub-human realms of suffering. *Sotāpanna* literally means "Stream-winner"—he has entered the stream that leads surely to Nibbāna. After that comes the disciple who has reached the next stage, by weakening the next two fetters, four and five. He is called a *Sakadāgāmi* or "Once-returner," because even if he fails to reach Nibbāna in the current life, he is bound to do so in the next birth. Then comes the *Anāgāmi*, who has completely destroyed all the first five fetters; he is called *Anāgāmi* or "Non-returner" because if he does not gain Nibbāna before he dies he will reach it in his next birth, which takes place in *Suddhāvāsa* or the Pure Abodes. There he attains *Arahantship*, and passes straight to Nibbāna without returning to the sensuous planes. The fourth and last stage is of course that of the *Arahant*, who has broken all the fetters, burned out all the defilements and brought the grasping-formations to an end. For him there is no rebirth.

Mr. T: So Nibbāna is attained when these Ten Fetters are broken?

U: Yes, in this present life itself all the stages can be accomplished.

Mr. T: Then cannot Nibbāna rightly be called the "Kingdom of Heaven"? Doesn't that also mean the ending of suffering?

U: Right thinking depends so much, you know, on the right use of words. That is why we try to be as exact as possible in terminology when we present Buddhist ideas. What exactly do people mean by "Heaven"? If that question could be settled, the answer could be found at once. If in thinking of "Heaven" we mean what is intended by the phrase "Heaven lies within us," then there certainly is a likeness to the Buddhist concept of Nibbāna as it is experienced whilst the *Arahant* is still in the flesh. That is the subjective "Heaven," the state of mind that knows its own happiness and security, and is fully detached from the troubles of earthly life. But if "Heaven" means a place of bliss which is a kind of superior copy of the best of life on earth, it does not correspond to Nibbāna at all. Buddhism recognizes heavens of that kind, but Nibbāna is above and beyond them. Those heavens are impermanent—and there indeed one might find a correspondence between them and the heaven of which it is said, "Heaven and earth shall pass away, but my words shall not pass away"[11] in the Christian scriptures. Those words are better fitted to a Buddhist than Christian setting, since the Buddhist heavens and hells are subject to the law of impermanence and causality, but the Dhamma which teaches that law is everlasting. Universes arise and pass away, but the law remains the same forever. And Nibbāna, which is outside the realm of condition and causality, also remains unchanging. So, as Buddhists, we should simply amend the phrase to "Heaven and earth shall pass away, but the Law of Causality shall not pass away." Nibbāna does not come into it at all, because it is not within the causal law. It cannot be compared to any idea of a heaven in which phenomenal personality, with its inevitable arising, decay and destruction, continues to manifest.

Mr. T: I see. But now there is another comparison I should like to make. It concerns what is meant by *saddhā*. If the Buddha's teaching requires faith, is not a Christian justified in arguing that it is merely a matter of developing the faculties to become able to perceive the truth of the revealed dogmas of the Christian Church, and so there is no difference between Buddhism and revealed religion in that respect?

U: *Saddhā* means confidence more than faith. When we are sick and go to a physician, why do we believe—or at least hope—that he can cure us?

Mr. T: Well, I suppose because he has got his degrees, has an established practice and has shown his capability by curing others.

U: Exactly. And for the same reason when we wish to learn any art or science we go to a teacher whose ability has been shown in practice. Doesn't that mean that we have confidence in the doctor or teacher?

Mr. T: Yes, of course.

U: But it does not come from direct knowledge that he can cure or teach us? There is no absolute certainty about it?

11. Matt. 24:350

Mr. T: No, we can be absolutely certain only after the event.

U: Then it can also be called faith, can't it?

Mr. T: Yes.

U: But "faith" is a rather emotionally-loaded word, which we usually reserve for the mysteries of religion. It implies belief not confirmed by reason—even belief in defiance of reason. Now a Buddhist's confidence in the Buddha is just the kind we have in a good physician or teacher. It is not blind faith, because we have substantial grounds for it. The doctrine the Buddha offers us is one that we can believe in first of all intellectually, because it conforms to what we can see and prove empirically as to the nature of the world. And, like the physician, the Buddha has effected his cures. We know that his method is effective in putting an end to suffering because it has done so for so many people during the last 2,500 years. It is, one would say, a very old, established practice indeed. So we have that much confidence in the Buddha's Dhamma before we start on the treatment. It does not ask us to believe in any improbable dogmas, and certainly not in anything that goes against fundamental reason. It is not based on myths, or legends, but on observed facts of experience—the truths of impermanence, suffering and non-self. Those cardinal truths, irrespective of miracles or revelations, attest to the solid foundation of Buddhism in the knowledge of things as they are. And since everything else in the Dhamma springs logically from those three facts of observation in a coherent and articulated system, we surely have the most emphatic reason for feeling confidence in the Physician and Teacher. And lastly, it invites us to "come and see" for ourselves. We are asked only to suspend our doubts until such time as we have clear proof, by direct experience, that the Teaching is true. This comes with the first attainment, after which doubt (*vicikicchā*) cannot arise anymore.

Mr. T: That, I see, is quite different from making faith a prerequisite of revelation. When one considers how many of the finest intellects in the Christian Church have struggled against doubt, blaming themselves for their inability to believe and fearing that the longed-for revelation will be withheld from them because of it, one realizes what a stumbling block this demand for unquestioning faith can be. Now that you have entirely satisfied me on that point, I shall be glad if you can clear up another matter for me. Does the Buddha teach that the world is a dualism of good and evil, as Manichaeism is supposed to do?

U: That is not a question that can be answered with a plain yes or no. To begin with, we should suppress the emotional overtones that accompany such words as "good" and "evil."

Mr. T: Why?

U: Because they interfere with our view, which should be as far as possible detached, objective and scientific. In any case, "good" and "evil" are very loose terms. What is good for one person may be evil for another. Man exterminates pests and certain kinds of animals for his own "good" (as he imagines), but the effect so far as the animals are concerned is decidedly evil. So it is, even with actions concerning man and man. It is extremely difficult to make a hard and fast division between what is good and what is evil—a distinction that will remain valid for all occasions and eventualities. These are words that really describe different viewpoints, rather than fixed qualities.

Mr. T: But still, we do know in a broad general way what is meant by good and evil.

U: No doubt. But can we always be agreed as to what is good or evil in specific instances? Can we, when our own interests are in conflict with those of someone else? Practical experience shows that we cannot, so long as the feeling of selfhood sways our judgement. If we could, human beings would live in a greater measure of peaceful agreement than they have ever shown themselves able to do. The fact is that we all measure good and evil according to the way events afford us either pleasure or pain. So, for the purpose of this discussion it would be better if we were to substitute some other terms for "good" and "evil." They are really too subjective to be very helpful in our present enquiry. In Buddhism, where "evil" denotes the pain inherent in life it is defined as "suffering." Where it denotes moral wrong it is called "unwholesome action" (*akusala-kamma*). These terms are on the whole much more satisfactory for a precise treatment of the subject than are the "good" and "evil" of theology.

Mr. T: Yes, I grant that they are more precise. But suppose, then, we were to define "evil" broadly as whatever causes pain to living beings, and "good" as whatever gives them pleasure?

U: Well, we can accept that definition for the moment, and try to find an answer to your question along those lines. Only I must ask you to remember that it is still not an entirely satisfactory definition, because things that give pleasure are not always good. Very often they are bad in themselves, or they bring "evil" consequences to ourselves or to others. But let us see what the believers in dualism themselves meant by their distinction. The Manichaean idea of two powers or cities, light and darkness, was derived from Zoroastrianism, which postulated two coeval, co-eternal and equally potent powers in the world—the creator of all good, Ahura Mazda, and the force of evil, Ahriman. It explained the presence of good and evil side by side as the inveterate opposition of these two equally matched personages. It was a ditheism, and as such it overcame the difficulties that present themselves when belief in one single Creator-god makes him necessarily responsible for both good and evil in the world. The Zoroastrian and Manichaean position was to some extent more logical than that of monotheism; but it had one unhappy result, which was that the power of evil tended to receive as much worship, if not more, than the power of good. This was really unavoidable; it followed upon the recognition that there is on the whole more evil than good in the world.

Mr. T: I'm not altogether prepared to agree with that.

U: Perhaps not. But remember that in Christianity also, the Devil is called "the Prince of this world." And also I must ask you to bear in mind, again, that when I use the word "evil" I intend it to mean whatever is painful and a source of suffering and grief. Don't be led away by those emotional overtones I warned you about at the start!

Mr. T: Hmm... Well, exactly how did the Zoroastrians measure good and evil?

U: I'm afraid they measured it just as most people always do. "Good" was what was beneficial to them, or seemed so; "evil" was what was harmful. In the Pahlavi scriptures, Ahura Mazda goes about creating things for the good of man, such as crops, fruit trees, fair weather and so on. Ahriman follows behind him creating blight, locusts, storms, disease and floods. Everything that Ahura Mazda creates Ahriman mars. But you can see that this concept of what is good and evil is a very narrow and parochial one. It is all centred about man and his needs. Suppose that we consider it from the point of view of the locusts, rats and other vermin that Ahriman is supposed to have brought into being. To them, the works of Ahura Mazda and Ahriman would appear equally good—except that they would regard man as the creation of the evil spirit. But the dualists never gave that a thought. They were concerned only with themselves and their own welfare. And of course they had no idea of the balance which nature preserves, in which every species of living being plays a part in the general economy of the world.

Mr. T: Meaning...?

U: Meaning that, for example, if man succeeds in utterly exterminating one form of pest, another, which the destroyed pests formerly kept in check, increases—with perhaps even more harmful effects than before. This is a fact that man never realized until he was able to make practical experiments in the wholesale destruction of parasites, predatory animals and the like. And even in the question of weather, the Zoroastrians of course did not realize that storms and fair weather alike are all part of the climatic system of the earth, and that you cannot have one without the other. So you see that what they meant by "good" and "evil" was really nothing more than the balance of opposites. By personalizing these they made two deities in eternal conflict.

Mr. T: Scientists believe now that in course of time we shall be able to control the weather...

U: And when that comes about it will be just another complication, just another source of conflict, in human life. For when one section of people needs dry weather for crops, another will want rain. If control of weather is practised on a regional basis it can only be a further cause of international tension, by interfering with world economics. Artificially produced dry weather in one region would probably cause floods in another.

Mr. T: Yes, I can see that man's power of controlling his environment artificially holds even greater dangers than those we confront now. However, to return to the main subject: the only point of dualism, then, is that it absolves God of responsibility for suffering?

U: Yes—but at the cost of admitting the existence of another power as mighty as God, if not mightier. So the omnipotence of God is abandoned. That supposed infinity of power can be reserved to a god only by attributing to him good and evil in at least equal measure. But very few monotheists are prepared to go along with Jacob Boehme when he speaks of "the evil that is in God."[12]

Mr. T: Truly, it does seem that God's omnipotence and infinite love are mutually exclusive ideas. They cannot both be the attribute of one and the same deity. Yet the Vedāntists claim to have an answer to that, don't they?

U: Yes, an answer of a sort. But it practically amounts to denying the existence of evil as an objective reality. It holds that all things emanate from God—therefore all things are "good." And as a logical corollary of this, there is left no moral distinction between good and evil, right and wrong, either. This is actually what the teaching of the *Bhagavad Gīta* amounts to.

Mr. T: Dear me! Is that really so? Someone told me that what the *Bhagavad Gītā* teaches is pure Buddhism!

U: No, its ethical teaching is rather the opposite of the Buddha's. The *Gītā* tries to show that one may be a full Yogi whilst engaging in all the activities, good and bad, of the world. It is a sustained argument to the effect that violence is not necessarily evil kamma. According to this theory, morality is solely a matter of social obligations; a man's moral duty is whatever his caste, or station in life, requires of him. If he is of the warrior caste by birth, it is his moral duty to kill even his own relatives and preceptors, should occasion arise. The *Gītā's* teaching is expressly that so long as such actions are performed without desire for or clinging to the results (a psychological impossibility, by the way), but are made an offering

12. In his later works, e.g., the *Mysterium Magnum,* Jacob Boehme developed his theory of evil as being a direct outcome of the divine manifestation, the "wrath side" of God.

to God, there is no sin attached to them. Buddhism denies this argument absolutely. But don't let us digress. Dualism, as we have seen, is an escape from the difficulties created by monotheism. But Buddhism does not postulate any supreme consciously-acting power, either of good or evil.[13] It teaches only the supreme law of cause and effect. It is in the working out of that law, in all its inescapable necessity, that man, judging from his own standpoint, finds these two apparently opposite effects which he labels "good" and "evil." But the causal law is an operation of nature; in itself it is neither good nor evil. We may liken it to the law of gravity; without gravity nothing could remain in place on the surface of the earth. So then you will say the law of gravity is "good." But supposing you fall from a high building? Then, because it causes your death, the law of gravity is "evil"?

Mr. T: All right—I get your point. What we call good and evil are simply two aspects of one and the same law, which is in itself completely neutral. And from that Buddhism derives the principle of kamma and *vipāka*, actions and results, as you explained previously.

U: Yes. It may seem to you that I laboured the point, but you must admit that if I hadn't gone into it as I did, you would not have been ready to accept it merely on a dogmatic statement such as "good and evil are necessary and complementary to one another."

Mr. T: You are right—I shouldn't. But doesn't Buddhism regard man's nature as a sort of dualism of good and evil?

U: In man's nature there are the lower instincts, summarized as greed, hatred and delusion, all three of which are brought into play in man's character of an animal struggling for survival and seeking

13. Māra, the personified evil of Buddhism, appears in the texts sometimes as a real person, sometimes as an externalisation of the mental defilements, often in the plural form. It is as a real person that he tempts the Buddha at the time of Enlightenment and later, to pass into *Anupādisesa-Nibbāna* without fulfilling his mission. But at no time after the Enlightenment does Māra appear to the Master in the guise of the grosser fetters; his temptation of the Buddha, whose defilements are eradicated, can only be on the highest level—the temptation to accept his *Parinibbāna* at once. This, the Buddha's concern for suffering humanity did not permit.

sensual satisfaction. But man is potentially something greater than this. He has higher aspiration, a higher scale of values, and so these two aspects of his nature come into play alternately. Buddhism teaches us to eliminate the lower nature and systematically to cultivate the higher. By that means man can become greater than the gods. He can become a *visuddhi-deva*—a god by purification.

Mr. T: Isn't that the same as becoming God, or becoming "one with God"?

U: Not at all. In those ideas God still has a personal identity and attributes. He is supposed to be the creator or source of all that is. As I have said before, there is no place for a god of that kind in Buddhism.

Mr. T: Well, since we are back again on the subject of God, what is the harm in developing the love of God, as the Christians and Vedāntists do? Is not love the noblest and most liberating sentiment? And if belief in, or worship of God—even if it is only a matter of faith, or even if he does not exist—helps us to develop love, isn't that a good thing?

U: As I pointed out in answer to one of your earlier questions, the idea of a supreme Godhead can be used to cover up some self-centred wish of one's own, as the wars of religion in the past have amply proved. Armies intent on pillage have marched into battle "in the name of God"; rulers have oppressed their subjects and subverted all human rights—"in the name of God"; ecclesiastical authorities have tortured and burned people alive for daring to disagree with their doctrines, all "in the name of God." And why is this? Obviously it is because nobody really knows anything about this God—what his will is, or how he expects man to act in any given situation. Every theistic religion differs on these questions. Therefore the Buddha likened the love of God to loving a woman one has never seen, whose form and characteristics one does not know, and whose very existence is in doubt. He dismissed this kind of love as foolishness.[14] The love of a being whose attributes exist only in one's own imagination is at the best an unprofitable expenditure of the affections. One is most likely loving an image of one's own desires. Is not such love offered in the lively expectation

14. *Tevijja Sutta* of the *Dīgha Nikāya* (*The Wheel*, No. 57/58).

of getting some reward from the deity? If God is needed only as a peg on which to hang one's love, what happens when the peg is nothing but an illusion? Buddhism teaches that it is far better to fix on real living beings as objects of *mettā bhāvanā*.[15] One then has something concrete and external to oneself on which to focus the concentrated mind of goodwill. You must see that it is easy to love a fabrication of one's own imagination, especially an image constructed in the form of a loving father and protector, but it is not so easy to love beings who have their own independent existence—an existence that may possibly be hostile to one's own. That is the real test of whether love is genuine and disinterested or not. It is the cultivation of that kind of universal benevolence—entirely unconnected with any expectation of return or reward—that Buddhism prescribes as the real development of the heart of loving-kindness. This is the love that liberates. But the love of an imaginary being, a projection of one's own dreams, can never lead a man out of ignorance into the highest Enlightenment.

Mr. T: No doubt the love of God, when it is harnessed to institutional and sectarian religion, often does give undesirable results, but isn't an ascetic who tortures himself out of devotion to a god still doing a good action? Isn't devotion spiritually profitable?

U: The Buddha was most emphatic on that point. Having tried to gain liberation by the most extreme asceticism himself, without result, he was in a position to speak with authority on it. The very first declaration he made, before preaching the Dhamma, was that the two extreme courses, self-indulgence and self-torture, were equally low, base and unprofitable. Self-torture is not conducive to sound health of mind or body. It can only bring on hallucinations and mental derangement, or, if the mind is stronger than the body, a physical breakdown before the mind gives way. That is what actually happened to the *Bodhisatta* himself; his weakened body collapsed and he could go no further on that path, but due to his strong mental powers his brain remained clear. But tell me this: why, in any case, should it be supposed that God is pleased by self-torture? Does he take delight in seeing men make wrecks of themselves?

15. *Mettā Bhāvanā*: the meditation on universal benevolence, one of the four *Brahma Vihāras* (*The Wheel*, No. 6/7).

Mr. T: No... No I must say, it doesn't seem likely.

U: Indeed, one would think that human life was painful enough, without voluntarily inflicting more suffering on oneself. But very often such extreme asceticism is itself the outcome of a pathological condition of the mind. Haven't you noticed how, in history, those given to self-torture were equally ready to torture others on the slightest provocation?

Mr. T: That's true—the Grand Inquisitor with a hair shirt under his habit!

U: Violence towards oneself is never very far from violence towards others. Buddhism condemns them both. It is not one of the cults of blood. But the self-torture of Hindu ascetics was originally not undertaken out of devotion to God, but to gain power through the strengthening of the will, so that the gods themselves could be brought under compulsion. This is made very clear in the old Hindu stories of gods and ascetics, the *Purānas*. It is all part of the cult of power which underlies the Hindu system. The idea was that a man could make his will stronger than the gods, by mortification of the flesh. It is only in early Christianity that we come across the paradoxical notion that a god of love can be pleased by self-torture. And in Christianity it did not gain widespread credence because the contradiction was too self-evident. It was so far from being universally approved that on several occasions the Vatican took action to suppress a sect of self-torturers, the flagellants; possibly because those who were eager to torture themselves could not be expected to fear torture from others.

Mr. T: Really? When did that happen?

U: Oh, some time between 1349 and 1389, in Italy. The leader of the sect was burned at the stake by order of the Pope. You can read about it in W. M. Cooper's *Flagellation and the Flagellants,* written in 1908. But in any case, the belief that the ego can be overcome by mortification of the body has no psychological justification whatever; on the contrary, egoism is more likely to be increased by it. The pride of the ascetic in his asceticism is a byword. There are several allusions to it in the Buddhist texts. When Devadatta, the renegade bhikkhu, proposed stricter rules for the Sangha, one of the reasons he gave was that "people esteem asceticism." The Buddha rejected his proposals decisively.

Mr. T: Can you quote me anything the Buddha said on the subject?

U: Certainly. In the *Dhammapada,* verse 141, you will find this:

> "Neither wandering naked, nor matted hair, nor dirt, nor fasting, nor lying on the raised ground, nor smearing the body with dust, nor (the ascetic pose of) squatting can purify a mortal who has not overcome doubt."

And again, in verse 394:

> "Of what use is your matted hair, O wicked man? Of what use is your deer skin? Within you is a thicket (of passion); only outwardly are you clean!"

Mr. T: Thank you. I am bound to agree that rigorous self-mortification may be undertaken out of vanity and a desire for renown, and even if at the beginning the motive was a higher one it may in the end produce spiritual pride. And it does seem to me that the idea of self-torture is quite out of keeping with the modern spirit, which looks with suspicion on all forms of fanaticism.

U: I am glad you have grasped those points. Buddhism recommends a life of simplicity and austerity for the subduing of the passions. It is the Middle Way of moderation and sanity— a sound and healthy regimen that carries the full authority not only of the Buddha's personal experience but also the great weight of sane opinion throughout the ages. All truly great men have led simple, even spartan lives, practising self-restraint and avoiding all those excesses which encourage sensuality and dissipate vital energy. By such means the mind is kept clear, unclouded by the passions that warp judgement, yet the body is not deprived of anything necessary for its healthy and efficient functioning. That is the ideal life which Buddhism enjoins on everyone, monk and layman alike, but more strictly of course on the bhikkhu.

Mr. T: That is very reasonable indeed, and must meet with the approval of all sensible people. But now, leaving aside what we were talking about just now, the love of God, which you have made me realise is of little value because in loving God each man is really loving a being of his own conception, fashioned in the likeness of his own desires and often with his own defects— leaving that aside, isn't the whole of the Buddha's Teaching simply love?

U: The whole of the Buddha's Teaching, as he often said, is simply the fact of suffering, its cause, its cessation and the way to make it cease. Love, which is an attitude towards other beings, has an object and is therefore bound up with concepts; it can never on its own produce the insight-knowledge which is the crown of the Buddhist achievement. Love is an instrument—a necessary instrument—for eliminating the erroneous concept of selfhood and all the mental defilements that spring from self. And besides, it is a special kind of love that must be cultivated—not the self-assertive, possessive emotion that people usually mean by love. The Pāli word *mettā* corresponds more closely to the Greek *agape*. It means universal, dispassionate benevolence. It is not the love we feel for any particular person who happens to be pleasing or agreeable to us. Still less is it the love that is associated with sensuality. And it is not a mere passing emotion, but a fixed attitude of mind, something which has become habitual through constant cultivation.

Mr. T: But just how does the Buddha's teaching of love differ from that of Christianity or Vedānta? Isn't that the kind of love they teach, also?

U: There are very important differences. Christianity says: "Love your enemies, and those that despitefully use you," and here there is a strong affinity with the teaching of the Buddha. But Christian love is confined to God and human beings; it does not include the lower forms of life, which according to Christian belief are created for man's use and pleasure. Now when I say this it is just to serve as a reminder of fact. In practise, many Christians show great love and kindness to animals, but this does not alter the fact that the Christian religion does not call for it. Those people are extending love beyond the bounds required by their religion—or perhaps some of them substituting the love of animals for the love they cannot feel for their own kind. However that may be, it is only certain kinds of animals they love—those that are useful or agreeable to them. Others they hunt and kill without compunction. But in any case, when we are dealing with matters of doctrine we should never let ourselves be influenced by the behaviour of the followers of the various creeds; we should go straight to the teaching itself. Again, Christianity does not call on its followers to love the Devil, or the damned souls in hell; but Buddhism excludes nobody. The beings in the states of suffering are the greatest objects of compassion, and Buddhists are taught to share with them the merit of their good deeds, that their pains may be alleviated. And another difference is that Buddhist *mettā* is not an emotion which can turn into anger and violence, into furious denunciations of sinners and threats of eternal punishment. The love taught by Christianity always has its reverse aspect—loving righteousness involves hating evil. The injunction to "hate the sin but love the sinner" is really meaningless. It is impossible because the sinner and his sin cannot be separated a man *is* his character, his personality, his actions. The fallacy of this idea of hating the sin but loving the sinner is shown in the fact that the God himself does not love sinners. If he did, he would not cast them into hell. He loves them only when they repent—that is, when they cease to be sinners. Even God, it seems, cannot separate a man and his deeds in such a way that he can save the man and send only his deeds to hell!

Mr. T: Do you know, I never thought of that before! It is really appalling the way we accept meaningless words as being profound wisdom, simply because we never stop to think out whether they have a meaning or not... And so we go on deceiving ourselves. We use words as a sort of plaster, to cover up truth and reality, instead of using them to clarify our ideas. Really, it is shocking when one realizes it.

U: I am afraid the language of theology is designed more to that end than any other. That is what has put theology into irreconcilable opposition to philosophy in the West. To be quite plain, Christianity does not offer any reasoned basis for its teaching of love. No attempt is made to explain to man why he should love his enemy. It is simply given as a commandment of God; yet it is quite clear that the God himself does not continue to love those who persist in rebelling against him. Jesus himself often denounced sinners in anything but loving speech, as Bertrand Russell has pointed out in one of his essays. And one is bound to remember that this God who cannot forgive has not really been injured by the sinner. How can a puny mortal do any real injury to the "Eternal and Almighty God"? But the enemy a man is commanded to love and forgive is one who has done a very real injury to him, and may inflict another in the future. So what can one deduce from that?

Mr. T: That man is expected to be more loving and forgiving than God. That seems to me the sole and inescapable answer.

U: Yes, exactly.

Mr. T: But—but... Oh, dear... Excuse me—I feel a bit bewildered. These things seem so plain now—and yet—how was it I never thought of them before?

U: In the case of Vedānta, again, love is directed mainly towards a God—one who is conceived either as endowed with qualities, the personalised or *Saguṇa Brahman*, or as being "qualityless," the neuter or *Nirguṇa Brahman*. No matter which of these two aspects of godhead may be its object, what I have already said about the love of God applies here as well. So far as the love of real beings is concerned, it is limited, for all but ascetics and yogis, by the obligations of caste. We have already referred to the teaching of the Bhagavad Gīta concerning the duty of a *kshatriya*, one of the ruling warrior caste, and how it involves taking life, and I have said that the Buddha, who was himself a *kshatriya*, opposed this concept of duty absolutely. Buddhism makes no compromise on this question; the first of the Five Precepts, which is the undertaking to abstain from killing, shows how literally the spiritual love towards all beings is to be cherished and observed by the follower of the Buddha.

Mr. T: Buddhism is certainly very consistent. Its theoretical view of life—if I may use the expression—and its ethics are all of a piece. I have not found such a closely-knit integration of the two in any other religion.

U: That is because the ethics of Buddhism spring logically and inevitably from its view of the cosmos as a whole. When the law of cause and effect with which we are familiar in the physical world is expanded to include the world of moral values, then a consistent and homogeneous system is the inevitable result.

Mr. T: Yet I wonder whether the moral rules can always be applied consistently.

U: In what respect?

Mr. T: Well, you referred just now to the First Precept, to abstain from killing. But is it possible for man to live in health and comfort on this planet without taking life in one way or another? Even to raise crops for food, vermin and pests have to be exterminated. And what about bacteria? For example, does the treatment of germ-borne diseases by antibiotics involve a breach of the First Precept?

U: It may seem strange to you, but that question touches on an important point in Buddhist ethical psychology. The first fact we have to grasp about kamma is that it is primarily intention. That, incidentally, is how craving comes to be implicated in actions. A kamma, in the sense of a deed that bears good or bad results to the doer, is an action performed knowingly, in full awareness of its immediate consequences, and desiring those consequences. With more remote effects we can hardly be concerned, because often they are beyond our control. We cannot be held morally responsible for them. But we are responsible for whatever it is we wish to do, when our intention is carried out. So the Buddha said: "Kamma, I declare, O monks, is volition." We are not responsible for any effects, good or bad, which we have not intended. Do you follow me so far?

Mr. T: Yes, of course. That is plain common sense.

U: Nevertheless, one Indian school of thought holds otherwise.[16] Anyway, in consonance with its teaching of kamma as volition, Buddhism states that for an act of killing to be complete and kammically potent, four conditions must be present. There must be the knowledge that the creature is living, the intention of killing it, the act of killing and the creature's death. Here, by the way, I must point out also that the intention of killing alone

16. Jainism, the teaching of Mahāvīra, a contemporary of the Buddha, holds that even involuntary actions constitute kamma, so that release from saṃsāra can be gained only by abstaining from all activities. Mahāvīra is the Nigaṇṭha Nātaputta of the Buddhist texts.

does not constitute the kamma of killing. It only does so when it is followed by the act and its result. The thought of killing is an unwholesome mental kamma, but it does not amount to killing unless it produces the actual deed. All the same, thoughts of killing should always be avoided because the thought is father to the deed.

Mr. T: Yes, quite so. But what bearing does this have on the use of antibiotics?

U: Just this: all medical practice, from the earliest times, must have included preparations whose action was that of destroying bacteria. But since it was not then known that the action of these herbal and other decoctions was to kill minute forms of life which caused the disease, those who employed the medicines were not aware that they were taking life. Their sole intention was to cure sickness. So they were certainly not guilty of conscious killing and no evil kammic consequences would follow for them. But we today are no longer unaware of the bacteriological causes of disease, and when we give treatment we are knowingly taking life. It is in the light of that knowledge that we have to consider your question.

Mr. T: Yes, indeed. It seems that modern science has complicated life for us in this way, as well as in so many others.

U: Well, of course there are systems of medicine which do not employ any of the products of animal life and do not aim directly at destroying bacteria. They simply help the body's vital powers of resistance and natural processes then overcome the bacteria. An organism can protect itself very well by its own method of producing antibodies.

Mr. T: But still I don't think it is going too far to say that there are certain diseases which are too malignant and swift in their onslaught to be dealt with in that fashion.

U: Yes, I will grant that. In such cases it is imperative to destroy the bacteria or the virus before it kills the patient. It is one of the dilemmas which are perpetually lying in wait for those who live and act in the world. A bhikkhu who is solely bent on attaining Nibbāna will not care about the preservation of his life to the extent of involving himself in unwholesome moral action. Ideally, he will take the view that if, through some bad kamma of the past, he is to die before attaining Nibbāna, he should resign himself to it; if he is not, his body will deal with the disease in its own way. But when we are considering the case of ordinary people, we have to look at it from a different standpoint. There is, as you know, one law for the world—the law of self-preservation—and another law for those who seek Nibbāna— the law of self-renunciation. Those who still follow the law of the world keep the Precepts according to their capacity. If they break them they do so in full awareness of the consequences to themselves. For the Buddha has distinctly taught, "Such and such is wholesome action, and such is its good result; such and such is unwholesome action, and such is its evil result." But also he has said, "He whose evil deed is covered by a good deed (*kusalena pithīyati*) illumines this world like the moon emerging from clouds".[17] This was in reference to Aṅgulimāla, who abandoned a life of violence, renounced the world and became an *Arahat*. After his attainment, Aṅgulimāla had to endure great distress as the result of his past deeds, but by having cut off the round of his rebirths at that point he saved himself from æons of suffering in hell. But Aṅgulimāla's sin was that of taking many human lives, and in force of kamma the killing of bacteria can in no wise be compared to that. There is, indeed, a scale of values accorded to the moral culpability involved in the taking of life, and sub-microscopic organisms are at the bottom of the scale. There is a mitigating element, also, in the fact that the foremost intention of the doctor who administers the antibiotics or other bacteria-destroying drugs is to cure the patient. Therefore, the unwholesome mental factor of hatred, which is present in all acts that have killing as their direct objective, is lacking. The suffering that is alleviated is far greater than any pain inflicted on the bacteria, if indeed there is any at all. We may apply the same principle to all other acts which, although they result in death to certain organisms, are not primarily performed with that intention, but are carried out for the welfare of higher organisms such as man. But still I must repeat that one who is intent on his own ultimate and lasting good will eschew all such actions.

---

17. *Dhammapada* v. 173. Dhp. Com. XIII, 6.

Mr. T: I understand. It is in the end a question of personal choice—whether we choose the immediate good, which is not enduring, or the ultimate good, which is the only real and permanent good.

U: Yes, and there is still another aspect of this problem, which is really a very complex one. It is that if man were to lead a more natural, healthy life, eating pure, unadulterated food and living in accordance with Dhamma, he would have less need—possibly none at all—for antibiotics, sera prepared from living animals and all the other treatments that depend upon animal experimentation. The bad kamma that is generated by these methods of investigating and treating disease, particularly by vivisection, is itself one of the causes of man's increasing proneness to disease, and so a vicious circle is set up. Man will never succeed in conquering disease by torturing animals. The proof of this lies in the fact that by mutation and adaptation nature produces new strains of micro-organisms which are impervious to the old treatments. New variations of the diseases then make their appearance, and further experiments on animals are carried out, to find new remedies. It has even been questioned recently whether vaccination is really effective against smallpox. This is strange indeed, considering that vaccination has been used effectively for the past hundred years. If there is any room at all for doubt in the matter it can only mean that something has changed. If a new strain of the virus is beginning to appear, medical science is more or less back where it started so far as smallpox is concerned. First the new strain will have to be isolated, then experiments will have to be made on more unfortunate animals to produce a new vaccine—and so the wheel of kamma and vipāka goes on drearily and endlessly turning.

Mr. T: Then you do not deny altogether that experiments on living animals have contributed to our understanding and treatment of disease?

U: No, certainly not. To deny it would be to go against all the clear evidence. But I say most emphatically that it is not the right way of dealing with the problem. Man brings diseases on himself by weakening the natural resistance of his body through unnatural and unwholesome living, through contaminated atmosphere, food denatured and adulterated by chemical preservatives and, last but not least, through wrong thinking and acting—and then he subjects animals to unspeakable torture in order to find remedies for his self-produced ailments. Such a course can never be morally defensible; in the light of the law of kamma it is seen to be self-destructive.

Mr. T: I am sure you are right in saying that many of our diseases would vanish if we led healthier and more natural lives. And in view of what we know now about psychosomatic sicknesses most people would agree that our bodies would be healthier if our minds were better regulated. The trouble is that people don't know how to set about straightening out their minds.

U: That is where Buddhism could help them. Do you know that the Buddha expressly said that sickness increases when people live without regard for the moral law? There is a definite connection between disease and the moral standards of the people in general. In a very real sense, disease is the outward and visible sign of an inward corruption. I do not mean that all sick people are wrongdoers in this present life, but that the prevalence of sickness in a society is an index of declining moral standards which affect every member in some degree. Does that seem improbable to you?

Mr. T: No, I cannot say that it does. Psychiatry has even gone some way towards establishing it as a scientific fact. Anyway, we have enough data to show that there is a connection. But now, with your permission I should like to go back for a moment to the subject of intention which you were explaining in connection with kamma. Doesn't an absolutely pure motive justify *any* action?

U: If you mean by that, "does the end justify the means," the answer is "no." An action that is bad in itself can never produce good, no matter what the motive may be. It is not *any* action that can be performed with a pure intention, only a good one, so that in Buddhism the question does not arise.

Mr. T: What I had especially in mind is whether killing for mercy is not justified. Supposing, for example, that an animal is in dreadful pain and cannot be relieved, surely it is merciful to put the creature out of its misery?

U: Well, I will ask *you* a question now. Are you in favour of euthanasia for human beings in similar circumstances?

Mr. T: As a matter of fact, I had a discussion on that subject with a friend recently. He is a deeply religious man while I, as you will have gathered, am a bit of a freethinker. On the whole, and with some important reservations, I argued in favour of a human being's right to take his own life if he is suffering from a painful and incurable disease.

U: But you weren't, I suppose, in favour of someone else taking the responsibility of "putting him out of his misery"?

Mr. T: Only with his knowledge and consent. After all, a man is a rational and responsible creature, whereas an animal is not.

U: Let us leave animals out of it for a moment, please. What position did your religious friend take?

Mr. T: As you would suppose, he argued that life is a divine gift, something which man cannot bestow or restore, and so no one has any right to terminate his own life, or get another person to do it. And he also maintained that human suffering has a purpose and meaning; it is a trial or purgation. Pain is something sent by God, which man should bear in patience and resignation to the divine will. I replied that might be so or not, but it was a very slender possibility on which to doom countless people to a life of torment. If he really believed in the purgation theory he should also be against the administering of sedatives and anaesthetics. The only point I would concede was that euthanasia could be a very dangerous instrument, and should only be resorted to under very strict conditions.

U: Well, now I know your ideas on the subject as it concerns human beings, let us return to the animals. Buddhism holds that the pain of animals is also not without meaning. If it is the result of previous bad kamma in a human life it will have to run its course until the kammic potency is exhausted, which means that even though we may succeed in ending it by taking the animal's life, we are only causing an interruption in the current of resultant experience. The suffering will be resumed again in some other life, until the whole of the bad kammic force is expended. Buddhism does not make the distinction that theistic religion makes between man and animals by claiming that man's suffering has a meaning and purpose, whereas that of the animals has none. If the pain is caused by past kamma no outside agency can prevent it running its course. That is the first point to be considered. The next is that Buddhist psychology shows that no act of killing can be carried out without the arising of a thought of ill-will or repugnance. At the moment when the lethal act takes place, when the thought of killing becomes transformed into deed, whatever motive may have been in the mind previously is superseded. If it were not so, if in that critical moment the mental impulse of aversion did not arise, the deed could not be done. It may seem to you that putting an animal into a gas receptacle is a detached and passionless deed; but nevertheless the psychic genesis of the act is an impulse of aversion. The plain truth is that when a man performs what he believes is a mercy-killing it is because the pain of the animal is repugnant to him; it disturbs his mind and he experiences subconsciously a dislike of the object that has aroused the disagreeable sensation. Below the threshold of awareness he transfers his hatred of the pain to the animal, which then becomes the symbol of the pain and the object on which he vents his feeling of resentment. So, whether considered from the standpoint of the animal's welfare or that of the "mercy-killer," the deed is a mistaken and unwholesome one. Buddhism teaches that we should endeavour, as far as possible, to treat a sick animal as we should a sick human being—to alleviate its suffering as much as we can, but not to interfere with the working out of its kammic life-pattern. It could well be that if the evil kammic result, the vipāka, is allowed to run its full course here and now, the animal might be reborn in a higher state when the present life has come to its natural end. But that could not happen if its life were to be cut short with a residue of bad vipāka still to be undergone.

Mr. T: I am really surprised to find that Buddhist psychology is so profound and searching.

U: It has to be, because the seeking out and recognition of motive is its primary concern. It is, you must remember, essentially an *ethical* psychology. That is why some of its terms and classifications seem a little strange to the Western mind.

Mr. T: But does Buddhism consider that all pain is the result of bad kamma?

U: No. Some forms of suffering are the mere result of being a living organism. They are the price we pay for our existence in saṃsāra, the condition brought on by our craving. So we can never tell precisely whether a particular affliction is the result of past kamma or not. In any case, even a disease which has kamma for its principal cause must also depend to a certain extent on physical conditions to bring it about. If that were not so, Buddhism would have no use for medicine or surgery. But on the contrary, we should regard every disease as being possibly curable, so long as there is life in the patient. If it is caused by kamma, we cannot tell at what point the bad *vipāka* may come to an end and the patient recover. Many people have lived to a ripe age after having been given only a few months of life by their doctors. It would be a mistake to blame the doctors for such apparent errors; their prognosis may have been perfectly correct by all the clinical evidence available at the time they made it. Yet cases have been known in which the most incredible physical restorations have come about quite naturally after the patient has been given up for lost.

Mr. T: I feel bound to say that the Buddhist explanations of all these obscure matters are more convincing than any I have yet come across. They throw light in the most unexpected places. There is no reply to this! The interest I felt at the beginning has increased tremendously, and I now wish to go into Buddhism in greater detail. Is it necessary for me to learn the *Pāli* language to get a true insight into the Dhamma?

U: Not at the beginning. You can get an excellent general idea of Buddhism without that, provided you are careful in your choice of books. But as you go deeper in your studies you will find it necessary to acquire a vocabulary of certain *Pāli* technical terms, because for many of these there are no really satisfactory equivalents in English. You will learn them as you go along. Then as you proceed further you will probably feel a desire to learn the language, if only to be able to compare translations with the original texts and so clear up doubtful points for yourself. Not all interpretations of Buddhism, or even translations, are equally reliable, you know.

Mr. T: I suppose not. It must be easy to make errors in interpreting a system so complex and in so many points different from anything the Western mind is accustomed to. Well, thank you again. I shall look forward to our next meeting, when I expect to have some further questions to ask you.

III

Well, Mr. Thompson, you are back again, I see. Just now I noticed you making an offering of flowers at the temple shrine. That is a very nice gesture, coming from a freethinker!

Mr. T: I felt I wanted to pay my tribute to the great Teacher.

U: People may have thought you were a visiting politician!

Mr. T: Never mind that. My offering was genuine. Having done some more reading since I saw you last, I am more than ever impressed by the Doctrine. Apart from everything else, it has a coherence and logic that are beautiful in themselves—the beauty one finds in mathematics or in the majestic inevitability of a Bach fugue. One feels that this truly is the law that holds the stars in their courses, that it presents things as they really are and that nothing in it could possibly be otherwise than as it is.

U: Yes, naturally. It is the law of the universe, the "thusness" of things, which in Pāli is called *tathatā*.

Mr. T: But now, to descend from the cosmic to the—er, mundane, I have just noticed some people making offerings of rice and other food to the Buddha-image. I have seen this done before, and it has always struck rather a jarring note to me. Offering flowers, incense and even pure water I can understand. But food... Surely they do not believe that the Buddha, who passed utterly away "into the state wherein there is no possibility of the grasping factors arising," as I have read, is in need of material human food? Or that the Buddha image can eat it?

U: Of course they do not. It is nothing more than a symbolic gesture. But if it is done with the right mental concentration it produces a good kammic impulse resembling that generated by giving food to the living Buddha. The Buddha-image is always just a substitute for the presence of the Teacher who is no longer with us.

Mr. T: Hmm... Well, that calls for rather more imagination than I can muster. I should prefer to see the food eaten by a hungry man. However, I realize that is just a point of view—perhaps my Western mind is too literal. Anyway, I am told the food is not wasted.

U: No, it is distributed to the poor after having been offered.

Mr. T: I am glad to know that. There are too many hungry children in the world for symbolic feedings to be justified, if they were to involve waste. It would be too costly an exercise of the imagination and I cannot believe that the Buddha would have approved of it.

U: Buddhists understand that very well. You need have no fear that Buddhism encourages heartless waste. The offering to the Buddha is simply a preliminary gesture; it really means that the food is to be given to the poor, in honour of the Buddha's teaching of *dāna,* generosity. If it were wholly a kind of make-believe it would be ritualism, which Buddhism condemns. You will remember that the third of the ten fetters, as I told you, is addiction to vain virtues and observances, or *sīlabbataparāmāsa.*

Mr. T: Yes, one of the things that I, and many others, find so attractive about Buddhism is that it dispenses almost entirely with the external trappings of religion, which to so many people today are tedious and meaningless. It seems to me that the only purpose which communal worship serves is to give people a sense of solidarity. They no longer get the kind of mystical exaltation which possibly people got from it in the past. But I have noticed one thing, which I want to ask you about. It seems to me that most of the Buddha's discourses, and his training in general, were given for the monks. What exactly does the laity get out of Buddhism?

U: That is a quite mistaken impression. Some of the most important of the Buddha's sermons were delivered to lay people—people of every walk of life, from kings to scavengers. One of the best known of the sermons to householders is the *Sigālovāda Sutta,*[18] which gives comprehensive advice on the good life that is as true today as when it was first uttered. And there are many others. In addition to that, nearly all the suttas give some counsel which can be beneficially applied by both monks and laymen.

18. Translated in *Everyman's Ethics* (*The Wheel,* No. 14).

They have a universal relevance. The Dhamma offers a code of living to everyone, the highest and best the world has ever known. It is a path to happiness, both here and in future states, which everyone can follow.

Mr. T: But can a layman attain Nibbāna?

U: He can go a long way towards it. If he goes as far as attaining one of the three stages of purification prior to *Arahantship* he will almost certainly lose all desire to continue with worldly life. He will then take the yellow robe if his responsibilities allow him to.

Mr. T: Ah, yes, of course—with the waning of desire that would be a quite natural result.

U: But of course it is much more difficult for a layman, surrounded by distractions and sensual enticements, to tread the path to the end. For him it is a considerable achievement if he can manage to observe the Five Precepts faithfully all his waking hours. But he should certainly put forth effort to do so and supplement his self-training by observing the eight or ten precepts[19] on Uposatha Days.

Mr. T: What are Uposatha Days?

U: I suppose the best term for them would be "retreat days," as that conveys the idea better than any other. They are not fast days in the sense of abstaining entirely from food. The Uposatha days fall on the new moon and full moon dates, and the days of the first and last lunar quarter. In practice it is usually the full moon days that are observed by lay people. On those days they withdraw themselves from all worldly concerns and take on the major precepts of a bhikkhu, including that of not eating after midday. They spend the day usually in a temple, meditating, hearing the Dhamma or discussing it quietly among themselves. It is a very beneficial practice, and one that was strongly urged by the Buddha. There is no special sabbatarian significance in the days; they are just the natural landmarks of the lunar calendar.

Mr. T: I should like an opportunity of doing that myself. Would there be any objection?

U: Of course not. I will gladly arrange for you to spend the next

19. Text in *The Mirror of the Dhamma* (*The Wheel*, No. 54).

full moon day here at this temple. Your meal will be provided, and if you would like to wear the customary white clothes I will see that you are properly fitted out.

Mr. T: That is very good of you, indeed. But is there any reason for wearing special clothes? Isn't that rather like the European habit of dressing up to go to church?

U: The white clothes are not essential. What is essential is the right mental attitude, and special clothes which by their colour symbolize purity, help to put us into the right frame of mind. So it is not just a mere convention. You might call it a psychological device.

Mr. T: Well, that helps. We have become conditioned to respond to satisfying phrases and the more solemn and scientific-sounding they are the better! Anyway, I see the point. One needs all the help one can get, to maintain a religious attitude of mind in these days. But, as we are on the subject of the Buddhist precepts, I notice that they are all stated negatively. Why should they not be positive? For instance, why should not the first precept, not to kill, be stated as a positive instruction to *respect* life or to *protect* it?

U: Because all morality must start by abandoning wrong actions. The precepts are actually positive injunctions to refrain from certain acts which are harmful. Old rubbish has to be cleared away before a new building can be erected. The Ten Commandments all begin with "Thou shall not—" Buddhism substitutes "I shall not—" because the precepts are undertaken voluntarily. The difference that is sometimes made between positive and negative virtues is largely an artificial one; all restraint from wrong action is a positive virtue. But out of these necessarily negative statements of what are really positive virtues there does emerge a concept of virtue which is actively manifested, which expresses itself in an outflow of tenderness for all that lives and suffers. There are four qualities of the heart which, when they are developed and magnified to their fullest, the Buddha declared, lift man to the highest level of being, where he abides like unto the gods. That is the literal meaning of the name *brahma-vihāra*,[20] which is given to them. They are *mettā*, *karuṇā*, *muditā* and *upekkhā*—benevolence,

20. *The Four Sublime States* (*The Wheel*, No. 6).

compassion, sympathy and equanimity. These are not only to be practised in daily life, but also to be cultivated as meditation exercises, when they produce full concentration of mind and *jhānic* consciousness. They are the keys which unlock the gates of rebirth in the Brahma worlds. In practice they represent the ultimate ethical ideal to which man can aspire in his relations with other beings, for they make no distinction between the hostile and the friendly, the sinner and the saint, the Brahmas of high heaven and the worm beneath the foot—as calm, pure, dispassionate love reaches out to all and encompasses all. This is how the Buddha described the practice of boundless loving-kindness in some passages from the *Karaṇīyametta Sutta*:

Whatsoever living beings there are,
Be they weak or strong ... small or large—
May all beings, without exception, be happy.
Whether they be visible or invisible,
Dwelling afar or near at hand,
Already born or about to be born—
May they all, without exception, be happy.

Just as a mother lovingly protects,
Even with her life, her only child,
So should one cherish boundless friendliness
And good will towards all living beings.
With heart of loving kindness grown immeasurable,
One should permeate the world, above, below
And transversely in all directions, with a love
Unobstructed, free from all envy and hate.

Here in the world this is the highest, holiest life.

Mr. T: Yes, that is positive enough, and active, so far as the mind is concerned. But what about turning thought into deed? If the loving-kindness is no more than a cerebral activity, an attitude of mind and nothing more, how can one be sure that it is a genuine feeling? If it is never put to practical test, in some situation that calls for self-sacrifice or active work for someone else's good, can one ever be certain that it is not self-deception? May one not be humbugging oneself, to put it crudely?

U: Not if one also practises self-examination and analysis, in the thorough way Buddhism teaches. If one does not do that—yes, there is a possibility of deceiving oneself. Some people do indeed manage to convince themselves that they have boundless loving-kindness, when their actions show very clearly—to everyone but themselves—that they have not. But that possibility is present in every idea one has of oneself. The only safeguard against it, as I have said, is the deep self-knowledge that comes of minutely examining one's thoughts and motives, impersonally and without bias in one's own favour.

Mr. T: But would it not prevent any such self-deception if, right at the start, the precepts were to be framed as I suggested: instead of the injunction not to kill, a positive instruction to respect and protect life?

U: I think a moment's reflection will show you that it would be quite impracticable. No one could literally obey an instruction to protect life, without making his own life impossible. He would be all the time going about trying to prevent butchers from slaughtering animals and gardeners from spraying their rose trees. And if he professed to obey the commandment (for that is what it would be) whilst knowing that he could not possibly carry it out, it would be just meaningless words. He would be left with no choice but to be a hypocrite. As for respecting life, if the phrase has any meaning at all it is surely covered by the resolve not to kill. I do not know in what other way we could show respect for life.

Mr. T: You surprise me! Why do you say "if the phrase has any meaning at all"?

U: Because to a Buddhist there is no concept of "life" in a collective sense; there are only living beings, individual organisms. And the life in them is not divine, or divinely bestowed; it is the result of past kamma actuated by craving. Therefore the Buddhist attitude is not one of respect, but of compassion. The phrase "reverence for life"[21] is not found in Buddhism; its place is taken by compassion for living beings.

---

21. Schweitzer's phrase: a concept which has led to much confused thinking and to serious contradictions between theory and practice in the ethical life.

Mr. T: I see you are determined to resist any theistic terms or ideas.

U: If I am, it is not for the sake of verbal quibbling, but in the interests of straight thinking. Tell me, now, can anyone seriously say that he has reverence for cockroaches or tuberculosis bacilli?

Mr. T: Hardly, I suppose.

U: Well then, you see for yourself the phrase is meaningless. It can only lead to confused thinking. And what would you say of a man who undertook to "protect" those forms of life?

Mr. T: Well—I surrender that point! But I am wondering whether it is any more feasible to feel compassion for them.

U: When they are considered as beings bound to the wheel of suffering *like oneself*, then there is true compassion. But it does not require that we should engage in fighting with other organisms to preserve their lives. In Buddhism kindness and compassion take the form of not interfering harmfully with the destinies of other beings, but of wishing them well. When they die, whether it be naturally or at the hand of someone else, may they be reborn in some happier state! If they live, may they be free from unnecessary suffering! Such thoughts as these reach as far as loving-kindness can go without entering into the conflict between one creature and another, and so changing its own nature. If sides are taken, hatred creeps in and the *mettā*, which to be illimitable must be without distinctions or biases, is marred—we are then back at the more primitive level of "loving the righteous but hating sinners," each being personified for us by some specific individual.

Mr. T: But then, to take a concrete example, what if we should happen to see a murder being committed? Are we to do nothing to prevent it?

U: In that case a Buddhist, like everyone else, will feel a spontaneous urge to go to the aid of the victim. But he should try by every means to avoid using force. If he cannot protect the victim by non-violent means, then it is for him to decide whether he shall use force or not, and if he does, how far he is prepared to go. He should never exceed the limits of strict necessity. Here I am speaking of the ordinary layman; the case of a bhikkhu, and particularly one who is striving earnestly to gain Nibbāna, and has renounced all other concerns and responsibilities for the sake of deliverance, is different. He should confine his intervention entirely to non-violent measures.

Mr. T: And if those fail?

U: Then they fail.

Mr. T: And the unfortunate victim dies! Then does Buddhism teach that it is more important for a man to preserve his own virtue, when by a lapse from his virtue he might save another's life?

U: It leaves the decision to the individual. It is for him alone to decide which he considers more important, and to act accordingly. But if he is one who is seeking the supreme good, the Buddha's words carry the greatest weight: "Let no one set aside his own good for that of another, however great it may be."

Mr. T: That is a hard teaching, it seems to me.

U: The point of it is that the one who is cultivating universal benevolence must not discriminate in any way. For him there should be no "aggressor" and no "victim," but only two beings equally caught up in the web of suffering, for whom he must feel equal compassion. The Buddha illustrated it in this way: You are one of four monks, practising *mettā bhāvanā* in a forest cave. One of the monks is friendly towards you, another is hostile, the third is neutral. Armed robbers appear at the entrance and demand that you shall give them one of your number to be sacrificed to their deity. Which of the monks shall you give—your enemy, your friend, the one indifferent to you, or *yourself*? The answer is "None—not even yourself." Your *mettā* for each must be equal and undiscriminating. If the robbers wish to commit a ritual murder you cannot prevent them, but they must choose the victim themselves. The moral responsibility is theirs alone. But now compare with this the *Jātaka* story in which the Bodhisatta gives his life to feed a starving tigress and her young. At first it would seem that two entirely different moralities are being taught. But it is not so. The Bodhisatta was accumulating good kamma by self-sacrifice; the meditating bhikkhus are striving to abolish all notions of distinction between self and others which stand in the way of boundless, undiscriminating *mettā*. Therefore none of them should discriminate against any of them, not even against oneself. His *mettā* for himself must be exactly the same as that which he feels for each of the others. The two parables show the distinction between the way of kamma and the way of the renunciation of kamma. In the *Jātaka* the virtue, or *pāramitā*, consisted of the accumulation of merit; the virtue of the bhikkhus consists of the abandoning of all merit except that of their *jhāna*.

Mr. T: That is a difficult point, but I think I understand it now. At least, I can see why the bhikkhu should not resort to violence, even to prevent a murder.

U: You see, there are two kinds of merit—that which brings a worldly result and that which leads to supramundane classes of consciousness.

Mr. T: Very well, then can you tell me how kamma will operate in the case of an ordinary person who chooses to use force to prevent a murder?

U: No one can calculate precisely the consequences of an act from the viewpoint of kamma. So much depends upon the actual state of the mind—on what wholesome or unwholesome mental concomitants are present—when the act is performed. But in the case of a layman who elects to use force in a situation of that kind for the sake of the victim, the bad kamma, if any, must be quite light—perhaps less than he generates in many of his daily activities. The fact that he is not acting from any selfish motive must mitigate it to a very great extent. If he should sustain injuries as the result of his intervention, the bad vipāka may be completely exhausted in the course of the pain he suffers then. And if he can by self-knowledge and control succeed in using the minimum of force necessary, without any impulse of anger or hatred towards the aggressor, but only feeling pity for the victim, then it is possible that there would be no bad kamma present at all. But to act in that utterly passionless manner is extremely difficult.

Mr. T: Now I am wondering just what kind of social effect such an attitude might be expected to have. Its bearing, I mean, on crime, on social abuses and—what is particularly relevant in these days when power movements and power-seeking groups threaten in some parts of the world to establish the rule of force—what weapon it leaves society to protect itself from such evils as, for instance, race-hatred and political persecutions. It seems there is no place in Buddhism for "righteous anger." How, then, are these evils to be counteracted? Does not moral indignation, the outspoken public condemnation of vices, cruelties and perverted ideologies, play a part in keeping society pure? Don't you think that a society which is too tolerant of obvious evils bears within it the germs of its own destruction?

U: We must never lose sight of the fact that the Dhamma is a teaching for individual salvation. It is hardly concerned with society as such because, as I pointed out in another connection, when individuals improve, society automatically improves as well. At the time when the Buddha lived and taught, the ordinary man had no say in the way society was held together, no influence at all in the affairs of the state, its laws or the trends of its development. When the Buddha wished to give advice concerning man's life within society he addressed himself to the kings, or to the elders who formed the governing bodies of the republics. It was they alone who held the reins of public affairs. And of course the problems they had to solve were relatively simple ones, and quite different from those that confront us now.

Mr. T: But it is just in those matters that man is most in need of guidance today.

U: Yes. For better or for worse, the private individual is now involved more deeply than ever before, in national affairs, and so he is the more responsible for what goes on in the society of which he forms a part. Since you have put this question, and it is one that cannot well be ignored, I shall try to answer it. But you must understand that what I shall say is my own opinion only; the sole authority I can claim for it is that it is an interpretation of the situation which I believe to be in accordance with Buddhist principles. You have asked me whether too much tolerance of obvious evils is not a dangerous weakness in society. I am bound to grant that it could be a source of danger. The moral indignation of which you speak does act as a corrective, if it is aroused for a just cause. When we admit that in the relative scale of worldly values every virtue can become a vice if it is carried to excess, it is not difficult to see that the virtues of the monastery and the hermit's cave can be harmful if they are practised in a society in which unwholesome and disruptive forces are at work. But Buddhism does not by any means advocate this. For the majority of people—those who bear voluntarily the responsibilities of worldly life—it teaches, as it has ever done, the middle way. Since they enjoy the rights, privileges and securities which society gives them, they own a duty to society in return, which is to keep it healthy. They are under a moral obligation to resist—using means that are in accord with Buddhist principles—whatever influences are manifestly evil and detrimental to society, or which threaten the welfare of their fellow-men. They should never, in any circumstances, tolerate cruelties, injustices or the oppression of the weak by the strong. There are today many means, short of physical violence, by which disapproval may be expressed, and if these are used effectively at the first appearance of vicious trends in society, the necessity of resorting to force later may be avoided. But if the weight of moral force is insufficient to stamp out some grave evil, then the state itself must take action. Even Asoka, who stands out as the pattern of a benevolent Buddhist king, did not disband his army or abolish the punitive laws that were necessary to guarantee his subjects' peace and security. Neither did the Buddha ever counsel a ruler to go to such extremes of non-violence; he simply called for a just and merciful administration of the realm, exhorting kings to look upon their subjects as their own children, for if the king and his ministers were good, the people would be good also, living as members of one united family.

Mr. T: I am relieved to know that Buddhism favours a realistic view of these matters, and does not expect us to take a neutral and complaisant attitude towards social evils; for if it did, I am afraid it would be of little service to mankind as a whole today. Now, you just mentioned kingdoms and republics in the India of the Buddha's time. Is there any indication as to which system the Buddha himself considered best?

U: No, not enough to base any theory of "rulership" upon. The republics appear to have resembled the Greek republican states; they were governed by a senate—not elected by the people, but composed of men of known character and tested ability, chosen by their peers. The Buddha never drew any comparison between the two systems. But in the Buddhist texts, when the ideal state is depicted it is under the rule of a *Chakravartin*, or world-monarch, a man of sublime wisdom and compassion who rules according to Dhamma. It is, in fact, a benevolent autocracy. But this state of things appears only at a phase of evolution when civilization is at its highest peak and it is possible to rule without bloodshed. It seems to be tacitly assumed that at other times "rulership" must share to some extent the defects of all *Saṃsāric* phenomena.[22] Buddhism has no belief in the perfectibility of human institutions—only in the perfectibility of individuals.

Mr. T: The idea of the *Chakravartin* seems to link up with the Messianic hope that is found in other religions—and his rule, perhaps, with the "Kingdom of God." How natural it is that men should long for a divine or semi-divine ruler—one who will guide them out of the wilderness into the green pastures of peace, and cause the lion to lie down with the lamb, here on this very earth, so stained with blood! It seems to me that this is one of the archetypal dreams of man, something universal and perennial among the varieties of human hope.

U: It may be not a dream but a memory.

Mr. T: You mean...?

U: There have been world-monarchs in the past cycles of the world, just as there will be in the future. Who knows what subconscious memories of them have crossed the portals of death and rebirth? Or what expectations may have been born of those dimly-remembered things?

Mr. T: Yes... it is possible. I feel now more than ever I did the depth and breadth of this experience we call life, how infinitely it extends all about us, how it stretches back into unimaginable vistas of time. It is a thing I never understood before. The other day I was reading a poem, and all at once I had a feeling that

---

22. In illustration of this it is related that the Bodhisatta was once born as the son of a powerful monarch. As an infant he saw his father in the counsel chamber condemning criminals to punishment and death. Horrified, the prince thought to himself: "If I inherit the kingdom I too will have to commit such acts, for to a ruler they are unavoidable." From that time on, he feigned dumbness to disqualify himself for the throne.

the words were living things, with a meaning greater than their sense. It seemed as though the walls of the room had suddenly, silently, slid away and there was voidness—just voidness—but it contained all that has ever been or will be. And it seemed to me that I knew everything, and had been one with that knowledge throughout all time... Strange... It seems to me that since I have been reading about Buddhism, thinking about it, something has grown to maturity in me, something that otherwise might never have come to the light... But I can neither describe it nor account for it. I can only say—perhaps I knew these things before.

U: Perhaps you did.

Mr. T: There is just one last question I want to ask. Just now you spoke of what should not be tolerated in society. It reminded me of a question I wanted to put to you earlier. What is the proper attitude for a Buddhist to take to other religions? Should it not be one of absolute tolerance? As I understand it, that is what the Buddha taught.

U: Perhaps you think that in answering some of your questions about Buddhism in relation to other faiths I have not been as tolerant as I might have been?

Mr. T: It had crossed my mind.

U: Well, in that case I am glad you have mentioned it. What do you yourself understand by religious tolerance?

Mr. T: I take it to mean not forcing others to give up their own beliefs—not using any kind of compulsion to make them change their religion; and, of course, not making any discrimination in one's attitude towards those of other faiths.

U: But do you think that reasoned, legitimate criticism of religious beliefs, with opportunity given to the other side to oppose you, constitutes intolerance?

Mr. T: Well—it could indicate an intolerant attitude of mind.

U: But in that case, can you name any single religious teacher, including the Buddha himself, who was not "intolerant"?

Mr. T: Actually, I thought the Buddha was the single exception.

U: Then you can never have read the many Suttas in which the Buddha discussed matters of doctrine and practice with other religious teachers or their followers. In those discourses, such as the *Brahmajāla*, *Ambaṭṭha*, *Soṇadaṇḍa*, *Kassapa*, *Sīhanāda*, *Poṭṭhapāda*, *Lohicca* and *Tevijja* Suttas in the *Dīgha Nikāya*, the Buddha courteously but very firmly refuted different kinds of wrong belief. Can you tell me how he could have taught anything at all if he had refused to make comparisons between his own doctrines and those of other teachers?

Mr. T: Hmm... No, I suppose he couldn't.

U: Exactly so. Having any kind of teaching to impart, must necessarily mean that some other teachings are contradicted. And supposing, further, that someone invites one to make a comparison between his religious beliefs and one's own, can one be called "intolerant" if the comparison does not turn out to be pleasing to him?

Mr. T: No, not really. Of course, a lot depends on how one expresses oneself.

U: More depends upon how sensitive the other person is about his faith. Buddhists are not particularly sensitive because they feel that Buddhism can be demonstrated rationally.

Mr. T: All right, I admit that "reasoned, legitimate criticism" is not intolerance—particularly if it has been asked for. But I take it that Buddhism is tolerant in the stricter sense that I mentioned first?

U: You had better have said "in the true sense," for when you said "not forcing others to give up their religion, and not making any discrimination against others on account of their faith" you were really defining true tolerance. That is the kind of tolerance the Buddha practised and advocated and which Buddhists have always followed. After he had refuted erroneous beliefs, the Buddha still maintained that a man had a right to continue holding those beliefs and that no one should attempt to coerce him out of them. And he went even further than that in teaching that all sincerely held beliefs should be respected, so long as they were not patently harmful doctrines. Buddhism in fact shows that all the great world-religions have some good moral principles which, if they are observed, will lead to a favourable rebirth. Doctrines may be erroneous, but if the actions they prompt are good and wholesome ones they will produce results as beneficial as those performed by a Buddhist. Morality based upon wrong views is called *diṭṭhinissita-sīla*; if it should happen to accord with morality based on right views its kammic action is the same, no matter what strange theories of the universe may have inspired it. The tolerance of Buddhism is grounded on two central facts: that happiness hereafter comes not through faith but through deeds; and Buddhism claims for itself no exclusive right of access to the heavenly realms. It claims only to show the sole way to exit from saṃsāra. So the Buddha taught us to approve and respect whatever is good in other teachings, and furthermore, not to feel anger if his own Dhamma is attacked. This is true tolerance, and it has been observed faithfully by Buddhists through 2500 years of the growth and expansion of the Dispensation or *Sāsana*. Buddhism has always spread in other ways than by conflict, violence and oppression. Surely that is a sufficient answer to your question. But it is certainly a mistaken idea of tolerance to believe that it forbids us to draw critical comparisons between the Dhamma and other religious teachings.

Mr. T: Yes, I see that now. There are some religions, you know, which hold that since they and they alone are in possession of absolute truth and the means of salvation, they should not tolerate error.

U: Yes, I know. Many crimes have been committed in the name of that doctrine. In reality the exaltation of intolerance is nothing but a cover for dogmatic beliefs that cannot meet the light of reasoned criticism.

Mr. T: Well, Buddhism can certainly do that. I am grateful to you for all the time you have spent over my questions. I am rather ashamed now to realize that several of them need not have been asked. I could have thought out the answers for myself, if I had chosen to do so.

U: Never mind. Don't we all need help and guidance? Come to me again, any time you wish.

Mr. T: I shall come on the next full moon day.

U: Good! And the white clothes...?

Mr. T: Please have them ready. I shall be happy to wear them.

U: And may you always be happy!

Mr. T: "May all beings, everywhere, be happy."

The Discourse Collection

Selected Texts from the Suttanipāta

Translated by

John D. Ireland

WHEEL PUBLICATION NO. 82

Introduction

The Suttanipāta, or "Discourse-collection," from which this selection has been compiled, contains some of the oldest and most profound discourses of the Buddha. The complete text has been translated at least three times into English, the most recent being by E. M. Hare under the title *Woven Cadences* (Oxford University Press, London, 1945). The Pali original consists mainly of verse interspersed with some prose passages and Hare has followed this arrangement by translating it into English blank verse. However, in the selection appearing below the aim has been to keep as near as possible to the original, and no attempt has been made to versify it.

This short anthology is arranged, as far as the material will allow, in a sequence of topics commencing with morality and general conduct leading up to insight and realisation.

The first discourse shows the distinction between the mode of conduct of the bhikkhu and the layman, both regarded as virtuous or good (*sādhu*). For, as it is said elsewhere:

> These two ways of life are not the same:
> that of a householder supporting a wife
> and one without worldly attachments...
>
> As a peacock never approaches the swiftness
> of a swan, so a householder cannot imitate a
> bhikkhu, a hermit meditating in the forest.

Sn vv. 220-221

The lay-follower is given the five precepts of abstaining from killing, stealing and so forth, and then the eight precepts observed on special occasions (*uposatha*, "observance days"). Also perhaps it is appropriate to commence with Dhammika's praising the Buddha, for these two, moral discipline and faith in the Buddha, are the basic requisites for making further progress on the Buddhist path.

The next two discourses (2, 3) deal with wrong and right conduct, pointing out the results both courses lead to.

One of the essentials for the practice of the Buddha's teaching is having "good friends" and the avoidance of those who hinder one's progress (4). The best friend is "He from whom a person learns the Dhamma" (5) and as such the Buddha is known as the "Good Friend" to all beings.

The next two (6, 7) give the practical training and the direction one should tend towards.

Continuous effort is needed to practice the Dhamma (8) and to inspire one there is no better example than the Buddha's own struggle (9). Then there are two contemplations on the transience of life and the futility of sorrowing over the natural course of events in this world (10, 11).

Two important discourses follow dealing with the misconception that purity can come from outside without our putting forth any effort (12) and with wrongly holding to views and opinions leading to contention and suffering (13). These two, together with the rest of what follows, are regarded as some of the oldest discourses of the Suttanipāta and contain much that is difficult to understand.

In the Parāyana-vagga, the last chapter of the Suttanipāta, sixteen *brāhmaṇas*—"famous throughout the world, meditators, delighting in meditation, and wise..." (v. 1009)—come to the Buddha and ask him various questions. Five of them are included here (14, 15, 16, 18, 19).

No. 17 may be compared with the *Sakkapañha Suttanta* (Dīgha-nikāya 21, translated as No. 10 in the Wheel Series), which contains a closely parallel series of questions and answers.

No. 20 consists of the concluding verses of a fairly long discourse and indicates the disparity existing between the realisation of the "Ariya," the Buddhas and their disciples, and the way of thinking usual to the ordinary people of this world.

A note ought to be included on the term "Dhamma," an important and frequent word in Buddhist literature and which has, in most cases, been left untranslated below for the reason that there is no equivalent word in English to cover all its various shades of meaning. It could be rendered by Law (cosmic and moral), Norm, Teaching, Doctrine, Scripture, Truth, Nature, Practice, Method, Conduct, Causality, etc., for these are all meanings of the term "Dhamma." But they all tend to fall short of a true definition. The Dhamma is the heart of the Buddha's teaching and without it Buddhism would be something quite dead, and yet it is not the exclusive possession of the historical religion. In addition, it has another set of meanings and is practically always used in this sense in the plural, as mental (and sensory) objects, ideas, things, phenomena, elements, forces, states, etc. In this latter sense however it has not been left untranslated below.

In conclusion I wish to acknowledge the valuable assistance given by the Ven. Nyanaponika Mahāthera in correcting several errors in the translation of this short anthology and in supplying much advice and commentarial literature used in formulating the notes.

John D. Ireland
London
February 1965

1. Dhammika

Thus have I heard. At one time the Lord was staying near Sāvatthī in the Jeta Grove at Anāthapiṇḍika's monastery. Now the lay-follower Dhammika with five hundred other lay-followers approached the Lord. Having drawn near and having saluted the Lord respectfully he sat down at one side. Sitting there the lay-follower Dhammika addressed the Lord as follows:

"I ask Gotama[1] of extensive wisdom this: How acting is a disciple virtuous—both the disciple who has gone from home to the homeless state and the followers who are householders? For you clearly understand the behaviour[2] of the world with the *devas* and the final release. There is none equal to you who are skilled in seeing what is profound. You are an illustrious Awakened One (Buddha). Having investigated all knowledge and being compassionate towards beings you have announced the Dhamma, a revealer of what is hidden, of comprehensive vision, stainless, you illuminate all the worlds.

"This Dhamma, subtle and pleasing and taught so clearly by you, Lord, it is this we all wish to hear. Having been questioned, foremost Awakened One, tell us (the answer). All these bhikkhus and also the lay-followers who have come to hear the truth, let them listen to the Dhamma awakened to (*anubuddha*) by the Stainless One as the *devas* listen to the well-spoken words of Vāsava."[3]

(The Lord:) "Listen to me, bhikkhus, I will teach you the ascetic practice (*dhamma dhuta*), the mode of living suitable for those who have gone forth. Do you all bear it in mind. One who is intent upon what is good and who is thoughtful should practise it.

"A bhikkhu should not wander about at the wrong time but should walk the village for food at the right time, as one who goes about at the wrong time is (liable to be) obsessed by attachments; therefore Awakened Ones do not walk (for alms) at the wrong

1. Gotama is the Buddha's clan or family name.
2. According to the commentary, the Pali term "*gati*" translated here as "behaviour" means either "trend of character" or "the destination of beings after death."
3. "Vāsava" is one of the several names for Sakka, ruler of the *devas* or gods. This is a poetical way of saying they should listen very attentively.

time.[4] Sights, sounds, tastes, scents and bodily contacts overwhelm (the minds of) beings. Being rid of desire for these sense objects, at the right time, one may enter (the village) for the morning meal. Having duly obtained food, going back alone and sitting down in a secluded place, being inwardly thoughtful and not letting the mind go out to external objects, a bhikkhu should develop self-control.

"If he should speak with a lay-disciple, with someone else or with another bhikkhu, he should speak on the subtle Dhamma, not slandering others nor gossiping. Some set themselves up as disputants in opposition to others; those of little wisdom we do not praise; attachments bind them and they are carried away by their emotions.[5]

"Having heard the Dhamma taught by the Sugata[6] and considered it, a disciple of him of excellent wisdom should wisely make use of food, a dwelling, a bed, a seat and water for washing the robe. But a bhikkhu should not be soiled by (clinging to) these things, as a lotus is not wetted by a drop of water.

"Now I will tell you the layman's duty. Following it a lay-disciple would be virtuous; for it is not possible for one occupied with the household life to realise the complete bhikkhu practice (*dhamma*).

"He should not kill a living being, nor cause it to be killed, nor should he incite another to kill. Do not injure any being, either strong or weak, in the world.

"A disciple should avoid taking anything from anywhere knowing it (to belong to another). He should not steal nor incite another to steal. He should completely avoid theft.

"A wise man should avoid unchastity as (he would avoid falling into) a pit of glowing charcoal. If unable to lead a celibate life, he should not go to another's wife.

"Having entered a royal court or a company of people he

---

4. The right time for going into the village to collect almsfood is in the forenoon. If a bhikkhu went about indiscriminately, "at the wrong time," he might see things or have experiences that would endanger his life of purity and cause him to revert to the lay life.

5. Literally, "they send the mind far."

6. *Sugata*, literally "well-gone," sometimes translated as the "Happy One," is an epithet of the Buddha.

should not speak lies. He should not speak lies (himself) nor incite others to do so. He should completely avoid falsehood.

"A layman who has chosen to practise this Dhamma should not indulge in the drinking of intoxicants. He should not drink them nor encourage others to do so; realising that it leads to madness. Through intoxication foolish people perform evil deeds and cause other heedless people to do likewise. He should avoid intoxication, this occasion for demerit, which stupefies the mind, and is the pleasure of foolish people.

Do not kill a living being;
do not take what is not given;
do not speak a lie;
do not drink intoxicants;
abstain from sexual intercourse;
do not eat food at night, at the wrong time;
do not wear flower-garlands nor use perfume;
use the ground as a bed or sleep on a mat.

"This is called the eight-factored observance made known by the Awakened One, who has reached the end of suffering.

"With a gladdened mind observe the observance day (*uposatha*), complete with its eight factors, on the fourteenth, fifteenth and eighth days of the (lunar) fortnight and also the special holiday of the half month. In the morning, with a pure heart and a joyful mind, a wise man, after observing the *uposatha*, should distribute suitable food and drink to the community of bhikkhus. He should support his mother and father as his duty and engage in lawful trading. A layman who carries this out diligently goes to the *devas* called 'Self-radiant.'"[7]

— vv. 376–378, 383–404

7. A class of heavenly beings (*deva*). A layman who practices this will, after death, be reborn as one of them.

2. Wrong Conduct

The practice of Dhamma,[8] the practice of continence,[9] mastery of this is said to be best if a person has gone forth from home to the homeless life. But if he is garrulous and, like a brute, delights in hurting others, his life is evil and his impurity increases.

A quarrelsome bhikkhu shrouded by delusion does not comprehend the Dhamma taught by the Awakened One when it is revealed. Annoying those practised in meditation, being led by ignorance, he is not aware that his defiled path leads to Niraya-hell. Falling headlong, passing from womb to womb, from darkness to (greater) darkness, such a bhikkhu undergoes suffering hereafter for certain.

As a cesspool filled over a number of years is difficult to clean, similarly, whoever is full of impurity is difficult to make pure. Whoever you know to be such, bhikkhus, bent on worldliness, having wrong desires, wrong thoughts, wrong behaviour and resort, being completely united avoid him, sweep him out like dirt, remove him like rubbish. Winnow like chaff the non-recluses. Having ejected those of wrong desires, of wrong behaviour and resort, be pure and mindful, dwelling with those who are pure. Being united and prudent you will make an end of suffering.

— vv. 274-283

3. Right Conduct

By developing what habit, what conduct, what actions may man be correctly established in and arrive at the highest goal?

He should respect his elders and not be envious of them. He should know the right time for seeing his teacher.[10] If a talk on Dhamma has started he should know the value of the opportunity and should listen carefully to the well-spoken words.[11]

---

8. Dhammacariya.

9. Brahmacariya, the divine-life, the practice of purity or chastity. Dhammacariya and Brahmacariya are two closely related terms. "Dhamma" being used here in the sense of virtue or good conduct.

10. That is, when needing their advice for dispelling mental defilements.

11. The phrase "well-spoken" (*subhāsita*) is a technical term in the Pali Canon.

When the time is right let him go to his teacher's presence, unassuming, putting aside stubbornness. Let him keep in mind and practise (what he has learned): the meaning and the text (of the Teaching), self-control and (the other virtues of) the Holy Life.[12] Delighting in the Dhamma, devoted to the Dhamma, established in the Dhamma, skilled in investigating the Dhamma,[13] let him not indulge in talk harmful to the (practice of) Dhamma. Let him be guided by well-spoken truths.

Abandoning the uttering of laughter and lamentation, giving up anger, fraud, hypocrisy, longing, conceit, violence, harshness, moral taints and infatuation: let him live without pride, self-controlled. Understanding is essential (for listening) to a well-spoken word. Learning and understanding are essential to meditation, but a man who is hasty and heedless does not increase his wisdom and learning.

Those who are devoted to the Dhamma made known by the Noble Ones (*ariyas*) are unsurpassed in speech, thought and action. They are established in peace, gentleness and concentration, and have reached the essence of learning and wisdom.

— vv. 324-330

4. On Friendship

One who, overstepping and despising a sense of shame, says, "I am your friend," but does not take upon himself any tasks he is capable of doing, is to be recognised as no friend. One who speaks amiably to his companions, but whose actions do not conform to it, him the wise know for certain as a talker not a doer. He is no friend who, anticipating conflict, is always alert in looking out for weaknesses.[14] But he on whom one can rely, like a child sleeping on its mother's breast, is truly a friend who cannot be parted from one by others.

It refers to sayings connected with Dhamma and concerning one's well-being, happiness and progress on the path.

12. The rendering follows the Commentary.

13. Or, "having discriminative knowledge of the Dhamma."

14. Such a person dislikes to be reproved, and when an occasion for this occurs he would wish to have a weapon with which to retaliate, and therefore, he takes note of one's weaknesses.

One who bears the human burden of responsibility, with its fruits and blessings in mind, he cultivates a cause[15] of joy and happiness worthy of praise. Having tasted the flavour of solitude and peace one is free from fear and wrongdoings, imbibing the rapture of Dhamma.

— vv. 253-257

5. The Simile of the Boat

He from whom a person learns the Dhamma should be venerated, as the *devas* venerate Inda, their Lord.[16] He (a teacher) of great learning, thus venerated, will explain the Dhamma, being well-disposed towards one. Having paid attention and considered it, a wise man, practising according to Dhamma, becomes learned, intelligent and accomplished by associating himself diligently with such a teacher.

But by following an inferior and foolish teacher who has not gained (fine) understanding of the Dhamma and is envious of others, one will approach death without comprehending the Dhamma and unrelieved of doubt.

If a man going down into a river, swollen and swiftly flowing, is carried away by the current—how can he help others across?

Even so, he who has not comprehended the Dhamma has not paid attention to the meaning as expounded by the learned, being himself without knowledge and unrelieved of doubt— how can he make others understand?

But if (the man at the river) knows the method and is skilled and wise, by boarding a strong boat equipped with oars and a rudder, he can, with its help, set others across. Even so, he who is experienced and has a well-trained mind, who is learned and dependable,[17] clearly knowing, he can help others to understand who are willing to listen and ready to receive.[18]

---

15. According to the Commentary, this joy-producing cause is strenuous effort (*viriya*).

16. "Inda" (Sanskrit "Indra") is another name for Sakka, the ruler of the gods.

17. He has a character which remains unperturbed by the vicissitudes of life (Comy.).

18. Possessing the supporting conditions for attaining the paths and fruits of stream-winning, once-returning, never-returning and final sainthood

Surely, therefore, one should associate with a good man who is wise and learned. By understanding the meaning of what one has learned and practising accordingly, one who has Dhamma-experience[19] attains (supreme) happiness.[20]

— vv. 316-323

6. Advice to Rāhula

Renouncing the five pleasures of sense that entrance and delight the mind, and in faith departing from home, become one who makes an end of suffering!

Associate with good friends and choose a remote lodging, secluded, with little noise. Be moderate in eating. Robes, alms-food, remedies and a dwelling—do not have craving for these things; do not be one who returns to the world.[21] Practise restraint according to the Discipline,[22] and control the five sense-faculties.

Practise mindfulness of the body and continually develop dispassion (towards it). Avoid the sign of the beautiful connected with passion; by meditating on the foul[23] cultivate a mind that is concentrated and collected.

Meditate on the signless[24] and get rid of the tendency to conceit. By thoroughly understanding and destroying conceit[25]

(Arahatta).

19. One who has fully understood or experienced the Dhamma by penetrating to its essence through the practice taught by a wise teacher (Comy.).

20. The transcendental happiness of the paths and fruits and of Nibbāna.

21. By being dragged back to it again by your craving for these things (Comy.).

22. The Vinaya, or disciplinary code of the community of bhikkhus.

23. The "foul," or *asubha-kammaṭṭhāna*, refers to the practice of contemplating a corpse in various stages of decay and the contemplation on the thirty-two parts of the body, as a means of developing detachment from the body and dispassion in regard to its beauty (or, "the sign of the beautiful," *subha-nimitta*).

24. The signless (*animitta*) is one of the three Deliverances (*vimokkha*) by which beings are liberated from the world. The other two are desirelessness (*appaṇihita*) and emptiness (*suññata*). The signless is connected with the idea of impermanence of all conditioned things (cf. *Visuddhi magga*, XXI 67f).

25. The word "*māna*" means both conceit and misconceiving.

you will live in the (highest) peace.

In this manner the Lord repeatedly exhorted the Venerable Rāhula.

— vv. 337-342

7. The Training

Violence breeds misery;[26] look at people quarrelling. I will relate the emotion agitating me.

Having seen people struggling and contending with each other like fish in a small amount of water, fear entered me. The world is everywhere insecure, every direction is in turmoil; desiring an abode for myself, I did not find one uninhabited.[27] When I saw contention as the sole outcome, aversion increased in me; but then I saw an arrow[28] here, difficult to see, set in the heart. Pierced by it, one runs in every direction, but having pulled it out one does not run nor does one sink.[29]

Here follows the (rule of) training:

Whatever are worldly fetters, may you not be bound by them! Completely break down sensual desires and practise so as to realise Nibbāna for yourself!

A sage should be truthful, not arrogant, not deceitful, not given to slandering others, and should be without anger. He should remove the evil of attachment and wrongly directed longing; he should conquer drowsiness, lassitude and sloth, and not dwell

26. *Attadaṇḍā bhayaṃ jātaṃ*: "Violence" (*attadanda*, lit.: "seizing a stick" or "weapons") includes in it all wrong conduct in deeds, words and thoughts. *Bhaya* is either a subjective state of mind, "fear," or the objective condition of "fearfulness," danger, misery; and so it is explained in the Comy. as the evil consequences of wrong conduct, in this life and in future existence.

27. Uninhabited by decay and death, etc. (Comy.).

28. The arrow of lust, hate, delusion and (wrong) views.

29. That is, sink into the four "floods" of sensual desire, continual becoming, wrong views and ignorance. These are the two contrasting dangers of saṃsāra, i.e., restless running, ever seeking after sensual delights and sinking or passively clinging to the defilements, whereby one is overwhelmed by the "flood." In the first discourse of the Saṃyutta-nikāya the Buddha says: "If I stood still, I sank; if I struggled, I was carried away. Thus by neither standing still nor struggling, I crossed the flood."

in indolence. A man whose mind is set on Nibbāna should not be arrogant. He should not lapse into untruth nor generate love for sense objects. He should thoroughly understand (the nature of) conceit and abstain from violence. He should not delight in what is past, nor be fond of what is new, nor sorrow for what is disappearing, nor crave for the attractive.

Greed, I say, is a great flood; it is a whirlpool sucking one down, a constant yearning, seeking a hold, continually in movement;[30] difficult to cross is the morass of sensual desire. A sage does not deviate from truth, a *brāhmaṇa*[31] stands on firm ground; renouncing all, he is truly called "calmed."

Having actually experienced and understood the Dhamma he has realised the highest knowledge and is independent.[32] He comports himself correctly in the world and does not envy anyone here. He who has left behind sensual pleasures, an attachment difficult to leave behind, does not grieve nor have any longing; he has cut across the stream and is unfettered.

Dry out that which is past,[33] let there be nothing for you in the future.[34] If you do not grasp at anything in the present you will go about at peace. One who, in regard to this entire mind-body complex, has no cherishing of it as "mine," and who does not grieve for what is non-existent truly suffers no loss in the world. For him there is no thought of anything as 'this is mine' or "this is another's"; not finding any state of ownership, and realising, "nothing is mine," he does not grieve.

To be not callous, not greedy, at rest and unruffled by circumstances—that is the profitable result I proclaim when asked

30. According to the commentary these four phrases, beginning with a "whirlpool sucking down," are all synonyms for craving (*taṇhā*) or greed (*gedha*), called the "great flood."

31. In Buddhism the title "Brāhmaṇa" is sometimes used for one who has reached final deliverance. The Buddha himself is sometimes called "the Brāhmaṇa."

32. Independent of craving and views.

33. "Dry out" (*visodehi*) your former, and not your matured kamma, i.e., make it unproductive by not giving room to passions that may grow out of the past actions.

34. Do not rouse kamma-productive passions concerning the future.

about one who does not waver. For one who does not crave, who has understanding, there is no production (of new kamma).[35] Refraining from initiating (new kamma) he sees security everywhere. A sage does not speak in terms of being equal, lower or higher. Calmed and without selfishness he neither grasps nor rejects.

— vv. 935-954

8. On Vigilance

Rouse yourself! Sit up! What good is there in sleeping? For those afflicted by disease (suffering), struck by the arrow (craving), what sleep is there?

Rouse yourself! Sit up! Resolutely train yourself to attain peace.[36] Do not let the king of death,[37] seeing you are careless, lead you astray and dominate you.

Go beyond this clinging,[38] to which *devas* and men are attached, and (the pleasures) they seek. Do not waste your opportunity. When the opportunity has passed they sorrow when consigned to Niraya-hell.

Negligence is a taint, and so is the (greater) negligence growing from it. By earnestness and understanding withdraw the arrow (of sensual passions).

— vv. 331-334

9. The Buddha's Great Struggle

When, near the river Nerañjarā, I exerted myself in meditation for attaining to security from bondage,[39] there came Namuci[40] speaking words of compassion:

---

35. Volitional acts, good or bad, manifesting in deeds of body, speech and mind leading to a future result.

36. "Peace" is a synonym for Nibbāna, the final goal.

37. The king of death (*maccurāja*), or Māra (death), is the personification of everything that binds us to this world and prevents the gaining of deliverance.

38. This clinging to pleasures of the senses.

39. *Yogakkhema*, a name for Nibbāna.

40. Namuci, meaning "He who does not let go" (his hold over beings easily), is a name for Māra, the Evil One.

"You are emaciated and ill-looking, you are near to death! A thousand parts of you belong to death and only a fraction of you is alive. Live, good sir! It is better to live. Living you may perform meritorious deeds. From practising celibacy and tending the sacrificial fire much merit is made, but what is obtained from striving? It is difficult to enter the path of exertion, it is difficult to do, difficult to maintain."

Māra spoke these words whilst standing in the presence of the Awakened One. To Māra speaking thus, the Lord replied:

"You who are the friend of the negligent, O evil one, for what reason have you come here? Those who still have use for merit Māra may consider worthwhile addressing. I have faith and energy and wisdom. Being thus bent on striving, why do you ask me to live? This wind will wither the currents of the rivers, why should not my exertion dry up even the blood? When the blood dries up, the bile and phlegm wither. On the wasting away of the flesh the mind becomes more and more serene and my mindfulness, wisdom and concentration are established more firmly. In me, who abides enduring such an extreme experience, the mind does not long for sensual pleasures. See the purity of a being!

"Sensual desire is your first army, the second is called discontent, the third is hunger and thirst, the fourth craving, the fifth sluggishness and laziness, the sixth fear, the seventh indecision, and the eighth disparagement of others and stubbornness: gain, fame, honour, prestige wrongly acquired and whoever praises himself and despises others—these, Namuci, are your armies, the Dark One's[41] striking forces. A lazy, cowardly person cannot overcome them, but by conquering them one gains bliss.

"I wear muñja-grass![42] Shame on life here in this world! It is better for me to die in battle than to live defeated. Some

---

41. The "Dark One" or Kaṇha (Sanskrit: Krishna) is another name for Māra. He is the Indian Cupid (Kāmadeva) and personifies sensual passions. He carries a lute (*vīṇā*), mentioned at the close, with which he captivates beings by his playing. His other equipment includes a bow, arrows, a noose and a hook.

42. Indian warriors used to wear a tuft of a certain grass, called *muñja*, on their head or headgear for indicating that they were prepared to die in battle and determined not to retreat.

recluses and brāhmaṇas are not seen (exerting themselves) here, so immersed are they (in worldliness). They are not aware of that path by which those of perfect conduct walk.

"Seeing the surrounding army ready and Māra mounted (on his elephant), I am going out to fight so that he may not shift me from my position. This army of yours which the world together with the *devas* is unable to subdue, that I will destroy with wisdom, like an unbaked clay-bowl with a stone. Having mastered the mind and firmly established mindfulness, I shall wander from country to country guiding many disciples. And they will be diligent and energetic in practising my teaching, the teaching of one without sensual desire, and they will go where, having gone, one does not grieve."

Māra: "For seven years I followed the Lord step by step but did not find an opportunity to defeat that mindful Awakened One. A crow flew around a stone having the colour of fat: 'Can we find even here something tender? May it be something to eat?'

"Not finding anything edible the crow left that place. As with the crow and the stone, we leave Gotama, having approached and become disheartened."

Overcome by sorrow his lute fell from his arm and thereupon the unhappy spirit disappeared from that place.

— vv. 425-449

10. On Decay

Short indeed is this life, this side of a hundred years one dies; whoever lives long even he dies from old age. People grieve for things they are attached to, yet there exist no permanent possessions but just a state of (constant) separation. Seeing this one should no longer live the household life. That which a man imagines to be his will disappear at death. Knowing this a wise man will have no attachment (to anything).

As a man awakened from sleep no longer sees what happened in his dream, similarly one does not see a loved one who is dead. Those people who were seen and heard and called by their names as such and such, only their names remain when they have passed away. Those greedy for objects of attachment do not abandon sorrow, grief and avarice, but sages having got rid of possessions live perceiving security. For a bhikkhu with a detached mind, living in a secluded dwelling, it is right, they say, that he no longer shows himself in the abodes (of existence).[43]

A sage who is completely independent does not make close friends or enemies. In him sorrow and selfishness do not stay, like water on a lotus leaf. As a lotus is not wetted by water, so a sage is not affected by what is seen or heard, nor by what is perceived by the other senses. A wise man is not deluded by what is perceived by the senses. He does not expect purity by any other way.[44] He is neither is pleased nor is he repelled (by the six sense-objects).

— vv. 804-813

11. The Arrow

Unindicated and unknown is the length of life of those subject to death. Life is difficult and brief and bound up with suffering. There is no means by which those who are born will not die. Having reached old age, there is death. This is the natural course for a living being. With ripe fruits there is the constant danger that they will fall. In the same way, for those born and subject to death, there is always the fear of dying. Just as the pots made by a potter all end by being broken, so death is (the breaking up) of life.

The young and old, the foolish and the wise, all are stopped short by the power of death, all finally end in death. Of those overcome by death and passing to another world, a father cannot hold back his son, nor relatives a relation. See! While the relatives are looking on and weeping, one by one each mortal is led away like an ox to slaughter.

In this manner the world is afflicted by death and decay. But the wise do not grieve, having realised the nature of the world. You do not know the path by which they came or departed. Not seeing either end you lament in vain. If any benefit is gained by

43. There is a play on words here: "*bhāvanā*," besides meaning "an abode of existence," also means "a house." So as well as saying, he is not reborn into any realm of existence, the passage also indicates he lives secluded and does not associate with people in the village.

44. By any way other than the Noble Eightfold Path (Comy.).

lamenting, the wise would do it. Only a fool would harm himself. Yet through weeping and sorrowing the mind does not become calm, but still more suffering is produced, the body is harmed and one becomes lean and pale, one merely hurts oneself. One cannot protect a departed one (*peta*) by that means. To grieve is in vain.

By not abandoning sorrow a being simply undergoes more suffering. Bewailing the dead he comes under the sway of sorrow. See other men faring according to their deeds! Hence beings tremble here with fear when they come into the power of death. Whatever they imagine, it (turns out) quite different from that. This is the sort of disappointment that exists. Look at the nature of the world! If a man lives for a hundred years, or even more, finally, he is separated from his circle of relatives and gives up his life in the end. Therefore, having listened to the Arahant,[45] one should give up lamenting. Seeing a dead body, one should know, "He will not be met by me again." As the fire in a burning house is extinguished with water, so a wise, discriminating, learned and sensible man should quickly drive away the sorrow that arises, as the wind (blows off) a piece of cotton. He who seeks happiness should withdraw the arrow: his own lamentations, longings and grief.

With the arrow withdrawn, unattached, he would attain to peace of mind; and when all sorrow has been transcended he is sorrow-free and has realised Nibbāna.

— vv. 574-593

12. On Purity

"Here I see one who is pure, entirely free of sickness. By seeing him a man may attain to purity!"

Convinced of that and thinking it "the highest," he believes it to be knowledge when he contemplates "the pure one."[46] But if by sights man can gain purification or if through such knowledge he could leave suffering behind, then, one who still has attachments

45. The Perfect One, i.e., the Buddha.

46. This refers to the old Indian belief in "auspicious sights" (*diṭṭha-maṅgala*), the belief that by merely beholding something or someone regarded as a holy object or person, purity, or whatever else is desired, may be gained.

could be purified by another.[47] However, this is merely the opinion of those who so assert.

The (true) brāhmaṇa[48] has said one is not purified by another, nor by what is seen, heard or perceived (by the other senses), nor by the performance of ritual observances. He (the true brāhmaṇa) is not defiled by merit nor demerit. Having given up what he had (previously) grasped at, he no longer engages in producing (any kamma). Having left a former (object) they attach themselves to another, dominated by craving they do not go beyond attachment. They reject and seize, like a monkey letting go of a branch to take hold of another.

A person having undertaken a ritual act goes this way and that, fettered by his senses. But one with a wide wisdom, having understood and gone into the Dhamma with his experience, does not go this way and that. For a person indifferent towards all conditions, whatever is seen, heard or cognised, he is one who sees it as it really is and lives with clarity (of mind). With what could he be identified in the world?

They do not speculate nor pursue (any notion), they do not claim perfect purity. Loosening the knot (of clinging) with which they are bound, they do not have longing anywhere in the world. The (true) brāhmaṇa who has gone beyond limitations, having understood and seen there is no longer any assumption for him, he is neither disturbed by lust nor agitated by revulsion. For him there is nothing upheld as "the highest."

— vv. 788-795

13. On Views

A person who associates himself with certain views, considering them as best and making them supreme in the world, he says, because of that, that all other views are inferior; therefore he is not free from contention (with others). In what is seen, heard, cognised and in ritual observances performed, he sees a profit for

47. By another method, other than that of the Noble Eightfold Path (Comy.); but it could also mean, "by the sight of another person."

48. That is, the Buddha.

himself. Just by laying hold of that view he regards every other view as worthless. Those skilled (in judgement)[49] say that (a view becomes) a bond if, relying on it, one regards everything else as inferior. Therefore a bhikkhu should not depend on what is seen, heard or cognised, nor upon ritual observances. He should not form a view through knowledge or rites. He should not present himself as equal to, nor imagine himself to be inferior, nor better than, another. Abandoning (the views) he had (previously) held and not taking up (another), he does not seek a support even in knowledge. Among those who dispute he is certainly not one to take sides. He does not recourse to a view at all. In whom there is no inclination to either extreme, for becoming or non-becoming, here or in another existence, for him there does not exist a fixed viewpoint on investigating the doctrines assumed (by others). Concerning the seen, the heard and the cognised he does not form the least notion. That brāhmaṇa[50] who does not grasp at a view, with what could he be identified in the world?

They do not speculate nor pursue (any notion); doctrines are not accepted by them. A (true) brāhmaṇa is not guided by ritual observances. Such a one, gone beyond, does not fall back on views.

— vv. 796-803

14. Ajita's Questions

The Venerable Ajita: "By what is the world enveloped? Because of what is it not known? With what do you say it is soiled? What is its great fear?"

The Lord: "The world is enveloped by ignorance, Ajita. Because of wrongly directed desire and heedlessness it is not known (as it really is). It is soiled by longings and its great fear is suffering."

Ajita: "Everywhere flow the streams.[51] What is the obstruction for the streams, tell me the restricting of them, by what are they cut off?"

49. That is, the Buddhas and their disciples who have realised the goal.

50. That is, a perfected one.

51. "The streams" are cravings flowing out towards pleasurable and desirable objects in the world.

The Lord: "Whatever streams are in the world, it is mindfulness that obstructs them and restricts them, and by wisdom they are cut off."

Ajita: "It is just wisdom and mindfulness. Now mind-and-body, sir, explain this: where does it cease?"

The Lord: "This question you have asked, Ajita, I will answer for you: where mind-and-body completely cease. By the cessation of consciousness they cease."[52]

Ajita: "Those who have fully understood the Dhamma, those who are training and the other individuals here,[53] explain their (rule of) conduct."

The Lord: "Not craving for sensual pleasures and with a mind that is pure and tranquil,[54] a bhikkhu should mindfully go forth, skilful in all situations."

— vv. 1032-1039

15. Puṇṇaka's Questions

The Venerable Puṇṇaka: "To him who is free from craving, who has seen the root (of things)[55] I have come with a question:

---

52. This question and answer refer to the doctrine of dependent-arising (*paṭicca-samuppāda*). Where rebirth-consciousness (*paṭisandhi-viññāṇa*) does not arise there is no establishment of an individual (mind-and-body, *nāmarūpa*) in a realm of existence, nor the consequent appearance of old age and death and the other sufferings inherent in life.

53. "Those who have fully understood" are Arahants (perfected ones), who have reached the highest goal. "Those who are training" are those noble beings (*ariya*) who are working towards and are assured of that goal. The other individuals are ordinary beings (*puthujjana*) who have not yet reached assurance.

54. The word *anāvilo* means pure, clear, tranquil, unagitated, unmuddied, etc. In the Dhammapada v. 82, the wise are compared to a deep lake with this quality.

55. "The root of unwholesome actions, etc." (Comy.). There are six roots or basic conditions in a person leading to the performance of unwholesome (unskilled) and wholesome (skilled) actions: greed, aversion, delusion, non-greed (renunciation, detachment), non-aversion (love) and non-delusion (wisdom). The Buddha has seen and understood this as it really is.

for what reason did sages, warriors, brāhmaṇas and other men prepare, here in this world, various sacrificial gifts for the gods (*devatā*)? I ask the Lord this, let him tell me the answer."

The Lord: "Whatever sages, warriors, brāhmaṇas and other men, Puṇṇaka, prepared various sacrificial gifts for the gods, they did so in the hope of this or that (future) existence, being induced by (the fact of) old age and decay."

Puṇṇaka: "By preparing various sacrificial gifts for the gods, being zealous in sacrificing, do they cross beyond birth and decay, Lord?"

The Lord: "They hope and extol, pray and sacrifice for things of the senses, Puṇṇaka. For the sake of such reward they pray. These devotees of sacrifice, infatuated by their passion for existence,[56] do not cross beyond birth and decay, I say."

Puṇṇaka: "If these devotees of sacrifice do not cross beyond birth and decay through sacrifice, sir, then by what practice does one cross beyond birth and decay in this world of gods and men?"

The Lord: "He who has comprehended in the world the here and the beyond, in whom there is no perturbation by anything in the world, who is calm, free from the smouldering fires,[57] untroubled and desireless—he has crossed beyond birth and decay, I say."

— vv. 1043-1048

16. Mettagū's Questions

The Venerable Mettagū: "I ask the Lord this question, may he tell me the answer to it. I know him to be a master of knowledge and a perfected being. From whence have arisen these many sufferings evident in the world?"

The Lord: "You have asked me the source of suffering. Mettagū, I will tell it to you as it has been discerned by me. These many sufferings evident in the world have arisen from worldly

56. Or, "burning with lust for life."

57. The three "fires" of greed, aversion and delusion. This is a punning reference, also to be seen in the previous note, to the brāhmaṇa's sacrificial fire.

attachments. Whoever ignorantly creates an attachment, that stupid person comes upon suffering again and again. Therefore a man of understanding should not create attachment, seeing it is the source of suffering."

Mettagū: "What I did ask, you have explained; now I ask another question. Come tell me this: how do the wise cross the flood, birth and old age, sorrow and grief? Explain it thoroughly to me, O sage, for this Dhamma has been understood[58] by you."

The Lord: "I will set forth the Dhamma, Mettagū, a teaching to be directly perceived,[59] not something based on hearsay, by experiencing which and living mindfully one may pass beyond the entanglements of the world."

Mettagū: "I rejoice in the thought of that highest Dhamma, great sage, by experiencing which and living mindfully one may pass beyond the entanglements of the world."

The Lord: "Whatever you clearly comprehend, Mettagū, above, below, across and in between, get rid of delight in it. Rid yourself of habitual attitudes[60] and (life affirming) consciousness.[61] Do not continue in existence. Living thus, mindful and vigilant, a bhikkhu who has forsaken selfish attachments may, by understanding, abandon suffering, birth and old age, sorrow and grief, even here in this life."

Mettagū: "I rejoice in the words of the great sage. Well explained, O Gotama, is the state of non-attachment.[62] The Lord has surely abandoned suffering as this Dhamma has been realised by him. They will certainly abandon suffering who are constantly admonished by you, O sage. Having understood, I venerate it, Noble One. May the Lord constantly admonish me also."

The Lord: "Whom you know as a true brāhmaṇa, a master of knowledge, owning nothing, not attached to sensual (-realm) existence, he has certainly crossed this flood. Having crossed beyond he is untainted and freed from doubt. One who has discarded this

---

58. The Pali word *vidito* also means "found out, discovered."

59. *Diṭṭhe dhamme*: to be seen for oneself in this life or here and now. It is an expression used of Nibbāna.

60. Or, "fixed views."

61. Or, "kamma-producing consciousness."

62. That is, Nibbāna.

clinging (leading) to renewal of existence is a man who has realised the highest knowledge. Free from craving, undistressed, desireless, he has crossed beyond birth and old age, I say."

— vv. 1049-1060

17. Further Questions

"From what arise contentions and disputes, lamentations and sorrows, along with selfishness and conceit, and arrogance along with slander? From where do these various things arise? Come tell me this."

"From being too endeared (to objects and persons) arise contentions and disputes, lamentations and sorrows along with avarice, selfishness and conceit, arrogance and slander. Contentions and disputes are linked with selfishness, and slander is born of contention."

"What are the sources of becoming endeared in the world? What are the sources of whatever passions prevail in the world, of longings and fulfilments that are man's goal (in life)?"

"Desires are the source of becoming endeared (to objects and persons) in the world, also of whatever passions prevail. These are the sources of longings and fulfilments that are man's goal (in life)."[63]

"Now what is the source of desire in the world? What is the cause of judgements[64] that arise; of anger, untruth, doubts and whatever other (similar) states that have been spoken of by the Recluse (i.e., the Buddha)?"

"'It is pleasant, it is unpleasant,' so people speak in the world; and based upon that arises desire. Having seen the appearing and disappearing of material things a man makes his judgements in the world.[65] Anger, untruth and doubts, these states arise merely because

63. Man's longings, hopes and aspirations and their satisfaction are his refuge giving him an aim in life.

64. Judgements or evaluations of things motivated by craving for them or by opinions of them as being desirable or otherwise.

65. The "appearing" of the pleasant and the "disappearing" of the unpleasant are judged to be "good." The "appearance" of the unpleasant and the "disappearance" of the pleasant are judged to be "bad."

of the existence of this duality.[66] Let a doubter train himself by way of insight to understand these states as taught by the Recluse."

"What is the source of thinking things as pleasant or unpleasant? When what is absent are those states not present? What is the meaning of appearing and disappearing? Explain the source of it to me."

"The pleasant and the unpleasant have their source in sense-impression. When this sense-impression is absent, these states are not present. The idea of appearing and disappearing is produced from this, I say."

"What is the source of sense-impression? From what arises so much grasping? By the absence of what is there no selfish attachment? By the disappearance of what is sense-impression not experienced?"

"Sense-impression is dependent upon the mental and the material. Grasping has its source in wanting (something). Want not being present there is no selfish attachment. By the disappearance of material objects sense-impression is not experienced."

"For whom does materiality disappear? How do pleasure and discomfort cease to be? Tell me how it ceases so that I may be satisfied in my mind that I have understood it."

"His perception is not the ordinary kind, nor is his perception abnormal;[67] he is not without perception nor is his perception (of materiality) suspended,[68] to such a one materiality ceases.[69] Perception is indeed the source of the world of multiplicity."

---

66. That is, of the pleasant and the unpleasant.
67. He is neither insane nor mentally disturbed (Comy.).
68. He has not attained the state of cessation of perception and feeling (*saññā-vedayita-nirodha*) nor the immaterial absorptions (*arūpajjhāna*) (Comy.). In the former perception completely ceases, but in the latter there is still the perception of an immaterial object.
69. According to the commentary what remains after these four negations is the state of one who has reached the highest of the fine-material absorptions (*rūpajjhāna*) and is in the process of attaining the first immaterial absorption. This answers the question "for whom does (the perception of) materiality disappear?" And as "pleasure and discomfort" have previously been stated to "have their source in sense-impression," in other words, the perception of material objects, the second question is answered too.

"What we asked, you have explained. We now ask another question. Tell us the answer to it. Do not some of the learned declare purification of the spirit[70] as the highest state to be attained? And do not others speak of something else as the highest?"[71]

"Some of the learned do declare purification of the spirit as the highest. But contrary to them some teach a doctrine of annihilation. Those clever ones declare this to be (final liberation) without basis of life's fuel remaining. Knowing that these (theorists) rely on (mere opinions for their statements) a sage investigates that upon which they rely. Having understood and being free (from theories) he will not dispute with anyone. The wise do not enter into any existence."

— vv. 862-877

18. Mogharāja's Question

The Venerable Mogharāja: "Twice have I asked Sakka[72] but the Seeing One has not answered me. I have heard a divine sage replies when asked a third time. I do not know the view of the greatly famous Gotama concerning this world, the next world and the Brahma-world with its deities. To him of supreme vision I have come with a question: how should one regard the world so that one is not seen by the King of Death?"

The Lord: "Look upon the world as empty,[73] Mogharāja, ever mindful; uprooting the view of self you may thus be one who overcomes death. So regarding the world one is not seen by the King of Death."

— vv. 1116-1119

70. The term "spirit" (*yakkha*) is equivalent here to "being" or "man."

71. An alternative rendering of this sentence could be: "Do not some of the learned declare (the immaterial attainments) as the highest state, as man's purification?"

72. The name "Sakka" is used here as a title for the Buddha. It means, "a man of the Sakya clan." The Buddha is also sometimes called Sakyamuni, "the sage of the Sakyas."

73. In the Saṃyutta-nikāya (S IV 54) the Venerable Ānanda asks: "How is the world empty, venerable sir?" And the Lord replies: "Because, Ānanda, it is empty of a self or what belongs to a self, therefore it is said, 'the world is empty.'"

19. Pingiya's Request

The Venerable Pingiya: "I am old and feeble, the comeliness of youth has vanished. My sight is weak and I am hard of hearing. I do not wish to perish whilst still confused. Teach me the Dhamma by understanding which I may abandon birth and decay."[74]

The Lord: "Seeing heedless people afflicted and suffering through their bodies, Pingiya, you should be heedful and renounce body so as to not come again to birth."

Pingiya: "In the ten directions—the four quarters, four between and those above and below—there is nothing in the world not seen, heard, sensed or understood by you. Teach me the Dhamma by understanding which I may abandon birth and decay."

The Lord: "Seeing men caught in craving, Pingiya, tormented and afflicted by old age, you should be heedful and renounce craving so as to not come again to birth."

— vv. 1120-1123

20. The Noble One's Happiness

"See how the world together with the *devas* has self-conceit for what is not-self. Enclosed by mind-and-body it imagines, 'This is real.' Whatever they imagine it to be, it is quite different from that. It is unreal, of a false nature and perishable. Nibbāna, not false in nature, that the Noble Ones[75] know as true. Indeed, by the penetration of the true, they are completely stilled and realise final deliverance.

"Forms, sounds, tastes, scents, bodily contacts and ideas which are agreeable, pleasant and charming, all these, while they last, are deemed to be happiness by the world with its *devas*. But when they cease that is agreed by all to be unsatisfactory. By the Noble Ones, the cessation of the existing body[76] is seen as happiness. This is the reverse of the outlook of the whole world.

"What others call happiness, that the Noble Ones declare to

---

74. *Jarā*: decay, decrepitude, old age

75. The Noble Ones or *ariyas* are the Buddhas and their disciples.

76. The "existing body" (*sakkāya*) is a term for the five aggregates as objects of grasping.

be suffering. What others call suffering, that the Noble Ones have found to be happiness. See how difficult it is to understand the Dhamma! Herein those without insight have completely gone astray. For those under the veil (of ignorance) it is obscured, for those who cannot see it is utter darkness. But for the good and the wise it is as obvious as the light for those who can see. Even though close to it, the witless who do not know the Dhamma, do not comprehend it.

"By those overcome by attachment to existence, those who drift with the stream of existence, those in the realm of Māra, this Dhamma is not properly understood. Who other than the Noble Ones are fit to fully understand that state, by perfect knowledge of which they realise final deliverance, free from defilements?"[77]

— vv. 755-765

77. *Anāsava*; the defilements or *āsava*, literally, "out-flows," are dissipations: of energy in the form of sensual desire, becoming (the perpetuation of existence), views and ignorance and are the same as the four "floods" mentioned earlier. One who has destroyed the defilements (*khīṇāsava*) is another name for an Arahant or Perfected One.

With Robes and Bowl

Glimpses of the Thudong
Bhikkhu Life

by

Bhikkhu Khantipālo

WHEEL PUBLICATION NO. 83/84

"As the bird takes his wings
whithersoever it flies,
so the bhikkhu goes
with robes and bowl."

Verses for Thudong-faring

From the Suttanipāta

Selected verses of the *Rhinoceros Sutta* from *Woven Cadences* (*Suttanipāta*), translated by E. M. Hare, and published in *Sacred Books of the Buddhists Series* by the Pali Text Society. Other verses are used below in this booklet.

Put by the rod for all that lives,
Nor harm thou anyone thereof;
Long not for son—how then for friend?
Fare lonely as rhinoceros.

Love cometh from companionship;
In wake of love upsurges ill;
Seeing the bane that comes of love,
Fare lonely as rhinoceros.

In ruth for all his bosom friends,
A man, heart-chained, neglects the goal;
Seeing this fear in fellowship,
Fare lonely as rhinoceros.

Tangled as crowding bamboo boughs
Is fond regard for sons and wife:
As the tall tops are tangle-free,
Fare lonely as rhinoceros.

The deer untethered roams the wild
Whithersoe'er it lists for food:
Seeing the liberty, wise man,
Fare lonely as rhinoceros.

Casting aside the household gear,
As sheds the coral-tree its leaves,
With home-ties cut, and vigorous,
Fare lonely as rhinoceros.

Seek for thy friend[1] the deeply learned,
Dhamma-endued, lucid and great;
Knowing the needs, expelling doubt,
Fare lonely as rhinoceros.

The heat and cold, and hunger, thirst,
Wind, sun-beat, sting of gadfly, snake:
Surmounting one and all of these,
Fare lonely as rhinoceros.

Crave not for tastes, but free of greed,
Moving with measured step from house
To house, support of none, none's thrall,
Fare lonely as rhinoceros.

Free everywhere, at odds with none,
And well content with this and that:
Enduring dangers undismayed,
Fare lonely as rhinoceros.

Snap thou the fetters as the snare
By river denizen is broke:
As fire to waste comes back no more,
Fare lonely as rhinoceros.

And turn thy back on joys and pains,
Delights and sorrows known of old;
And gaining poise and calm, and cleansed,
Fare lonely as rhinoceros.

Neglect thou not to muse apart,
'Mid things by Dhamma-faring aye;
Alive to all becomings' bane,
Fare lonely as rhinoceros.

As lion, mighty-jawed and king
Of beasts, fares conquering, so thou,
Taking thy bed and seat remote,
Fare lonely as rhinoceros.

1. "'Friend" here signifies the Good Friend (*kalyāṇa-mitta*), as the meditation-master is called.

Poise, amity, ruth and release
Pursue, and timely sympathy;
At odds with none in all the world,
Fare lonely as rhinoceros.

Leaving the vanities of view,
Right method won, the Way obtained:
"I know! No other is my guide!"
Fare lonely as rhinoceros.

With Robes and Bowl

Preamble

The Bhikkhu Life— The Thirteen Austere Practices

The Triple Gem or the Three Precious Ones are the highest ideals of the Buddha dhamma. To the Lord Buddha, to the Holy Dhamma (Teaching) and to the Noble Sangha (Order of Monks) are given veneration by all Buddhists since they aspire to mould their lives according to the qualities represented by these three ideals.[2]

In the English language, there are now a number of books describing the life of the last Buddha, Gotama, also many explaining what is meant by the ideal of Buddhahood. Likewise, we have an ever-growing flood of literature, translations, commentaries and so forth, to help us understand what is Dhamma. Much less information, however, is to be found on the Sangha, especially upon the bhikkhu-life of the present day. Of course those living in Buddhist countries where the Sangha is established will know more about it than will those who follow the Buddha's Path in other lands. It is to give the latter a picture of bhikkhu-life that this book is written, besides keeping before the eyes of those living in Buddhist land, the best traditions of the Sangha.

While Buddhadhamma is a way for everyone, bhikkhu or lay-follower, naturally the bhikkhus, since they have fully devoted themselves to its practice, have more opportunity to penetrate to the heart of the Teaching.

To do this, they must, as indeed anyone who wishes to do so, obtain experience in its three trainings (*ti-sikkhā*): learning (*pariyatti*), practice (*paṭipatti*) and penetration (*paṭivedha*). These lead on one from the other, thus making both of the first two necessary. Without learning, one's practice (of keeping the precepts, meditation) is liable to stray away from Correct Understanding (*sammā-diṭṭhi*). Without

2. See *The Wheel* No. 76, *The Threefold Refuge*, by Nyanaponika Thera.

practice, learning is just barren as far as the fruits of penetration are concerned.

Commentaries written later upon the ancient Buddha-word give new names to learning and practice, calling the former book-work (*gantha-dhura*) and the latter insight-work (*vipassanā-dhura*). It may have been already in early times that a tendency appeared to concentrate upon either one or the other as though they were alternative ways rather than complementary steps. This tendency, which has persisted into the present, seems to be an expression of human frailty, for it is much easier to study the scriptures and become learned,[3] while largely setting aside the practice, especially meditation, than it is to get down and practise all that has been learned.

This separation is, however, far from absolute since many bhikkhus gain a groundwork of learning and then leave the city temples where they have studied for a meditation teacher's forest dwelling, there to take up the practice which will lead, in due course, to penetration of the Dhamma.

Although one may gather something of the life of the insight-work bhikkhus from ancient sources, nothing seems to have been written regarding them in the present day. Hence this short account which attempts to outline their life as found in Thailand (the position in other Buddhist countries is unknown to the writer).

A bhikkhu undertaking insight-work bases his life upon three great foundations. These are:

Firstly, strict observance of the *rules of training* (as contained in the Discipline (Vinaya) which he has undertaken to keep at the time of his Acceptance (the higher ordination—*upasampadā*). He is one who takes the earnest exhortation of Lord Buddha to heart:

"Devoted to virtue should you dwell, O Bhikkhu, devoted to the discipline of the Sangha and restrained by that discipline! Perfect should be your conduct and behaviour! Seeing danger in even the slightest fault, you should train yourself in the rules which you have accepted."

Secondly, he follows his meditation teacher in the application of the *austere practices* (*dhutaṅga* in Pali and *thudong* in Thai),

3. For the life of the "book-work" bhikkhu, see *Buddhism,* Ch. V: 3, edited by R. Gard.

being guided by him as to how and to what extent he should practise them. The first foundation above ensures purification and the removal of obstacles while the second gives rise to strong renunciation and to contentment with little. Thus both become good, indeed necessary, bases for the third foundation of his life, the actual *meditation practice* (*bhāvanā*).

* * *

Something should now be said about these austere practices.[4] Lord Buddha refused to allow extreme asceticism, with which he had experimented before his Enlightenment. However, he did recognize that a certain degree of austerity would be useful in the training of bhikkhus. For instance, we find that in the Four Supports (*nissaya*) recited to a bhikkhu upon the occasion of his ordination, he is to: (1) wear rag robes, (2) eat almsfood, (3) dwell at the foot of a tree, (4) have fermented cow's urine for medicine.

Further, we see from the lives of many bhikkhus in the time of Lord Buddha that the *dhutaṅgas* were widely practised, for the early Sangha was a community in which the wandering, meditative life was the normal one. As examples we have the greatly venerated Mahā-Kassapa, who was acclaimed by Lord Buddha as the foremost among those who lead austere lives; while the first of his disciples to gain insight into the Dhamma, Añña Koṇḍañña, dwelt secluded throughout his life in the depths of the forest.

With the establishment of permanent monasteries, which began even in Lord Buddha's days, together with the necessity of preserving the Buddha-word, memorizing and learning came to have increased importance. Not all learned bhikkhus practised and thus *dhutaṅgas* were left for those who wished to practise meditation.

It was also stressed that for a person whose character was strongly rooted in hatred (*dosa*), these austere practices would not be appropriate, being liable to increase self-hatred. On the other hand, with characters rooted in greed (*lobha*), faith (*saddhā*) and mixed-rooted (so-called "balanced") characters, the *dhutaṅgas* could help greatly in the cultivation of renunciation and contentment.

The differences between a *dhutaṅga* bhikkhu and one who

4. Fully described in the *Path of Purification* (*Visuddhimagga*), Ch. II.

practises severe asceticism (some yogis in Hinduism, some Christian monks, etc.) are worth noting. The latter start with some species of view that there is a permanent spiritual entity (*ātman,* soul) enclosed in, or even imprisoned by, the fleshly body begotten of and begetting further the so-called "lusts of the flesh." Holding to such a view, the body becomes something despicable and then hateful as it seems to thwart one's search for the spiritual. Then follows "mortification of the flesh" to quell the evil arising from the possession of such a body (see for instance, the case of Henry de Suso [Heinrich Seuse] related in William James' *Varieties of Religious Experience*). Such attempts to "control" desires are really only extreme examples of repression effected by means of self-inflicted torture. To begin to do this, one must hold a view which hates the body and the outcome of such asceticism will be greatly increased body-hatred. Masochistic tendencies, where present, will also be gratified. All this can hardly be said to indicate a healthy psychological state and Lord Buddha has many times criticized these ways as unskilful (*akusala*). His words found in the Dhammapada (verse 304) show the insufficiency of "exterior" asceticism, which must fail to accomplish salvation.

> "What is the use of your matted hair, O witless man! What use your garment of antelope's hide? Within you is a tangle (of passions); outwardly you clean yourself."

In Buddhist Teaching, the interdependence of mind-body (*nāma-rūpa*) is emphasized. Moreover, it is the mind which has charge at the helm, while materiality (*rūpa*) is a passenger. As the Dhammapada stresses in its first and second verses:

> "Mind precedes all states and is their chief, they are all mind-wrought..."

A Buddhist knows that he has acquired his present body through his own craving (*taṇhā*) and that it is in the *mind* that one must look to find the source of all unskill, including all types of greed and all hatred whether for self or other. The *dhutaṅgas* are therefore a mainly physical discipline with a psychological basis and are invaluable as a complement to the greater part of the Dhamma, which is a psychological discipline based on materiality (i.e., the "possession" of a human body). The thudong bhikkhu thus makes use of these practices in so far as they help him to discipline himself in the promotion of skilful mental states like renunciation and contentment.

These thirteen austere practices allowed by Lord Buddha[5] have been characterized as a moderate and sane ascesis; they are as follows:

I. Refuse-rag-wearer's practice (*paṃsukulik'aṅga*)—wearing robes made up from discarded or soiled cloth and not accepting and wearing ready-made robes offered by householders.

II. Triple-robe-wearer's practice (*tecīvarik'aṅga*)—having and wearing only three robes and not having additional allowable robes.

III. Alms-food-eater's practice (*piṇḍapātik'aṅga*)—eating only food collected on *piṇḍapāta* or the almsround while not accepting food in the monastery or offered by invitation in a layman's house.

IV. House-to-house-seeker's practice (*sapadanik'aṅga*)—not omitting any house while going for alms; not choosing only to go to rich households or those selected for some other reason as relations, etc.

V. One-sessioner's practice (*ekāsanik'aṅga*)—eating one meal a day and refusing other food offered before midday. (Those Gone Forth may not, unless ill, partake of food from midday until dawn the next day.)

VI. Bowl-food-eater's practice (*pattapiṇḍik'aṅga*)—eating food from his bowl in which it is mixed together rather than from plates and dishes.

VII. Later-food-refuser's practice (*khalupacchābhattik'aṅga*)—not taking any more food after one has shown that one is satisfied, even though lay people wish to offer more.

VIII. Forest-dweller's practice (*āraññak'aṅga*)—not dwelling in a town or village but living secluded, away from all kinds of distractions.

IX. Tree-root-dweller's practice (*rukkhamulik'aṅga*)—living under a tree without the shelter of a roof.

X. Open-air-dweller's practice (*abbhokāsik'aṅga*)—refusing a

5. The *Buddhist Dictionary* notes: "These thirteen ascetic exercises are all, without exception, mentioned in the old sutta texts but never in one and the same place—MN 5 and 112; A V 181–190." Niddesa has eight of them at Nidd I 188. edn.

roof and a tree-root, the practice may be undertaken sheltered by a tent of robes.

XI. Charnel-ground-dweller's practice (*susānik'aṅga*)—living in or nearby a charnel field, graveyard or cremation ground.

XII. Any-bed-user's practice (*yathāsanthatik'aṅga*)—being satisfied with any dwelling allotted as sleeping place.

XIII. Sitter's practice (*nesajjik'aṅga*)—living in the three postures of walking, standing and sitting and never lying down.

It will be noticed that the *dhutaṅgas* help a bhikkhu to find contentment with the first three of his four requisites (*paccaya*): robes (nos. I, II), almsfood (III-VII) and shelter (VIII-XIII); the fourth of his requisites, not covered here, is medicine.

As regards their present practice in Thailand, III, V, VI and VII are most commonly found amongst thudong (*dhutaṅga*) bhikkhus. Having and wearing only three robes is also widely practised (II). Individual thudong bhikkhus may gather rags, stitch them together, dye and then wear them, although made-up robes are so plentiful that this is not so common (I). The fourth practice is the normal kind of almsround in many Thai villages where every house gives a spoonful or so of rice to every bhikkhu. In the towns, IV is not practised, it being more usual for bhikkhus to have a few houses where he is invited to call each day. All thudong *vihāras* comply with VII. The next two are practised subject to the conditions of the weather, for fierce sun or torrential rain makes them both impossible. The eleventh may be recommended by a teacher for the practice of some of his disciples according to character, while XII is a special aspect of that contentment which all bhikkhus must cultivate. The last *dhutaṅga* has been mentioned below as a communal practice in some *vihāras* upon uposatha-day. When a bhikkhu practises this individually, he will usually only do so after consulting his teacher and, lest conceit arise, he will take care that others do not know that he practises in this way. It is likewise true of all these practices that they are to be undertaken in seclusion and a real *thudong* bhikkhu always shuns the public gaze. The *Buddhist Dictionary* says, quoting the *Puggala-paññatti*: "These exercises are however properly observed if they are taken up only for the sake of frugality, of contentment, of purity, etc."

The Thai word for *dhutaṅga*, "thudong," however, has a rather wider connotation than that of these *dhutaṅga* practices themselves. It is applied to anything connected with them and thus we have: thudong-vihāra, thudong-bowl, thudong-life and so on. As the *dhutaṅgas* may be practised either strictly, middlingly, or mildly, according to the standards laid down in the *Visuddhimagga*, so there are many variations in thudong practice, and different teachers place different emphases, and therefore different vihāras have different conditions.

For 2500 years and more, this thudong life has been lived by bhikkhus in many different lands. Not much can be found to record their life since those who take the thudong way are not usually writers and carry out their practice in seclusion. In Thailand, many of the ancient records, religious and secular, were destroyed in the conflagration of the capital Ayuthaya in 1767 CE. Still, we know that there were before that time many *āraññika* (forest-dwelling) bhikkhus. Probably our oldest records now are the temple wall paintings from the early reigns of the present dynasty. They illustrate thudong bhikkhus undertaking the thirteen practices according to the three grades of strictness.

At the present time there are a good number of vihāras where this way of life with its three foundations is taught by experienced teachers. Most of them prefer to be well away from the commotion of city life, the distractions and luxuries of which are far removed from the thudong ideal.

Finally, it is interesting to record that a large stupa (or *cetiya*—"relic-monument") with thirteen white pinnacles piercing the blue sky, is now being completed in a large thudong vihāra named after that great Indian monarch who helped in widely disseminating the Buddha's Teaching, the Emperor Asoka. In the topmost *cetiya* will be enshrined relics of Lord Buddha, whose life was this very thudong way, while below will be placed the ashes of a famous meditation teacher who had followed his Great Master's way with devotion, until his recent death.

Daily Life

"Control of the senses, contentment, restraint according to the Pātimokkha and association with friends who are noble, energetic and pure in life, these are the very basis of the holy life for the wise bhikkhu."

"The bhikkhu who abides in the Dhamma, who delights in the Dhamma, meditates on the Dhamma, and who bears the Dhamma well in mind, does not fall away from the sublime Dhamma."

—Dhp 375, 364

It is rather difficult to write about the thudong bhikkhu's daily life as the conditions in which they live are so different. However, there are certain features of this life which are general and these may be taken as a basis for this outline.

The material which is presented in this and succeeding sections is composite in origin, some of it being experience heard from others and more again being stories told of others. Therefore we shall speak of "the bhikkhu" or "our thudong bhikkhu" and present all these varied sources under this anonymous label. While doing this, it should be borne in mind that much of what will be said is quite common experience for those following the thudong life.

Wherever the thudong bhikkhu is, whether in a cave, in the forest, or in some other solitary place, his day begins early and with stirred-up vigour he rises. All is quiet except for the night-sounds of some insects and perhaps the swishings of bats—and at such a time, long before dawn, say, two or three o'clock, conditions are excellent for the practice of meditation. Of course, our bhikkhu, unless he is very skilled, will have to shake off Māra (the personification of evil) in the guise of sloth-and-torpor (*thīna-middha*), for this aspect of the Evil One would urge him to loll abed until daybreak. Instead he rises and after refreshing himself, fixes his mind upon his meditation subject which he had put down the night before upon going to sleep. Making the triple prostration to the Three Jewels, quietly intoning, "*Namo tassa...*" and perhaps the Three Refuges, the bhikkhu, his mind rightly directed and guarded, settles into his meditation. The extent to which he is able to fix his mind upon his subject, to prevent the arising of the five hindrances[6] (*pañca nivaraṇa*) and make it more and more one-pointed, will depend of course upon his own progress and ability. The two greatest obstacles which he will encounter will be the sloth-and-torpor already mentioned above, and distraction (*uddhacca*); and between these two his mind is liable to vacillate as Odysseus' boat dodging between Scylla and Charybdis. Being wrecked upon one or the other will be a common experience for him in the beginning. When he finds his mind to be like a fountain bubbling up ideas, fantasies, memories, anticipations and so forth, he sits firmly upon his seat unmoving employing mindfulness (*satipaṭṭhāna*) until the mind becomes quiet. But when sleepiness creeps into his mind and interferes with his bodily posture, then he gets up and practises his meditation while walking up and down. If he is settled for some time in a cave or in the forest, he will have made his walking place (*caṅkamana*) even, and neither too long nor too short. Pacing steadily up and down, sleepiness leaves both mind and body and after some time, with the mind made one-pointed, he may try standing practice. After bringing the mind to a fully quiet and one-pointed condition in this position, he may return to fruitful practice sitting-down.

His practice will be concluded when the cockerels, birds or alarm clock inform him that daybreak is at hand. Then, if he has them, he will offer a candle and a few sticks of incense and, having reverently prostrated, our bhikkhu will intone his morning *pūja* to the Buddha, Dhamma and Sangha. The standard formulas for this, found so many times in the Pali Canon, gain deeper and deeper meanings which become clear to him as his devotion (*saddhā*) deepens and as his practice makes progress. Indeed, when our bhikkhu's calm is well established, the slowly chanted phrases do not disturb at all and they may even be the basis for insight (*vipassanā*). He may supplement these standard chants with others selected according to individual preference or tradition: among the latter will be the meditation chant upon the 32 parts of the body, the Pali of each repulsive part being followed by a translation into his own language, just to make their significance quite clear. This may well be balanced by the meditation chants of loving-kindness (*mettā*), first filling himself with this spirit to get rid of inward conflict and then spreading out his loving-kindness

6. See *The Wheel* No. 26, *The Five Mental Hindrances.*

to other beings.[7] It is also usual to chant the Recollection-before-use of the Four Requisites of a bhikkhu (robes, almsfood, shelter and medicines). The reason for doing this is that the true purposes of the requisites then readily come to mind during the day when he is actually using them. Finally, our bhikkhu chants a sincere wish that the merits which have accrued through this chanting be made over for the good of all beings. Perhaps, being in Thailand, he may use the beautiful, *"Yā devatā santi vihāravāsinī...,"* even more excellent when intoned in the rising and falling *"sarabhañña"* style of chanting. This chant is now beloved in Thailand since, apart from the merits of its meaning and the euphony of style, it was composed by the greatly respected and deeply religious king, Phra Chom Klao, known to the West as King Mongkut (reigned 1851–1868).

Now is the time for our bhikkhu to prepare himself to obtain that medicine which will allay but not cure the greatest disease—hunger. He will see that his bowl is in order, clean and tightly bound in its sling. Then rolling his two upper robes together (*uttarāsaṅga* and *saṅghāṭi*), he is ready to set out. A few remaining possessions may be secured by him in his bag and hung up in some safe place to await his return; however, his three robes should go with him since in ancient days cloth was not always easy to obtain and even now the double outer "cloak" (*saṅghāṭi*) is expensive to make and must thus be guarded carefully.

Many things may happen on his almsround (*piṇḍapāta*), the subject of another booklet in this series.[8] His almsround is not only to collect food for himself since it serves two other important aspects in Buddhist life. On the one hand he gives lay-people a chance to make merit (*puñña*) by their acts of giving, while on the other he trains himself in many good qualities at this time, for as he goes his way collecting food, so he cultivates humility, loving-kindness and compassion, mindfulness and perhaps his meditation subject.

Having taken sufficient food to last the day and knowing at the same time moderation in quantity, the bowl has then to be washed and dried carefully so that it will not rust, returned to its

7. For many of these chants see Wheel No. 54: *The Mirror of the Dhamma.*

8. See Wheel No. 73: *The Blessings of Piṇḍapāta.*

sling and tied to its stand, being then ready to be taken anywhere.

If the bhikkhu is temporarily resident in one place, he will then engage in some walking up and down. This is in accordance with one of the discourses of Lord Buddha which recommends this form of meditation exercise to ward off sleepiness after having taken what is usually a substantial meal. Having thus established himself once again in mindfulness, he may take up any work which has to be done. It is difficult to list all the possible jobs that he may do at this time but readers should realize that he tries to be as self-sufficient as is practicable. Even though he has but few things (see section on "Wandering"), these have to be kept in good repair. For instance, it is important for him to keep his robes mended. Going through jungles, thorns catch and tear and there is always ordinary wear and tear; in fact, the thudong bhikkhu is well aware of the household truth—"A stitch in time saves nine." A thudong bhikkhu's robes are usually well-patched and look as though they have seen long service. Or he may make certain things from bamboo or wood, and many a thudong bhikkhu is very skilful at such manufacture. A bowl-stand is needed or the bamboo shafts of his *crot* (umbrella cum mosquito net) must be replaced, or he may make quantities of toothbrush-and-picks out of bitter wood to give to other bhikkhus. Our thudong bhikkhu may be conversant with the medicinal properties of the herbs, trees and climbers which grow all about him, and compound from these, with honey, milk, red peppers and fruits, medicines for many diseases. Then again, he may manufacture out of tins, wire, and fine white cloth, a collapsible candle-lamp which no wind can blow out; or perhaps he is gifted in the ability to carve and if so he may fashion small pieces of hardwood or ivory into images of Lord Buddha. He may, if he lives in a cave, like to adorn the mighty walls of his residence with drawings of the Buddha all executed in simple colours from the earth round about.

If there were many thudong bhikkhus in this world, they would truly be the bane of modern commerce, which insists that man's happiness depends on having many things and that he buys them in particular and new brands from others. Quite contrary to all this is the thudong bhikkhu, whose ways are directly set against the worldly stream where it is not a multitude of things impermanent which bring happiness—but contentment with little. Thus lightened of the clutter of things he goes more swiftly towards his goal of Enlightenment.

Or, if his *piṇḍapāta* has been long and his food got with difficulty, he may feel bodily tiredness and lie down mindfully. This is usually done by lying on the right side, placing a supporting roll of robes (or pillow if he has one) under the upper half of the body, the head being supported in the palm of the right hand while the elbow of that arm rests on the ground. This was the lying posture recommended by Lord Buddha, and balanced thus, it is not possible to go to sleep while mindfulness will be maintained.

Whenever he feels that his body is light, all tiredness gone, we should picture our thudong bhikkhu sitting down cross-legged upon his sitting-cloth and arousing mindfulness and all the other salutary factors of meditation, and then striving to succeed, or perhaps succeeding in his subject of meditation. He may sit for many hours at a stretch especially if he is skilled, or he may vary his sitting with more walking and even, if his back becomes tired, with lying down. The latter posture can only be practised during the day as sleep is liable to overcome him if he lies down during the hours of darkness. He may also find it helpful in moments of mental stress or when he is experiencing too much of the monkey-mind.

His meditation time will take him round to early evening when, the heat of the day over, it is the usual time to do the sweeping. If he lives in a meditation-vihāra there may be large areas to sweep. If in a hut in the forest, then only his hut and its surroundings. But this work is quite unnecessary for one who is living under his *crot* wherever he has pitched it and he will probably not have a broom anyway. General mindfulness at this time is accompanied by the "sweeping reflection": Just as this broom is sweeping away dust, so may this meditation practice sweep away the defilements (*kilesa*). There are some other excellencies to sweeping: for instance, it is a chance to test the strength of the calm (*samatha*) which has been developed mostly in the sitting posture. Also it is good exercise for the body after sitting still most of the day. Our, bhikkhu does his sweeping rhythmically and silently.

Next comes the time for bathing, perhaps in a forest pool or river. Taking his bathing-cloth our thudong bhikkhu goes—not with the worldly idea of enjoying the water but bearing in mind an aspect of his body's repulsiveness which makes it necessary to bathe. He reflects: Having got this body through craving (*taṇhā*), one has daily to wipe off the sweat which oozes out of it, and the dirt which sticks to it, otherwise it would quickly become evil-smelling and unbearable both to oneself and to others. This also applies to his robes, which require washing frequently, while at this time he may occasionally have to dye his robes.

Returning, still bearing his meditation subject in mind if he is able, there may be some allowable drink awaiting him at his abode to refresh him further. *Nains* (novices) are expert at preparing these from jungle fruits adding sugar or honey, while if hunger disturbs him much, one of the bitter fruits allowed in the Vinaya may be taken with salt, sugar and perhaps some chilli. Before he takes these, he will reflect carefully upon the real reason for doing so, according to the passage repeated in his morning *pūja*.

If we were watching him, we should soon notice the care that he takes so that no small creatures come to destruction. Before he pours out his drink, he inspects the glass to see whether ants or other insects are inside. If there are, he removes them very gently to a safe place. In lifting the glass and putting it down, he takes the same care and even when a mosquito alights on his body, it is not squashed but blown away, for even the smallest creatures must not come to death either through his intention or through negligence. Harmlessness (*ahiṃsa*) has for him many practical applications.

The time has come now for his evening meditation and taking his seat refreshed in body, he makes further endeavours in governing the mind. Perhaps before he begins, Lord Buddha's oft-repeated exhortation comes to mind: "What a master can do for his disciples, wishing them well, out of compassion and sympathy, that I have done for you. Here, O bhikkhus, are the roots of trees and secluded places. Practise meditation, O bhikkhus! Be not negligent lest you regret it later! This is my exhortation to you." And so we may imagine him sitting long into the night, as long in fact, as he can keep off sleepiness. When this becomes too pressing, he lights a candle and some incense and begins his night chanting. If he knows much Pali, this may continue for a long while softly and steadily proceeding with that euphony peculiar to this ancient language. It is recorded in commentarial stories that the gods came to listen to the Pali chanting of those bhikkhus living in wild places, who had pure hearts.

At last finishing, after again making over all merits for beings' happiness (for one should not have greed even for merit), he lies down mindfully bearing in mind his meditation subject and the necessity of arising early to proceed with his practice.

The Hand of Death

> "Ere long, alas, will this body lie upon the earth, unheeded and lifeless, even as a useless log."
>
> —Dhp 41

Living in sylvan solitudes is not always, alas, ideal, for *dukkha* must show its fangs from time to time to remind our bhikkhu, if indeed he needs reminding, that it is in a world subject to birth and death that he lives. Having got himself into the condition of being born, he and all other beings will surely die.

This lesson he learned from close acquaintance, for he recently lost a good companion. He was an intelligent young man recently ordained as a *nain*, one who would have been well capable of understanding the Dhamma. He was able to live the thudong life and to enjoy it to his profit—a not inconsiderable combination of factors.

His life ended suddenly when he was about twenty years old, for he fell over a forty-foot cliff and dashed his brains upon the rocks below. Our bhikkhu was the first person to reach the *nain* after having raced down a circuitous path. Little enough could he do. Telling another *nain* to run into the nearest village for a stretcher, he knelt beside his only other companion on the rocky hill where they lived. The *nain's* breathing still functioned but in great, irregular gasps. Blood, already clotted, oozed from the sundered skull and trickled from many other cuts and bruises upon the body, arms and legs. Death was near at hand.

Taking a rosary from his bag, the bhikkhu opened one of the *nain's* hands and placed it there. It would thus act as a skilful object of touch (*phassārammaṇa*), if the *nain's* touch-consciousness still functioned. After sprinkling him with cooling water, he began to intone the suttas (discourses) for protection (*paritta*). This he did so that there would also be a skilful sound-object (*saddārammaṇa*) upon which the *nain's* death-consciousness (*cuti-citta*) could be concentrated. Though he tried to chant steadily and evenly, to give confidence to the dying *nain*—if indeed he heard him—his voice was not without trembling.

The minutes drew on and after the opening salutation of "Namo tassa...," the *Karaṇīyametta Sutta* (on loving-kindness), the *Mahā-maṅgala Sutta* (on the greatest blessings), and the *Ratana Sutta* followed each other.[9] As the closing words of the last sutta: "*saṅghaṃ namassāma, suvatthi hotu*" (to the Sangha let us bow: may bliss abound!)—as these words were softly chanted upon the shimmering air, a last breath arose and gaspingly fell—and the body was still. His good companion had passed on according to his kamma and as the bhikkhu earnestly vowed: "May it truly be to a better state of affairs than this!" After that, if only to relieve his own mind—and who knows, perhaps his erstwhile friend could still hear him in his new condition—he intoned further the *Buddha-jayamaṅgala* stanzas with their refrain of: "By the power of this (truth) may you be endowed with victory and blessings."

It is widely believed in Buddhist lands that merits (*puñña*) are transferable, providing that one has a compassion deep enough with others and a wisdom grown great. For the well-faring of the dead *nain*, his friend made over to him all and any merits which he might have accumulated, including those gathered by the recitation of these hallowed scriptures.

* * *

We take up the story again three days later when bhikkhus have gathered for reciting the traditional chants for the dead. The father of the dead *nain* has also arrived. The chanting is solemn indeed and rolls on sonorously through the tropic night, spreading its peaceful sound far beyond the range of the pressure lamps which light up but a small circle in the bamboo forest. Seated upon mats covering the ground lay-people listen reverentially with joined palms (*añjali*), while the chanting proceeds. Our bhikkhu, seated with others upon some other mats, concentrates all his attention upon the chanting, making it proceed not from the throat but

9. For these discourses, see Wheel No. 54: *The Mirror of the Dhamma.*

deep down from the heart.

At its conclusion, there is some informal talk upon Dhamma especially regarding death and kamma, and then more general conversation opens concerning what arrangements should be made. A Westerner might notice, if one had been present, that, although this ceremony roughly corresponded to a funeral service, no one was weeping or even looking particularly sad—and certainly not the father of the late *nain*. Whatever tears there had been over his death, they were long since over and quickly stopped by such Buddhist recollections as the fact that rebirth takes place according to kamma and that nothing of this can be changed by weeping. And again, the injunction to live in the present without attachment to the past, which is irreclaimably gone. And the reflection that rebirth may already be accomplished and (it is always sincerely hoped) be superior in happiness to this state; would it not be strange to be miserable because someone else was now more happy than he was in this life? Putting aside all self-pity, which makes for most of the tears at death, a good Buddhist concentrates upon the situation *now* and sees what can best be accomplished in the present.

The conversation has turned to the customary presentation, in this case by the father, of robes (*cīvara*) upon the death of a relative. Sometimes ready-made robes are laid upon the coffin and received by bhikkhus as *paṃsukūla* (intentionally cast-off cloth); at other times, white cloth is similarly given to be made up into robes. The strictest practice and one which is followed by a few thudong bhikkhus is to take cloth which has been used as a corpse-wrapping and make this into robes—this is a practice from the time of Lord Buddha and such robes may truly be called "rag-robes."[10] Our bhikkhu wishes to benefit from the present circumstances so as to obtain such a robe. The father of the dead *nain* has already bought about twenty yards of white cloth for *paṃsukūla* robes. This has then to be inserted into the coffin and then to be extracted at the time of burning. Later, our bhikkhu will cut it up and sew it to make the traditional patchwork pattern and the robes that he makes from this cloth will ever remind him

10. *Paṃsukulik'aṅga* (refuse-rag-wearer's) practice, the first *dhutaṅga*—see Preface.

of death, by stains and smell for some time and for longer by the memory of how they were obtained.

The next day, food being finished, our bhikkhu turns his attention to the large coffin which rests under some trees. Candles and incense, the Buddhist symbols respectively of Enlightenment and of the perfume of strict morality (*sīla*), are burning round about. As he approaches the coffin, the smell grows stronger—îthe peculiarly repulsive smell of a human body's decay, which spreads its sweetly sickening odours for many yards about. It is not without some apprehension of what he will see upon raising the lid that he proceeds, for he has read the descriptions of bodily decay as used for meditation purposes but reading does not satisfy him, the bhikkhu wishes to see for himself.

Lifting the lid, he gazes within and is immediately and deeply impressed that these descriptions as found for instance in the *Satipaṭṭhāna Sutta*,[11] are but poor substitutes for beholding the real thing. His companion in life was a handsome young man, even with his hair shaved off: this body which lay before him was quite as hideous as temple wall-paintings sometimes show and emphasized for him that words are quite inadequate for portraying such sights.

So, the young *nain* with unblemished body and pleasing face died but three days before and now what does our bhikkhu perceive? His companion is certainly not there! This puffed, distorted, oozing mass, bluish in colour, is not the *nain* he knew! Nothing resembles him. Three days have sufficed to change everything. Gaining this insight and the perception of impurity in even living bodies—what to speak of dead ones—he continues with the work he has set out to do. The body is already covered by the stained robes of the late *nain* and the white cloth is laid over this. Having completed his work, he reseals the coffin to await the time of cremation. As the lid is replaced so the stench grows less but the whole experience has burned itself deep into his mind and will not lessen. Indeed, he may develop it into a fruitful meditation when he sees with inward sight his *own* body not only as liable to such a condition but actually experiences the body (not then "his" body) as *being* in such a state.

11. See Wheel No. 19: *The Foundations of Mindfulness.*

Climbing back to his dwelling high above the forest, he muses: Where such a terrible sight as this can be found so soon originating from apparently pleasing conditions—where such and worse can be found—what sort of world is this? Who will waste their lives after such a perception? Who will longer be deluded by the sugar-coating of the world's sense-attractions after seeing thus? Will they not rather sense the bitter pill beneath? Is this not the time to turn away from those conditions giving rise to this bitterness? Is it not the time to devote oneself to that Dhamma which is "lovely at its beginning, lovely in its middle course, and lovely at its ending"? Some such thoughts as these, our bhikkhu thinks.

For those who can do more, this is the time to join those millions who have gone forth like our bhikkhu with robes and bowl, rejecting all that the world values, and seeking to reject both ignorance and craving *(avijjā-taṇhā)*, those twin conditions for bitterness, to win in the Dispensation of the Conqueror, that Enlightenment which he also won. So urges the Enlightened One:

"Shed thou householder's finery,
As coral tree its leaves in fall:
And going forth in yellow clad,
Fare lonely as rhinoceros.

And rid of passion, error, hate,
The fetters having snapped in twain
Fearless when as life ebbs away
Fare lonely as rhinoceros."

Thudong Abodes

> "The bhikkhu who has retired to a solitary abode and has calmed his mind and who comprehends the Dhamma with insight—in him there arises a delight that transcends all human delight."
>
> —Dhp 373

Our bhikkhu will live anywhere that is conducive to his practice of meditation and to winning insight, but certain types of abode are generally more suitable for him than others.

From ancient times a favourite dwelling-place of the thudong bhikkhu has been a cave; indeed this is really the best environment, providing that a suitable one can be found. Not all are good for meditation and our bhikkhu upon arriving at a cave new to him would inspect it with the following points in mind.

People are very fond of making caves into shrines—and some of these are very beautiful with hundreds or thousands of Buddha-figures of different sizes ranged about the cave, sitting on blocks of stone and stalagmite near to the floor and gazing down compassionately from apparently inaccessible niches near the lofty roof. Such caves and others more rustic acquire fame as places of pilgrimage in proportion to their beauty and ease of approach. Now, if our bhikkhu were to make his sitting place in some such cave, he would surely be disturbed by the people visiting the shrine. Apart from the noise that they make, some would certainly approach him, perhaps trying to engage him in ordinary conversation, or coming to ask for charms or blessings, since popular ideas of "holiness" are rather less exacting or rather more vague than the freedom from the fetters (*saṃyojana*) which mark a Noble One (*ariya*) according to the Pali Canon. Therefore, if he does not wish for such interruptions, not yet wanting even to instruct in Dhamma, much less to engage in worldly matters, he will avoid all such caves.

Apart from people, bats are also fond of caves in the dark depths of which they live in their thousands. They also make noises, cheeping and swishing about, but their noises are much less objectionable than is the smell of their dung. This is very good for growing plants but less agreeable to a meditator's nose.

Usually, they will not live near to the cave entrance, especially if the sun comes in and so, other conditions being favourable, our bhikkhu may live there.

Other conditions include sound and heat. In this noisy age, rackety iron boxes of various shapes travel over land, water and through the air and their sound is surprisingly hard to escape from. It is understandable therefore that caves adjacent to airfields, motorways or railways will also be avoided.

The great advantage of a cave in a tropical country is its equable temperature. Cool even on the hottest days of the hot season, and warm in the coldest nights of the cold weather, it is very favourable for a meditating bhikkhu. Caves which have wide openings to the south or west are therefore less suitable for the hot weather. Other inconveniences to consider are the danger of falling rocks and the presence of carbon dioxide. Also, it sometimes happens that earth godlings (*bhumma-devata*) take up their residence in caves and not all of them will welcome a bhikkhu staying there as this will interfere with their pleasures. Indeed, there are stories of bhikkhus being evicted by spirits but there is at least one instance of an experienced bhikkhu (lately a famous meditation teacher in this country) who sat night after night in a cave defeating all the efforts of godlings to oust him. Our bhikkhu, if he is wise, seeks for the protection of any gods there abiding when he first arrives at a cave. With gods giving their blessing to his efforts, meditation certainly becomes easier; while, if the opposite should occur, it may be impossible.

Finally, a consideration of great importance: its distance from the nearest village. As most thudong bhikkhus go to collect alms every day and as bhikkhus are not allowed to store food, so a village must be within walking distance. How far this is depends upon the vigour and age of our bhikkhu. Half a mile or a mile's distance is desirable in any case being thus beyond village noises but it does happen that a cave otherwise ideal may be too far from the village for the bhikkhu to walk there and back. In this case villagers will help the bhikkhu by taking their food out half-way.

He may find that living in a cave is a little eerie at first and should any "fear, trembling or hair-raising" take place, no doubt he will at least remember the *Metta Sutta* (Lord Buddha's discourse on loving-kindness). Also well-fitted for recitation at such a time is the *Discourse on the Flags* (*Dhajagga Sutta*), where the medicines recommended for fear are the Recollections of the Buddha, Dhamma and Sangha. If our bhikkhu is still better read in the Pali Canon, he will remember the *Discourse on Fear and Dread* (*Bhayabherava Sutta* in *Majjhima Nikāya*), where Lord Buddha describes the way in which he trained himself to be mindful of fear while he was yet a Bodhisatta (Wisdom-being striving for Buddhahood).

What sort of picture do we get of our bhikkhu in his cave? If he is staying long he will probably have built himself a bamboo or wooden pallet above which will hang his *crot*. To one side somewhere hang his bag and candle-lamp. Near to him will be a water flask and, if it is dark, possibly a torch. His bowl is placed securely on a flat rock while any robes which he is not using are folded up neatly upon his pallet. He is sitting quietly facing the direction of his head when lying down.[12] If one were to watch intently, it would be difficult to detect even breath movements in his body, swathed as it is in rather shabby patched robes of faded ochre. Above him, the roof vaults in great arches and mysterious hollows half-lit by the dim light. Steady and distant is the dripping of water which makes through long ages great columns slowly joining roof and floor. Sunlight filters through a leafy screen for a few minutes and is gone and perhaps a bee drones in but finding little of interest soon finds its way out. All is very still, very silent.

* * *

He who sits alone, sleeps alone, walks alone,
who is strenuous and subdues himself alone,
will find delight in the solitude of the forest.[13]

—Dhp 305

Caves are by far the best abode but they, especially ideal ones, are rare so that we should go on to describe something of the more common "home" of thudong bhikkhus—the forest.

---

12. Because if he has a small Buddha-figure or Dhamma-book, it will be placed respectfully near to his head.

13. This verse summarizes the eighth *dhutaṅga* practice (*āraññik'aṅga*)—see Preface.

The advantages of dwelling in the forest are several. First, there is much of it in many Buddhist countries. Then, as it is the sort of place where most men do not like to live (except they are secure and comfortable in a strong house), the thudong bhikkhu is not likely to be disturbed, not at any rate by his fellow men. Like other thudong abodes, it conduces to contentment with little; also, it makes very necessary the development of *mettā* or loving-kindness.[14]

Besides advantages, there are quite a number of possible hindrances to practise while forest-dwelling. For instance, *mettā* is made rather essential by the presence of all sorts of potentially antipathetic creatures, the most dangerous of which are snakes. This is certainly emphasized in the Pali canon by the presence of a special chant, the *Khanda Paritta*, in which the person chanting stresses that he has *mettā* towards and does no harm to all creatures including four species of snakes.

There is a little story to illustrate this. An old Buddhist nun was living in a small hut close to the jungle. Her hut had one doorway and she usually sat on the bamboo floor for meditation against the opposite wall. She was quite accustomed to see the tails of large lizards appear out of the thatch overhead where they lived. Occasionally they fell out but being quite harmless, they would scamper away quickly. One day, hearing such a bump on her floor, she opened her eyes but instead of seeing a lizard, there was an angry snake of the most poisonous species coiling and uncoiling itself. Instantly recollecting the meditation on *mettā*, she pervaded herself and the whole hut with this spirit. The snake, which lay between her and the door and had been threatening to strike her, now quietly coiled up and after a few minutes slithered out of the doorway. This anecdote illustrates quite a common occurrence for one dwelling in the jungle: how a meditator can be brought into close proximity with the untamed animal world. Is it necessary to stress further the value of *mettā* in such surroundings?

While the power of Lord Buddha's *mettā* was so great that he could calm the rutting wild elephant Nalagiri, there have been many thudong bhikkhus up to modern times who have lived continuously in the forest developing the *Brahma-vihāras*[15] (the

14. See Wheel No. 7: *The Practice of Loving-kindness.*

15. See Wheel No. 6: *The Four Sublime States.*

Divine Abidings in loving-kindness, compassion, sympathetic joy and equanimity), and with whom forest animals became friends. For the man who has love—and no fear because no hatred—of other creatures, those creatures will not fear him. In this connection there are a number of Jātaka stories which tell of the Bodhisatta's life in the forest when, living in a hermitage, all manner of animals became his companions.

Still, there do seem to be some creatures which do not respond so well to *mettā* and therefore, returning to the case of our thudong bhikkhu, he will be wise not to spread his sitting cloth over the entrance to an ants' nest, nor to pitch his *crot* near places where stagnant water lies. Regarding the latter, he would be courting the attention of vast numbers of hungry mosquitoes. The *crot* is an effective protection against these but it can be hot inside while cooler air blows without. So if a place can be found fairly free of mosquitoes, at least during the day, our bhikkhu will abide more happily. As to ants, they come in all shapes and colours and a good range of sizes and mill about everywhere and our bhikkhu knows that it is safe to assume that all bite, so it is well to stay away from their roads, tunnels and doorways. A few drops of paraffin sprinkled round his sitting-cloth will ensure that he is fairly secure against invasion.

Unless the forest is really ancient with dense shade, our bhikkhu will experience extremes of heat and cold unknown to the cave-dweller. In the hot season the sun blazes down from out of the cloudless sky overhead and the small shade of his *crot* will be insufficient. Even under a tree, at least in open forest, hot winds are liable to blow and make life less pleasant.[16] The conditions in a densely-shaded rainforest rather resemble cave-dwelling but there is an increase of biting life to reckon with as well as the rainfall.

Forest-dwelling is only possible for the thudong bhikkhu all the year round if he has a small hut to supplement the protection of his *crot*.[17] During the three months of the Rains Retreat (*Vassa*—approximately July to September), he must in any case dwell with

16. The practice of the ninth *dhutaṅga* (*rukkha mulik'aṅga*) is therefore possible at some places and times. See Preface.

17. Thus limiting the practice of the tenth *dhutaṅga*, (*abbhokāsik'aṅga* open-air-dweller's) practice, to the dry season and cool places: see Preface.

a roof over his head. It is quite common for thudong bhikkhus to have a small wood and bamboo hut built by a supporter in some favourable place in the forest and to dwell there either alone or with a *nain* or boy to assist him.

Forest life is very far from silent, for, quite apart from the occasional noises of the larger animals, smaller ones, especially insects, keep up an almost continuous racket. Cicada and grasshopper-like creatures, although small, manage to produce incredible volumes of sound sometimes resembling that of railway trains! The only times when they are silent is when presumably they are sleeping. This is during the heat of midday and afternoon and during the middle watch of the night. Unfortunately this quietness coincides with the times when human beings also are most inclined to sleep.

However, forest conditions vary very much and our bhikkhu will not find all the unfavourable conditions together, but since this world is one level of saṃsāra, there are bound to be one or more flies in the ointment.

We may think of him on a moonlit night in the hot weather. A cooling wind blows, stirring the trees many of which are leafless, while filling the air with the fragrance of some tree's blossoms. A little bamboo hut stands raised upon wooden legs and upon its open platform a boy sleeps. The bhikkhu paces up and down his walk which is some thirty feet long and made under tall trees. The dark end of it is lit by his candle-lamp hanging from a tree while the moon lights up the rest. Light is necessary since thick, tubular millipedes have their homes on either side of his walk and also like to wander upon its smooth and freshly-swept surface.

Our bhikkhu finishes his walking and contemplatively returns to his hut. Mounting the bamboo ladder to the platform, he stops before the door to his tiny room. Over the door is fixed a polished wooden board upon which the following words are cut and coloured:

Handa dāni bhikkhave, āmantayāmi vo:
Vayadhammā saṅkhārā, appamādena sampādetha'ti.

"Pay attention, O bhikkhus, I exhort you:
Going to destruction are all compounded things,

With heedfulness make an effort!"

These are the last recorded words of Lord Buddha, his final exhortation to the thudong bhikkhus of those days.[18]

For our thudong bhikkhu, now they not only have the significance of being the last instructions, since his own practice—and perhaps realization—accord well with them.

> "Should one find a sagacious man who points out faults and reproves, as if indicating a hidden treasure, let one associate with such a wise person. It is always better and never worse for him who cultivates the acquaintance of such a one.
>
> "Let him admonish, instruct and shield one from evil; a dear one is he to the good, detestable to the wicked."
>
> —Dhp 76-77

The greatest teachers of the thudong tradition have very often wandered all their lives, never settling down long in any one place except for the annual Rains Retreat, or when extreme old age forced them to do so. Some have never founded vihāras (monastic residences), leaving this to those of their disciples who had an aptitude for such work.

Our bhikkhu, however, especially if he still requires guidance, may live in a thudong vihāra. This will be rather different from the ordinary run of vihāras where bhikkhus usually live two or three together in large huts (*kuṭi*), or even if they live singly, their residences will be crowded closely together being built about an open hall (*sāla*). A thudong vihāra is distinguished by having the huts set so that from one, another cannot be seen. This is not difficult as wood, bamboo and thatch blend easily into the jungle. In each hut, one bhikkhu lives and orders his time according to his practice and ability.

Our bhikkhu will not often meet others resident there—once or twice a day at most. The first time is when all gather in the hall to prepare themselves for *piṇḍapāta*, while the second may be in the evening when some fruit drink is served. At this time also, the venerable teacher of meditation may give some instruction as he sees fit. General instructions, for instance upon matters of

18. See Wheel No. 67–69, p. 75

Vinaya (monastic discipline), will be given to the community of resident bhikkhus every Holy Day (*uposatha*—the full and half moon days) after the recitation of the *Pātimokkha* (the bhikkhus' Fundamental Precepts).

If our bhikkhu wishes for individual instruction in some matter, he will approach his teacher after the evening instruction has been given and, after saluting him with the triple prostration, he will question him respectfully. If we were present in the hall, pillared with roughly shaped tree trunks and lit by candles burning before the gilded and painted shrine of Lord Buddha, we should notice the great respect which he pays to his teacher. He sits in a respectful position never pointing his feet towards the teacher and he always raises his joined palms (*añjali*) when speaking to the teacher, while, when the latter speaks to him, he places them clasped together in his lap and listens attentively. Our bhikkhu's teacher is for him one who has experienced some degree of the Dhamma in his own heart and not merely read about it out of books. Such teachers are therefore accorded great veneration and anyone going to such a teacher, yet not making the usual salutations, would probably be regarded as being difficult to teach—because of the presence of strong conceit.[19]

In some thudong vihāras, usually those inclined to less strict observance, there is communal meditation and *pūja* in the morning before *piṇḍapāta* and again in the evening. Some teachers favour this while others prefer their disciples to lead a more solitary life. Both may be valuable to our bhikkhu according to his character and progress.

Upon *uposatha*-nights it is also a feature in some thudong vihāras, to chant Lord Buddha's discourses all through the night, the bhikkhus not sleeping.[20] This may be interspersed with some instructions from the meditation master and perhaps by the individual practice of walking. Where practice already goes deep, this chanting, slow and rhythmic, may well be an aid to attainment in meditation.

---

19. For an interesting case of this in ancient times see the "*Sutra of Hui Neng* (*Wei Lang*) and the master's encounter there with Bhikkhu Fa-Ta.

20. This is a modification of the thirteenth *dhutaṅga* (*nesajjik'aṅga*—the Sitter's Practice). See also Preface.

Regarding this, there was once a twelve-year-old boy who sat down one evening with other pious lay-people who were practising meditation while the bhikkhus chanted. He knew nothing about how to practise, nor had he ever sat in meditation posture before. But a very great meditation-master lived there at that time and was leading the bhikkhus in chanting. These factors all combining led that boy through successive stages of mental concentration until he reached complete meditation (*appanā samādhi*). He was still sitting rapt in stillness when the bhikkhus prepared to go collecting *piṇḍapāta*. The meditation-master upon seeing him, decided, not unnaturally, that the boy would make a good disciple. After rousing him, and giving him the precepts, the boy lived in that vihāra learning the way from his master.

One bhikkhu, well-practised in meditation, was famous for the easy control he had over his body. Sitting down in the temple at eight o'clock upon *uposatha*-nights, he would not even find it necessary to change his posture until six o'clock the next morning. He never got up from his seat, his gaze never wandered anywhere, he just concentrated upon chanting from the heart, being completely absorbed in this.

Our bhikkhu will be encouraged by his teacher to live with him until such times as the latter feels that he has sufficient knowledge of the Dhamma and strong enough meditation to go off on his own, to practise in cave or forest. There are disciples who like to stay with their teachers until death parts them. There are others who want to go off quickly and practise alone. It sometime happens that the latter experience one of the ecstatic absorptions (*jhāna*) and conclude from this, since they lack sufficient Dhamma-knowledge and the guidance of their teacher, that they have won a noble (*ariya*) attainment. Sometimes such bhikkhus proclaim this out of ignorance and gain quite a following; however, their fame soon dwindles for one cannot pretend, intentionally or otherwise, to be an arahant (an accomplished sage), or even to have reached one of the lower stages of ariyan attainment.

A famous teacher once had a pupil who esteemed himself to be an arahant but the former knew that he was not so but that his mind was really overcome by the perversions (*vipallāsa*). Now this teacher had another pupil who, although he could neither read nor write, had such experience of Dhamma that many consider that he was really an arahant. He lived alone in a cave and seldom spoke and when he did so, he uttered only words of Dhamma, never mere pleasantries. The famous teacher was in the habit of sending any of his pupils who became deluded to this great pupil, of whom he thought very highly. So he sent his deluded disciple to him. The first and only words which the great pupil spoke to the deluded one were: "Sit here." The former gave the latter no instruction; he only sat in meditation with him day and night only rarely breaking off for the barest necessities. After two weeks of this rigorous treatment, the deluded one at least gained the insight that he was not after all an arahant and then returned to live with his teacher. In this way he was cured of this manifestation of the perverted mind (*vipallāsacitta*).

Living in a monastery, at least for some time, will enable the thudong bhikkhu to make his meditation practice grow strongly and that "fear, trembling and hair-raising," which he might easily experience in other more remote surroundings, are less likely to arise there. He has the guidance of the Good Friend (*kalyāṇa-mitta,* as the meditation teacher is called), and the companionship of the good, that is of fellow-bhikkhus and *nains* who are likewise striving to accomplish the goal of complete liberation of the mind. In this way he has the best possible environment for progress in his meditation and may stay with his teacher for many years. This is particularly true if the pupil finds just the right teacher who can instruct him in the right way to go. For just as pupils vary as to the proportions of differing defilements in their characters, so teachers vary with regard to different attainments and ability.

> "Just as a storm cannot prevail against a rocky mountain, so Māra can never overpower one who lives devoted to the meditations on impurity (of the body), who is controlled in senses, moderate in eating and endowed with faith and earnest effort."
>
> —Dhp 8

* * *

What can we say of other bhikkhu abodes? Generally the thudong bhikkhu looks with disfavour upon living on a mountain—unless, that is, there happens to be a village near and at approximately the same altitude. Our bhikkhu knows that his bowlful of rice is quite heavy enough, especially after a long walk, without having to haul it up a mountain path. Whenever bhikkhus ceased to rely on *piṇḍapāta*, as for instance in China, they were able to live upon mountain heights in peace and solitude.

Among abodes recommended in the *Path of Purification* is the charnel-field or bone yard. This is said to be an excellent abode for greed (*lobha*) characters. It appears to have been a common custom in ancient India to take corpses to a special part of the forest and to leave them there to go to their dissolution. Thus a thudong bhikkhu lighting upon such a place might be able to see all the various stages of decay of the body—as they are described in detail in the above work.[21] Such was, of course, an unforgettable lesson upon the fate of his own body.

Nowadays, in this country, boneyards like this cannot be found, for burning the body sooner or later has taken the place of the natural process of its return to the component elements. Therefore it is now almost impossible to live in this environment and the best that can be done is to dwell near a burning ground. Usually there will not be much of bones remaining, only piles of ashes; still there is for many the fear of spirits (*peta*) to overcome. It is commonly assumed that such a birth follows a human one and that the hungry ghost or spirit lurks about near to its former body, sometimes with evil intent while others are supposed to be more kindly disposed. This may sometimes happen when peta-birth actually follows the human one because of peta-like kamma, but popular belief assumes that this is invariable.

However this may be, a certain amount of caution is required before dwelling in such a place. If our bhikkhu is of imaginative disposition, he must have his imagination well under control before dwelling in a burning-ground. An uncontrolled imagination coupled with loneliness, the natural noises of the night and the dimly lighted surroundings can result in an unbalanced mind.

A good many years ago now, there was a *nain* recently ordained and fifteen years of age. His meditation master sent him

21. See Ch. VI, "Foulness as a Meditation Subject." This is also *susānik'aṅga* (Charnel-ground-dweller's) practice, the eleventh *dhutaṅga*. See Preface.

to dwell overnight in the local burning-ground-cum-graveyard which was well out of the village, in the jungle. Not knowing that it is proper to inspect such a place in full daylight first, noting how all the rocks, trees, tombs, etc., are placed—he arrived there only at dusk. After laying a cloth to sit upon and hanging up his *crot*, he began to look around. Finding a suitable place to walk up and down, he decided to begin his meditations in this way. As he was turning round, at one end, out of the corner of his eye, he saw a great black phantom looming up, its jagged arms outstretched, the claw-like fingers ready to seize him. In fear and trembling he continued his walking and so great was his terror of the unknown "thing" that he did not sit or lie down all that night but walked and stood meditating (with a glance every so often to see that "it" had not moved). When dawn came, the "thing" became less black and menacing, slowly resolving itself into a stricken tree-trunk!

As custom has changed so much that the boneyard is no longer to be found, there was in this country many years ago a senior bhikkhu who decided to remedy this lack. This teacher dwelt in a little vihāra in a patch of woodland outside a small town and near the old capital of Ayuthiya. Very few bhikkhus stayed in his vihāra for after they had seen what they came to see, he sent them away to practise on their own. And what did they see?

This teacher had constructed a flower garden and all round it he had built a high wall pierced by only one door and that was padlocked. The flowers that grew in this garden were very special ones, special bhikkhu flowers. The flowers of lay men are of gorgeous colours, entrancing shapes and subtle perfumes but these flowers for bhikkhus, although they also had their colours, shapes and perfumes, were rather different. Inside the garden there were constructed a number of open troughs covered by glass frames from one end of which rose a long pipe. When a man died in the town, the teacher would go and personally carry away the body, slinging it over his shoulder. Taking it to his garden he would lay it in a trough and cover it with a frame.

When a bhikkhu desiring a subject of meditation came to him, he would be told by the teacher that he only instructed in the Cemetery Contemplations. At first the teacher would go with him into the garden during daylight and let him select a suitable "flower" for his meditations. Then he let the bhikkhu go in there alone, to fix the subject in his mind. Finally, he was permitted to go in at night and spend the hours of darkness meditating upon his "flower." Then having settled the meditation subject firmly in his mind, the teacher would tell the bhikkhu to go and to meditate alone. Before he went, he would receive instructions upon a further aspect of the meditation which emphasized that it was not a body "out there" which was to be seen, even in the mind. It was his own body which had to be seen with insight as bloated, festering, or just dry bones, according to the stage of decay selected. Thus were bhikkhus of that time enabled to free themselves from the deluded identification of this body as being "myself" or as "mine"—by the special exertions of this teacher.

Every teacher, as we mentioned before, has his own characteristic ways, both of instruction and of conduct. If our bhikkhu went to a certain teacher, a disciple of a yet more famous master, he would have to put forth energy if he wished to live with him. This teacher lived in a little ramshackle hut—he would not let lay-people build him anything else—in a small jungle vihāra and was about eighty-five years old. It was his practise to begin his working day at five o'clock when he would vigorously start to sweep the vihāra grounds. Then, when it was light, he went out to collect food. Returning, he ate a single meal of small quantity and for the rest of the day drank only water. Besides the two normal *pūjas*, he made a third one in the middle of the night. To do this, he slept from ten o'clock until midnight—and never used a mosquito net—and then got up for *pūja*, after which he slept again for another two hours. Arising vigorous, he would sit in meditation until the sweeping time. His appearance was hale and it appeared that he might very well carry on with his way of life for another twenty years at least!

Stories about teachers are endless and this short account could never contain a tithe of them. So we must let these few suffice as examples and close this section on thudong abodes.

Wandering

"Those who exert themselves and are mindful, delight not in any abode. They are like swans that abandon their like, leaving home after home behind."

—Dhp 91

Today, when it is possible to go quickly everywhere by some conveyance or other, why wander? What is the purpose of the thudong bhikkhu who, alone or with one or two companions, prefers to go his way on foot? There are quite a lot of reasons why wandering in this manner is preferred. For example, the wanderer goes quietly and at whatever speed he wishes. He is not brought into contact with others who might disturb his contemplative way and he may stay at a place just as long as it pleases him—and leave it when he wishes. Also, he is uninvolved with other people, no arrangements has he to make for them while he gives trouble to none. In fact, his is the way of freedom. Then again, he reflects that this way of travel was used by his great Master in the forty-five years of his teaching in India and has been that of countless other bhikkhus seeking Enlightenment. The modern ways of travelling are good for getting to places quickly but not so good for gaining Enlightenment. There is distraction enough in the mind without churning it up still further—some such thoughts he thinks.

Reasons for wandering are also rather various and we are only concerned with those motivated by the search for Enlightenment. The real purposes are threefold: to be able to dwell in solitary places for meditation; to visit meditation-masters who often stay far into the country or forest; or to go on pilgrimage to some famous shrine.

While the first and second have already been touched upon, the third needs a few more words. By pilgrimage to a shrine is meant the desire that arises in some bhikkhu who has taken to thudong life, to visit and make his *pūja* at a great stupa (reliquary monument) where are enshrined some remains of Lord Buddha or the arahants. Or perhaps to go to some famous temple where an exceptionally beautiful image of the Enlightened One is enshrined. All this he does with the idea that merit is gained from such actions and indeed, if our thudong bhikkhu, or anyone else, goes on such pilgrimages single-mindedly and in deep devotion, the results for his own development in the Dhamma are bound to be fruitful.

If he wanders every day, especially if the weather is hot, the way rough or both, his power of meditation must be very strong indeed, or it will suffer from the impact of these external conditions. Tiredness of the body after walking only four or five hours can be a great obstacle in the way of peaceful practice. Therefore, either he will walk one day and then finding a suitable place, stop there for three or four days, or, if he wishes to reach a definite place by a certain time, then he puts by his practice of mental calm (*samatha*) and takes up the full-time application of mindfulness (*Satipaṭṭhāna*) in its various aspects.[22]

Besides the necessity of strong *samādhi*, it is quite sure that he must have a strong body able to endure blazing sun, heat, sweat, rough ways, insects and cuts and bruises. These latter, together with blisters, are not infrequent in thudong life and can make his way very difficult. If he goes without sandals, rocks will cut and thorns pierce his feet, or going with them, the feet must be very hard or they will surely be chapped.

Strength of body is required so that he can carry comfortably his few essentials. What does a wandering thudong bhikkhu carry? First of all, there are his eight essentials which are a bhikkhu's only possessions. They are: three robes (one waist-cloth, one upper robe and one double robe),[23] a bowl (usually of thin malleable iron with a brass cover), a waist-band to secure the waist-cloth, a needle and thread, razor (of cut-throat pattern), and lastly, a water-strainer. These items he must take with him or if he loses any of them, they should be made good as soon as possible. In the thudong life, all these things have their relevance—including the water-strainer which is a very important piece of equipment.

Besides these, there will be certain other things which he is sure to have: a water flask or kettle, his *crot*, a sitting cloth

22. For these see: Wheel No. 60: *The Satipaṭṭhāna Sutta and Its Applications* and *The Heart of Buddhist Meditation*, Nanaponika Thera, Rider and Co., London.

23. Having only three robes is the *ticīvarik'aṅga* (triple-robe-wearer's) practice—the second *dhutaṅga*; see Preface.

and one for bathing and probably a bhikkhu-bag containing a few additional articles. Among these may be a candle-lamp, one or two medicines, toothpick-cum-brushes, perhaps a small folding clock and a penknife. He may also carry a copy of the Pātimokkha (his Fundamental Precepts) in Pali with a translation into his own language and some small book on the teaching, such as the Dhammapada. All these together make up a good weight and generally he will only want to carry them before the sun gets too high and in the late afternoon or evening when it is setting.

How then should we picture our bhikkhu as he makes his way by footpaths and stony tracks, through deep forest or open rice fields? He wears two of his robes, the double-thick one being usually wrapped and stowed inside his bowl, unless it is very cold. His bowl is secured in its sling and tied tight to its stand, while the strap of the sling passes over one shoulder. His sitting cloth and a few other things may also be put inside while the bathing-cloth forms an additional outer protection for the bowl. His bag, the *crot* in its sling and the water flask, hang from the other shoulder. A thudong bhikkhu does not wear his robes long but hitches them rather high and so passes more easily through streams and over mountains. If he is in open country and the sun is shining, he may place any handy piece of cloth on his head, although this is always removed in accordance with the Vinaya's injunctions when passing by houses or through villages. The sandals on his feet are stout ones—they have to be to take all the knocks that his feet would otherwise suffer. In this way he goes, mindful of and joyful in the Dhamma.

He may go alone or with a *nain* or small boy following, or he may be with one or two other bhikkhus. Probably they will not be walking very close together but prefer to be rather well-spaced so that mindfulness does not suffer, nor conversation tend to break up their silence. Every so often, at least in forests, one of the bhikkhus will spot some refreshing fruit tree and then they may turn in that direction and after gathering the wild fruits—providing that it is not yet twelve o'clock—sit eating them while taking a well-earned rest. Certain bitter fruits, such as the emblic myrobalan, may be taken after midday as they have medicinal properties and our bhikkhu will be glad of these to help quench his thirst in the heat of the afternoon.

A few thudong bhikkhus *en marche* in some ways resemble a small detachment of soldiers. They both have uniforms, they both carry all their needs along with them and in both cases the senior leads and the juniors follow, but here the resemblance ends. The former wear the robe of peace, of harmlessness towards all living beings and all their possessions speak of a pacific way of life. No guns do they carry, but *crots,* no grenades, but almsbowls. The wandering bhikkhu has conquered eastern Asia by these means, without dissension, without resort to violence, without wars but with loving-kindness and compassion. And those mighty empires which ambitious and victorious men have raised one after the other, by the use of force, shattering opponents by wars innumerable—all this might and glory have passed away, have crumbled to defaced stones and time-smoothed coins found in distant jungles. But the Dispensation of the Conqueror who practised and preached a morality based upon non-violence, this empire of peace has endured. What is the message here for the empire makers, political or economic, of the present day? What has this Dhamma to say to those who think of their lives as a fight against others? Upon this matter, the Dhammapada has the following verse:

> "Though he may conquer a thousand thousand men in battle, yet he is indeed the noblest victor who would conquer himself."
>
> —Dhp 103

Our wandering bhikkhu may decide at the end of his day whether he will stay the night in the forest, or cave or other suitable place, or whether, the country proving unfavourable, he will go to the nearest village. If he elects in favour of the latter, it may well be that in approaching the village in the evening light, some villagers will see him. Then some pious laymen will approach him and saluting him respectfully, relieve his shoulders of bowl and *crot* and invite him to stay for the night in the village vihāra, or where there is no established residence for bhikkhus in the "hall" (*sāla*). Word will soon get round the village that a venerable thudong bhikkhu has arrived and people will then come to the hall bringing with them things for his comfort—a pillow, mat and of course, tea. In Thailand at any rate, this means "water-tea" (literally translated), or as Westerners would say, Chinese tea. He may also be offered honey or sugar to refresh himself and while he does this, people will sit upon a lower level of the hall and respectfully enquire where he has come from, where he will be going to, how long he has been a bhikkhu (how many Rains-Retreats?)—and so forth. If our bhikkhu wishes, or has the gift of teaching, the general conversation may well be turned towards Dhamma and the lay-people will sit listening intently and perhaps putting a question now and then upon some point which they do not understand.

Whenever there is time during the informal gathering, or when people have departed, our bhikkhu will have to see about patching up his skin bag which is so liable to become punctured even though he takes great care. Villagers will give him more medicines, often of their own manufacture, if those he carries do not suffice. His various wounds, usually very small matters, may nevertheless give him plenty of room for reflection upon the nature of the body. A small pimple soon grows into a large sore and an insignificant cut quickly pulsates with oozing pus; and he remembers that each day he chants: "There are in this body: *kesa*-hair of the head, *loma*-hair of the body ... and so forth, to ... *taco*-skin, *maṃsaṃ*-flesh ... *pubbo*-pus, *lohitaṃ*-blood..." His cuts and blisters are reminders for him that the bag of skin holds much which, although usually hidden from ordinary sight, is liable to erupt and compel attention. The thudong bhikkhu gives attention here willingly whereas the worldly attitude is to turn away from and try not to consider such nasty things. Our bhikkhu, however, knows that the seeing of all these parts of the body, traditionally thirty-two in number, as they really are—that is, as a danger, as repulsive and as liable to decay—leads him towards freedom from the "own-body-view" (*sakkāya-diṭṭhi*) and towards that state where the body is viewed quite impersonally and as a collection of processes, acting and reacting. At best, it will be seen, after insight into its nature has been experienced, as an instrument of the Dhamma.

Towards such insight and mature understanding, our bhikkhu strives, and he will, if he has still energy enough, sit in meditation after the last villager has departed and, attaining calm, shift his attention to these thirty-two messy parts, or some one or two of them, endeavouring to develop insight. Perhaps he may vow before taking his rest: "Oh, may this body be devoted to the Dhamma, may it become a Dhamma-instrument." And his night will be spent peacefully, no dreams will disturb him and he will awake refreshed, the body ready for active service in the Dhamma when he takes up his meditation subject again in the cool of the morning.

When it is fully light, many villagers will come to the hall to make merit, which means that our bhikkhu will not have to go out for *piṇḍapāta*. Every house will send a bowl of rice and some other food to accompany it and perhaps he may get sweets and fruits as well. One person from each house will place one or two spoons of rice into his bowl as it stands upon the raised platform-floor. When they have finished, the other food, together with his bowl will be reverently given into his hands—for a bhikkhu should not take any food which has not actually been offered in this way. The senior layman may well ask him for the Three Refuges and the Five Precepts, and the giving of these being completed, our bhikkhu will intone a chant (*yathā vārivāha pūrā paripūrenti...*) whereby the merits made by the laity are formally dedicated to the happiness and comfort of the hungry ghosts (*peta*). Before he begins his meal, he remembers that this food is one of the four requisites (*paccaya*) and the proper reason why he will eat it. His meal over and his bowl washed, he sets out again upon his way.

Generally, however, the serious wanderer will prefer, wherever conditions permit, to spend his nights in the forest where his own quiet of mind will be better company for him than many people. Of course, he will not get good tea, nor honey—nor the other comforts of the village hall but if he has practised diligently, he will have comforts enough and far superior to those who have not sat in meditation. He will be able to sit as long as he can in the cool of the night, without interruption if he has chosen a site far enough removed from the village.

So our bhikkhu stays out of sight and hearing until he appears the next morning in the village upon his round for *piṇḍapāta*. Of course, there will be no special food for him as there would be if he had stayed in the hall. He will just get the ordinary fare. As he has cultivated contentment, he will not care whether it is finest culinary art or plainest village rice—it is all the same to him.[24]

24. *Piṇḍapātik'aṅga* (alms-food-eater's) practice, the third *dhutaṅga*; see Preface.

He will find a considerable difference in the villages along his way; some will be prosperous, while others are poor, some tidy and others uncared for, and so on. And he will not always be welcome; though this will be very unusual, it does happen, especially where villagers are for some reason without bhikkhus to guide their lives. When he chances upon such a village, if he is an ordinary bhikkhu, he will have a good opportunity to test the strength of his patience, while if he is a teacher, he may stop there for some time and, using all his skill, teach the people what is wrong with the way that they are going and what is the right way to fare through life.

Turning now to another matter, we should mention here the custom among thudong bhikkhus of making certain vows (*adhiṭṭhāna*). It may be that the vow is made to observe a definite practice among the thirteen ascetic modes (*dhutaṅga*), such as refraining from lying down for a certain number of days, weeks or months. A wandering bhikkhu may vow never to stay in a hall such as we have described, or to go on some pilgrimage by foot all the way, not accepting proffered transport—and so forth.

Regarding this last vow, there is a story. A few years ago, a Thai bhikkhu of about fifty years of age made a vow to walk from Bangkok to the holiest place for Buddhists, the "Diamond Throne" (the Buddha's Seat of Enlightenment) at Buddha Gaya in India. So he set off with bowl and robes and a few other things such as we have described. He took no money upon his pilgrimage, neither did he worry about such modern encumbrances as passports and visas. Falling in with a party of Mon bhikkhus going to make their *pūja* at the Shwe Dagon Pagoda in Rangoon, he went with them and from there made his slow progress up the length of Burma. Two Rains Retreats he spent upon the way and still he had not reached India. Finally, he crossed the Indo-Burmese border in the wild hills of Nāgaland and there some Nāgas, who had probably never seen a bhikkhu before and took him for a spy, severely beat him, taking away even his robes and bowl. Fortunately, he was able to recover these, although his few other things were gone, and so limping, he made his way down to the Assamese plain. Knowing not a word of any Indian language and having to rely on *piṇḍapāta,* which is not so easily got in India, his first concern was to get someone to write on a piece of paper in Hindi and

Bengali: "I am a Buddhist bhikkhu. I collect cooked food which is to be placed in this bowl. May you be well and happy." This piece of paper he showed everywhere he went so that people would understand what he required. Luckily he was a vegetarian and not troubled regarding food. After many months of walking, he came to Buddha Gaya. His vow was fulfilled after two and a half years: he had wandered to good purpose.

There is wandering in this way with some profitable end in view and there is also an aimless wandering. The thudong bhikkhu wanders (*carati*) in order to put an end to wandering (*saṃsarati*). He wanders purposefully in the Dhamma-faring so as to come to an end of the infinitely long wandering in birth-and-death (*saṃsāra*). He has taken up this way of life, that of a homeless one, because he sees the dangers which beset all who drift in the currents of *saṃsāra*. Birth and death, ageing and disease afflict all beings who are like so many pieces of driftwood dashed about by the ocean waves, first this way and then that—but never getting anywhere and forever at the mercy of wind and water. As driftwood, so beings do not know why they are here and instead of trying to probe this matter, they invent all sorts of fanciful explanations.

Our bhikkhu sees, if only to some extent and for part of the time, that beings are overcome by the poisons of the three roots of unskill (greed, hatred and delusion) and that these blind them and make them the prey of all the worldly conditions which they experience. And so they go, pulled this way and that by the results of their own actions (*kammaphala*), leaping from birth to birth. He knows that beings do not always spiritually evolve, but that devolution is always possible—into states where darkness is complete, the black night of ignorance (*avijjā*), where the lamp of the Dhamma is no longer discernible.

"Why wander blindly in this round of woes?" thinks our bhikkhu. "Why wander on and on to such states as will be difficult to escape from (as for instance, animal-birth)?" Perhaps he calls to mind a picture painted by a master of old[25] which shows a long, long track winding from the distance into the foreground and from thence out of our ken. This track so tortuous passes through an unbeautiful landscape of shattered, spiky rocks, smitten, storm-

25. The reverse panels of a diptych by Hieronymus Bosch.

struck trees, fire-blackened grass and earth, and here and there lying about are bones—a skull bone here, a leg bone there. Along this dreadful track there comes a man, his clothes all in tatters, a wide-brimmed pilgrim's hat upon his head and a staff held skew-wise in one hand. His face bears all the marks of foolishness, from his eyes, which are wandering and not fixed upon his way before him, to his mouth set in the most imbecile smile imaginable. He has wandered all down that long way, grinning foolishly at the bones which would warn him if only he would heed them. He has wandered long, infinitely long and he will wander longer—uncomprehending. He sees no other way to go but the dreary track in front of him.

Our bhikkhu (and all those who earnestly take to this Dhamma) is one who is determined no longer to wander aimlessly but to be one who marches along the high road to freedom, that glorious bliss-bestowing Way, the Noble Eightfold Path.

Companionship and the Solitary Life

If one find friend with whom to fare,
Rapt in the well-abiding, apt,
Surmounting dangers one and all,
With joy fare with him mindfully.

Finding none apt with whom to fare,
None in the well-abiding rapt,
As rajah quits the conquered realm,
Fare lonely as rhinoceros.

A good deal has already been written upon companionship while leading the holy life and this need not be repeated. The point that is really important is whether one makes progress best in the Dhamma-company of others, or whether one's mentality and progress are sufficiently strong and mature to "fare lonely as rhinoceros."

One who has the company of others has many chances to learn from them. Not only from his teacher but from other bhikkhus, and not only from them, from *nains*, in fact, from everyone with whom he has contact. Every person is one's teacher, if only there is the facility and humility to learn from them and in all situations. From the wise, our thudong bhikkhu upon his Dhamma-pilgrimage learns wisdom. But also from those lacking in good qualities, he learns how not to behave, he learns through their mistakes and reflects upon himself: "Now, is this unskilful way of speech or bodily action to be found in me, or not?"

He also learns more humility from this mindfulness of others' action, for while perceiving some fault of others, he does not make this an opportunity for the arising of pride. When noting greed in someone else, besides the above reflection upon his own behaviour, perhaps he can add the thought: "But he has (for instance) a very strong devotion." In other words, he learns through his contact with fellow Dhamma-farers to see their good qualities also and to strive to bring those excellencies to perfection in his own personality.

Through the effort that he makes, we should note certain qualities which, being present to the extent that his training has been successful, mark him out as one who has indeed taken the following to heart:

> "Good is restraint in eye, good is restraint in ear, good is restraint in nose, good is restraint in tongue.
>
> "Good is restraint in action, good is restraint in speech, good is restraint in thought, restraint everywhere is good. The bhikkhu restrained in every way is freed from all suffering."
>
> —Dhp 360-361

> "We should notice that all his actions were marked by this moderation. If we saw him in company, he would be one who laughed but little for he will have to some extent perceived the truth in the following: When the world is ever ablaze, why this laughter, why this jubilation?"
>
> —Dhp 146

But we should not from this gain the impression of a gloomy saintliness or that his face would be forbiddingly harsh, for our bhikkhu has made loving-kindness and compassion (*mettā-karuṇā*) grow and will upon occasion smile gently. Likewise, his speech is marked by a softness of expression and lack of rough words. He would be inclined to speak to others upon the Dhamma and be little attracted to other subjects except where they touched upon what for him is all-important: the Way to Enlightenment.

Besides contact with teachers and other bhikkhus he may have a *nain* as his companion or perhaps a boy who wishes to train for ordination later. If a suitable boy can be found and is given the going-forth to become a *nain* then he will be of great help to the thudong bhikkhu. "Suitable," here means that he feels a genuine urge to live not only the holy life but also to live it in the sort of places where thudong bhikkhus live. He must also be devoted to the bhikkhu with whom he lives, looking upon him as his teacher. Suitability includes as well the ability of the *nain* or boy to practise meditation, for living in the wilds with few or no books and out of range of the sense-distractions of the towns, such boys must be able to employ themselves through at least part of the day without disturbing the bhikkhu. There are, in Buddhist countries particularly, numbers of boys who, one supposes, have practised meditation in past lives and who take to it in this one as ducklings to water.

The *nain* or boy helps in so many ways that it would not be possible to list them all. He is ever-solicitous for the well-being of bhikkhus and never loses an opportunity for doing them some service. In particular this applies to the teacher of the *nain* and to any other bhikkhus whom he particularly respects—for their wisdom, patience, gentleness, learning, energetic striving or whichever other fine qualities are manifest in them. In the training of the *nain*, helpfulness towards others and humility to learn from them are prime qualities.

Whenever our thudong bhikkhu finds the occasion proper to instruct or correct, he will find if he has a really good *nain* that he will listen with ears open wide to the former, while accepting the correction humbly and with a good heart. It does happen even with the best of *nains* that he will make some mistake, particularly regarding carelessness. Then the bhikkhu will quietly admonish the *nain* and perhaps prescribe some punishment-work (*daṇḍa-kamma*) for him to do—and the *nain* gently smiling accepts his work, which is often sweeping, and sets about it with a right good will.

Such a novice, keen for the training, is positively avid for Dhamma and listens particularly to stories with great attention. As there is no lack in Buddhist literature of stories to illustrate points of training, *nains* soon come to have a fund of such material both of the Buddha-time and from later Buddhist history. Thus begins the Dhamma-education of what will probably be a good thudong bhikkhu.

What then of one who chooses to live alone? Two points stand out: Positively his character must be deep and resourceful enough to surmount all the obstacles he may encounter, while on the negative side, his defilements (*kilesa*) must be sufficiently held in check by his culture of mindfulness (*sati*) and meditation (*samādhi*).

It is no good living in the wilds boorishly unrestrained as in the case of venerable Gulissāni.[26] On the contrary, our bhikkhu knows that the greatest restraint is needed as there is no longer any companion to upbraid or advise him whenever this is necessary. He has then to be his own instructor and this is plainly impossible unless such excellent qualities as mindfulness, shame (*hiri*) and fear of blame (*ottappa*) are well-developed.

Our bhikkhu who wishes to taste solitude must also be sure that he does so for the right reasons. There are those people who like to live by themselves simply because they cannot bear their fellow men. Their solitary life is thus based upon the root of hatred (*dosa*). Far different must be the thudong bhikkhu's reason for desiring loneliness. He wishes to course deep in the Dhamma and have no drags, no ties whatever, which might prevent his increasing perception of its truth. His whole life revolves around the Dhamma and he has, or wishes to develop, the central thought of Dhamma, that is, of the three signata of existence (*tilakkhaṇa*—impermanence, suffering and non-self).[27]

To do this his emotional nature must be mature and this, in Buddhist practice, means the development of the divine abidings (*brahma-vihāra*), each one of which replaces a certain aspect of emotional instability. Thus hatred is replaced by loving-kindness; indifference to others' sufferings is remedied by compassion; envy by sympathetic joy with others' happiness; while involvement with and attachment to others is, in maturity, replaced by equanimity. Even if our bhikkhu cannot yet reach to the heights of equanimity, at least his gentleness and compassion must have grown to some degree. He has almost placed himself outside the

26. See Gulissāni Sutta, Majjhima Nikāya, No. 69.

27. See Wheel No. 20: *The Three Signata.*

world of men, and he is sure therefore to have greater contact with animals than do most men and he may, especially if in him purification is well advanced, have visions of the gods (*devatā*). Many are the stories of old told about both sorts of contact. From the context of stories in which the gods appear to bhikkhus it is apparent that they do so because the latter's spiritual development has approached or surpassed that of those gods. It is these divine abidings which make possible this meeting of worlds.

Stories of extraordinary affection between thudong bhikkhus and animals are also frequent. In this country at the end of the Ayuthiya period (ended CE 1767), there were numbers of forest-dwelling bhikkhus who, like the sages of old, would dwell hermit-like surrounded by animals and birds. Deer in particular came to love the companionship of these hermits, who could only attract animals thus because of the loving-kindness which they had made grow in their hearts and the consequent absence of hatred and fear.

Two other qualities are necessary for the solitary dweller: patience and energy. He will hardly be a thudong bhikkhu at all if he has not the former. Living-conditions for him are many and not all of them are perfect all the time. Although he has backed out of the rough waters of attachments to persons, places and things, he still lives in this world imperfect and must patiently cope with whatever trials he encounters. With patience he trains his mind so difficult to bring under control and with patience he notes the gradual relaxation of the defilements (*kilesa*). He comes to know that his dispensation (*sāsana*) is as Lord Buddha instructed:

> "Just as the great ocean deepens not suddenly but shelves out gradually, so this Teaching is gradual and understanding of it gradually deepens."

He has patience in seeing that his efforts are gradually rewarded. "Efforts" means energy, rather necessary for many aspects of strenuous thudong life, as our bhikkhu knows. If he did not make any effort in his chosen way of life, then a speedy decline would follow, in which the defilements, for the weakening and ultimate breaking of which he was leading this life, would re-assert themselves and once more tighten their stranglehold upon him.

The thudong bhikkhu makes efforts, too, to maintain his observance of the Vinaya and in particular of the Fundamental

Precepts (*Pātimokkha*) pure and unbroken. Even more diligent must be the observance of the solitary bhikkhu who can ill afford to let slide any of the precepts. If he does so, he will find that his meditation is disturbed by thoughts of the broken precepts and to mend matters he must go and obtain purification of his fault through confession of it to another bhikkhu.

He has also to stir up energy to maintain and develop further his meditative practice. Without effort, instead of going from strength to strength in meditative calm and insight (*samatha-vipassanā*), he would be liable to slip backwards practising less and less every day.

With patience to hold in check agitation and energy to ensure that slothfulness does not lay on its benumbing touch, our solitary thudong bhikkhu has a good chance of making balanced progress along the way.

Pali scriptures mention another kind of solitariness; after his practice of bodily seclusion (*kāya-viveka*) together with the mental withdrawal experienced in deep meditation (*citta-viveka*), he may come to possess this lasting solitude. The man with craving (*taṇhā*) present is said to be accompanied by a second one (*dutiya*), whereas one in whom craving is absent, having been totally eradicated through insight (*vipassanā*), is an arahant who abides in the ultimate solitude from all substrates producing continued existence (*upadhi-viveka*).

Our thudong bhikkhu strives to use his solitude in forest or cave, in order to be rid of his companion in all *saṃsāric* wandering—craving, and being without this second one to know the true solitude of Dhamma-truth. When he has achieved this, then indeed he may abide anywhere, and whether forest or city it will make no difference to him.

This was the pattern in Lord Buddha's life, first the long meditative seclusion followed by his carrying of the torch of Enlightenment for all to see. Sometimes, in those long years of teaching the Enlightened One would betake himself to the forests for a time. Then he would return to the vihāras quite near to the important towns of those days or wander among the villages meeting kings and "outcastes," priests and princes and discoursing to all without exception, for the potential of Enlightenment lay within all men, having no regard whether he was estranged from society and labelled an "outcaste" or esteemed by people as a priest (*brahmin*) of "pure" lineage.

Thus, in following the thudong life our bhikkhu is making his efforts, however small, to follow in the way his Master trod. To him, the life of the Enlightened One is not something remote, for it is illuminated to some extent by his own experience and is always a great source of precious inspiration and guidance. It shows him what can be achieved and gives him the courage to face all dangers and go forth to make the attempt for this highest achievement. As Lord Buddha assures all people:

> "Those who are always meditative and ever steadfastly persevering, the wise ones realize Nibbāna, the bond-free, the highest."
>
> —Dhp 23

Postscript

As much as can easily be written of the thudong bhikkhu's life is contained in these sketches. Just as the flavour of soup is not to be told even in one thousand pages, so the real flavour of this ancient way cannot be conveyed by words. Soup is to be tasted; the thudong life is to be lived. If it sounds hard, one must remember that its rewards are great, and in the field of Dhamma-endeavour, nothing is gained without effort. The world wants everything quick-and-easy but the fruits of the holy life are thus only for those who have already put forth their energy, already striven hard for the goal. Truly Lord Buddha promises in the *Discourse on Mindfulness* (*Satipaṭṭhāna Sutta*) that the noble attainment of the arahant may be experienced within seven days. There is also the phrase found: "Instructed in the morning, he attains in the evening." Such promise and statements depend upon individual capacities and whether the practice of mindfulness is strong and complete enough and, moreover, they only apply providing that there is the ability to renounce this world completely. Nibbāna, the supreme goal, is not to be got at while anything, even the most subtle *dhamma*, is still clung to. Behold, says the Exalted One:

> "Come behold this world,

Like unto a royal chariot,
Wherein fools flounder,
But where the wise find no attraction."

—Dhp 171

The thudong bhikkhu makes efforts to be among the wise who have cast aside all embroilments with things, people and the three periods of time. He has few things among which he can flounder and he tries vigorously to cut off all that might tie him to people. He strives also to win for his own his Master's realization regarding the three times:

"The past is like a dream,
The present as clouds appears,
Mirage-like is the future."

All bonds, however arising, he tries to shatter. He is inspired by the Enlightened One's exhortations that a mortal disease (ignorance, *avijjā*) requires a drastic remedy. He has gone forth from home and family, from all the dear decorations of life, to don the ancient yellow robe of patches, to have little and want less, to pursue the sublime way shown by the Buddha with every energy he possesses. While unenlightened he wants only one "thing"—Enlightenment.

When he wishes to take the step of going-forth (*pabbajjā*, to become a *nain*), he thrice utters these words: "Give leave, venerable sir, and having given me these robes, out of compassion let me go forth for the extinction of suffering and the realization of Nibbāna."

If he is serious in his quest he tries even amid life's diffusion, not to forget these words, not to forget the reason why he is wearing the three robes. They are a great reminder that Enlightenment is his aim and that the well-being of others is best upheld by penetration of Enlightenment by oneself. This thudong way, although it seems to be devoted only to the good of the bhikkhu undertaking it, actually stands at the beginning of his progress along the way.

Lord Buddha emphasized: "Who, stuck in the mud, can pull out another stuck in the mud?" Later, when some mastery is gained in the Dhamma, then is time to aid others and only then can one actually help them effectively.

It is this straightforward attitude to the Dhamma among members of the Sangha and devoted lay-people which has been responsible for the spread of the Dhamma in Eastern Asia, from Sri Lanka to Siberia, from Afghanistan to Japan. And to spread the Dhamma outwardly, it must first be spread inwardly, in one's own heart. The Sangha unencumbered by worldly lumber, has just this work. It is the Sangha in fact which has everywhere in the past been the backbone of the Buddhist religion. It is the mainstay of knowledge of the Dhamma and it is the spearhead of applying that Dhamma to the living of the holy life. Efforts made to spread Buddhism in the present must therefore take account of these two factors: the necessity of having those who have experienced Dhamma for themselves as guides, as meditation masters; and the importance of the Third Jewel, the Sangha, which must be made to grow strongly since it provides the opportunity for devoted effort to win that Dhamma and the subsequent teaching of others which may follow.

Such effort is made particularly by the thudong bhikkhu as we have tried to show. This is not to say that others having practices different from those outlined here do not make efforts toward Enlightenment. Of course they do, but here we have only been concerned with this particular aspect of bhikkhu life. Still, from the high esteem in which the genuine thudong bhikkhu has always been held in Buddhist lands and the fact that his life most nearly approaches that of the original Sangha it would not seem a mistake to regard the thudong way as being first among other modes of bhikkhu life.

Among the bhikkhus, it is those who have realized for themselves the truth of the Dhamma and who are therefore qualified to teach others; it is they who are the elect. Of course, they do not write books and are often difficult to find but certainly they are the heartwood. Where they are to be found, in whatever Buddhist land or anywhere else, there the Buddhadhamma truly lives, for the light of that Dhamma burns brightly in their hearts. Wherever they are, there Dhamma not only lives, but can also grow. For the Dhamma does not grow by the numbers of its adherents according to governments' statistics, nor by the number of its temples, not yet even by the quantities of yellow robes worn: no, it grows heartwise from teacher to pupil, through the former's instructions and the latter's application.

The thudong life is one way to this growth. The Dhamma is not secret, for it is open to all who have ears to hear, and the Sangha exists for all those who would devote their lives to Dhamma. The Way is there, the Way is always there—but who will tread it?

* * *

> "Grounded on practice (*paṭipatti*), sire, is the Dispensation of the Teacher, in practice is its essence. It will last so long as practice does not disappear."
>
> — Venerable Nāgasena's reply to King Menander (Milinda) in "Milinda's Questions" (*Milindapañhā*) p. 1986, translated by I. B. Horner.

Appendix: The Ariyavaṃsa Sutta

Introduction

Here follows a translation which is based on Woodward's translation of the Pali text (PTS) in *Gradual Sayings II* and the Thai translation of the Aṅguttara Nikāya. In this re-translation, great help has been given by Ven. Nāgasena Bhikkhu of Wat Benchamabopitr in Bangkok.

This sutta which we call the *Discourse on the Noble Lineages,* has a very celebrated history. It will be immediately obvious that its content is an inspiration for the thudong bhikkhu and for those who are neither thudong nor bhikkhu, it has as its message that of contentment with a sufficiency of this world's goods while warning any who cultivate this attitude to guard against pride arising ("I am pure, they are not...").

The Commentary states that, under the first three of the Noble Lineages, all of the Vinaya Collection (of rules and regulations for the Sangha) may be expounded. Under the fourth heading, which concerns mental development by way of meditation and the subsequently arising desire to relinquish all states connected with the unskilful *(akusala)* factors, under this Lineage may be explained all the Discourses *(sutta)* and Buddhist psychology *(Abhidhamma).* That such exposition actually took place is attested by many references in the history of Sri Lanka. It seems that such was the fame of this Discourse that thousands would flock from near and far to hear skilled bhikkhus expound it. As the reader will see, it is a short sutta but evidently during its preaching practically all topics in the vast range of the Pali Canon could be brought under the headings which it gives. Such preaching sometimes continued for many days and was a popular subject for exposition during the Rains Retreat. Some traces of this tradition are still to be found in Sri Lanka. (For this information, see Ven. W. Rāhula's *History of Buddhism* in Ceylon, Colombo. 1959.)

Long before the days of the Commentaries (c. fifth century CE), there is another possible reference to this sutta. It occurs in the list of seven Dhamma passages recommended for study by bhikkhus and bhikkhunīs (nuns), *upāsakas* and *upāsikās* (lay men and women), by the Emperor Asoka in his Bhabru Edict. There it is called the "Aliyāvāsani," which many scholars equate with the *Ariyavaṃsa Sutta*. That the great emperor should have singled out this text for the study of those who follow the Buddha Way is indeed fitting and it is as appropriate for its study now as it was over two thousand years ago.

In Thailand at the present time, it is one of a selection of suttas and other chants which come up regularly each month for chanting in temples after the evening *pūja*. Needless to say, it is highly esteemed by thudong bhikkhus, many of whom know it by heart.

In the translation following, passages in parantheses are explanations drawn from the Commentary or from the Thai translation, which somewhat enlarges upon the Pali text. It is hoped that this most ancient teaching upon the thudong life will be of some interest after the preceding account of the Noble Lineages in the present time.

The Discourse on the Noble Lineage

Thus have I heard: At one time the Lord was dwelling near Sāvatthī at the Jeta Wood in Anāthapiṇḍika's Park. Then the Lord addressed the bhikkhus, saying: O bhikkhus!

Yes, Lord, responded those bhikkhus.

Then the Lord said—

Here, O bhikkhus, are these Four Lineages of the Noble Ones (Fully Awakened Ones, Silent Buddhas and Disciples)—foremost (among lineages such as nobles, priests, merchants, etc.), (practised from) days of old, traditional (to the family of Noble Ones), (handed down from) time immemorial, neither separated from them now nor were they separated in the past (as inseparable from the life of Noble Ones), neither stained now nor shall they be reckoned impure in the future, and never are they despised by wise recluses and brahmins.

1. Here, O bhikkhus, a bhikkhu is content with this or that robe and he speaks in praise of contentment with any kind of robe (as those made up from rags cast off, oddments of cloth, corpse-wrappings, etc.). He does not search for robes in an unbecoming way (by hints, indications, round-about talk, or any

other intimations) and if he does not obtain them, he is not cast down. When he has got them, he is not attached to them, is not fascinated by them, nor has he any desire for them. Seeing the peril (in robes acquired by wrong means) and skilled in avoiding this, he just makes use of them. Yet he does not exalt himself because of his contentment with any kind of robes (thinking, I wear rag-robes, etc.), nor does he look down upon others (thinking, these bhikkhus wear fine robes made up by householders, etc.).

O bhikkhus, whatever bhikkhu is skilled in this (matter of contentment and in explaining to others the advantages of contentment), who is not lazy (slipping thereby into luxurious living), who clearly comprehends and is mindful (of the fact that he wears the robes only to ward off cold, heat, the sting of fly and mosquito, the touch of wind and burning sun and creeping things, and to conceal the body), then he is indeed well established in this foremost Noble Lineage as handed down from time immemorial.

2. Then again, O bhikkhus, a bhikkhu is content with this or that almsfood and he speaks in praise of contentment with any kind of almsfood (as that collected from door to door, not favouring the rich, nor discriminating against the poor man's food). He does not search for almsfood in an unbecoming way (by hints, by indicating his likes, etc.) and if he does not obtain it, he is not cast down. When he has got it, he is not attached to it, is not fascinated by it, nor has he any desire for it. Seeing the peril (in almsfood acquired by wrong means) and skilled in avoiding this, he just makes use of it. Yet he does not exalt himself because of his contentment with any kind of almsfood (thinking, I eat only almsfood and only once a day, etc.), nor does he look down upon others (thinking, these bhikkhus take meals by invitation and eat twice before noon, etc.).

O bhikkhus, whatever bhikkhu is skilled in this (matter of contentment and in explaining to others the advantages of contentment), who is not lazy (slipping thereby into luxurious living), who clearly comprehends and is mindful (of the fact that he eats almsfood not for amusement, intoxication, beauty or embellishment but just enough for the support and continuance of his body, for the ending of discomfort and for helping on the life of purity), then indeed he is well established in this foremost Noble Lineage as handed down from time immemorial.

3. Then again, O bhikkhus, a bhikkhu is content with this or that shelter and he speaks in praise of contentment with any kind of shelter (as living at a tree-root, in the forest, or in a cave, etc.). He does not search for shelters in an unbecoming way (by asking supporters to provide him with spacious quarters, furnished, etc.) and if he does not obtain it, he is not cast down. When he has got it, he is not attached to it, is not fascinated by it, nor has he any desire for it. Seeing the peril (in a shelter acquired by wrong means) and skilled in avoiding this, he just makes use of it. Yet he does not exalt himself because of his contentment with any kind of shelter (thinking, I sleep in any place available), nor does he look down upon others (thinking, these bhikkhus live in well-built, well-furnished quarters, in vihāras, etc.).

O bhikkhus, whatever bhikkhu is skilled in this (matter of contentment and in explaining to others the advantages of contentment), who is not lazy (slipping thereby into luxurious living), who clearly comprehends and is mindful (of the fact that the shelter is only to ward off cold, heat, the sting of fly and mosquito, the touch of wind and burning sun and creeping things, and for protection against adverse climatic conditions and for abiding in seclusion), then he is indeed well established in this foremost Noble Lineage as handed down from time immemorial.

4. Then again, O bhikkhus, a bhikkhu has development (of wholesome mental states) as a source of happiness and he delights in it; he has abandoning (of evil mental states) as a source of happiness and he delights in it. By having the happiness from development and by the delight thereof; by having the happiness from abandoning and the delight thereof, he does not exalt himself (thinking, I enjoy the tranquillity of transic concentration, or of insight, etc.), nor does he look down upon others (thinking, these bhikkhus are not striving to develop the supermind or for the superwisdom—*adhicitta*, *adhipaññā*, etc.).

O bhikkhus, whatever bhikkhu is skilled in this (matter concerning restraint of the senses, the threefold good conduct in thought, word and action, the four foundations of mindfulness, the seven factors of enlightenment, leading to deliverance by wisdom; who is therefore also skilled in abandoning the five hindrances and who has finally rid himself of the three roots of unskill—greed, hatred, delusion; and who can explain the way whereby all this is accomplished for the benefit of others), who is not lazy (thereby giving up striving for attainment), who clearly comprehends and is mindful (that both development and abandoning are practised only for the one purpose of insight and Enlightenment—never for gaining magic powers, etc.), then he is indeed well established in this foremost Noble Lineage as handed down from time immemorial.

These, O bhikkhus, are the Four Lineages of the Noble Ones; they are foremost, practised from days of old, traditional, handed down from time immemorial, neither separated from the life of Noble Ones now nor in the past, neither stained now nor shall they be reckoned impure in future, and are never despised by wise recluses and brahmins.

Moreover, bhikkhus, possessing these Four Lineages of the Noble Ones, a bhikkhu may dwell in the East, or in the West, in the North or in the South, and in whatever place he dwells, accidie (boredom in matters spiritual) cannot overpower him, but he will overcome accidie. Why so? O bhikkhus, such a one is a steadfast sage who has overcome both accidie (with seclusion, quietness, etc., and with skilled mental states) and delight (in evil ones that arise while living in seclusion and practising meditation. That is, by the contentment plus humility taught in the first three Noble Lineages, the evil of accidie is overcome—a truly contented mind is never bored; and by development, abandoning and humility taught in the fourth Noble Lineage, the bond of delighted attachment is broken).

Thus spoke the Lord. The Welfarer, the Teacher then said further:

Accidie does not overpower the sage.
(Because of its weakness) it cannot overpower him.
(Instead), the sage overcomes accidie,
It is he alone who overcomes it.

What hindrances can obstruct one for whom
All kamma is dispelled and given up?
Who could blame one as pure
As ornament of Jambu gold?

Even the gods of him speak praise!

Even by Brahmas is he praised!

Glossary

The following Thai words are used in this essay:

Thudong—(pronounce *toodong*, from Pali, *dhutaṅga*: austere practices), the wandering, ascetical, solitary and meditative life of some bhikkhus in Thailand.

Crot—a large brown umbrella with an attachable mosquito net.

Nain—(from Pali, *sāmaṇera*), a novice, often under 20 years old, who observes the 10 Precepts.

A few Pali words are used occasionally:

Bhikkhu—a fully ordained member of the sangha over the age of 20, training himself in the observance of the Pātimokkha, that is, the monastic Code of Discipline. Nearest English translation of *bhikkhu* is "monk"—*never* "priest"!

Sangha—the community or order of bhikkhus open to people of all races who desire to lead the holy life in the Dispensation of the Buddha.

Vihāra—The Buddhist equivalent of a "monastery" (i.e., where bhikkhus live), but this English word conjures up so many misleading ideas that the Buddhist term "vihāra" has been preferred throughout.

Pūja—veneration, worship. In Buddhist practice this is done with the idea of increasing the skilful qualities (such as wisdom and devotion) in one's own mind. Propitiation of forces outside oneself (gods, etc.) is quite foreign to Buddha dhamma.

Kamma—intentional action, or willed, volitional action. (In Buddhism, *never* the result of action.)

Buddhism in Thailand

Its Past and Its Present

by

Karuna Kusalasaya

WHEEL PUBLICATION NO. 85/86

Buddhism in Thailand

Its Past and Its Present

People all over the world who are interested in Buddhism and keep in touch with its news and activities must have heard of the Buddha Jayanti celebrations held a few years ago in all Buddhist countries, including India and Japan. It was in 1957 or, according to the reckoning of some Buddhist countries, in 1956, that Buddhism, as founded by Gotama the Buddha, had completed its 2,500th year of existence. The Buddhist tradition, especially of the Theravāda or Southern School such as now prevails in Myanmar, Sri Lanka, Cambodia, Laos and Thailand, has it that on the completion of 2,500 years from its foundation, Buddhism would undergo a great revival, resulting in its all-round progress, in both the fields of study and practice. Buddhists throughout the world, therefore, commemorated the occasion in 1956–57 by various kinds of activities such as meetings, symposiums, exhibitions and the publication of Buddhist texts and literature.

As to whether or not the tradition mentioned above has any truth behind it, the future alone will testify. However, judging from news received from all corners of the globe, it is no exaggeration to say that mankind is taking an ever-increasing interest in Buddhism. As a matter of fact, since the end of the Second World War interest in Buddhism as evinced by people in Europe, America and Australia has reached a scale unheard of before. Any casual perusal of journals on Buddhism in any of these continents will convince the readers of this statement. It is a matter worth noticing that after the end of the First World War, also, Buddhism made great headway in Europe and elsewhere. This phenomenon can perhaps be best explained by the fact that mankind's spiritual thirst is more sharpened by calamities like war, and that in times of distress mankind realises Truth better.

"The Land of Yellow Robes"

Thailand is perhaps the only country in the world where the king is constitutionally stipulated to be a Buddhist and the upholder of the Faith. For centuries Buddhism has established itself in Thailand and has enriched the lives of the Thais in all their aspects. Indeed, without Buddhism, Thailand would not be what it is today. Owing to the tremendous influence Buddhism exerts on the lives of its people, Thailand is called by many foreigners "The Land of Yellow Robes," for yellow robes are the garments of Buddhist monks. In view of the increasing interest the world is taking in Buddhism and in view of the fact that Thailand is one of the countries where Buddhism still exists as a living force it will not, perhaps, be out of place to know something of the story of how this great faith reached that country.

Buddhism in Thailand: Its Past

Different opinions exist about when, exactly, Buddhism reached that part of the world now officially known as Thailand. Some scholars say that Buddhism was introduced to Thailand during the reign of Asoka, the great Indian emperor who sent Buddhist missionaries to various parts of the then known world. Others are of the view that Thailand received Buddhism much later. Judging from archaeological finds and other historical evidence, however, it is safe to say that Buddhism first reached Thailand when the country was inhabited by a racial stock of people known as the Mon-Khmer, who then had their capital, Dvārāvati, at a city now known as Nakon Pathom (Sanskrit: *Nagara Prathama*), about 50 kilometres to the west of Bangkok. The great pagoda at Nakon Pathom, Phra Pathom Chedi (*Prathama Chetiya*), and other historical findings in other parts of the country testify to this fact as well as to the fact that Buddhism, in its varied forms, reached Thailand at four different periods, namely:

- i. Theravāda or Southern Buddhism
- ii. Mahāyāna or Northern Buddhism
- iii. Burma (Pagan) Buddhism
- iv. Sri Lanka (Laṅkāvaṃsa) Buddhism

We shall now proceed to study each of these periods in detail.

I. Theravāda or Southern Buddhism

That the first form of Buddhism introduced to Thailand was that of Theravāda (The Doctrine of the Elders) School is proved by various archaeological remains unearthed in the excavations at Nakon Pathom, such as the Dharma Chakra (Wheel of Law), the Buddha footprints and seats, and the inscriptions in the Pali language, all of which are in rocks. Such objects of Buddhist veneration existed in India before the introduction of the Buddha image, which appeared later as a result of Greek influence. Buddhism, therefore, must have reached Thailand during the third century BCE, and it must have been more or less the same form of Buddhism as was propagated by the great Buddhist Emperor Asoka. This form of Buddhism was known as Theravāda or Hīnayāna (the Lower Vehicle) in contradistinction to the term Mahāyāna (the Higher Vehicle); the two schools having sprung up soon after the passing away of the Buddha. When worship of the Buddha image became popular in India, it also spread to other countries where Buddhism had already been introduced. This is borne out by the fact that many Buddha images, especially those of the Gupta style, had been found in the ruins of Nakon Pathom and the neighbouring cities. Judging from the style of the Buddha images found, it can also be assumed that the early Buddhist missionaries to Thailand went from Magadha (in Bihar State, India).

To support the view that the first form of Buddhism introduced to Thailand was that of the Theravāda School as propagated by Emperor Asoka, we have evidence from the Mahāvaṃsa, the ancient chronicle of Sri Lanka. In one of its passages dealing with the propagation of the Dhamma, the Mahāvaṃsa records that Asoka sent missionaries headed by Buddhist elders to as many as nine territories. One of these territories was known as Suvarṇabhūmi, where two Theras (elder monks), Soṇa and Uttara, were said to have proceeded.

Now opinions differ as to where exactly this land of Suvarṇabhūmi is. Thai scholars express the opinion that it is in Thailand and that its capital was at Nakon Pathom, while scholars of Burma say that Suvarṇabhūmi is in Burma, the capital being at Thatōn, a Mon (Peguan) town in Eastern Burma near the Gulf of Martaban. Still other scholars of Laos and Cambodia claim that the territory of Suvarṇabhūmi is in their lands. Historical records in this connection being meagre as they are, it would perhaps be of no avail to argue as to the exact demarcation of Suvarṇabhūmi. Taking all points into consideration, one thing, however, seems clear beyond dispute. That is, Suvarṇabhūmi was a term broadly used in ancient times to denote that part of Southeast Asia which now includes Southern Burma, Thailand, Laos, Cambodia and Malaya. The term *suvarṇabhūmi* is a combination of the words *suvarṇa* and *bhūmi*. Both are Sanskrit words; the former means gold and the latter stands for land. Suvarṇabhūmi therefore literally means Golden Land or Land of Gold. Keeping in view the abundance of nature in that part of Asia just referred to, the term seems but appropriate.

The reason why scholars of Thailand express the view that the capital of Suvarṇabhūmi was at Nakon Pathom was because of the archaeological finds unearthed in the area surrounding that town. Nowhere in any of the countries mentioned above, not even at Thatōn in Burma, could one find such a large and varied number of ancient relics as were found at Nakon Pathom. By age and style these archaeological objects belong to the times of Emperor Asoka and the later Guptas. Even the Great Stupa (Phra Pathom Chedi) at Nakon Pathom itself is basically identical with the famous Sāñchī Stupa in India, built by Asoka, especially if one were to remove the Shikhara or upper portion. Many Thai archaeologists are of the opinion that the Shikhara was a later addition to the pagoda, a result, so to say, of the blending of the Thai aesthetic sense with the Indian architectural art. Moreover, the name Pathom Chedi (Pali: *Paṭhama Cetiya*) means "First Pagoda," which, in all probability, signifies that it was the first pagoda built in Suvarṇabhūmi. This would easily fit in with the record of the Mahāvaṃsa—that Theras Soṇa and Uttara went and established Buddhism in the territory of Suvarṇabhūmi at the injunction of Emperor Asoka. Taking cognizance of the fact that Asoka reigned from 269 to 237 BCE,[1] we can reasonably conclude that Buddhism first spread to Thailand during the third century BCE. It is interesting to note in this connection that the history of the penetration of Indian culture to Southeast Asia also started more or less during the same period.[2]

1. *The History of Buddhist Thought*, E.J. Thomas, London, 1933.
2. *The Discovery of India*, Jawaharlal Nehru, New York, 1946, Chapter V (XVI).

II. Mahāyāna or Northern Buddhism

With the growth of Mahāyāna Buddhism in India, especially during the reign of King Kanishka, who ruled over Northern India during the second half of the first century CE, the sect also spread to the neighbouring countries, such as Sumatra, Java and Kambuja (Cambodia). It is probable that Mahāyāna Buddhism was introduced to Burma, Pegu (Lower Burma) and Dvārāvati (now Nakon Pathom in Western Thailand) from Magadha (in Bihar, India) at the same time as it went to the Malay Archipelago. But probably it did not have any stronghold there at that time; hence no spectacular trace was left of it.

Starting from the beginning of the fifth century CE, Mahāyāna Buddhist missionaries from Kashmir in Northern India began to go to Sumatra in succession. From Sumatra the faith spread to Java and Cambodia. By about 757 CE (Buddhist Era: 1300) the Srivijaya king with his capital in Sumatra rose in power and his empire spread throughout the Malay Peninsula and Archipelago. Part of South Thailand (from Surāsthāni downwards) came under the rule of the Srivijaya king. Being Mahāyāna Buddhists, the rulers of Srivijaya gave much encouragement and support to the propagation of Mahāyāna Buddhism. In South Thailand today we have much evidence to substantiate that Mahāyāna Buddhism was once prevalent there. This evidence is in the form of stupas or *chetiyas* and images, including votive tablets of the Buddhas and Bodhisattas (Phra Phim), which were found in large number, all of the same type as those discovered in Java and Sumatra. The *chetiyas* in Chaiya (Jaya) and Nakon Sri Thammarāth (Nagara Sri Dharmarāja), both in South Thailand, clearly indicate Mahāyāna influence.

From 1002 to 1182 CE kings belonging to the Suryavarman dynasty ruled supreme in Cambodia. Their empire extended over the whole of present-day Thailand. Being adherents of Mahāyāna Buddhism, with a strong mixture of Brahminism, the Suryavarman rulers did much to propagate and establish the tenets of the Northern School. There is an interesting stone inscription, now preserved in the National Museum at Bangkok, which tells us that in about 1017 CE (BE 1550) there ruled in Lopburi, in central Thailand and once a capital city, a king who went from Nakon Sri Thammarāth who traced his ancestry to Srivijaya rulers. The king had a son who later became the ruler of Kambuja (Cambodia) and who, more or less, kept Thailand under the suzerainty of Cambodia for a long time. During this period there was much amalgamation of the two countries' religions and cultures. The stone inscription under consideration probably refers to one of the Suryavarman kings who had blood relationship with the Srivijaya rulers.

From the inscription just referred to we also learn that at that period the form of Buddhism prevalent in Lopburi was that of Theravāda, and that Mahāyāna Buddhism, already established in Cambodia, became popularized in Thailand only after Thailand had come under the sway of Cambodia. There are no indications, however, that the Mahāyāna School superseded the Theravāda in any way. This was due to the fact that Theravāda Buddhism was already on a firm basis in Thailand when the Mahāyāna School was introduced there. That there were monks of both schools, Theravāda and Mahāyāna, in Lopburi during those days is indicated in a stone inscription in the Cambodian language found in a Brahmanic Temple within the vicinity of Lopburi city itself.

Much of the Brahmanic culture which survives in Thailand till today could be traced to its origin from Cambodia during this period. Many of the Cambodian kings themselves were zealous adherents of Brahminism and its ways of life. This period, therefore, can be termed Mahāyāna Period. Sanskrit, the sacred language of the Hindus, took its root deep in Thailand during these times.

III. Burma (Pagan) Buddhism

In 1057 CE King Anuruddha (Anawratha) became powerful in the whole of Burma, having his capital at Pagan (Central Burma). Anuruddha extended his kingdom right up to Thailand, especially the Northern and Central parts, covering areas now known as Chiengmai, Lopburi and Nakon Pathom. Being a Theravāda Buddhist, Anuruddha ardently supported the cause of Theravāda, which Burma, like Thailand, at first received directly from India through missionaries sent by Emperor Asoka. However, at the time under consideration, Buddhism in India was already in a state of decline, and as contact between Burma and India was then faint, Theravāda Buddhism, as prevalent in Burma at that time, underwent some changes and assumed a form somewhat different from the original doctrine. This, at a later stage, became what is known in Thailand as Burma (Pagan) Buddhism. During the period of King Anuruddha's suzerainty over Thailand, Burmese Buddhism exercised great influence over the country, especially in the north where, owing to proximity, the impact from Burma was more felt.

It is significant that Buddhist relics found in North Thailand bear a striking Theravāda influence, whereas those found in the South clearly show their Mahāyāna connections dating back from Srivijaya days. To a great extent this is due to the fact that, in their heyday of suzerainty over Thailand, the Burmese under Anuruddha were content with Upper Thailand only, while leaving the South practically to be ruled by their Khmer (Cambodian) vassals whose capital was at Lopburi.

From the beginning of the second century BCE the Thai people, whose original homeland was in the valleys between the Huang Ho and the Yangtze Kiang in China, began to migrate southwards as a result of constant friction with the neighbouring tribes. In the course of their migration, which lasted for several centuries, they became separated into two main groups. One group went and settled in the plains of the Salween River, Shan States, and other areas and spread on as far as Assam. This group of Thais is called Thai Yai (Big Thai). The other main group moved further south and finally settled in what is today termed Thailand. The latter group of Thais is called Thai Noi (Small Thai). The Thais in present-day Thailand are actually the descendants of these migrant Thais. Of course, in the course of their migration, which, as said above, continued off and on for a long time, there had been a great deal of mixture of blood through intermarriage, which was only natural. We should always bear in mind that there are several ethnic groups scattered through the length and breadth of Southeast Asia from times immemorial. But even today we can trace the language affinity of the Thais living in widely scattered areas such as Assam, Upper Burma, Southern China, Shan States, Laos, North Vietnam and Thailand.

After struggling hard for a long time the Thais were able to establish their independent state at Sukhothai (Sukhodaya) in North Thailand. This was probably about 1257 CE (BE 1800).

It was during the period of their movement southwards that the Thais came into contact with the form of Buddhism as practised in Burma and propagated under the royal patronage of King Anuruddha. Some scholars are of the opinion that as Mahāyāna Buddhism had spread to China as early as the beginning of the Christian Era, the Thais, while still in their original home in China, must have already been acquainted with some general features of Buddhism. As the Thai migrants grew in strength their territory extended and finally they became the masters of the land in succession to Anuruddha, whose kingdom declined after his death. During the succeeding period, the Thais were able to exert themselves even more prominently in their southward drive. Thus they came into close contact with the Khmers, the erstwhile power, and became acquainted with both Mahāyāna Buddhism and Brahmanism as adopted and practised in Kambuja (Cambodia). Much of the Brahmanic influence, such as religious and cultural rites, especially in the court circles, passed on from Cambodia to the Thais during this period, for Hinduism was already firmly established in Cambodia at that time. Even the Thai scripts, based on Cambodian scripts, which, in turn, derived their origin from India, were invented by King Rām Kamhaeng of Sukhothai during the period under consideration.

Of the period under discussion it may be observed in passing that Northern Thailand, from Sukhothai District upwards, came much under the influence of Burma (Pagan) Buddhism, while in the central and southern parts of the country many Mahāyāna beliefs and practices, inherited from the days of the Suryavarmans and the Srivijayas, still persisted.

IV. Sri Lanka (Laṅkāvaṃsa) Buddhism

This is the most important period in the history of the spread of Buddhism to Thailand, for it witnessed the introduction to that country of that form of Buddhism which remains dominant there until today.

About 1153 CE (BE 1696) Parākramabāhu the Great (1153–1186 CE) became king of Sri Lanka, known in ancient days as Lanka. A powerful monarch and a great supporter of Theravāda Buddhism, Parākramabāhu did much to spread and consolidate the Dhamma of the Lord in his island kingdom. He caused (according to some scholars of Southern Buddhism) the Seventh Buddhist Council[3] to be held under the chairmanship of Kassapa Thera, of Dimbulāgala in order to revise and strengthen the Doctrine and the Discipline (Dhamma and Vinaya).

As a result of the efforts of King Parākramabāhu the Great, Buddhism was much consolidated in Ceylon and the news spread to neighbouring lands. Buddhist monks from various countries, such as Burma, Pegu (Lower Burma), Kambuja, Lannā (North Thailand) and Lanchang (Laos) flocked to Ceylon in order to acquaint themselves with the pure form of the Dhamma. Thailand also sent her bhikkhus to Ceylon and thereby obtained the *Upasampadā Vidhi* (Ordination Rite) from Ceylon, which later became known in Thailand as Laṅkāvaṃsa. This was about 1257 CE (BE 1800). Apparently the early batches of bhikkhus, who returned from Ceylon after studies, often accompanied by Ceylonese monks, established themselves first in Nakon Sri Thammarath (South Thailand), for many of the Buddhist relics bearing definitely Ceylonese influence, such as stupas and Buddha images, were found there. Some of these relics are still in existence today. News of the meritorious activities of these monks soon spread to Sukhothai, then the capital of Thailand, and King Rām Kamhaeng who was ruling at the time, invited those monks to his capital and gave them his royal support in propagating the Doctrine. This fact is recorded in one of the king's rock inscriptions, dated about 1277 CE. Since then Ceylon (Sinhala) Buddhism became very popular and was widely practised in Thailand. Some of the Thai kings, such as King Maha Dharmaraja Lithai of Sukhothai dynasty and King Borom Trai Lokanath of the early Ayudhya Period, even entered the Holy Order or Bhikkhu Sangha according to the Ordination Rite of Lankāvaṃsa Buddhism by inviting a patriarch from Ceylon, Mahāsāmi Saṅgharāja Sumana by name, to be the presiding monk over his *Upasampada* (Ordination) ceremony. Many monasteries,

3. The counting of the Buddhist Councils (Saṅgāyana or Saṅgīti) differs in the several Theravāda countries. In Sri Lanka, the above-mentioned Council is numbered as the fifth; and in Burma, its place is taken by the Council of Mandalay (1871), while the last Council in Rangoon (1954–1956) is counted as the sixth. [*Editor*.]

stupas, Buddha images and even Buddha footprints, such as the well-known one at Sraburi in central Thailand, were built in accordance with the usage popular in Ceylon. The study of Pali, the language of Theravāda or Southern Buddhism, also made great progress, and in all matters dealing with the Dhamma the impact of Ceylon was perceptibly felt.

However, there had been no antagonism between the different forms of Buddhism already in existence in Thailand and the Lankāvaṃsa, which had been introduced later from Ceylon. On the contrary they seemed to have amalgamated peacefully, and all had adjusted themselves to one another's benefit. This is evident in all religious rites and ceremonies of Thailand. Indeed, somewhat characteristic of the Buddhists, there had been a spirit of forbearance in all matters. For instance, even today Brahmanic rites thrive side by side with Buddhist ceremonies in Thailand and Cambodia, especially in the royal courts.

History repeats itself. Years after, when in Ceylon under King Kirtisri (1747–1781 CE) the *Upasampadā* Ordination was lost due to a decline of Buddhism and upheavals in the country, Thailand (during the reign of King Boromkot, 1733–1758 CE) was able to repay the debt by sending a batch of Buddhist monks under the leadership of Upāli and Ariyamuni Theras, who in the course of time established in Ceylon what is known as the "Siyāmopali Vaṃsa" or "Siyam Nikāya," or Siamese Sect, which still is a major sect in that country. Upāli worked and died in Sri Lanka, the country he loved no less than his own.

Today, for all purposes, Thailand can be termed a Theravāda Buddhist country. There are, of course, a few Mahāyanā monks and monasteries, but they are mostly confined to foreign communities, chiefly the Chinese. All, however, live at peace and co-operate with one another.

So much for the past of Buddhism in Thailand.

Buddhism in Thailand: Its Present

According to the census taken in 1960 the population of Thailand numbers 25,519,965. Of this number 94 per cent are Buddhists (the rest are mostly Muslims and Christians). This fact itself demonstrates more than anything else how influential Buddhism is in Thailand. In their long history of existence the Thais seem to have been predominantly Buddhists, at least ever since they came into contact with the tenets of Buddhism. All the Thai kings in the recorded history of present-day Thailand have been adherents of Buddhism. The country's constitution specifies that the King of Thailand must be a Buddhist and the Upholder of Buddhism.

The term "The Land of Yellow Robes" has not been inappropriately applied to Thailand, for two things strike most foreigners as soon as they set foot in that country. One is the Buddhist temple with its characteristic architecture, and the other is the sight of yellow-clad Buddhist monks and novices, who are to be seen everywhere, especially in the early hours of dawn when they go out in great numbers for alms. The two sights inevitably remind the foreigners that here is a country where Buddhism is a dominant force in the people's life. Indeed, to the Thai nation as a whole, Buddhism has been the mainspring from which flow its culture and philosophy, its art and literature, its ethics and morality and many of its folkways and festivals.

For clarity and convenience we shall divide the study of the present state of Buddhism in Thailand into two parts, namely, the Bhikkhu Sangha or the Holy Order and the Laity.

I. The Bhikkhu Sangha or the Holy Order

The Bhikkhu Sangha or the Holy Order of Buddhist monks has been in existence in Thailand ever since Buddhism was introduced there. According to the 1958 census there were in the whole kingdom of Thailand 159,648 monks, 73,311 novices and 20,944 monasteries or temples. These are scattered throughout the country, particularly more numerous in the thickly populated areas. The Bhikkhu Sangha of Thailand, being of Theravāda or Southern School, observes the same set of discipline (Vinaya) as the Bhikkhu Sanghas in other Theravāda countries such as Sri

Lanka, Burma, Laos and Cambodia. In spite of the fact that the government allots a yearly budget for the maintenance and repair of important temples and as stipends for high ranking monks, almost the entire burden for the support of the Sangha and the upkeep of the temples rests with the public. A survey entitled "Thailand Economic Farm Survey" made in 1953 by the Ministry of Agriculture of the Government of Thailand gives the religious cash expenses of the average Thai rural family per year as ranging from 5 to 10 per cent of its total annual cash income. It may be added here that the report concerns the average Thai rural family, and not the urban dwellers, the majority of whom, in Thailand as elsewhere, are less inclined to religion than the country folks.

Two Sects or Nikāyas

There are two sects or Nikāyas of the Buddhist Order in Thailand. One is the Mahānikāya and the other is the Dhammayuttika Nikāya. The Mahānikāya is the older and by far the more numerous one, the ratio in the number of monks of the two sects being 35 to 1. The Dhammayuttika Nikāya was founded in 1833 CE by King Mongkut, the fourth ruler of the present Chakri Dynasty who ruled Thailand from 1851 to 1868 CE. Having himself spent twenty-seven years as a bhikkhu, the king was well versed in the Dhamma, besides many other branches of knowledge, including Pali, the canonical language of Theravāda Buddhism. The express desire of the king in founding the Dhammayuttika Sect was to enable monks to lead a more disciplined and scholarly life in accordance with the pristine teachings of the Buddha. The differences between the two Nikāyas are, however, not great; at most they concern only matters of discipline, and never of the Doctrine. Monks of both sects follow the same 227 Vinaya rules as laid down in the Pātimokkha of the Vinaya Piṭaka (the Basket of the Discipline), and both receive the same esteem from the public. In their general appearance and daily routine of life too, except for the slight difference in the manners of putting on the yellow robes, monks of the two Nikāyas differ very little from one another.

Organisation of the Sangha

Formerly, and in accordance with the Administration of the Bhikkhu Sangha Act (BE 2484, CE 1943), the organisation of the Sangha in Thailand was on a line similar to that of the state. The Sangharaja or the Supreme Patriarch is the highest Buddhist dignitary of the kingdom. He is chosen by the king, in consultation with the government, from among the most senior and qualified members of the Sangha. The Saṅgharāja appoints a council of Ecclesiastical Ministers headed by the Sangha Nāyaka, whose position is analogous to that of the prime minister of the state. Under the Sangha Nāyaka there function four ecclesiastical boards, namely, the Board of Ecclesiastical Administration, the Board of Education, the Board of Propagation and the Board of Public works.

Each of the boards has a Sangha Mantri (equivalent to a minister in the secular administration) with his assistants. The four boards or ministries are supposed to look after the affairs of the entire Sangha. The Ecclesiastical Ministerial Council, which, by the way, corresponds to the Cabinet, consists of ten members, all senior monks of the Sangha. In addition to this, there is a Consultative Assembly (Sangha Sabhā), equivalent to the National Assembly, the members of which number 45, selected from various important monasteries. The Sangha Sabhā acts as an Advisory Body to the Ecclesiastical Ministerial Council. Below the Sangha Sabhā the administration of the Sangha continues to correspond to the secular administration of the country. All monks and novices (*sāmaṇeras*) have to live in monasteries, which are scattered throughout the country. Each monastery has its abbot appointed by the Ecclesiastical Ministerial Council in consultation with local people. It may be pointed out here that all religious appointments in Thailand are based on scholarly achievements, seniority, personal conduct and popularity, and contacts with monks further up in the Sangha.

There is a Department of Religious Affairs in the Ministry of Education which acts as a liaison office between the Government and Sangha. In general the Department of Religious Affairs works in co-operation with the Ecclesiastical Ministerial Council on all matters affecting the Sangha. For instance, it issues all legal directives concerning the entire community of monks; it keeps record of the Sangha's property, such as lands, etc.; it maintains facts and figures with respect to monks and monasteries. The Religious Affairs Department also prepares the annual budget for the upkeep of the Sangha functionaries and the maintenance and repair of temples, etc. It may be added here that all temples and monasteries are state property.

In 1962, the administration of the Bhikkhu Sangha Act of 1943 was abolished; a new one was enacted instead. By virtue of the new act, the posts of Sangha Nāyaka, Sangha Mantris and Sangha Sabhā were abolished. In place of these there is a Mahāthera Samāgama (Council of the Elders) headed by the Saṅgharāja himself and consisting of not less than four and not more than eight senior monks (Mahātheras) of the two sects (Nikāyas). The Mahāthera Samāgama, in collaboration with the Department of Religious Affairs, directly governs the entire Sangha.

Education of Monks

As is well-known, the original idea of men's entering monkhood during the Buddha's time or shortly later was to attain liberation from worldly existence in accordance with the teaching of the Master. Such an idea, of course, springs from man's feeling of aversion to things mundane. In other words, in those far-off days, men entered monkhood with the sole intention of ridding themselves of life's miseries and of obtaining spiritual freedom or Nirvana. Instances of such self-renunciation are found in the holy books of the Buddhists. With the passage of time, as is only natural, many of the ideals and practices of the early followers of the Buddha underwent modifications. Today, over 2,500 years after the passing away of the Buddha, though the ideal of becoming a Bhikkhu still remains very lofty among Buddhists of all lands, yet in practice it must be admitted that there have been many deviations from the Master's original admonitions with regard to the whys and wherefores of man's entering monkhood. Generalisation of any subject matter is often dangerous but it will not be far from truth to say that today, in Thailand as in other Buddhist countries, the practice of Buddhist males entering monkhood is to a considerable extent prompted rather by the dictation of custom, the wish for an education and other external considerations than by the desire to attain emancipation. Yet there are also many who join the Sangha through genuine love for a religious life and religious studies, or out of the wish to be of service to Buddhism and their country. Finally, in the Thai Sangha also those are not entirely lacking whose life is vigorously devoted to the aim of ultimate emancipation and to the guidance of others towards that goal. There have been, and still are, saintly and able meditation masters in Thailand, with a fair number of devoted disciples in Sangha and laity. There are also still monks—the so-called Thudong bhikkhus—who follow the ancient way of austere living embodied in the "strict observances" or *dhutaṅgas*.[4]

In view of the above facts, there are two categories of Buddhist monks in Thailand. One comprises those who become monks for long periods, sometimes for life, and the other those who enter the Order temporarily. To serve in the monkhood even for a short period is considered a great merit-earning attainment by the Thai Buddhists. Even kings follow this age-old custom. For instance, the present ruler, H.M. King Bhumibol Adulyadej, also observed the custom for a period of half a month some time ago. Government officials are allowed leave with full pay for a period of four months in order to serve in monkhood. The idea is to enable young men to gain knowledge of Buddhism and thereby to become good citizens. Life as a monk gives them practical experience of how an ideal Buddhist life should be. In rural districts the general tendency is still to give more deference to those who have already served in monkhood. Such people are supposed to be more "mature" than those who have not undergone the monk's life. Moreover, in Thailand wats (monasteries and temples) used to be and are still regarded as seats of learning, where all men, irrespective of life's position, could go and avail themselves of education benefits. This is especially so in the case of economically handicapped males of the countryside. Instances are not lacking in which people have climbed high up on life's status ladder after obtaining an education while in monkhood. There are neither religious restrictions nor social disapproval against monks' returning to lay life if and when they find themselves unable to discharge their duties as monks.

---

4. See *The Wheel* No. 83/84: *With Robes and Bowl. Glimpses of the Thudong Bhikkhu Life*, by Bhikkhu Khantipālo.

Cases exist in which, for some reason or the other, men have entered monkhood more than once, although such practice cannot be said to be in the esteem of the public. Looked at from this viewpoint, the institution of entering monkhood in Thailand, apart from being a way of gaining moral and spiritual enlightenment, is a social uplift method by which those not so fortunately placed in life could benefit. Judged from the ideal of adopting a monk's life as enunciated by the Buddha, whether or not such practice is commendable, is a different story. The fact is that even today, when modernism has penetrated deep into Thailand, about one half of the primary schools of the country are still situated in wats. With sex and crimes on the increase in the country, the cry for living a better Buddhist life is being heard more and more distinctly in Thailand today.

The traditional education of monks and novices in Thailand centres mainly on the studies of the Buddhist Doctrine (Dhamma) and Pali, the language in which the Theravāda scriptures are written. Of the former, the study of the Doctrine, there are three grades with examinations open to both monks and laymen. Those passing such examinations are termed "Nak Dhamma," literally meaning one who knows the Dhamma. The latter, i.e. the study of Pali, has seven grades, starting with the third and ending with the ninth grade. Students passing Pali examinations are called "Parian" (Pali: Pariñña = penetrative knowledge); in the Thai language the word "Pariñña" is used to mean academic degree. For example, monks and novices passing the first Pali examination are entitled to write "P. 3" after their names.

Generally the Dhamma and the Pali studies go hand in hand and take at least seven years to complete. The stiffness of the two courses, especially that of the Pali language, can be guessed from the fact that very few students are able to pass the highest grade, the Parian 9, in any annual examination. In the good old days, when living was less competitive than now, passing of even the lower Dhamma and Pali examinations used to be of much value in securing good government posts. But now things are quite different; even those successful in the highest Pali examination, the ninth Grade, find it difficult to get suitable employment.

Of late there has developed a new outlook in the education of monks in Thailand. With the rapid progress of science and with the shrinking of the world, Buddhist leaders of Thailand, monks as well as laymen, are awakened to the necessity of imparting broader education to members of the Sangha, if the Sangha is to serve the cause of Buddhism well, "for the gain of the many, for the welfare of the many." As a result of the new outlook there now function in Bangkok two higher institutes of learning exclusively for monks and novices. One is the Mahāchulālongkorn Rājvidyālaya, and the other is the Māhamongkut Rājvidyālaya. Both are organised on a modern university footing and both seem to be making satisfactory progress towards that direction. Inclusion in the curriculum of some secular subjects not incompatible with monks' discipline (Vinaya) is among the notable features of these two institutes; the aim is to give an all-round education to monks in order to enable them to be of better service to the cause of Buddhism amidst modern conditions.

So much for the education of "long-term" monks. As for those who enter the Order temporarily, mostly for a period of three rainy months during the Vassa, or Buddhist Lent, the education is brief and devoted to the main tenets and features of Buddhism only. As pointed out above, such people enter monkhood either by their own genuine desire for knowledge of the Dhamma, by the dictum of custom or, as generally is the case, by the two reasons combined. Monks of this category return to lay life again as soon as the Lent is over. This is the reason why accommodations in monasteries (wats) are usually full during the Lenten period. Nowadays, owing to the pressure of modern life, the custom of temporarily entering monkhood is not so rigorously observed by people living in urban areas as by those in the countryside. The custom has its parallel in Burma, Cambodia and Laos, where Theravāda Buddhism prevails.

Wats and Monks

The word "wat" means monastery and temple combined. It is the residence of monks and novices. There are about 21,000 wats in the whole of Thailand. In Bangkok alone there are nearly two hundred wats. Some big wats in Bangkok have as many as 600 resident monks and novices. Wats are centres of Thai art and architecture. Thai culture, to a considerable extent, flows from wats. Wat-lands and constructions thereon are donated by royalty, wealthy people and the public in general. The wat is the most important institution in Thai rural life. The social life of the rural community revolves around the wat. Besides carrying out the obvious religious activities, a wat serves the community as a recreation centre, dispensary, school, community centre, home for the aged and destitute, social work and welfare agency, village clock, rest-house, news agency and information centre. A wat is headed by a "Chao Avas" (the abbot), who is responsible for the maintenance of the wat discipline, the proper performance of religious services and rituals, and the general welfare of the inmates. Besides monks and novices, there are also the "temple boys" in wats, who assist monks and novices in various ways, such as bringing and arranging food, cleaning dormitories, washing yellow robes, etc. Usually these boys are related to resident monks in one way or another, and their stay is free of charge. Most of them are students whose homes are far away and who would, otherwise, find it impracticable to get education. This is especially so in Bangkok, where accommodation is difficult to get and where all higher seats of learning of the country are situated. The census taken in 1954 reveals that there are as many as 119,044 temple boys in Thailand, which indeed is not a small figure. The institution of the wat, in itself a gift of Buddhism, therefore contributes in no small measure to the social welfare and progress of the Thai Buddhists. The benefits in this respect, of course, are more apparent among the lower strata of society than in the case of the fortunate few on the top.

Apart from engaging themselves in doctrinal studies and observing disciplinary rules (Vinaya) in general, monks are expected to be "friends, philosophers and guides" of the people. Preaching to masses face to face or over the radio is one of the commonest ways by which monks help the promotion of moral stability among various members of the society. It may not be out of place to reiterate the fact that Buddhism lays great stress on the necessity of leading a morally good life in order to obtain happiness in life here and hereafter. In most of the ceremonies and rituals, whether private or public, monks' co-operation and benediction are indispensable. Indeed, in the life of the average Thai Buddhists, from the cradle to the grave, monks are persons to whom they constantly turn for moral support.

The role of monks in rural districts is even more important, for there the local wat is not only the religious but also the social centre of the community. It is at the wat that people come together and experience a sense of comradeship. Religious rituals and ceremonies held at wats are always accompanied by social activities: they are occasions for people, especially the young, to enjoy themselves in feast, fun and festivities. This aspect of the religious service helps the common folks to relax and satisfies their needs for recreation. Not a few matrimonial alliances started from contacts at wat premises. Acting as a moral and ethical example, monks are the most venerated persons in the countryside Thai society, remaining very close to the hearts of the people. In times of crisis, it is to monks that people bring their problems for counsel and encouragement. With few exceptions, the Sangha has well justified this attitude of respect and honour shown to it on the part of the laity and, on the whole, has lived up to the dignity of the Faith.

II. The Laity

Throughout its over 2,500 years of existence Buddhism has been closely connected with the lay community. In Pali the word for a male lay-devotee is "*Upāsaka*" and "*Upāsikā*" is its female equivalent. In the history of Buddhism, right from the time of its founder, there have been numerous "*Upāsakas*" and "*Upāsikās*" whose faith in the Teachings of the Master have contributed largely to the dissemination of the Doctrine. Names of the Buddha's munificent followers like Anāthapiṇḍika, Visākhā, Asoka, Kanishka, etc., are on the lips of Buddhists even today. Without the patronage of Emperor Asoka, Buddhism probably could not have spread so far and the course of its history might have been different. In India, the land of its birth, as well as in most of the countries where its Message has been accepted, Buddhism has received unstinted support from people of all classes, especially the ruling class. History of the movements of Buddhism in China, Japan, Burma, Ceylon, Tibet, etc., amply justifies this statement. In the case of Thailand too, ever since its introduction to that country, Buddhism has been warmly received and patronized by kings and commoners alike. It is well-known that many of the Thai rulers, not satisfied with being mere lay-devotees, got themselves ordained into monkhood and became famous for their erudition in the Dhamma. King Mongkut, Rama IV, probably stands out as most distinguished among this class of royal devotees. The custom of Thai males entering the Sangha also contributes much to the better understanding and co-operation between the lay community and the monkhood. After all, personal experience is better than mere theoretical knowledge.

The Buddha himself, in one of his discourses, exhorted his followers to discharge their duties well so as to enable the Dhamma to endure long in the world. One of the duties of the lay followers, as taught by the Master, is to look after the needs of monks. Hence, it is the traditional practice with lay-followers in all Buddhist countries, especially those following Theravāda Buddhism, to see that monks do not suffer from lack of the four requisites, namely food, clothing, shelter and medicine. Although in the present age of competitive economy, life in any field is not so easy, nobody can say in fairness that monk-life in Thailand suffers greatly from shortage of the above four requisites. As bhikkhus are not allowed to follow any occupational activities, it is clear that they entirely depend on the laity for their existence. In return for this spontaneous support offered them by the public, monks are expected to live exemplary lives for the benefit of themselves as well as of those who look to them as teachers and guides. We have already seen what moral influence monks have upon the people.

Co-operation between the laity and the bhikkhu Sangha in Thailand is close and spontaneous. To a very great extent this is due to the fact that in an average Thai family some of its members are certain to be found who have for some time served in the Sangha. To the masses yellow robes are symbolic of the Master, and bhikkhus are upholders of the Dhamma, to be deferred to in all circumstances. It is interesting to note that bhikkhus or *sāmaṇeras* found guilty of committing crimes are formally divested of their yellow robes before legal action is taken against them by the state, and this is done invariably under permission of the chief monk or the abbot.

"To do good" (*kusala kamma*) is a cardinal point in the teachings of Buddhism. Consequently the idea of performing meritorious deeds is very deeply ingrained in the minds of Buddhists. Ways of doing good or making merit (*puñña*) among the Thai Buddhists are numerous. A man gains merit each time he gives alms to monks or contributes to any religious rituals. To get ordination into monkhood even for a short period, of course, brings much merit. Besides, there are other ways of merit-earning, such as releasing caged birds or freeing caught fishes, plastering gold leaf on Buddha statues or religious monuments, contributing to the construction of a new temple or the repair of an old one, etc. "The Law of Kamma" that each action has its corresponding result and the belief in rebirth are two important factors in moulding positive attitudes towards life among the Buddhists. Though "Nibbāna" (Sanskrit: Nirvana), the highest goal in Buddhism, is aspired to by all good Buddhists, the vast majority of them still think it is not so easy to reach and that they will be reborn again in this world, in heaven or in some other world, or—at the very worst—in hell. Hence, as long as they live they must try to do good in order to ensure good results in this very life as well as in the life to come. "Be a light unto yourself. Each man must strive for his own salvation"—these were the Master's final words. In view of this, Theravāda Buddhism is often said to have individualistic temper. Nevertheless, it is very tolerant, as the long history of its existence will prove. Indeed, the characteristic tolerance of Buddhism, for instance in Thailand, has always permitted the absorption of many beliefs and practices from other sources which have often served to supplement or expand its concepts or to fill gaps. Animism and Brahmanism may be cited in this connection, the two being important supplements of popular Buddhism in Thailand. A foreign writer has rightly observed that the attitude of the Thai masses towards their religion is of an easy-going nature. They do not bother to distinguish among the various components of their religion; for them it is all of a piece. Only the sophisticated few are concerned with doctrinal logic and purity. Of course, they too know much about its legends, its festivals, its ideals and its general message that "good will render good." On the whole it can be said that the Thais enjoy their religion. Religious observances are to them as social and recreational as sacred occasions. And for the vast majority, Buddhism suffices in that it enables them to feel and believe and enjoy.

Buddhist Organisations and the Revival of Buddhism

Organisations among the lay Buddhists of Thailand are recent establishments. Prominent and oldest among them is perhaps the Buddhist Association of Thailand, under royal patronage, which now is about thirty years old, having been established in 1933. Having its head office in Bangkok, it maintains branch organisations in almost all major districts of Thailand. Its membership is open to both sexes, irrespective of class, creed and colour. The aim and object of the Buddhist Association of Thailand are to promote the study and practice of Buddhism and to propagate its message in and outside Thailand. Besides arranging regular lectures and discussions on topics concerning the Dhamma, the association also publishes a monthly journal in the Thai language on the teachings of the Buddha.

Another organisation is the Young Buddhists Association, which came into being at the close of the Second World War. As its name implies, the Young Buddhists Association takes care of the interests of the young in matters concerning Buddhism. Its primary object is to encourage the young to imbibe the tenets of Buddhism and to live a virtuous life. Chief among its activities are arranging regular lectures and discussions on the Dhamma, issuing publications on subjects dealing with Buddhism in general, and sponsoring meetings of the young on the platform of Buddhism. The Young Buddhists Association also has branches in the districts.

As said earlier the end of the Second World War saw a great revival of interest in Buddhism throughout the world. Even in countries like Thailand, where the Doctrine of the Awakened One has been traditionally accepted for generations, people seem to be increasingly eager to know more about the Dhamma. Strange as it may seem, this is partly due to the interest the Occidental world has taken in Buddhism. In times past religion has been more or less regarded in Thailand as "solace of the old." But with the impact of the West in most matters and with the general interest shown towards Buddhism by Western intelligentsia, the Buddhists of Thailand, especially the younger generations who came into contact with the West, began to evince an inquisitive attitude towards their religion—a heritage which they have all along accepted as their own but which they have cared little to know about its true value. This is no attempt to belittle the exceedingly great importance the Thais attach to their religion. But human nature being what it is, the saying "Familiarity breeds contempt" is in most cases not very far wrong. In the Thai language also we have a proverb "klai kleua kin dang," which may be rendered in English as "to have the folly to resort to alkali when one is in possession of salt."

Having taken root on the soil of Thailand for centuries, Buddhism has naturally attracted many appendages to its fold, some of which are not quite in conformity with the teachings of the Master as contained in the Canon (*Tipiṭaka*). Many leaders of Buddhist thought in Thailand have, therefore, come forward to try to purify the Dhamma of the many impurities that have crept into it. Notable among the reform groups are the Dhammadāna Association in Jaiya, South Thailand, under the leadership of Buddhadāsa Bhikkhu, and the Buddha Nigama of Chiengmai (North Thailand) started by Paññānanda Bhikkhu. The two organisations are showing good efforts in the field of awakening the Buddhists of Thailand to the pristine teachings of the Buddha as treasured in the Pali *Tipiṭaka*. The mission is admittedly a difficult one but already a promising start has been made in this direction. Much will also no doubt depend on how things transpire in other spheres of human activities, chiefly economic, social and political. The present is an age of conflict— conflict between mind and body, between spirit and matter. Man must find harmony between the two if peace be his aim in life. And to this task of finding harmony within man Buddhism could contribute in no small measure.

The Greater Discourse on Voidness

The Mahāsuññatā Sutta
(Majjhima Nikāya No. 122)
And Its Commentary

Translated from the Pāli by

Ñāṇamoli Thera

From the Translator's Posthumous Papers

WHEEL PUBLICATION NO. 87

Introduction

Retire within yourselves; but first prepare yourselves to receive yourselves there. It would be madness to trust yourselves to yourselves if you do not know how to control yourselves. There are ways of failing in solitude as well as in company.

Montaigne

Often when the mind is tired and stale it needs the comfort and encouragement of a soothing kind. At other times such treatment can induce in it a false sense of security, and then it has to be jolted, woken up, even frightened if necessary, and injected with a sense of urgency. This discourse does precisely that. It does not offer comfort (which will be found elsewhere in the canon). It urges forced marches to the goal, with awareness of present dangers as encouragement.

In more than one place in the canon the Venerable Ānanda, the Buddha's faithful attendant, whose gentle concern with others' welfare led him now and then to neglect his own advancement to arahantship, suffers reproof for this wholly amiable trait. This discourse opens with a rebuke. And though elsewhere he is singled out for praise as the foremost of all the disciples in learning and remembering the discourses, he is here told that it is not enough merely to know about these things; they must be practised and put into effect. And the end carries a warning against underestimating the risks.

Voidness, the subject of the discourse, is not defined. It may be assumed, though, that the Venerable Ānanda, who remembered all the discourses he had heard, could recall others in which it is defined in the sense intended here. Similarly, the doctrine of no-self, which is the basis of such voidness, is taken for granted. (The explanation is in the commentaries, though not in the commentary to this sutta, which relies on commentaries to earlier suttas in the Majjhima Nikāya for some of its material.) The discourse is concerned only with the purpose for which those already defined doctrines should be used, and not with the way in which we use them.

The discourse can be misunderstood if it is forgotten that the Buddha has described his teaching as having only one taste, that of deliverance, just as the sea has only one taste, that of salt (Udāna 5); and that he said of becoming: "Just as even a little dung stinks, so I do not recommend even a little becoming, not for so much as a finger snap" (AN 1 xviii. 13). And to understand its full force it must not be forgotten that one who ends selfish clinging (which maintains becoming), and reaches arahantship, figures as one who has achieved the good which surpasses all others for the benefit of the world. "To protect oneself, bhikkhus, the foundation of mindfulness should be cultivated. To protect another the foundation of mindfulness should be cultivated. One who protects himself protects another; one who protects another protects himself. And how, bhikkhus, does one who protects himself protect another? By cultivation, development, and repeated practice. And how, bhikkhus, does one who protects another protect himself? By patience, harmlessness, kindness and forbearance" (S V 169).

The Mahāsuññatā Sutta is mentioned in the commentaries as one of the *paṭipadā* suttas (see the Commentary to Majjhima No. 3), one of which would be adopted by a bhikkhu as a guide in the particular mode of practice (*paṭipadā*) that suited his temperament. Others of these *paṭipadā* suttas give prominence to such qualities as restraint and patience (MN 3), purity through the seven stages of purification (MN 24), and so forth. Here seclusion is stressed.

Ñāṇamoli Thera

Namo Tassa Bhagavato Arahato Sammāsambuddhassa

The Greater Discourse on Voidness

("Mahāsuññata Sutta"; Majjhima Nikāya No. 122)

1. Thus I heard: At one time the Blessed One was living in the country of the Sakyans, at Kapilavatthu in Nigrodha's park.

2. Then when it was morning, the Blessed One dressed and taking his bowl and robe went into Kapilavatthu for alms. After he had returned from his almsround, after his meal, he went to spend the day at the dwelling of Kāḷakhemaka the Sakyan. On that occasion, however, there were many resting places prepared in the dwelling of Kāḷakhemaka the Sakyan. When the Blessed One saw this, he thought: "There are many resting places prepared in the dwelling of Kāḷakhemaka the Sakyan; do many bhikkhus live there?"

3. But on that occasion the Venerable Ānanda was engaged with many bhikkhus in making robes at the dwelling of Ghaṭā the Sakyan. Then when it was evening, the Blessed One rose from meditation and he went to the dwelling of Ghaṭā the Sakyan: on arriving there he sat down on the appointed seat; when he had done so, the Blessed One said to the Venerable Ānanda: "There are many resting places prepared in the dwelling of Kāḷakhemaka the Sakyan; do many bhikkhus live there?"

4. "Many resting places, Venerable Sir, are prepared in the dwelling of Kāḷakhemaka the Sakyan; many bhikkhus are living there. A time for making robes is permitted to us, Venerable Sir."

5. "A bhikkhu, Ānanda, does not shine forth by delighting in company, enjoying company, devoted to delight in company, delighting in society, enjoying society, finding satisfaction in society.

6. "Indeed, Ānanda, that a bhikkhu delighting in company, enjoying company, devoted to delight in company, delighting in society, enjoying society, finding satisfaction in society should come to obtain the bliss of renunciation, the bliss of seclusion, the bliss of peace the bliss of enlightenment at will, without trouble

and in full, that is not possible. But when a bhikkhu lives alone, apart from society, that he may be expected to obtain the bliss of renunciation, the bliss of seclusion, the bliss of peace, the bliss of enlightenment at will, without trouble and in full, that is possible.

7. "Indeed, Ānanda, that a bhikkhu delighting in company, enjoying company, devoted to delight in company, delighting in society, enjoying society, finding satisfaction in society should enter upon and dwell in either the temporary, or the permanent and unshakeable, delectable mind deliverance, that is not possible. But when a bhikkhu lives alone, apart from society, that he may be expected to enter upon and dwell in the temporary, or the permanent and unshakeable, delectable mind deliverance, that is possible.

8. "I do not see, Ānanda, even one material form that, because of the change and alteration of that material form, will not cause sorrow and lamentation, pain, grief, and woe to arise in him who delights and takes pleasure therein.

9. "But this is the abiding, Ānanda, discovered by the Perfect One, that is, to enter upon and dwell in voidness internally by not bringing to mind any sign. If the Perfect One, Ānanda, dwelling therein by that abiding, is visited by bhikkhus or bhikkhunis, by men or women lay disciples, by kings or kings' ministers, by other sectarians or their followers, on such occasions, Ānanda, since his mind tends to seclusion, inclines to seclusion, is bent on seclusion, is detached, delights in renunciation and has put an end to all states that give rise to cankers, the Perfect One will assuredly give only such talk as is associated with dismissal.

10. "Therefore, Ānanda, if a bhikkhu should wish, 'May I enter upon and dwell in voidness internally,' that bhikkhu must settle, steady, unify and concentrate his mind internally.

11. "And how, Ānanda, does a bhikkhu settle, steady, unify and concentrate his mind internally?

"Here, Ānanda, a bhikkhu, secluded from sense desires, secluded from unprofitable things, enters upon and dwells in the first jhāna, which is accompanied by applied thought and sustained thought, and is filled with rapture and bliss born of seclusion.

"With the subsiding of applied and sustained thought, he enters upon and dwells in the second jhāna, which possesses internal serenity and singleness of mind and is without applied thought and without sustained thought, and is filled with rapture and bliss born of concentration.

"With the fading away of rapture, he dwells in equanimity, mindful and fully aware, and he feels with his mental faculties that bliss, of which the Noble Ones say: 'He who has equanimity and is mindful dwells happily'; thus he enters upon and dwells in the third jhāna.

"With the abandoning of bodily bliss and bodily pain, and with the disappearance of previous joy and grief, he enters upon and dwells in the fourth jhāna, which is neither painful nor pleasant and possesses mindfulness purified by equanimity.

"Thus, Ānanda, does a bhikkhu settle, steady, unify and concentrate his mind internally.

12. "He brings to mind voidness internally. While bringing to mind voidness internally, still his mind does not enter into voidness internally, nor does it become settled, steady and resolute. When that is so, Ānanda, the bhikkhu understands thus: 'While bringing to mind voidness internally, still my mind does not enter voidness internally, nor does it become settled, steady and resolute.' Thus he is possessed of full awareness therein.

"He brings to mind voidness externally...

"He brings to mind voidnesss internally and externally...

13. "He brings to mind the imperturbable. While bringing to mind the imperturbable, still his mind does not enter into the imperturbable, nor does it become settled, steady and resolute. When that is so, Ānanda, the bhikkhu understands thus: 'While bringing to mind the imperturbable, still my mind does not enter into the imperturbable, nor does it become settled, steady and resolute.' Thus he is possessed of full awareness therein.

14. "That bhikkhu, Ānanda, must then continue to settle, steady, unify and concentrate his mind internally in that same sign of concentration as before.

15. "He brings to mind voidness internally. While bringing to mind voidness internally, his mind enters into voidness internally, becomes settled, steady and resolute. When that is so, Ānanda, the bhikkhu understands thus: 'While bringing to mind voidness internally, my mind enters into voidness internally, becomes settled, steady and resolute.' Thus he is possessed of full awareness herein.

"He brings to mind voidness externally...

"He brings to mind voidness internally and externally...

16. "He brings to mind the imperturbable. While bringing to mind the imperturbable, his mind enters into the imperturbable, becomes settled, steady and resolute. When that is so, Ānanda, the bhikkhu understands thus: 'While bringing to mind the imperturbable, my mind enters into the imperturbable, becomes settled, steady and resolute.' Thus he is possessed of full awareness therein.

17. "If, Ānanda, dwelling in this way, a bhikkhu's mind inclines to walking, he walks: 'Walking thus, the evil, unprofitable states of covetousness and grief will not invade me.' Thus he is possessed of full awareness therein.

18. "If, Ānanda, dwelling in this way, a bhikkhu's mind inclines to standing, he stands: 'Standing thus, the evil, unprofitable states of mind will not invade me.' Thus he is possessed of full awareness therein.

19. "If, Ānanda, dwelling in this way, a bhikkhu's mind inclines to sitting, he sits...

20. "If, Ānanda, dwelling in this way, a bhikkhu's mind inclines to lying down, he lies down...

21. "If, Ānanda, dwelling in this way, a bhikkhu's mind inclines to talking he resolves: 'Such talk as is low, vulgar, base, ignoble, as leads to harm, as leads not to revulsion, to fading away, to cessation, to pacification, to direct knowledge, to enlightenment, to Nibbāna; that is to say, talk of kings, robbers, ministers, armies, alarms, battles, food, drink, clothing, beds, garlands, perfumes, relatives, vehicles, villages, towns, cities, countries, women, heroes, street inhabitants, wells, the dead, trivialities, the origin of the world, the origin of the sea, whether things are so or are not so—in such talk I shall not indulge.' Thus he is possessed of full awareness therein.

22. "But, Ānanda, he resolves: 'Such talk as is concerned with effacement, as favours the mind's release, as leads to complete revulsion, to fading away, to cessation, to pacification, to direct knowledge, to enlightenment, to Nibbāna; that is to say, talk on wanting little, on contentment, seclusion, aloofness from contact, strenuousness, virtuous conduct, concentration, understanding deliverance, knowledge and vision concerning deliverance—in such talk I shall indulge.' Thus he is possessed of full awareness

therein.

23. "If, Ānanda, dwelling in this way, a bhikkhu's mind inclines to thinking, he resolves, 'Such thoughts as are low, vulgar, base, ignoble, as lead to harm, as lead not to revulsion, to fading away, to cessation, to pacification, to direct knowledge, to enlightenment, to Nibbāna; that is to say, thoughts of lust, of ill-will, of cruelty—in such thoughts I shall not indulge.' Thus he is possessed of full awareness therein.

24. "But, Ānanda, he resolves, 'Such thoughts as are noble, as lead forth from the round of rebirths, and lead on rightly to the destruction of suffering for him who practises them; that is to say, thoughts of renunciation, non-ill-will, non-cruelty—in such thoughts I shall indulge.' Thus he is possessed of full awareness therein.

25. "There are, Ānanda, these five cords of sense-desire. What five? Visible objects cognizable by the eye that are sought after, desired, pleasing, gratifying, associated with desire and productive of greed; sounds cognizable by the ear...; odours cognizable by the nose...; flavours cognizable by the tongue...; tangible objects cognizable by the body that are sought after, desired, pleasing, gratifying, associated with desire and productive of greed. These are the five cords of sense-desire wherein a bhikkhu should constantly review his own mind thus: 'Does there arise in me any mental attachment concerned with any source of defilement among these five cords of sense-desire?'

26. "If, Ānanda, while reviewing, the bhikkhu understands, 'There arises in me mental attachment concerned with some source of defilement among these five cords of sense-desire,' then the bhikkhu understands thus: 'Greed for the five cords of sense-desire is not abandoned in me.' Thus he is possessed of full awareness therein.

27. "But if, Ānanda, while reviewing, the bhikkhu understands: 'There does not arise in me any mental attachment concerned with any source of defilement among these five cords of sense-desire,' then the bhikkhu understands thus, 'Greed for the five cords of sense-desire is abandoned in me.' Thus he is possessed of full awareness therein.

28. "There are, Ānanda, these five aggregates as objects of clinging, wherein a bhikkhu should dwell contemplating arising and passing away: 'Thus is matter, thus its arising, thus its passing

away; thus is feeling, thus its arising, thus its passing away; thus is perception, thus its arising, thus its passing away; thus are formations, thus their arising, thus their passing away; thus is consciousness, thus its arising, thus its passing away.'

29. "In one who dwells contemplating arising and passing away of these five aggregates as objects of clinging, the conceit 'I am,' based on these five aggregates as objects of clinging, is abandoned. This being so the bhikkhu understands thus: 'The conceit "I am," based on the five aggregates as objects of clinging, is abandoned in me.'

"Thus he is possessed of full awareness therein.

30. "These, Ānanda, are states of wholly profitable origin; they are noble, supramundane, inaccessible to the Evil One.

31. "What do you think, Ānanda? With what aim in view is a disciple justified in seeking the Master's company, even if resisted?"

32. "Our doctrines [*dhammā*], Venerable Sir, have their roots in the Blessed One; they have the Blessed One as their leader, have the Blessed One as their refuge. It would be good if the meaning of these words would occur to the Blessed One; having heard it, the bhikkhus will bear it in mind."

33. "A disciple, Ānanda, is not justified in seeking the Master's company for the sake of expositions of discourses and stanzas. Why is that? For long, Ānanda, these doctrines have been heard by you, borne in mind, recited by word, reviewed by the mind, thoroughly mastered by the understanding. But such talk as is concerned with effacement, as favours the mind's release, as leads to complete revulsion, to fading away, to cessation, to pacification, to direct knowledge, to enlightenment, to Nibbāna; that is to say, talk on wanting little, contentment, seclusion, aloofness from contact, strenuousness, virtuous conduct, concentration, understanding, deliverance, knowledge, and vision concerning deliverance—for the sake of such talk, Ānanda, a disciple is justified in seeking the Master's company, even if resisted.

34. "Yet when this is so, Ānanda, there comes to be the teacher's undoing, there comes to be the pupil's undoing and there comes to be the undoing of the dweller in the life of purity.

35. "And how, Ānanda, comes to be the teacher's undoing? Here, Ānanda, some teacher retires to a secluded abode: to the forest, the root of a tree, a rock, a hill cleft, a mountain cave, a

charnel ground, a woodland solitude, an open space, a heap of straw. While dwelling thus in retreat, priests and laymen from town and country visit him. When that happens, he goes astray, hungers, succumbs to craving and reverts to abundance. This teacher, Ānanda, is said to be undone by the teacher's undoing. He has been struck down by evil unprofitable things that bring defilement; cause continued becoming; conduce to misery; result in pain; and produce future birth, ageing and death. Thus, Ānanda, there comes to be the teacher's undoing.

36. "And how, Ānanda, does there come to be the pupil's undoing? A pupil of that teacher, emulating the teacher's seclusion, retires to a secluded abode .... Thus, Ānanda, there comes to be the pupil's undoing.

37. "And how, Ānanda, does there come to be the undoing of the dweller in the life of purity? Here, Ānanda, the Perfect One appears in the world, Accomplished, Fully Enlightened, endowed with clear vision and virtuous conduct, sublime, knower of worlds, incomparable leader of men to be tamed, teacher of gods and men, Enlightened, Blessed. He retires to a secluded abode: to the forest, the root of a tree, a rock, a hill cleft, a mountain cave, a charnel ground, a woodland solitude, an open space, a heap of straw. While dwelling thus in retreat, priests and laymen from town and country visit him. When this happens, he does not go astray, nor hunger, nor succumb to craving, nor revert to abundance. But a disciple of this teacher, emulating his teacher's seclusion, retires to a secluded abode .... While dwelling thus in retreat, priests and laymen from town and country visit him. When this happens, he goes astray, hungers, succumbs to craving and reverts to abundance. This dweller in the life of purity, Ānanda, is said to be undone by the undoing of the dweller in the life of purity. He has been struck down by evil, unprofitable things that bring defilement; cause continued becoming, conduce to misery; result in pain; and produce future birth, ageing and death. Thus, Ānanda, there comes to be the undoing of a dweller in the life of purity. And herein, Ānanda, the undoing of a dweller in the life of purity has a more painful result, a more bitter result, than the teacher's undoing or the pupil's undoing, and it even leads to rebirth in the states of woe.

38. "And herein, Ānanda, bear yourselves towards me in amity,

not in hostility; long shall that be to your welfare and happiness.

39. "And how, Ānanda, do disciples bear themselves in hostility towards the Master, not in amity? Here, Ānanda, compassionate and seeking their welfare, the Master teaches the Truth [Dhamma] to the disciples out of compassion: 'This is for your welfare, this is for your happiness.' His disciples do not want to hear, do not give ear, do not lend their minds to knowledge; erring, they turn aside from the Master's teaching. Thus do disciples bear themselves in hostility towards the Master, not in amity.

40. "And how, Ānanda, do disciples bear themselves in amity towards the Master, not in hostility? Here, Ānanda, compassionate and seeking their welfare, the Master teaches the Truth to the disciples out of compassion: 'This is for your welfare, this is for your happiness.' His disciples want to hear, give ear, lend their minds to knowledge; nor, erring, do they turn aside from the Master's teaching. Thus do disciples bear themselves in amity towards the Master, not in hostility.

"Therefore, Ānanda, bear yourselves in amity towards me, not in hostility; long shall this be for your welfare and happiness.

41. "I shall not, Ānanda, treat you as the potter treats the raw damp clay. Repeatedly admonishing, repeatedly testing, I shall speak to you, Ānanda. He who is sound will stand the test."

So said the Blessed One. Glad at heart, the Venerable Ānanda rejoiced at his words.

Commentary

(What follows is a translation of the Commentary to the Majjhima Nikāya 122 in the *Papañcasūdanī*, supplemented where necessary, and as indicated, with paragraphs from other commentaries to earlier *Majjhima Nikāya* discourses.)

1. Thus I heard: The Mahāsuññata Sutta. (Comy. to MN 122) Herein, *in the country of the Sakyans* means in the country so named; for that country came to be known as Sakyan because it was the Sakyan princes' residence. But the origin of the Sakyans has been handed down in the Commentary to the "Ambaṭṭha Sutta" (DN 3). *At Kapilavatthu*: in the town so named; for that town was called Kapilavatthu ("Kapila land") because it had been the sage Kapila's residence. That was the village on which he depended for alms. *In Nigrodha's park*: the Sakyan named Nigrodha. When the Blessed One had come to Kapilavatthu at the time of the foregathering of his relatives, Nigrodha had a dwelling place made in his own park and assigned to the Blessed One. It means that he was living in it. (Commentary to MN 14)

2. *Of Kāḷakhemaka* (of "Black" Khemaka): He was called "Black" because of the colour of his skin; but his name was Khemaka. *Dwelling*: a dwelling (monastery) made in that same Nigrodha's park, in one part, by erecting a surrounding wall, building a gate house, constructing dwellings [like those called *haṃsa-vaṭṭaka*?], such as a meeting hall, a refectory, and so forth. *Many resting places*: bed, chair, mattress, pillow, straw mat, leather mat, spread grass, spread leaves, spread straw and so forth were prepared. They were placed bed touching bed ... spread straw touching spread straw, so that it resembled the dwelling place of bhikkhus who have formed themselves into a society. *Do many*: The Blessed One has no doubts, because of the complete destruction of all his defilements during the Session of Enlightenment. The question is a rhetorical one, and the word "do" is merely rhetorical. No one who is uncertain gets to the acme of attainment. Before this, it seems, the Blessed One had not seen ten or twelve bhikkhus living in one place. Then it occurred to him: "This social life is developed to the utmost in the round of becoming. As water collects into rivers, so social life is developed

by beings in hell, in the animal world, in the realm of ghosts and in the Asura group; and also in the human world, the divine world and the Brahmā world. For hell is ten-thousand leagues across and is crammed with beings like a tube packed with bath powder. There is no counting or reckoning the beings in the place of torture by the fivefold binding [see MN 129 and 130]; likewise in the places of paring with adzes and so forth [see MN 129 and 130]. Such is the way they roast in society. As to the animal world there is no counting or reckoning the termites in a single termite hill; and likewise ants in each ants' nest. Such is social life in the animal world too. And there are ghost cities a quarter or half a league across crowded with ghosts. Such is social life in the ghost realm, too. The ten-thousand league sphere of Asura demons is like an earring or hole when the needle is put into the ear [?]. Such is social life in the Asura group too. As regards the human world, there were 5,700,000 in the large clans living at Sāvatthī, and inside and outside Rājagaha 1,800,000 people [18 *koṭis*]. Such is social life in certain places of the human world too. Beginning with the earth deities, there is social life in the divine world and the Brahmā world also. Each deity has two and a half *koṭis* of dancers, even up to nine *koṭis*. Also there are ten thousand Brahmās living in one place."

Thereupon he thought: "For four incalculable ages and a hundred thousand aeons the Perfections have been fulfilled by me for the purpose of undoing living in societies. And as soon as these bhikkhus have formed themselves into a society and get to delight in society, they will act contrary to that." Then feeling concern for the Dhamma, he thought again: "If it were possible to announce a training precept that two bhikkhus should not live in one place I would do so; but that is not possible. So I shall expound the discourse called The Great Way of Voidness, which, for training clansmen, will be like an announced training precept, like a full-length looking glass placed at the city gate. After that, just as Khattiyas [nobles] and so on, seeing their blemishes in that looking glass get rid of them and become unblemished, so indeed, even for 5,000 years after I have attained complete extinction, clansmen delighting in solitude will make an end of the suffering due to the round of becoming by harkening to this discourse and avoiding society." And the number of clansmen who, by harkening to this discourse and avoiding society, have, as though fulfilling the Blessed One's wish, made an end of suffering and attained complete extinction is past reckoning. For in the Vālikapiṭṭhi Monastery [in Sri Lanka] the Abhidhamma scholar called the Elder Abhaya, after reciting this discourse together with a number of bhikkhus on the occasion of taking up residence for the rainy season, exclaimed: "The Fully Enlightened One enjoins us to act thus; and what are we doing?" And by avoiding society and delighting in solitude all of them attained arahantship within that same rainy season. This discourse is called the "breaker-up of societies."

3. *Of Ghaṭā*: of the one so named. *At the dwelling*: This dwelling, too, was built like Kāḷakhemaka's dwelling, in a part of Nigrodha's park. *Making robes*: the repairing of those already made by patching, washing, and so forth, old and dirty ones; and it is also the making up of unmade ones by arranging and sewing cloth provided for the purpose of robes. Both are right, but here making up of unmade ones is intended, for people had given the Elder Ānanda material for robes, which is why he was doing work on robes there with a number of bhikkhus.

4. And those bhikkhus, sitting from the time announced for the needle work in the morning, get up from it some time unannounced, thinking: "When the sewing is finished we shall set our resting places in order." They had not set them in order, as "It is our time for robe making." The Elder, it seems, thought: "Surely it is those resting places that have not been arranged by those bhikkhus that will have been seen by the Blessed One; consequently the Master is displeased and desires to give a severe reproof. I will be a support for those bhikkhus." That is why he spoke as he did. But the intention here is this: "Venerable Sir, these bhikkhus are living in this way not just because they delight in being busy, but on account of robe-making."

5. *A bhikkhu, Ānanda, does not shine forth*: "Ānanda, whether it is an instance of being busy or whether it is an instance of robe-making or not, still a bhikkhu who delights in company does not shine forth. Do not be a support where there is no occasion for support." Here, *company* is gathering with one's own community; *society* is gathering with different sorts of people. So whether he delights in company or in society, in either case a bhikkhu who likes the fullness of society, who is bound by the ties of society,

does not shine forth. But it is when a bhikkhu sweeps out his daytime quarters after his meal and, after washing his feet well, takes up his basic meditation subject and devotes himself to delight in solitude, he shines forth in the Enlightened One's Dispensation.

6. *The bliss of renunciation*: the bliss in him who has renounced sense-desires. *The bliss of seclusion* is the bliss of seclusion from sense-desires too. But what leads to the pacification of greed and so forth is *the bliss of peace*, what leads to the enlightenment due to the path is the *bliss of enlightenment. Obtain ... at will*: one who obtains his desire, who obtains his wish without trouble; one who obtains without pain; one who obtains in abundance.

7. *Temporary*: free from defilement on any occasion of full absorption. *Delectable*: agreeable. *Mind deliverance*: the mind deliverance of the fine-material and immaterial worlds. For it is said: "The four absorptions [jhāna] and the four immaterial attainments, these are the temporary liberation." *Permanent*: not deliverance from defilements occasionally but rather deliverance which is perpetual and supramundane. For it is said: "The four noble paths and the four fruitions of recluseship, these are the permanent liberation." *Unshakeable*: not to be shaken by defilements.

So far what has been said? A bhikkhu who delights in company, who is bound by the ties of society, will be unable to produce either mundane or supramundane special qualities. But by avoiding society and delighting in solitude he can do so. For just as in the case of the Bodhisatta Vipassi, as long as he wandered during seven years surrounded by eighty-four thousand homeless ones, he was unable to produce the special quality of omniscience; but by avoiding society and delighting in solitude he climbed to the summit of enlightenment and produced the special quality of omniscience in seven days. Also as long as our Bodhisatta wandered with the Group of Five during six years he was unable to produce the special quality of omniscience; but when they left him, by delighting in solitude he climbed the summit of enlightenment and produced the special quality of omniscience.

8. Having thus pointed out the lack of attainment of special qualities of one who delights in company, he said: *I do not see, Ānanda*, etc., in order to point out how this flaw arises. Here, *one material form* is a physical body. *In him who delights ... therein*: in him who delights through greed for that material form; *will not*

cause ... to arise: that would not cause these things to arise in him who delights in that material form: "I do not see any such material form." And then they arise, too, as they did in Sañjaya owing to the changed state of Sāriputta and Moggallāna, called their coming to the discipleship of Him of the Ten Powers [see *Vinaya Mahā Vagga*]; as they did in Nātha-puta owing to the changed state of the householder Upāli [see MN 71]; and as they did in the rich man in the *Piyajātika Sutta* [see MN 87].

9. *But this ... Ānanda*: What is the sequence of meaning? For the purpose of removing the occasion in which any unintelligent bhikkhu newly gone forth should say: "The Fully Enlightened One leads us away from society like cattle sent into a field, and he exhorts us to solitude, but he himself lives surrounded by kings, kings' ministers, and so on," he began this part of the teaching in order to show that the Perfect One is alone even when sitting in the midst of a community extending over a world sphere.

Any sign: any sign [mark] of visible objects and so forth [of materiality, and so forth]. *Internally*: internally as regards place of occurrence. *Voidness*: fruition attainment through Voidness [Commentary to MN 122].

Fruition attainment is called voidness firstly in virtue of its own special quality .... But Nibbana as its object is also called voidness as it is void of greed, hate and delusion .... It is also explained according to the way of coming to the path; for insight is called "void" and "signless" and "desireless." Herein, when a bhikkhu, after laying hold of formations as impermanent and seeing them in their impermanent aspect, causes emergence of the path in the impermanent aspect, his insight leading to emergence is called signless [*animitta*]. When after laying hold of them as painful and seeing them in their painful aspect, it is called desireless [*appaṇihita*]. When, after laying hold of them as no-self and seeing them in their aspect of no-self, he causes emergence of the path in the aspect of no-self, it is called void [*suñña*]. Herein the path due to signless insight is called signless and the fruition of the signless path is called signless. Likewise, the desireless and the void [Commentary to MN 44].

His mind tends to seclusion: tends to Nibbāna. It has put an end to, is without remainder of, unsupported by, dissociated from, states which give rise to cankers. *Associated with dismissal*:

associated with such words as "You may go." But at what periods did the Blessed One speak thus? Either during the period of activity following the meal, or during the period of activity in the first watch [of the night]. For after the meal the Blessed One adopts the lion's pose in the Perfumed Cell and then he rises and sits absorbed in fruition attainment. At that time the community gathers for the purpose of hearing the Dhamma. Then the Blessed One, who knows the time, comes forth from the Perfumed Cell and goes to the Enlightened One's exalted seat and he teaches the Dhamma. Then, not exceeding the time, like one judging the cooking of a medicinal oil, he dismisses the community with his mind inclining to seclusion. Also in the first watch of the night, he dismisses the community thus: "The night is well advanced; now it is time to do as you think fit." For since reaching enlightenment even the Buddhas' twofold five-door-consciousness incline to Nibbāna. [The twofold five-door consciousness are the kamma-resultant eye-, ear-, nose-, tongue- and body-consciousness, each with either a pleasant or an unpleasant object, as explained in the *Visuddhimagga*, Ch. XIV. The sub-commentary (*Ṭīkā*) to the *Papañcasūdanī* comments: "The two fivefold consciousness incline to Nibbāna owing to the mind-consciousness being intent upon it. For it is owing to the thoroughness of the Buddhas' full-understanding of formations that only the repugnant aspect appears evident even in refined objects which come into focus. How much more so in the others? The mind inclines only to Nibbāna because of Nibbāna's extreme peacefulness and sublimity, just as one who is harassed by thirst inclines to a place where there is cool water."]

10-11. *Therefore, Ānanda*: because dwelling in voidness is peaceful and sublime, therefore. *Internally*: only internally as to the range of object (that is, not externally).

12. *Voidness internally*: in himself internally; the meaning is: produced in regard to his own five aggregates [Commentary to MN 122].

"And which, friend, is the mind-deliverance of voidness? Here, friend, a bhikkhu, gone to the forest or to the root of a tree or to an empty place, considers thus: 'This is void of self or property of a self'" [MN 43].

Of self: void of self, called personality, man, person, and so on. *Or property of a self*: Void of anything belonging to self called requisite of robes and so forth... The mind-deliverance of voidness belongs to the sense-sphere as to plane, and its object is formations; for it is insight that is here meant by "voidness" [Commentary to MN 43].

Possessed of full awareness: fully aware through successfully knowing the meditation subject. *Externally*: in regard to another's five aggregates. *Internally and externally*: at one time internally, at another time externally.

13. *The imperturbable* [*āneñjā*: this is a term for the four immaterial attainments of the sphere of boundless space, and so forth]: he brings to mind the imperturbable immaterial attainment [resolving]: "I will become one who is Both Ways Released" [*ubhato-bhāga-vimatto,* that is, one who has attained both all eight meditative attainments and arahantship].

14. *In that same sign of concentration as before* is said with reference to jhāna treated as the basis for insight. For when one who has emerged from a basic jhāna which is still unfamiliar, and brings to mind voidness internally, his mind does not enter into voidness. Thereupon, thinking: "How about another's continuity [of aggregates]?" he brings it to mind externally. There also it does not enter into it. Thereupon thinking: "How about at one time in my own continuity and another time in another's continuity?" he brings to mind internally and externally. There also it does not enter into it. Thereupon, desiring to become one who is Both Ways Released, thinking: "How about the immaterial attainment?" he brings to mind the imperturbable. There also it does not enter into voidness. Now in that case he should not give up his effort and go following after supporters and so on, but the same basic jhāna should be thoroughly brought to mind again and again. Thus he said, "In that same" and so on, in order to point out that it is like a tree cutter's axe that does not have its effect; but by resharpening the edge the axe may cut. Similarly, his repeatedly bringing to mind the basic jhāna will have its effect in regard to the meditation subject.

15-16. Now in order to point out that, when one has practised this, his bringing to mind succeeds in respect to whatever he brings to mind, he *enters into*.

17. *Dwelling in this way*: in this way consisting of serenity [concentration] and insight [*samatha-vipassanā*]. *Thus he is possessed*

of full awareness therein: so, when the meditation subject succeeds while he is walking, he is possessed of full awareness through knowing that his meditation subject has succeeded.

18-20. *Lies down*: stretches himself out. Here, after walking for any given length of time, now knowing, "I am able to walk for so long," he should stand, without breaking the sequence of postures; and so in each section [Commentary to MN 122].

21. *Talk of kings* is talk about kings proceeding like this: "Mahāsammata, Mandhātu, Dhammāsoka had so much power" and so on. So too in the case of *robbers*, and so on. As regards these, such talk as "such and such a king is handsome, good looking" and so forth, is both worldly talk and "animal talk" [that is, pointless]. But if it proceeds, "So and so who was so powerful came to destruction," it keeps within the meditation subject. And as regards robbers, talk about Mūladeva or Meghamāla being so powerful and about their deeds thus: "Ah, what heroes!" is worldly talk and "animal talk." And as regards *battles*, it is "animal talk" when it is instigated by satisfaction of sense-desires thus: "In the Bhārata battle, and so forth, so and so was killed thus, was wounded thus"; but when it proceeds, "even they came to destruction," then talk in each case conforms to a meditation subject. Moreover it is wrong to talk about *food* and so forth according to satisfaction of sense-desires thus: "We chewed, we ate, we drank, we used what looked like this, smelt like this, tasted like this, was like this to touch." But it is right to talk of it meaningfully thus: "Formerly we gave food, drink, clothing, beds, garlands and perfumes that looked like this and so forth to the virtuous; we made such an offering at the shrine." As regards *relatives* and so on, it is wrong to say, according to satisfaction of sense-desires, "our relatives are brave, capable" or "formerly we went about in vehicles like this." But it should be said meaningfully thus: "Even those relatives of ours have passed away" or "formerly we gave sandals like this to the Order." *Villages*: it is wrong to talk of villages as good or bad to live in, or easy or hard to get alms in, or according to satisfaction of sense-desires thus: "The inhabitants of such and such a village are brave, capable." But it is right to talk meaningfully thus: "They have faith, they have confidence" or "They have come to destruction and have passed away." So too in the case of *towns, cities and countries.* Talk of *women* is wrong when instigated by satisfaction of sense-desires

and is about appearance, figure, and so forth; it is right only if it proceeds thus: "They have faith, confidence" or "they have come to destruction." Talk of *heroes* is wrong if it is in accordance with satisfaction of sense-desires thus: "The soldier called Nandamitta was a hero"; it is right only if it proceeds thus: "He had faith" or "He has come to destruction." Talk of *street inhabitants* is wrong if it accords with satisfaction of sense-desires thus: "The people of such and such a street are easy to live with, brave, capable"; it is right only if it proceeds thus: "They have faith" or "They have come to destruction." Talk of *wells* is said of talk of places for getting water, or it is talk of women water-carriers. It is wrong when concerned with satisfaction of sense-desires thus: "She is pretty, she is clever at dancing and singing"; it is right only if it begins, "She has faith, has confidence." Talk of the *dead* is talk of past relatives; the definition here is the same as that for present relatives. Talk of *trivialities* is meaningless talk of different kinds that is not included in those already dealt with and still to be dealt with. Talk of *the origin of the world* is talk of the Lokāyatas,[1] sophists [*vitaṇḍa*] and chatter of the kind beginning, "This world was created by whom? It was created by so and so." "A crow is white because its bones are white." "A crane is red because its blood is red." *Talk of the origin of the sea* is meaningless talk of the sea's origin of the kind beginning thus: "Why [is it called] sea [*samudda*]? Because it was excavated by the god Sāgara. Because he marked it with the seal [*muddā*] of his hand saying, 'The ocean [*sāgara*] has been excavated by me, it is called sea [*samudda*].' "*Whether things are so or are not* so is talk asserting that for some meaningless reason or other there is consequently existence; there is consequently non-existence. And here "existence" is eternity and "non-existence" is annihilation; "existence" is increase, "non-existence" is diminution; "existence" is sense-pleasure, "non-existence" is self-mortification. So with this talk on *whether things are so or are not so*, "animal talk" is of thirty-two kinds [Commentary to MN 76].

In such talk I shall not indulge. Thus he is possessed of full awareness: thus he is one who practises full awareness through knowing "*I shall not indulge.*" In the second paragraph he is one who practises full awareness through knowing, "In such talk I

1. A Lokāyata is a philosopher who engages in cosmological speculations.

shall indulge." This bhikkhu's serenity and insight are fresh,[2] and for the purpose of guarding them the seven kinds of suitable things are needed:

"Abode, resort, and speech, and person,
The food, the climate, and posture,
Select and cultivate of each
The kind that is most suitable."
This is said for the purpose of pointing these out.

22. [For the ten kinds of suitable talk see below.]

23-24. As regards the two paragraphs dealing with thoughts, full awareness should be understood as knowing respectively the not thinking and the thinking of the thoughts.

25. Having thus stated two of the paths by the abandoning of wrong thoughts, he now said: *There are, Ānanda, these five cords of sense-desire,* and so on, speaking of the insight for the third path. *Concerned with any source of defilement*: concerned with any reason whatever among these five cords of sense-desire for the arising of defilements. *Attachment*: unabandoned defilement which appears as attachment.

26. *Then*: it being present. *Possessed of full awareness*: possessed of full awareness through knowing the success of the meditation subject.

27. In the second paragraph, *possessed of full awareness* means possessed of full awareness through knowing the success of the meditation subject. For when he reviews thus: "Is desire and greed in regard to these five cords of sense-desire abandoned in me or not?" and knows that it is not abandoned, this bhikkhu exerts energy and abolishes it by means of the path of Non-Return. Thereupon, when he reviews after emerging from the fruition which follows next upon the path, he knows that it is abandoned. He is possessed of full awareness through knowing that, is what is meant.

28-29. Now speaking of the arahant path, he said, *There are, Ānanda, the five aggregates as objects of clinging*, and so on. *Is*

---

2. According to the *Visuddhimagga*, "fresh [or weak] insight" (*taruna vipassani*) extends as far as the Contemplation of Danger, but from the Contemplation of Revulsion onwards it is "strong insight." (See Chapter xxi.)

abandoned means that the conceit "I am," the desire, the inherent tendency to assert "I am" based on materiality, is abandoned; likewise that based on feeling and so on. Full awareness should be understood as previously stated.

30. *These, Ānanda, are states* is said with reference to the states of serenity [*samatha*] and insight [*vipassana*] and path and fruition set forth above. *Of ... profitable origin*: come from what is profitable. For profitable states can be both profitable and derived from the profitable, that is to say, the first jhāna is profitable, the second jhāna is both profitable and derived from the profitable; the sphere of nothingness is profitable and the sphere of neither-perception-nor-non-perception is both profitable and derived from the profitable; the sphere of neither-perception-nor-non-perception is profitable and the path of Stream-entry is both profitable and derived from the profitable; the path of Non-Return is profitable and the path of arahantship is both profitable and derived from the profitable. Likewise the first jhāna is profitable and states associated therewith are both profitable and derived from the profitable; the path of arahantship is profitable and the states associated therewith are both profitable and derived from the profitable. *Noble*: free from defilements and purified. *Supramundane*: beyond the world and purified. *Inaccessible to the Evil One*: inaccessible to Māra, the Evil One. For Māra does not see the mind of a bhikkhu who sits absorbed in the eight attainments when they are made the basis of insight. Nor is he able to know the consciousness that occurs in dependence on that as object. That is why "inaccessible" is said.

31–32. *What do you think*. Why did he say this? He said it in order to point out that there is one advantage in society. *In seeking the Master's company*: in going to, in frequenting.

33. *A disciple, Ānanda, is not*: Here, though one who is well-taught [who has studied much] has been compared by the Blessed One to a soldier possessed of the five weapons in the passage "The well-taught noble disciple, bhikkhus, abandons the unprofitable and develops the profitable, he abandons the reproachable and develops the irreproachable; and so he safeguards himself" [A IV 109]. Nevertheless, since he who does not, after learning the scriptures, practise in conformity with them, lacks those weapons, but he who does so has them, he therefore said "a disciple, Ānanda,

is not," and so on, pointing out that he is not justified in seeking his company with that aim alone in view.

Now, in order to point out with what aim in view the Master's company should be sought, he said, *But such talk as is* and so on. So in this sutta, the ten examples of talk [that is, talk of wanting little, of contentment, and so forth] are given in three places: *in such talk I shall indulge* [Paragraph 22] they are given by way of the suitable and the unsuitable; in the passage *for the sake of expositions of discourses and stanzas* [Paragraph 33] they are given as scriptures learned by ear; and *in this place* [Paragraph 33] they are given directly, as something to be fulfilled. Therefore one who explains the ten examples of talk in this sutta should do so pausing here for that purpose. [The "ten examples of (suitable) talk" are treated in detail in the Commentary to MN 24.]

34. Now because there are some who dwell alone and who are not successful in getting at the meaning of the scriptures, he therefore said, *Yet when this is so, Ānanda* and so on, pointing out the disadvantage in solitude with reference to that. Here, *Yet when this is so, Ānanda* means when this solitary state exists. The teacher is a teacher who is a sectarian outside the Dispensation.

35–37. *Be the teacher's undoing*: the undoing of the teacher is by the undoing due to defilements that have arisen inside him. So with the other kinds of undoing. *He has been struck down*: they [that is, the unsuitable things] have killed him; the death of his special qualities and virtues (not his physical death) is stated by this.

38. But why is it said that *the undoing of the dweller in the life of purity* has a more painful result, a more bitter result, and it even leads to rebirth in states of woe? Going into homelessness outside the Dispensation brings small gain; there is no outstandingly great or special quality to be developed there, but only the eight [meditative] attainments and the five supernormal powers beginning with the miraculous powers. Accordingly, just as there is no great suffering for one who falls from the back of a donkey (his body merely gets covered with dust), so, since in a sect outside the Dispensation he falls only from worldly special qualities [*lokiya-guṇa*], it is not said in this way of the first two kinds of undoing. But going into homelessness in the Dispensation brings great gain. Here the outstandingly special qualities are the four paths, the four fruitions, and Nibbāna. Accordingly, just as when a noble youth,

wellborn on both parental sides, traversing a city and seated in the place of honour on the back of an elephant, falls from the elephant's back, he comes to great suffering; so, since in falling away from the Dispensation he falls away from the expectation of the [aforesaid] nine supramundane special qualities [*lokuttara-guṇa*], it is said in this way of the undoing of the dweller in the life of purity.

39–40. *Therefore:* the construing should be done both with the preceding meaning and with the following meaning thus: because the undoing of the dweller in the life of purity leads to greater suffering than the other two kinds, because the practice of hostility [towards the Blessed One, see the *Discourse* (Paragraphs 38–39)] for long leads to harm and suffering, but the practice of amity [towards the Blessed One] leads to welfare. *In amity*: by the practice of amity. *In hostility*: by the practice of hostility.

Erring, they turn aside from the Master's teaching: one who transgresses on purpose even by as much as an offence of wrongdoing [*dukkata*] or wrong speech [*dubbhāsita*] is called one who "errs, turns aside."

It is one who does not so transgress that is called one who "does not err, does not turn aside."

41. *I shall not, Ānanda, treat you as:* I shall not behave towards you like. *Raw*: unbaked. *Damp clay*: a raw, not quite dry pot. For a potter takes the raw, not quite dry, clay pot gently with both hands lest it should break. Accordingly, I shall not behave towards you as the potter behaves towards the damp clay. *Repeatedly admonishing*: after advising once I shall not be silent; I shall advise and instruct by repeatedly admonishing. *Repeatedly testing*: by repeatedly testing for flaws. Just as the potter tests for those that are cracked, split or faulty among the baked pots and puts them aside, and he takes only those that are well-baked after he has tapped them again and again, so I too shall advise and instruct by repeatedly testing. He who is sound will stand the test: he among you thus advised by me, who is sound, through having reached the path and its fruition, will stand the test. Furthermore the worldly special qualities as well are here intended by "sound."

The rest is clear throughout. (Commentary to MN 122)

Buddhist Meditation and Depth Psychology

by

Douglas M. Burns

WHEEL PUBLICATION NO. 88/89

Introduction

Mind is the forerunner of all (evil) conditions.
Mind is their chief, and they are mind-made.
If, with an impure mind, one speaks or acts,
Then suffering follows one
Even as the cart wheel follows the hoof of the ox.

Mind is the forerunner of all (good) conditions.
Mind is their chief, and they are mind-made.
If, with a pure mind, one speaks or acts,
Then happiness follows one
Like a never-departing shadow.

These words, which are the opening lines of the Dhammapada, were spoken by Gotama Buddha 2500 years ago. They illustrate the central theme of Buddhist teaching, the human mind.

Buddhism is probably the least understood of all major religions. Indeed, from an Occidental viewpoint we might well question whether it warrants the title of religion. In the West we are accustomed to thinking of theology in terms of God, revelation, obedience, punishment, and redemption. The themes of creation, worship, judgement, and immortality have been major concerns in the Christian heritage and are virtually inseparable from our concept of religion. Against such a cultural background Western man views Buddhism and in so doing unconsciously projects his own concepts, values, and expectations. Erroneously he perceives ceremonies and bowing as examples of worship or even idolatry.

He may extol its scientific world view or abhor and condemn its "atheism." The Buddha is vaguely equated with God or Jesus, and meditation is suspected of being a hypnotic approach to mysticism or an escape from reality.

However, such erroneous notions of the Dhamma, the Teaching of the Buddha, are not entirely the result of Western ignorance and ethnocentrism. Before his demise the Buddha predicted that within a thousand years his doctrine would fall into the hands of men of lesser understanding and would thereby become corrupted and distorted.[1] Such has been the case throughout much, if not most, of the Orient. Ritual has replaced self-discipline, faith has replaced insight, and prayer has replaced understanding.

If the basis of Christianity is God, the basis of Buddhism is mind. From the Buddhist viewpoint, mind or consciousness is the core of our existence. Pleasure and pain, good and evil, time and space, life and death, have no meaning to us apart from our awareness of them or thoughts about them. Whether God exists or does not exist, whether existence is primarily spiritual or primarily material, whether we live for a few decades or live forever—all these matters are, in the Buddhist view, secondary to the one empirical fact of which we do have certainty: the existence of conscious experience as it proceeds through the course of daily living. Therefore Buddhism focuses on the mind; for happiness and sorrow, pleasure and pain, are psychological experiences. Even such notions as purpose, value, virtue, goodness, and worth have meaning only as the results of our attitudes and feelings.

Buddhism does not deny the reality of material existence, nor does it ignore the very great effect that the physical world has upon us. On the contrary, it refutes the mind-body dichotomy of the Brahmans and says that mind and body are interdependent. But since the fundamental reality of human existence is the ever-changing sequence of thoughts, feelings, emotions, and perceptions which comprise conscious experience, then, from the viewpoint of early Buddhism, the primary concern of religion must be these very experiences which make up our daily lives. Most significant of these are love and hate, fear and sorrow, pride and passion, struggle and defeat. Conversely, such concepts as vicarious atonement, Cosmic Consciousness, Ultimate Reality, Buddha Nature, and redemption of sins are metaphysical and hypothetical matters of secondary importance to the realities of daily existence.

Therefore, in Buddhism the most significant fact of life is the First Noble Truth, the inevitable existence of *dukkha. Dukkha* is a Pali word embracing all types of displeasurable experience—sorrow, fear, worry, pain, despair, discord, frustration, agitation,

1. *Buddhism,* by Richard A. Gard. New York: George Braziller, Inc., 1961, pp. 207–8.

irritation, etc. The Second Noble Truth states that the cause of *dukkha* is desire or craving. In various texts this cause is further explained as being threefold—greed, hatred, and delusion. Again, on other occasions the Buddha divided the cause of suffering into five components—sensual lust, anger, sloth or torpor, agitation or worry, and doubt. On still other occasions he listed ten causes of *dukkha*—belief that oneself is an unchanging entity; scepticism; belief in salvation through rites, rules, and ceremonies; sensual lust; hatred; craving for fine-material existence; craving for immaterial existence; conceit; restlessness; and ignorance. The Third Noble Truth states that *dukkha* can be overcome, and the Fourth Truth prescribes the means by which this is achieved.

Thus, with the Fourth Noble Truth, Buddhism becomes a technique, a discipline, a way of life designed to free people from sorrow and improve the nature of human existence. This aspect of the Dhamma is called the Noble Eightfold Path, and includes moral teachings, self-discipline, development of wisdom and understanding, and improvement of one's environment on both a personal and social level. These have been dealt with in previous writings and for the sake of brevity will not be repeated here. Suffice it to remind the reader that this essay is concerned with only one aspect of Buddhism, the practice of meditation. The ethical, practical, and logical facets of the teaching are covered in other publications.

If the cause of suffering is primarily psychological, then it must follow that the cure, also, is psychological. Therefore, we find in Buddhism a series of "mental exercises" or meditations designed to uncover and cure our psychic aberrations.

Mistakenly, Buddhist meditation is frequently confused with yogic meditation, which often includes physical contortions, autohypnosis, quests for occult powers, and an attempted union with God. These are not concerns or practices of the Eightfold Path. There are in Buddhism no drugs or stimulants, no secret teachings, and no mystical formulae. Buddhist meditation deals exclusively with the everyday phenomena of human consciousness. In the words of the Venerable Nyanaponika Thera, a renowned Buddhist scholar and monk:

> In its spirit of self-reliance, Satipaṭṭhāna does not require any elaborate *technique* or external devices. The daily life is its working material. It has nothing to do with any exotic

cults or rites nor does it confer "initiations" or "esoteric knowledge" in any way other than by self-enlightenment.

Using just the conditions of life it finds, Satipaṭṭhāna does not require complete seclusion or monastic life, though in some who undertake the practice, the desire and need for these may grow.[2]

Lest the reader suspect that some peculiarity of the "Western mind" precludes Occidentals from the successful practice of meditation, we should note also the words of Rear Admiral E. H. Shattock, a British naval officer, who spent three weeks of diligent meditation practice in a Theravada monastery near Rangoon:

> Meditation, therefore, is a really practical occupation: it is in no sense necessarily a religious one, though it is usually thought of as such. It is itself basically academic, practical, and profitable. It is, I think, necessary to emphasize this point, because so many only associate meditation with holy or saintly people, and regard it as an advanced form of the pious life... This is not the tale of a conversion, but of an attempt to test the reaction of a well-tried Eastern system on a typical Western mind.[3]

Reading about meditation is like reading about swimming; only by getting into the water does the aspiring swimmer begin to progress. So it is with meditation and Buddhism in general. The Dhamma must be lived, not merely thought. Study and contemplation are valuable tools, but life itself is the training ground.

The following passages are attempts to put into words what must be experienced within oneself. Or in the words of the Dhammapada: "Buddhas only point the way. Each one must work out his own salvation with diligence." Meditation is a personal experience, a subjective experience, and consequently each of us must tread his or her own path towards the summit of Enlightenment. By words we can instruct and encourage but words are only symbols for reality.

---

2. *The Heart of Buddhist Meditation*, by Nyanaponika Thera. London: Rider & Co., 1962, p. 82.

3. *An Experiment in Mindfulness*, by E.H. Shattock. New York: E. P. Dutton & Co., Inc., 1960, pp. 17, 19.

The Goals of Meditation

Before discussing the techniques of meditation, it is important that we first define its goals. That is, why does one meditate? What does one hope to achieve?

The ultimate goals of meditation are the ultimate goals of Buddhism, i.e., realisation of Nibbāna and the abolition of *dukkha* or suffering. Nibbāna, however, is beyond the realm of conceptualisation and all other forms of normal human experience. Therefore, we have no certainty that it exists until we ourselves have progressed to realising it as a direct experience transcending logic and sense perception. Nibbāna can thus be defined as that which is experienced when one has achieved ultimate moral and psychological maturation. Little more can be said.

Therefore the Buddha said relatively little about Nibbāna and instead directed most of his teachings towards two lesser goals which are empirical realities of readily demonstrable worth. These were, first, the increase, enhancement, and cultivation of positive feelings such as love, compassion, equanimity, mental purity, and the happiness found in bringing happiness to others. Secondly, he advocated the relinquishment and renunciation of greed, hatred, delusion, conceit, agitation, and other negative, unwholesome states.

As we gain in experience and self-understanding, and as we acquire full appreciation for the nature and quality of our own feelings, we find that the positive feelings (love, compassion, etc.) are satisfying, meaningful, and wholesome experiences in and of themselves. That is, they have their own inherent worth and intrinsic value independent of any world view or religious dogma. Conversely, greed, hatred, lust, etc., are agitating, discomforting experiences (i.e., *dukkha*) which when present preclude a full realisation of the happiness born of love and equanimity. Thus the realisation of positive feelings and the relinquishment of negative feelings are the major goals and motivations of meditation.

While Nibbāna and an end of suffering are the primary goals of meditation and the realisation of positive feelings is a secondary goal, there are also several tertiary goals which must be achieved before the higher ones can be fully realized. These are non-attachment, insight, and concentration.

Non-attachment is freedom from craving and freedom from infatuation for sensual experience. It is not a state of chronic apathy nor a denial of sense perception existence. Rather it is psychological liberation from our "enslaving passions and our addictions to sensual and emotional pleasures." Thus non-attachment is akin to freedom, equanimity, and serenity.

Insight is a word with two meanings, both of which are sought in Buddhist meditation. In its classical Buddhist usage insight (*vipassanā*) means full *awareness* of the three characteristics of existence, i.e., impermanence, suffering (*dukkha*), and impersonality. Otherwise stated, this means full realisation of the fact that all things in the universe are temporary and changing; the human psyche is no exception and thus is not an immortal soul; and as a consequence suffering is always inevitable, for no state of mind, pleasant or unpleasant, can endure forever. The word "*awareness*" is italicised here to distinguish it from mere conceptual knowledge, which is usually insufficient to have lasting effect upon one's feelings and values.

In its psychiatric usage insight means gaining awareness of those feelings, motives, and values which have previously been unconscious. Repressed feelings of guilt, fear, lust, and hatred may lurk in the hidden recesses of our minds and unconsciously shape our lives until such time as they are brought into awareness. And unless they are brought into awareness, we cannot effectively deal with them. In Buddhism this version of insight is included under the heading of mindfulness and will be discussed later.

Concentration involves the ability to keep one's attention firmly fixed on a given subject for protracted periods of time, thus overcoming the mind's usual discursive habit of flitting from subject to subject. As we shall see, concentration is one of the earliest goals of Buddhist meditation.

Preparations

The initial endeavour in Buddhist meditation is to quiet the mind and enhance detachment and objectivity. For only when the mind has stilled its perpetual ruminating and has momentarily abandoned its fascination for sensory experience can it readily become aware of the unconscious feelings and motivations which shape our thoughts, speech, and behavior. Furthermore, only with detached objectivity and its ensuing insights can we readily confront and renounce unwholesome feelings. On the other hand, we do not achieve complete calmness and detachment so long as we harbour unwholesome feelings and unconscious emotional conflicts. Thus the process is reciprocal: the more we quiet the mind, the more we gain insight and relinquishment of undesirable feelings. The more we relinquish such feelings and resolve emotional conflicts, the more we quiet the mind and approach perfect calmness, detachment, and objectivity.

The obscuring of unconscious feelings by preoccupation with thoughts and actions is demonstrated in a variety of neurotic symptoms. Most characteristic are obsessive compulsive reactions; these occur in persons who are desperately trying to repress overpowering impulses of fear, anger, lust, or guilt. In order to achieve this repression they divert nearly all their attention to some repetitious mental or physical activity, which is conducted in a compulsive, ritualistic manner. If prevented from performing their defensive rituals, they often become acutely anxious and even panic as their unconscious feelings begin to come into awareness. Less severe examples of the same defensive phenomena are seen in persons who are chronically anxious and are continuously focusing their worries on minor concerns of exaggerated importance such as unpaid bills, social commitments, and alleged physical ills. They, too, rarely relax and are forever busy with petty chores.

These neurotic symptoms are strikingly similar to an increasingly common way of life in Western society. Our ever-expanding populations with their accompanying advertising, mass entertainment, socialising, industrialisation, and emphasis upon success, sensuality, and popularity have produced an environment in which we are forever bombarded with an increasing number of sensory and emotional stimuli. The opportunities for solitude and introspection have diminished to the point that now solitude is often viewed as either depressing or abnormal. This is not to assert that the majority of our citizens are involved in a frantic endeavour to escape from their inner selves. Such is no doubt the case with many, but there still remains a sizeable percentage of people who are involved in the same frenzy only because they have conformed to the social norm and have been lured into a habitual fascination for television, jazz, sports, and the countless other forms of readily-available entertainment. Such persons are not necessarily precluded from relative happiness and emotional well-being.

The point to be made, however, is that the conditions of modern living are such as to pose several obstacles to successful meditation. These are threefold: psychological, material, and social. These same obstacles are present to a lesser degree in traditionally Buddhist cultures and must be considered before discussing meditation itself.

Psychological Obstacles

It is virtually impossible for a busy person with manifold worldly ambitions to suddenly and voluntarily quiet his mind to the point of removing all discursive thoughts. In a matter of minutes, if not seconds, the meditator will find himself either planning, reminiscing, or daydreaming. Therefore, before one begins meditation, some amount of moral development and self-discipline should be achieved. In the words of one of the Buddha's disciples:

> "Those salutary rules of morality proclaimed by the Exalted One, for what purpose, brother Ānanda, has he proclaimed them?"
>
> "Well said, brother Bhadda, well said! Pleasing is your wisdom, pleasing your insight, excellent is your question! Those salutary rules of morality proclaimed by the Exalted One were proclaimed by him for the sake of cultivating the four foundations of mindfulness (i.e., meditation)." (SN 47:21)

In every Buddhist country only a minority of devotees undertake regular practice. The decision to meditate rests with each individual. Many wait until their later years when moral development has progressed and family obligations have been fulfilled. On the other hand, meditation facilitates wisdom and morality and can be of benefit to the layman as well as the monk.

In addition to adjusting one's daily routine and cultivating morality and wisdom, it is often profitable to take a few minutes before each meditation to put one's mind in a receptive condition.

This may be done by reflecting upon the goals and advantages of meditation or by reading or reciting some chosen passage of Buddhist literature or other appropriate writing. If drowsy, a brisk walk may freshen one's mind and can also allow one to think over and mentally dispense with matters which might otherwise be distracting. Also, if one has some necessary chores to perform which can be executed quickly and easily, doing these beforehand will reduce their interference with meditation.

Material Considerations

Much has been written in both ancient and modern literature about the physical and environmental factors conducive to successful meditation. Mostly these are matters of common sense, which each person must determine for himself on the basis of his own individual needs and predispositions. In the *Visuddhimagga* we read:

Food: sweet food suits one, sour food another.

Climate: a cool climate suits one, a warm one another. So when he finds that by using a certain food or by living in a certain climate he is comfortable, or his unconcentrated mind becomes concentrated, or his concentrated mind more so, then that food or that climate is suitable. Any other food or climate is unsuitable.

Postures: Walking suits one; standing or sitting or lying down another. So he should try them, like the abode, for three days each, and that posture is suitable in which his unconcentrated mind becomes concentrated or his concentrated mind more so. Any other should be understood as unsuitable.[4]

Seclusion and isolation from noise are important considerations, especially for beginners. In an urban environment complete seclusion is rarely possible, but even relative seclusion is of value. How this is achieved must be determined by the practitioner's individual opportunities and circumstances. The time and duration of meditation will also vary with individual situations. Ideally one should choose a time when one's mind is alert. Fifteen to forty-five minutes is recommended for lay beginners, and many

4. *Visuddhimagga*, IV, 40–41. Translation by Bhikkhu Ñāṇamoli, *Path of Purification*, Colombo, 1956.

persons are of the opinion that it should be at the same time each day, preferably in the early morning. A good night's sleep and moderation in eating are valuable, but one should avoid an excess of fasting and sleep.

The preferred posture in both Asia and the West is the lotus posture or similar positions of sitting on the ground with legs folded. A cushion or other padding is desirable for comfort. These positions furnish maximum physical stability without the need of a back rest or other devices and are especially suitable if one intends to remain alert and motionless for protracted periods of time. However, many Occidentals are unaccustomed to this posture and are thus unable to assume it or can do so only with discomfort. With practise this difficulty is usually overcome; otherwise one can meditate seated on a chair. The eyes either can be closed or resting on some neutral object such as a blank place on the ground or a simple geometric shape at a distance of three or four feet.

Social Factors

In Burma meditation is discussed with interest and enthusiasm.[5] Men of national fame will take a leave of absence to further their training, and a practitioner is often greeted with the words, "And how are you progressing in your meditation? Have you reached such and such a stage yet?"

The antithesis is true in America, where meditation is poorly understood; in fact usually it is misunderstood. First of all, the relinquishment of worldly pursuits for the sake of spiritual and psychological gain is foreign to the prevailing values of both capitalist and socialist societies. Secondly, Americans often equate meditation with hypnotic trance, mysticism, or the occult. Consequently, the Occidental practitioner may conceal his practice to avoid social ridicule and religious antagonism. This problem is compounded by the existence of various quasi-religious and pseudo-scientific cults which often attract neurotics and social misfits with promises of occult powers, lasting happiness, and physical health. Such organizations often claim "esoteric"

5. *An Experiment in Mindfulness*, p. 8.

meditations and speak favorably (though ignorantly) of Hinduism and Buddhism. Too often Western impressions of Buddhism are gained either through these sources and their associated literature or through the unfavorable descriptions given by pro-Christian books, magazines, and newspapers.

Individual Variations

As we shall see, there are a variety of different meditation practices, each intended for specific individual needs. In traditionally Buddhist countries novices often seek a learned monk or meditation master and ask to be assigned a specific meditation subject. (Vism III. 62, 65, 121) In the Occident this is virtually impossible. Competent meditation masters are few and far between, and those masters who do visit our shores find that linguistic and cultural barriers prevent them from adequately appraising a novice's needs. Thus the Western Buddhist must fend for himself, relying on his own judgement and proceeding sometimes by trial and error. Here, again, we should note the words of the *Visuddhimagga:*

> For when a very skillful archer, who is working to split a hair, actually splits the hair on one occasion, he discerns the modes of the position of his feet, the bow, the bowstring, and the arrow thus: "I split the hair as I stood thus, with the bow thus, the bowstring thus, the arrow thus." From then on he recaptures those same modes and repeats the splitting of the hair without fail. So too the meditator must discern such modes as that of suitable food, etc., thus: "I attained this after eating this food, attending on such a person, in such a lodging, in this posture, at this time." In this way, when that (absorption) is lost, he will be able to recapture those modes and renew the absorption, or while familiarising himself with it he will be able to repeat that absorption again and again (Vism IV. 120).

Not only do meditation requirements differ from person to person, they also differ for the same person at different times. In the words of the Buddha:

> "Monks, suppose a man wanted to make a small fire burn up, and he put wet grass on it, put wet cowdung on it, put wet

sticks on it, sprinkled it with water, and scattered dust on it, would that man be able to make the small fire burn up?"—"No, venerable sir."—"So too, monks, when the mind is slack, that is not the time to develop the tranquillity enlightenment factor, the concentration enlightenment factor, and the equanimity enlightenment factor. Why is that? Because a slack mind cannot well be roused by those states. When the mind is slack, that is the time to develop the investigation-of-states enlightenment factor, the energy enlightenment factor, and the happiness enlightenment factor. Why is that? Because a slack mind can well be roused by those states.

"Monks, suppose a man wanted to extinguish a great mass of fire, and he put dry grass on it... and did not scatter dust on it, would that man be able to extinguish that great mass of fire?"—"No, venerable sir."—"So too, monks, when the mind is agitated, that is not the time to develop the investigation-of-states enlightenment factor, the energy enlightenment factor, or the happiness enlightenment factor. Why is that? Because an agitated mind cannot well be quieted by those states. When the mind is agitated, that is the time to develop the tranquillity enlightenment factor, the concentration enlightenment factor, and the equanimity enlightenment factor. Why is that? Because an agitated mind can well be quieted by those states." (SN 46:53)

There is no prescribed duration for the amount of time one should spend in meditation. The popular Western notion of Buddhist monks spending a lifetime with nearly every available moment dedicated to meditative seclusion is not supported by the recorded teachings of the Buddha nor the accounts of the daily activities of the Buddha and his followers. Nor is this the case with Theravada monks today, except during temporary periods of intensive training. As with all other aspects of meditation, the amount of time must be varied according to individual needs and circumstances.

One final point must be made before proceeding to the techniques of meditation. It is simply this: Meditation requires patience, persistence, and effort. For one who practises less than several hours a day, lasting and notable progress can only be achieved by months, if not years, of endeavour. There are no short cuts or magical formulae. Consequently, the aspiring practitioner should not expect quick results and before starting should decide if he sincerely intends to put forth the necessary time and effort. A decision not to meditate, however, in no way precludes one from progressing towards the same goals of insight, non-attachment, concentration, etc. Their full realisation requires formal meditation practise, but relative success may be acquired at a slower pace through cultivation of one's moral and intellectual faculties.[6]

The Techniques of Meditation

The seventh step of the Noble Eightfold Path is termed right mindfulness, also called the four foundations of mindfulness and Satipaṭṭhāna. The three terms are synonymous and encompass not only the most important aspects of Theravada meditation but also one of the unique and important features of all Buddhism. A full explanation of mindfulness or Satipaṭṭhāna is given in the Satipaṭṭhāna Sutta, which appears twice in the Pali Canon. The Buddha begins the discourse as follows:

> This is the only way, monks, for the purification of beings, for the overcoming of sorrow and lamentation, for the destruction of suffering and grief, for reaching the right path, for the attainment of Nibbāna, namely, the Four Foundations of Mindfulness.[7]

This same message he repeated frequently:

> Those for whom you have sympathy, O monks, those who deem it fit to listen to you—friends and companions, kinsmen and relatives—they should be encouraged, introduced to and established in the four foundations of mindfulness. (SN 47:48)

And again:

---

6. *The Foundations of Mindfulness.* Translation by Nyanasatta Thera. BPS Wheel No. 19.

7. *The Foundations of Mindfulness.* Translation by Nyanasatta Thera. BPS Wheel No. 19.

> There are three taints (*āsava* or cankers), O monks: the taint of sensuality, the taint of desire for renewed existence, and the taint of ignorance. For eliminating these three taints, O monks, the four foundations of mindfulness should be cultivated. (SN 47:50)

This same emphasis has persisted even to the present era in some sections of the Buddhist world, as described by the Venerable Nyanasatta Thera:

> The great importance of the Discourse on Mindfulness (i.e., the Satipaṭṭhāna Sutta) has never been lost to the Buddhists of the Theravada tradition. In Ceylon, even when the knowledge and practice of the Dhamma was at its lowest ebb through centuries of foreign domination, the Sinhala Buddhists never forgot the Satipaṭṭhāna Sutta. Memorizing the Sutta has been an unfailing practice among the Buddhists, and even today in Ceylon there are large numbers who can recite the Sutta from memory. It is a common sight to see on full-moon days devotees who are observing the eight precepts, engaged in community recital of the Sutta. Buddhists are intent on hearing this Discourse even in the last moments of their lives; and at the bedside of a dying Buddhist either monks or laymen recite this venerated text.[8]

Thus it seems a paradox that most Western texts on Buddhism merely list right mindfulness as one of the steps of the Eightfold Path and say little more except to redefine it by such terms as "right contemplation" and "right reflection." The reason is probably twofold. First, Satipaṭṭhāna cannot be as concisely explained as the other seven steps; for it is not a single step but includes instead several distinct meditation exercises. Second, to be properly understood the Satipaṭṭhāna Sutta must be examined from a psychological and psychiatric viewpoint. Most scholars of comparative religion are accustomed to approaching their studies from religious, ethical, or philosophical frames of reference, but none of these orientations applies here. If this sutta alone was to be filed on the shelves of a public library, it would most aptly be placed

8. *Foundations of Mindfulness,* p. 3.

adjacent to the archives of eclectic psychiatry and would have little in common with the classic writings of religion and philosophy. Even psychology would not be an appropriate category, for the sutta is not concerned with any theoretical or conceptual interpretation of the mind. It deals only with the empirical facts of conscious experience and prescribes the techniques for mental development. It is, therefore, not surprising that many Occidentals who have scanned the pages of the Satipaṭṭhāna Sutta have judged it confusing, meaningless, and sometimes morbid.

In addition to the two occurrences of the Satipaṭṭhāna Sutta, condensed versions of the same teaching appear several times in the Sutta Piṭaka.

The four parts of the four foundations of mindfulness are: contemplation of the body, contemplation of feelings, contemplation of mind, and contemplation of mental objects. The body contemplation is itself divided into six parts—breathing, postures, clear comprehension of action, repulsiveness, material components, and the cemetery meditations

Mindfulness of Breathing

The initial endeavour in Buddhist meditation is to calm and quiet the mind so that it is fully alert but has temporarily diminished the quantity of daydreaming, planning, reminiscing, and all other forms of verbal and visual thinking. This goal can only be approached gradually, and therefore the beginner should start his practice by focusing his attention on some quiet, readily available, rhythmic process. Respiratory movements are ideal for this purpose. Thus the first exercise of the sutta begins:

> Herein, monks, a monk, having gone to the forest, to the foot of a tree, or to an empty place, sits down cross-legged, keeps his body erect and his mindfulness alert. Just mindful he breathes in and mindful he breathes out. Breathing in a long breath, he knows "I breathe in a long breath"; breathing out a long breath, he knows "I breathe out a long breath"; breathing in a short breath, he knows "I breathe in a short breath"; breathing out a short breath, he knows "I breathe out a short breath." "Conscious of the whole (breath-) body, I shall breathe in," thus he trains himself. "Conscious of the whole

(breath-) body, I shall breathe out," thus he trains himself. "Calming the bodily function (of breathing), I shall breathe in," thus he trains himself. "Calming the bodily function (of breathing), I shall breathe out," thus he trains himself. As a skillful turner or his apprentice, making a long turn, knows "I am making a long turn," or making a short turn, knows "I am making a short turn," just so the monk breathing in a long breath, knows "I breathe in a long breath"; breathing out a long breath, he knows "I breathe out a long breath."...

The practitioner endeavours to keep his mind focused only on the act of breathing itself and not to think about breathing as a subject of intellectual contemplation. In other words, one attempts to give full attention to the reality of immediate experience and not become involved in speculations or contemplations *about* reality.

The theory is quite simple but the practice most difficult. In a typical case, at the beginning of his meditation the novice directs his attention solely to the process of breathing. Then after a few seconds, he inadvertently begins to think, "So far I am doing all right. My mind hasn't strayed from its subject." But at this very moment he has strayed from his subject. For now he is not concentrating but thinking about concentrating. If he does not catch himself (and he probably will not), the stream of consciousness will proceed something as follows: "My mind hasn't strayed from its subject. I'm doing better than yesterday. I wonder why? Maybe it's because I've finished all of my letter writing. I wonder if Marvin will answer the letter I sent him? He hasn't... Oh, oh! I've gotten off the subject. I'd better get back to it. But I'm not really back; I'm just thinking about it. I wonder how long it will take me..." And so on it goes, day after day, week after week until the practitioner begins to wonder if he is not seeking the impossible. Yet the fact remains that many thousands living today have achieved this degree of concentration. With little short of amazement, the Western novice reads the Venerable Nyanaponika Thera's remarks concerning Burmese Satipaṭṭhāna training: "Three to four hours of continuous mindfulness, i.e., without unnoticed breaks, are regarded as the minimum for a beginner undergoing a course of strict practice."[9]

9. *Heart of Buddhist Meditation*, p. 98.

The most widely practiced form of the breathing meditation is focusing attention at the nostrils where one feels the faint pressure of the ebb and flow of the breath. This technique is not mentioned in any of the recorded teachings of the Buddha or his disciples but has been popular at least since the time of Buddhaghosa in the fifth century A.D. In the words of Buddhaghosa:

> This is the simile of the gate-keeper: just as a gate-keeper does not examine people inside and outside the town, asking "Who are you? Where have you come from? Where are you going? What have you got in your hand?"—for those people are not his concern—but does examine each man as he arrives at the gate, so too, the incoming breaths that have gone inside and the outgoing breaths that have gone outside are not this monk's concern, but they are his concern each time they arrive at the (nostril) gate itself. (Vism VIII. 200)

And again, in the simile of the saw, the woodcutter's attention is focused only at the point of contact between the saw and the wood:

> As the saw's teeth, so the in-breaths and out-breaths. As the man's mindfulness, established by the saw's teeth where they touch the tree trunk, without his giving attention to the saw's teeth as they approach and recede, though they are not unknown to him as they do so, and so he manifests effort, carries out a task and achieves an effect, so too the bhikkhu sits, having established mindfulness at the nose tip or on the upper lip, without giving attention to the in-breaths and out-breaths as they approach and recede, though they are not unknown to him as they do so, and he manifests effort, carries out a task and achieves an effect. (Vism VIII. 202)

Modifications of the breathing meditation can be applied to suit individual requirements. In the early stages of practice many persons find that mentally counting the breaths enhances concentration. In these instances one is advised not to count less than five or more than ten. Upon reaching ten the counting starts over. By going beyond ten, the counting rather than the breathing is likely to become the subject of one's attention:

> Herein, this clansman who is a beginner should first give attention to this meditation subject by counting. And when counting, he should not stop short of five or go beyond ten or make any break in the series. By stopping short of five his thoughts get excited in the cramped space, like a herd of cattle shut in a cramped pen. By going beyond ten his thoughts take the number (rather than the breaths) for their support. (Vism VIII. 190)
>
> But how long is he to go on counting? Until, without counting, mindfulness remains settled on the in-breaths and out-breaths as its object. For counting is simply a device for settling mindfulness on the in-breaths and out-breaths as object by cutting off the external dissipation of applied thoughts. (Vism VIII. 195)

In the initial stages of practice one merely observes the process of breathing without attempting to change its rate or depth. Later, as concentration is achieved, the breathing is gradually and deliberately slowed in order to further quiet the mind. There is, however, no attempt to stop respiration as in certain yogic practices:

> When his gross in-breaths and out-breaths have ceased, his consciousness occurs with the sign of the subtle in-breaths and out-breaths as its object. And when that has ceased, it goes on occurring with the successively subtler signs as its object. How? Suppose a man struck a bronze bell with a big iron bar and at once a loud sound arose, his consciousness would occur with the gross sound as its object; then, when the gross sound had ceased, it would occur afterwards with the sign of the subtle sound as its object; and when that had ceased, it would go on occurring with the sign of the successively subtler sound as its object. (Vism VIII. 206–207)

It was a Burmese meditation teacher, Venerable U Nārada (Mingun Sayādaw) who, in the early part of this century, stressed the application of mindfulness of breathing as a means of cultivating direct awareness. It was he who gave the first strong impetus to the revival of Satipaṭṭhāna meditation in contemporary Burma. He passed away in 1955 at the age of 87 and is said by many to have realised Nibbāna.

A variation of the breathing meditation was developed by another Burmese monk, the Venerable Mahāsi Sayādaw, who was a pupil of the Venerable U Nārada. His technique involves focusing attention upon the respiratory movements of the abdomen instead of the sensation at the nostrils. This system has become popular in several parts of southern Asia. A revived interest in meditation has developed in that section of the world, especially in Burma, where numerous training centers have been established, and thousands of monks and lay people have received instruction.[10]

During meditation, when the practitioner finds that his mind has strayed from its subject, there should be no attempt to suppress or forcibly remove the extraneous thoughts. Rather he should briefly take mental note of them and objectively label them with some appropriate term. This may be done by thinking to himself "planning," "remembering," "imagining," etc., as the case may be. Then he should return to his original meditation subject. However, if after several tries the unwanted thoughts persist, he should temporarily take the thoughts themselves as the meditation subject. In so doing their intensity will diminish, and he can then return to his original subject. This same technique can be used for distracting noises. It can also be used for feelings of anger or frustration, which may develop as the result of unwanted thoughts or distractions. In these instances the meditator should think to himself "noise," or "irritation."[11] As the mind becomes quiet and verbal thinking begins to diminish, other stimuli come into awareness. Among these are sensations, such as itches and minor pains, which are always present but go unnoticed because attention is directed elsewhere. The same may occur with emotions such as worry or fear, and these we shall discuss in detail later. Pictures or visual scenes may arise and are often so vivid as to be termed visions or hallucinations. They often have the appearance of dreams or distant memories and differ from thoughts in that the meditator usually finds himself a passive spectator not knowing when such scenes will arise or what forms they will take. The meditator should first attempt to ignore these sensations, feelings,

10. *The Heart of Buddhist Meditation*, pp. 85–86.
11. Ibid., p. 97.

and pictures. This failing, he should label them "itching," "fear," "picture," etc., and lastly make them his meditation subject until they diminish.[12]

To be successful, meditation should not be an unpleasant experience. Strain and tension should be minimised. Therefore, if the practitioner finds himself becoming tense, irritable, or fatigued during meditation, he may wish to terminate the practice until he acquires a better state of mind.

Mindfulness of Postures and of Actions

Following mindfulness of breathing, the next exercise prescribed in the Satipaṭṭhāna Sutta is the development of the same clear awareness towards one's daily actions. Thus the Buddha continues:

> And further, monks, a monk knows when he is going "I am going"; he knows when he is standing "I am standing"; he knows when he is sitting "I am sitting"; he knows when he is lying down "I am lying down"; or just as his body is disposed so he knows it.
>
> And further, monks, a monk, in going forward and back, applies clear comprehension; in looking straight on and looking away, he applies clear comprehension; in bending and in stretching, he applies clear comprehension; in wearing robes and carrying the bowl, he applies clear comprehension; in eating, drinking, chewing and savoring, he applies clear comprehension; in attending to the calls of nature, he applies clear comprehension; in walking, in standing, in sitting, in falling asleep, in walking, in speaking and in keeping silence, he applies clear comprehension.

Here we note a similarity between early Buddhism and Zen. Or as the Zen master would say: "In walking, just walk. In sitting, just sit. Above all, don't wobble."

Usually while dressing, eating, working, etc., we act on habit and give little attention to our physical actions. Our minds are preoccupied with a variety of other concerns. In Satipaṭṭhāna, however, the practitioner devotes himself entirely to the situation

12. *An Experiment in Mindfulness*, pp. 52–55.

at hand. Persons interested in meditation are often heard to complain, "But I don't have time to meditate." However, the form of mindfulness we are now discussing can be practiced at all times and in all situations regardless of one's occupation or social and religious commitments.

As with breathing meditation, the primary intent of this discipline is to prepare one's mind for advanced stages of psychological development. However, a valuable by-product is that it can greatly increase one's proficiency at physical skills. In Japan, Zen practitioners have utilised it to achieve mastery in swordsmanship, archery, and judo. The Buddha himself is quoted: "Mindfulness, I declare, O monks, is helpful everywhere." (SN 46:53) And again:

> Whosoever, monks, has cultivated and regularly practiced mindfulness of the body, to whatever state realisable by direct knowledge he may bend his mind for reaching it by direct knowledge, he will then acquire proficiency in that very field. (MN 119)

For one engaged in strict monastic training, mindfulness of actions becomes a more formalised practice. Breathing and walking meditations often are alternated for periods of about thirty minutes each. In walking the monk paces slowly along a level stretch of ground and directs his attention fully to the movement of each foot, thinking: "lift"—"forward"—"down"—"lift"—"forward"—"down." This alternation of breathing and walking practice may last sixteen hours each day for a period of six or more weeks.

Repulsiveness, Material Components, and Cemetery Meditations

The last of the body meditations are designed to overcome one's narcissistic infatuation for one's own body, to abandon unrealistic desires for immortality, and to destroy sensual lust. To achieve these ends two principles are employed. First is vividly and repeatedly impressing upon one's mind the temporary, changing, and compounded nature of the body. Secondly one establishes and persistently reinforces a series of negative associations to the usually sensual features of the body. This latter process employs the same principles as behaviour therapy and Pavlovian conditioning. However, Satipaṭṭhāna differs from Pavlovian and behaviour therapy in that the conditioning is established by the meditator himself instead of an external agent.

Thus the Satipaṭṭhāna Sutta continues:

> And further, monks, a monk reflects on this very body, enveloped by the skin and full of manifold impurity, from the soles up, and from the top of the head hair down, thinking thus: "There are in this body hair of the head, hair of the body, nails, teeth, skin, flesh, sinews, bones, marrow, kidney, heart, liver, diaphragm, spleen, lungs, intestines, mesentery, gorge, feces, bile, phlegm, pus, blood, sweat, fat, tears, grease, saliva, nasal mucus, synovial fluid, urine."
>
> Just as if there were a double-mouthed provision bag full of various kinds of grain such as hill paddy, paddy, green gram, cow-peas, sesamum, and husked rice, and a man with sound eyes, having opened that bag, were to take stock of the contents thus: "This is hill paddy, this is paddy, this is green gram, this is cow-pea, this is sesamum, this is husked rice." Just so, monks, a monk reflects on this very body, enveloped by the skin and full of manifold impurity, from the soles up, and from the top of the head hair down, thinking thus: "There are in this body hair of the head, hair of the body, nails, teeth, skin, flesh, sinews, bones, marrow, kidney, heart, liver, diaphragm, spleen, lungs, intestines, mesentery, gorge, feces, bile, phlegm, pus, blood, sweat, fat, tears, grease, saliva, nasal mucus, synovial fluid, urine."
>
> And further, monks, a monk reflects on this very body however it be placed or disposed, by way of the material elements: "There are in this body the element of earth, the element of water, the element of fire (caloricity), the element of air."
>
> Just as if, monks, a clever cow-butcher or his apprentice, having slaughtered a cow and divided it into portions, should be sitting at the junction of four high roads, in the same way, a monk reflects on this very body, as it is placed or disposed, by way of the material elements: "There are in this body the elements of earth, water, fire and air."

This last paragraph is explained in the *Visuddhimagga:*

> Just as the butcher, while feeding the cow, bringing it to the shambles, keeping it tied up after bringing it there, slaughtering it, and seeing it slaughtered and dead, does not lose the perception "cow" so long as he has not carved it up and divided it into parts; but when he has divided it up and is sitting there he loses the perception "cow" and the perception "meat" occurs; he does not think "I am selling cow" or "They are carrying cow away," but rather he thinks "I am selling meat" or "They are carrying meat away"; so too this monk, while still a foolish ordinary person—both formerly as a layman and as one gone forth into homelessness—does not lose the perception "living being" or "man" or "person" so long as he does not, by resolution of the compact into elements, review this body, however placed, however disposed, as consisting of elements. But when he does review it as consisting of elements, he loses the perception "living being" and his mind establishes itself upon elements. (Vism IX. 30)

The last of the body meditations are the nine cemetery meditations. Numbers 1, 2, 5, and 9 respectively are quoted here. The remaining five are similar and deal with intermediate stages of decomposition:

> And further, monks, as if a monk sees a body dead, one, two, or three days, swollen, blue and festering, thrown in the charnel ground, he then applies this perception to his own body thus: "Verily, also my own body is of the same nature; such it will become and will not escape it."
>
> And further, monks, as if a monk sees a body thrown in the charnel ground, being eaten by crows, hawks, vultures, dogs, jackals, or by different kinds of worms, he then applies this perception to his own body thus: "Verily, also my own body is of the same nature; such it will become and will not escape it."
>
> And further, monks, as if a monk sees a body thrown in the charnel ground and reduced to a skeleton without flesh and blood, held together by the tendons...
>
> And further, monks, as if a monk sees a body thrown in the charnel ground and reduced to bones, gone rotten and

become dust, he then applies this perception to his own body thus: "Verily, also my own body is of the same nature; such it will become and will not escape it."

Similar meditations on the digestion and decomposition of food are listed in other sections of the Pali scriptures for the purpose of freeing the practitioner from undue cravings for food:

> When a monk devotes himself to this perception of repulsiveness in nutriment, his mind retreats, retracts and recoils from craving for flavors. He nourishes himself with nutriment without vanity... (Vism XI. 26)

While these meditations are intended to eliminate passion and craving they carry the risk of making one morbid and depressed. Therefore the Buddha recommended:

> If in the contemplation of the body, bodily agitation, or mental lassitude or distraction should arise in the meditator, then he should turn his mind to a gladdening subject. Having done so, joy will arise in him. (SN 47:10)

A cartoon in an American medical magazine shows four senior medical students standing together. Three are engaged in active conversation. Only the remaining one turns his head to take notice of a pretty nurse. The caption beneath the cartoon reads: "Guess which one has *not* done twelve pelvic examinations today." It is doubtful that many persons outside of the medical profession will appreciate the meaning, but to medical students and interns it speaks a reality. During his months of training in obstetrics and gynecology the medical trainee must spend many hours engaged in examining and handling the most repulsive aspects of female genitals. As a result he finds the female body becoming less attractive and his sexual urges diminishing. During my own years as a medical student and intern, this observation was repeatedly confirmed by the comments of my co-workers, both married and single. As we have seen, the same principle is utilised in the sections of the discourse on repulsiveness and the cemetery meditations.

Other aspects of scientific and medical training can produce results similar to those sought in the latter three body meditations. Chemistry, biochemistry, and histology foster an objective way of viewing the body which is virtually identical to the contemplation of elements. Anatomy, of course, is similar to the contemplation of repulsiveness. And in hospital training the persistent encounter with old age, debilitation, and death continuously reinforces the words of the cemetery meditations: "Verily, also my own body is of the same nature; such it will become and will not escape it." Similarly, in order to acquire a vivid mental image of the cemetery meditations, Buddhist monks occasionally visit graveyards to behold corpses in various stages of decay. (Vism VI) However, such experiences bear fruit only if one takes advantage of them and avoids the temptation to ignore and forget.

Discursive Meditations

Successful application of the Satipaṭṭhāna meditations requires developed concentration, which in turn necessitates many hours of practice. There are, however, a variety of discursive meditations and related practices which the lay devotee can utilize to notable advantage. Some of these are not meditations in the strict sense of the word and are commonplace in virtually all religions.

A hymn, a poem, a passage from the Dhamma, or a passage from any inspiring literature can temporarily elevate the mind and serve to cultivate wholesome feelings. Many Buddhists make a habit of setting aside a few minutes each day to reflect upon the Teaching or to either read or recite from memory some favored passage of the Dhammapada. For some, similar benefits may be gained from an evening stroll, a period of solitude in forest or desert, or a pause for contemplative relaxation in the midst of a hurried day. These latter three serve the added advantage of allowing one to reflect upon one's values and reappraise oneself.

Perhaps the most popular discursive meditation practised by Theravādin Buddhists is the meditation on love (*mettā*). It is often recited in the morning in order to create a wholesome mood for the rest of the day. (Vism IX) There are several versions, one of which is as follows:

> My mind is temporarily pure, free from all impurities; free from lust, hatred, and ignorance; free from all evil thoughts.
>
> My mind is pure and clean. Like a polished mirror is my stainless mind.

As a clean and empty vessel is filled with pure water I now fill my clean heart and pure mind with peaceful and sublime thoughts of boundless love, overflowing compassion, sympathetic joy, and perfect equanimity.

I have now washed my mind and heart of anger, ill will, cruelty, violence, jealousy, envy, passion, and aversion.

May I be well and happy!
May I be free from suffering, disease, grief, worry, and anger!
May I be strong, self-confident, healthy, and peaceful!

Now I charge every particle of my system, from head to foot, with thoughts of boundless love and compassion. I am the embodiment of love and compassion. My whole body is saturated with love and compassion. I am a stronghold, a fortress of love and compassion.

What I have gained I now give unto others.

Think of all your near and dear ones at home, individually or collectively, and fill them with thoughts of loving-kindness and wish them peace and happiness, repeating, "May all beings be well and happy!" Then think of all seen and unseen beings, living near and far, men, women, animals and all living beings, in the East, West, North, South, above and below, and radiate boundless loving-kindness, without any enmity or obstruction, towards all, irrespective of class, creed, color, or sex.

Think that all are your brothers and sisters, fellow-beings in the ocean of life. You identify yourself with all. You are one with all.

Repeat ten times—*May all be well and happy*—and wish them all peace and happiness.[13]

Another useful meditation for laymen is as follows:

May I be generous and helpful!
May I be well-disciplined and refined in manners!
May I be pure and clean in all my dealings!
May my thoughts, words, and deeds be pure!

---

13. *Buddhism in a Nutshell*, by Nārada Thera. Bambalapitiya, Ceylon: Asoka Dharmadutha Saṅgamāya, 1959, pp. 67–69.

May I not be selfish and self-possessive but selfless and disinterested!
May I be able to sacrifice my pleasures for the sake of others!
May I be wise and be able to see things as they truly are!
May I see the light of Truth and lead others from darkness to light!
May I be enlightened and be able to enlighten others!
May I be able to give the benefit of my knowledge to others!
May I be energetic, vigorous and persevering!
May I strive diligently until I achieve my goal!
May I be fearless in facing dangers and courageously surmount all obstacles!
May I be able to serve others to the best of my ability!
May I be ever patient!
May I be able to bear and forbear the wrongs of others!
May I ever be tolerant and see the good and beautiful in all!
May I ever be truthful and honest!
May I ever be kind, friendly, and compassionate!
May I be able to regard all as my brothers and sisters and be one with all!
May I ever be calm, serene, unruffled, and peaceful!
May I gain a balanced mind!
May I have perfect equanimity![14]

In the mind of a devout Buddhist, Gotama Buddha symbolises the embodiment of one's highest spiritual ideals. Consequently, the Buddha is often taken as a meditation subject.

> As long as (the meditator) recollects the special qualities of the Buddha in this way, "For this and this reason the Blessed One is accomplished... for this and this reason he is blessed," then on that occasion his mind is not obsessed by greed, or obsessed by hate, or obsessed by delusion; his mind has rectitude on that occasion, being inspired by the Perfect One. (Vism VII. 65)
>
> When a noble disciple contemplates upon the Enlightened One, at that time his mind is not enwrapped by lust nor by hatred nor by delusion and at that time his mind is

14. Ibid., pp. 70–71.

> rightly directed towards the Tathāgata. And with a rightly directed mind the noble disciple gains enthusiasm for the goal, enthusiasm for the Dhamma, gains the delight derived from the Dhamma. In him thus delighted, joy arises; to one joyfully minded, body and mind become calm; calmed in body and mind, he feels at ease; and if at ease the mind is composed. (AN 6:10)

The hazard in meditating on the Buddha, however, is that the unsophisticated meditator may not be aware of the psychological reasons for this exercise. In such a case the practice is likely to become a devotional one similar to those of non-Buddhist religions.

Mindfulness of Feelings, Consciousness, and Mental Objects

Some time ago I became acquainted with a Western Buddhist who for several years had made a daily practice of meditating on love. He confided that he had chosen this meditation subject because he was prone to frequent outbreaks of anger and chronic resentment; a "hate problem" he termed it. But despite years of meditation, the hatred had not diminished; the meditation had failed. Why? As our acquaintance broadened the answer became apparent. My friend had several poorly concealed intellectual and emotional deficiencies. He never once revealed that he acknowledged these; on the contrary, he displayed frequent attempts to bolster his self-image. Such attempts were invariably doomed to frustration, especially when his accomplishments and social poise were contrasted with those of others. By reacting with anger towards others he avoided the unpleasantry of looking at himself. In other words, his anger was a psychological defense through which he sought to maintain an illusion of self-esteem. Thus unconsciously he did not wish to relinquish his anger. To do so would be too painful, and to attack the anger by meditating on love was futile, for anger was only a symptom. The real problem lay much deeper.

To cure such hatred requires three things. First one must become aware of the existence of one's inadequacies and their accompanying humiliations; in other words, what is unconscious must become conscious. Second one must totally confront such unpleasant feelings and acknowledge them in their entirety. And finally one must relinquish the egotistical desire for self-exaltation. This last requirement is best achieved by objectively analysing the illusion of self and gaining full appreciation for the changing and compounded nature of the personality. In other words, one must acquire insight of both types discussed above under the goals of meditation. How can this be achieved?

Awareness of unconscious feelings is rarely obtained through logical deductions or rational explanations. A person who harbours these feelings will either refuse to believe what he is told or will come to accept it only as so much factual information devoid of emotional significance. An excellent illustration is the case of a forty-year-old woman who sought psychiatric help for severe feelings of fear, guilt, and depression. On examining her case it became apparent that her problem was largely due to repressed feelings of hatred for her mother, a very dominating and selfish woman. After much discussion the patient finally deduced that she indeed did hate her mother, and for the next two months she spoke knowingly and learnedly about her repressed hatred and resultant symptoms. Yet she improved not one bit. Then one day she entered the office shaking with rage and cried, "God, I hate that witch!" There was never a more vivid example of the difference between knowing and experiencing. Improvement quickly followed.

This example is typical of many psychiatric case histories. One sees patients who speak in the most erudite manner about Freud and Jung and adeptly employ psychiatric terminology. Yet this intellectual verbiage is often a subtle defense against facing their true feelings. Conversely, many unsophisticated and unlearned patients are quick to achieve insight and make rapid progress. Consequently, the skillful psychiatrist makes limited use of technical jargon and theoretical concepts. He asks questions often but answers few. This same technique is employed in Burmese and Zen meditation centers. The student is discouraged from making philosophical inquiries and is told: "Pursue your meditation, and soon you will see."[15]

---

15. *An Experiment in Mindfulness.*

> You may, Ānanda, also keep in mind this marvellous and wonderful quality of the Tathāgata (the Buddha): knowingly arise feelings in the Tathāgata, knowingly they continue, knowingly they cease; knowingly arise perceptions in the Tathāgata, knowingly they continue, knowingly they cease; knowingly arise thoughts in the Tathāgata, knowingly they continue, knowingly they cease. This, Ānanda, you may also keep in mind as a marvellous and wonderful quality of the Tathāgata. (MN 123)

In his earlier years Sigmund Freud experimented with hypnosis. He found it a useful tool in revealing unconscious feelings and conflicts to the *therapist,* but it was of little value to the patient. The reason was that hypnotic trance precluded the patient from consciously confronting and resolving his problems. Therefore, Freud abandoned hypnosis in preference to the now-standard procedures of psychiatry and psychoanalysis. These same findings and conclusions have often been repeated by later researchers and clinicians. Similarly, the Buddha rejected the use of trance states so common in yogic practice and developed a means by which people can acquire insight without the aid of a therapist or psychedelic drugs. Two approaches are employed.

The easier approach to insight is one which both monks and laymen can use regardless of meditative development. It consists in developing the habit of reflecting on one's feelings from time to time and detecting the motives which produce seemingly spontaneous words and deeds. "Why did I say that?" "Why am I tense when I meet so and so?" "I find myself disliking such and such a character in this novel. Why is that? Of whom does he remind me?"

For those who have progressed in the breathing meditation or made similar progress at quieting the mind, unconscious feelings become more readily accessible. As one begins to shut out sensory distractions and halt discursive thinking, more subtle sensations come into awareness. At first there may be only a vague feeling of anxiety, some unexplained sense of guilt, or a feeling of anger. Without recourse to verbal whys or hows and avoiding any speculative conjecture the meditator directs full attention to the feeling alone. He brings only the feeling itself into full awareness and allows no interfering thoughts, though later he will benefit by reflecting on it in a contemplative manner. It is at this point that repressed memories and emotional conflicts may come into awareness. Here also, meditation can be potentially dangerous for those whose personality structures are loosely constituted or who have repressed emotional problems of severe intensity. Usually, however, in these latter instances one's unconscious defenses will intervene and the meditator will terminate the practice because he feels anxious, or "can't concentrate," or "just quit because I felt like it."

Thus the last three sections of the Satipaṭṭhāna Sutta read as follows:

Mindfulness of feelings—the second of the four foundations of mindfulness:

> Herein, monks, a monk when experiencing a pleasant feeling knows, "I experience a pleasant feeling"; when experiencing a painful feeling, he knows, "I experience a painful feeling"; when experiencing a neutral feeling, he knows, "I experience a neutral feeling...

Mindfulness of consciousness—the third of the four foundations of mindfulness:

> Herein, monks, a monk knows the consciousness with lust, as with lust; the consciousness without lust, as without lust; the consciousness with hate, as with hate; the consciousness without hate, as without hate; the consciousness with ignorance, as with ignorance; the consciousness without ignorance, as without ignorance; the shrunken (i.e., rigid and indolent) state of consciousness as the shrunken state; the distracted (i.e., restless) state of consciousness as the distracted state; the developed state of consciousness as the developed state; the undeveloped state of consciousness as the undeveloped state...

Mindfulness of mental objects—the fourth of the four foundations of mindfulness:

> Herein, monks, when sense-desire is present, a monk knows, "There is sense-desire in me," or when sense-desire is not present, he knows, "There is no sense-desire in me." He knows how the arising of the non-arisen sense-desire comes to be; he knows how the abandoning of the arisen sense-

> desire comes to be; and he knows how the non-arising in the future of the abandoned sense-desire comes to be.
>
> When anger is present, he knows, "There is anger in me" (as above for sense-desire)... When sloth and torpor are present... When agitation and worry are present... When doubt is present... (as above).
>
> Herein, monks, when the enlightenment-factor of mindfulness is present, the monk knows, "The enlightenment factor of mindfulness is in me," or when the enlightenment factor of mindfulness is absent, he knows, "The enlightenment factor of mindfulness is not in me"; and he knows how the arising of the non-arisen enlightenment factor of mindfulness comes to be; and how the perfection in the development of the arisen enlightenment factor of mindfulness comes to be.

This paragraph on mindfulness is then repeated in the same wording for the remaining six enlightenment factors, i.e., investigation of reality, energy, happiness, tranquillity, concentration, and equanimity. These seven bear the title "enlightenment factors" as they are said to be the essential states for the realisation of Nibbāna.

Leaving the Satipaṭṭhāna Sutta for a moment, we note another of the Buddha's sayings:

> "Is there a way, monks, by which a monk without recourse to faith, to cherished opinions, to tradition, to specious reasoning, to the approval of views pondered upon, may declare the Final Knowledge (of Sainthood)?... There is such a way, O monks. And which is it? Herein, monks, a monk has seen a form with his eyes, and if greed, hate, or delusion are in him, he knows: 'There is in me greed, hate, delusion'; and if greed, hate, or delusion are not in him, he knows: 'There is no greed, hate, delusion in me.' Further, monks, a monk has heard a sound, smelled an odor, tasted a flavour, felt a tactile sensation, cognised a mental object (idea), and if greed, hate, or delusion are in him, he knows: 'There is in me greed, hate, delusion'; and if greed, hate, or delusion are not in him, he knows: 'There is in me no greed, hate, delusion.' And if he thus knows, O monks, are these ideas such as to be known by recourse to faith, to cherished opinions, to tradition, to specious reasoning, to the approval of views pondered upon?"

"Certainly not, Lord."

"Are these not rather ideas to be known after wisely realising them by experience?"

"That is so, Lord."

"This, monks, is a way by which a monk, without recourse to faith, to cherished opinions, to tradition, to specious reasoning, to the approval of views pondered upon, may declare the Final Knowledge (of Sainthood)."[16]

Thus far we have discussed how one achieves insight as the first step towards eliminating unwholesome feelings and motivations. Following insight one must totally confront these newly discovered feelings and acknowledge them fully and impartially. One must see their true nature devoid of any emotional reactions (such as guilt or craving) and devoid of preconceived notions about their good or evil qualities. In other words, complete attention is focused on the feeling itself in order that one may examine it objectively in its naked reality, free of any cultural and personal assumptions as to its desirability. This achievement results from the Satipaṭṭhāna practices described above.[17]

As an example, in a typical case of anger one is cognizant of being angry, yet a much greater amount of attention is directed outward. Most typically the angry mind quickly perceives and dwells upon the objectionable and offensive features of some other person (or persons). And in so doing indignation, resentment, and anger increase. These objectionable features of the other person may be fancied, exaggerated, or real, but in any case, were it not for the anger such preoccupations would not have arisen.

The Buddhist approach is to turn attention to the real problem—the anger. One reflects, "I am angry."... "I am doing this because I am angry."... "I am having these thoughts because I am angry." In so doing one avoids dwelling on alleged injustices, etc., and thereby does not intensify the hatred. This reflection continues, "This is anger."... "It is real; it is intense."... "It is a feeling."... "It has no reality outside of my own consciousness."... "Like all feelings, it will soon diminish."... "I experience it but am

16. SN 35:152. The reader will note that this passage also demonstrates the highly experiential aspect of Buddhist epistemology.

17. *The Heart of Buddhist Meditation*, pp. 68–70.

not compelled to act on it." With practise one finds that though anger still arises its effect is diminished. Its influence is no longer strong. In the case of painful emotions, such as humiliation, it is advantageous to also reflect, "This is most painful."... "I do not like it; but I can confront it."... "I can endure it."... "Even though it is unpleasant, I can tolerate it." In instances of greed and passion it is often fruitful to consider "Is this truly pleasurable?"... "Is it rewarding?"... "Am I now happy?"

It should be noted that this important technique can also be employed in the course of daily living without unusual powers of concentration or formal meditation practice.

In the words of the Buddha:

> There are three kinds of feeling, O monks: pleasant feeling, unpleasant feeling, and neutral feeling. For the full understanding of these three kinds of feelings, O monks, the four foundations of mindfulness should be cultivated. (SN 47:49)
>
> In pleasant feelings, monks, the inclination to greed should be given up; in unpleasant feelings the inclination to aversion should be given up; in neutral feelings the inclination to ignorance should be given up. If a monk has given up in pleasant feelings the inclination to greed, in unpleasant feelings the inclination to aversion, and in neutral feelings the inclination to ignorance, then he is called one who is free of (unsalutary) inclinations, one who sees clearly. He has cut off cravings, sundered the fetters, and through the destruction of conceit has made an end of suffering.

If one feels joy, but knows not feeling's nature,
Bent towards greed, he will not find deliverance.
If one feels pain, but knows not feeling's nature,
Bent towards hate, he will not find deliverance.
And even neutral feeling which as peaceful
The Lord of Wisdom has proclaimed,
If, in attachment, he should cling to it, this
Will not set free him from the round of ill.
But if a monk is ardent and does not neglect
To practise mindfulness and comprehension clear,
The nature of all feelings will he penetrate.
And having done so, in this very life

> *Will he be free from cankers, from all taints.*
> *Mature in knowledge, firm in Dhamma's ways,*
> *When once his life-span ends, his body breaks,*
> *All measure and concepts will be transcended.* (SN 36:3)

After getting rid of sensual cravings and after uncovering, confronting, and relinquishing unwholesome emotions, there remains only one fetter to be resolved. This is narcissism, the infatuation for one's self, which results in egotism, and an endless quest for social recognition and self-exaltation. Perpetuating this fetter is the illusion that one has a true or unchanging self, the "real me." In reality there is no such entity; instead there are only feelings, sensations, and emotions, and once we gain full appreciation of this fact, once it becomes a living reality to us, narcissism diminishes. Among the Buddha's teachings are numerous passages like the following:

> There is no corporeality, no feeling, no perception, no mental formations, no consciousness that is permanent, enduring, and lasting, and that, not subject to any change, will eternally remain the same. If there existed such an ego that is permanent, enduring, and lasting, and not subject to any change, then the holy life leading to the complete extinction of suffering will not be possible. (SN 22:96)
>
> Better it would be to consider the body as the ego rather than the mind. And why? Because this body may last for ten, twenty, thirty, forty, or fifty years, even for a hundred years and more. But that which is called "mind, consciousness, thinking" arises continuously, during day and night, as one thing, and as something different again it vanishes. (SN 12:61)

Such statements, however, are merely philosophical arguments through which one may intellectually accept this fact. Only by experiencing it as a living reality and by an impartial analysis of the self do we relinquish egotism. Thus in the Satipaṭṭhāna Sutta, after each of the six body meditations and after each of the meditations on feeling, consciousness, and mental objects, the following passage occurs. (Quoted here is the section on feelings. The words "body," "consciousness," and "mental objects" are substituted for the word "feelings" in their respective sections of the sutta.)

> Thus he lives contemplating feelings in himself, or he lives contemplating feelings in other persons, or he lives contemplating feelings both in himself and in others. He lives contemplating origination-factors in feelings, or he lives contemplating dissolution-factors in feelings, or he lives contemplating origination-and-dissolution factors in feelings. Or his mindfulness is established with the thought, "Feeling exists," to the extent necessary just for knowledge and mindfulness, and he lives independent, and clings to nothing in the world. Thus, monks, a monk lives contemplating feelings.

In the instance of anger, one would reflect: "This is anger."... "It is a feeling."... "I do not identify with it."... "It will eventually be replaced by another feeling, which in turn will be replaced by still another."... "I am a composite of various feelings; a changing aggregate of attitudes, values, and thoughts; no one of which is permanent."... "There is no eternal I." As such objectivity and detachment increases anger diminishes, for no longer is there an ego to be defended and no self which can be offended.

Except for a concluding section on the Four Noble Truths we have now discussed all but two portions of the Satipaṭṭhāna Sutta. These remaining two are included under the section on mental objects and are primarily intended to free one from sensual craving and the illusion of self:

> Herein, monks, a monk thinks: "Thus is material form; thus is the arising of material form; and thus is the disappearance of material form. Thus is feeling; thus is the arising of feeling; and thus is the disappearance of feeling. Thus is perception; thus is the arising of perception; and thus is the disappearance of perception. Thus are mental formations (i.e., thoughts); thus is the arising of mental formations; and thus is the disappearance of mental formations. Thus is consciousness; thus is the arising of consciousness; and thus is the disappearance of consciousness."
>
> Herein, monks, a monk knows the eye and visual forms, and the fetter that arises dependent on both; he knows how the arising of the non-arisen fetter comes to be; he knows how the abandoning of the arisen fetter comes to be; and he

knows how the non-arising in the future of the abandoned fetter comes to be.

This latter passage is repeated five times with "ear and sound," "nose and smells," "tongue and flavours," "body and tactual objects," and "mind and mental objects" respectively substituted where "eye and visual forms" appears above.

We have thus completed the Satipaṭṭhāna Sutta. In summary, it first prescribes mindfulness of breathing as a technique for quieting the mind and developing concentration. This same heightened awareness is then developed for all voluntary physical actions. Next are the meditations on repulsiveness, elements, and death, which are intended to free one from bodily attachment and lust; this is done by contemplating the temporary and changing nature of the body and by developing negative and unpleasant associations. The remaining three sections enable the practitioner to become fully aware of his thoughts, feelings, and emotions and to confront them impartially in their true nature. With each of these exercises, one also objectively notes that each facet of his own mind and body is temporary, compounded, and changing, and therefore there exists no immortal soul, unchanging essence, or true self.

One important fact should be noted. Neither in the Satipaṭṭhāna Sutta nor in any of the other seven steps of the Eightfold Path is advocated the denial or suppression of feelings. It is a widely spread and inaccurate belief that Theravada Buddhism attempts to destroy evil thoughts by forcing them from the mind. Suppression of undesirable thoughts is advocated in only a few parts of the Pali Canon and is to be used only in special cases when other measures fail.[18]

In southern Asia it is becoming a common practice for both monks and laymen to enter a meditation center for periods of from six to twelve weeks. Here one dons the white robe of an *upāsaka* and is removed from all social contacts and material possessions. Previous social status and identity soon come to have little meaning, thus minimising the effect of established habits and

18. *The Removal of Distracting Thoughts.* Translation by Soma Thera. BPS Wheel No. 21.

adaptations and thereby enhancing the opportunities for personal growth. The food is palatable but bland, and one eats and sleeps in moderation according to a strict schedule, and even eating and dressing become routine meditation practices. Virtually every waking moment is dedicated to meditation. Here progress is made at a rate impossible to achieve by setting aside an hour or two in the midst of a busy day. After his stay is over, the layman returns to family life and continues his daily one-hour practice. However, not all meditation centers are of high quality. Many are lax; a few are corrupt, and a few teach unorthodox meditations which are not truly Buddhist. Thus a person seeking entry should first make inquiries and would do well to avoid centers which make an effort to recruit Westerners for the sake of publicity and prestige. Satipaṭṭhāna meditation centers exist in North America, and courses are given in England.

The Eighth Step

The last step of the Noble Eightfold Path is termed right concentration and concerns the attainment of the four absorptions or *jhānas.* These states are achieved by an extreme degree of concentration and mental quietude beyond that usually sought through mindfulness of breathing. Yet, unlike Satipaṭṭhāna, the jhānas are not a prerequisite to Enlightenment. Some teachers say one may obtain Nibbāna without reaching the absorptions, and they alone will not produce Nibbāna. Also, there is the danger of one becoming enamoured with them and not striving for further progress. However, achieving the jhānas can facilitate one's progress.[19]

In these states all visual, tactile, auditory, and other sense impressions have ceased, while the mind remains alert and fully awake. The first jhāna is described as having five qualities absent and five present. Absent are lust, anger, sloth, agitation, and doubt. Present are a mild degree of conceptual thought, a mild degree of discursive thinking, rapture, happiness, and concentration. With the removal of all conceptual thought and discursive thinking one enters the second jhāna, which has the qualities of concentration,

19. *The Word of the Buddha*, by Nyanatiloka Mahāthera. Kandy: BPS, p. 79.

rapture, and happiness. Then with the abandonment of rapture, one enters the third jhāna in which only equanimous happiness and concentration remain. The distinctive factors of the fourth absorption are equanimity and concentration. This last jhāna is realised after giving up all joy and sorrow and is described as a state beyond pleasure and pain.[20]

> The jhānas are obtained by mindfulness of breathing with a steady, progressive quieting of the breath.[21] They may also be realised through the *kasiṇa* meditations and meditating on equanimity. (Vism III. 107)

At this point it is interesting to speculate on the phenomena of parapsychology. Despite the fraudulent and careless investigations which have been done in psychical research, there still remains a sizable number of reliable and carefully controlled studies (especially in England) which have demonstrated that people do, indeed, possess the faculties of telepathy, clairvoyance, and precognition (i.e., respectively, the abilities to read another's thoughts, to see or know distant happenings beyond the range of normal vision, and to foretell future events). In addition some researchers claim to have established the existence of psychokinesis, the power of mind over matter, but the evidence for psychokinesis is inconclusive and most experiments have failed to demonstrate its validity. Of those parapsychology subjects who have been tested to date, even the best guess incorrectly as often as correctly and are unable to determine which of their guesses are correct. That is, while being tested, the ESP subject is unable to distinguish between guesses and true extra sensory information.[22] One might wonder if the process of reducing sensory impressions and stilling discursive thoughts would enhance these psychic abilities.

According to the Pali texts there are five psychical powers which can be obtained through meditation. These five include psychokinesis, telepathy, and clairvoyance, plus two others. The additional two are the "divine ear" or clairaudience (the auditory

20. Ibid., pp. 80–81.

21. *The Heart of Buddhist Meditation*, p. 111.

22. *Psychical Research Today*, by D .J. West. Baltimore, Md.: Penguin Books, 1962.

counterpart of clairvoyance) and the ability to recall past lives.[23] Precognition itself is not listed among these but is mentioned in other sections of the Tipiṭaka. Reliable use of these powers is allegedly possessed only by those who have achieved the four jhānas either with or without Nibbāna.[24] Thus, like more worldly talents, Nibbāna alone does not produce them. (Vism XII. 11)

The most important consideration, however, is that Buddhism places very little emphasis on paranormal phenomena and regards them as by-products of spiritual development rather than goals. In fact, the novice is cautioned against experimenting with them, since they distract from one's true goals and in some cases can be obstructive or even dangerous. (DN 11)

> Supernormal powers are the supernormal powers of the ordinary man. They are hard to maintain, like a prone infant or like a baby hare, and the slightest thing breaks them. But they are an impediment for insight, not for concentration, since they are obtainable through concentration. So the supernormal powers are an impediment that should be severed by one who seeks insight. (Vism III. 56)

Other Forms of Meditation

The Satipaṭṭhāna exercises are by far the most valuable and widely practised of all the Theravada meditations. There are, however, a total of forty meditation subjects listed in the *Visuddhimagga* including those already mentioned, i.e., Satipaṭṭhāna practices and meditations on love, equanimity, repulsiveness of food, and the Buddha. The remaining subjects are the Dhamma, the Order of Monks, virtue, generosity, devas, peace, compassion, gladness, boundless space, boundless consciousness, nothingness, the base of neither perception nor non-perception, and the ten *kasiṇas*. Each of these subjects is intended for specific individual needs, and one should not attempt to undertake all forty. To do so would only dilute one's energies and retard progress.

---

23. *The Word of the Buddha*, pp. 67–68.
24. Ibid., p. 68.

A *kasiṇa* is an object (such as a clay disk, a flame, or color) which the practitioner looks at from a distance of about four feet. The eyes are alternately opened and closed until one has acquired a mental image of the object which is as vivid as the real one. (Vism IV. 30) The ten *kasiṇa* meditations develop the jhānas and do not enhance insight.

Meditation is not an exclusively Buddhist tradition. It is equally important in the Hindu religion and because the two schools employ similar techniques, they are often confused. Thus a comparison is warranted. Both advocate preparatory moral discipline, moderation in eating, quieting the mind, and abolition of selfish desires. The postures are similar, and the breathing meditation is practised by many yogis. Here, however, the similarities cease. Buddhism is concerned with the empirical phenomena of conscious experience, and thus its meditations are psychologically oriented. Hinduism, on the other hand, is mystically, religiously, and metaphysically inclined. Yogic meditation, therefore, has devotional aspects often including prayer. While Buddhism emphasizes motivations and insight, Hinduism speaks of Infinite Consciousness, Cosmic Reality, and oneness with God. To the Hindu, freedom from hatred is not so much an end in itself as it is a step towards Immortality. The following typifies Hindu writings:

> Retire into a solitary room. Close your eyes. Have deep silent meditation. Feel his (God's) presence. Repeat His name OM with fervor, joy and love. Fill your heart with love. Destroy the Sankalpas, thoughts, whims, fancies, and desires when they arise from the surface of the mind. Withdraw the wandering mind and fix it upon the Lord. Now, Nishta, meditation will become deep and intense. Do not open your eyes. Do not stir from your seat. Merge in Him. Dive deep into the innermost recesses of the heart. Plunge into the shining Atma (Soul) within. Drink the nectar of Immortality. Enjoy the silence now. I shall leave you there alone. Nectar's son, Rejoice, Rejoice! Peace, Peace! Silence, Silence! Glory, Glory! [25]

25. *Concentration and Meditation*, by Swami Sivananda. Himalayas, India: Yoga Vedanta Forest Academy, 1959, p. 314.

Another important difference concerns the visions that occur during meditation. The Buddhist regards these as psychological phenomena to be dealt with in the same way as distracting thoughts. The Hindu often interprets them as psychic experiences indicative of spiritual development. In the words of Swami Sivananda:

> Sometimes Devatas (gods), Rishis (sages), Nitya Siddhas will appear in meditation. Receive them with honor. Bow to them. Get advice from them. They appear before you to help and give you encouragement.[26]

A few passages in the *Tao-Te-Ching* suggest that the Chinese mystics discovered meditation independently of Buddhist and Hindu traditions:

> *Can you govern your animal soul, hold to the One and never depart from it?*
> *Can you throttle your breath, down to the softness of breath in a child?*
> *Can you purify your mystic vision and wash it until it is spotless?* (v. 10)

> *Stop your senses,*
> *Close the doors;*
> *Let sharp things be blunted,*
> *Tangles resolved,*
> *The light tempered*
> *And turmoil subdued;*
> *For this is mystic unity*
> *In which the Wise Man is moved*
> *Neither by affection*
> *Nor yet by estrangement*
> *Or profit or loss*
> *Or honor or shame.*
> *Accordingly, by all the world,*
> *He is held highest.* (v. 56)

> *To know that you are ignorant is best;*
> *To know what you do not, is a disease;*

26. Ibid., p. 171.

But if you recognise the malady
Of mind for what it is, then that is health.
The Wise Man has indeed a healthy mind;
He sees an aberration as it is
And for that reason never will be ill. (*v. 71*)[27]

The exact nature of early Taoist meditation will probably remain unknown, since later Taoism has intermingled with Mahayana Buddhism.

Mahayana Buddhist meditations include all the above mentioned Theravada practices plus others. The division of Mahayana into numerous and varied sects precludes any general statement about its practices. In some forms it bears similarities to Hinduism by virtue of devotional emphasis and prayer. In other schools this similarity is seen in the Mahayana concepts of Universal Mind, the Void, and Buddha Nature, which sometimes take precedence over the Theravada concerns of greed, hatred, and delusion. The curing of physical illness and the flow of spiritual forces through the body are other features of certain Mahayana practices:

> Vibrations (during meditation) show the free passage of the vital principle. As it passes through the stomach and intestines, it vibrates when the belly is empty. But when the belly is full, it ceases to vibrate. The breath reaches the lower belly more easily when the latter is full. Vibrations are not accidental but come from the vital principle circulating in the belly. As time passes, when your meditation is more effective and the vital principle flows freely, then these vibrations will cease.[28]

Of all the Mahayana schools, Zen places the greatest emphasis upon meditation. Zen practice is much like Theravada. It focuses on quieting the mind and shuns conceptual thinking in preference to direct experience. The postures are also similar, and the initial Zen practice usually involves attention to breathing. It does

27. *The Way of Life: Tao-Te-Ching.* Translation by R. B. Blakney. New York: The New American Library, 1955.
28. *The Secrets of Chinese Meditation,* by Charles Luk. London: Rider & Co., 1964, p. 187.

not include as wide a variety of different techniques. Zen places greater emphasis on the details of correct posture and, especially in the Soto school, contrasts with Theravada by preferring group meditation to individual practice. In order to cultivate a suitable state of mind, Zen meditation is often followed by chanting and gongs.

Perhaps the most significant difference is that, as compared to Theravada, Zen makes little mention of the need and means of dealing with motives, feelings, and emotions. It lays great emphasis upon freeing oneself from intellectualizing and conceptualizing in one's quest of "the Ultimate." But at the same time it offers scant advice on the means by which one overcomes unwholesome impulses or confronts mental hindrances that are emotional or motivational in origin.

Scientific Evaluations of Meditation

The Venerable Anuruddha, a disciple of the Buddha, once became ill with a painful disease. On that occasion several of the monks visited him and inquired:

> What might be the state of mind dwelling in which painful bodily sensations are unable to perturb the mind of the Venerable Anuruddha?
>
> [He replied:]
>
> It is a state of mind, brethren, that is firmly grounded in the four foundations of mindfulness; and due to that, painful bodily sensations cannot perturb my mind. (SN 52:10)

Throughout Buddhist history, there have been numerous other testimonies as to the benefits of Satipaṭṭhāna. Yet personal testimonies and case histories are subjective and prone to distortion. The reader may well wonder what, if any, scientific studies have been conducted. To date there are two areas of investigation which have given some evidence as to the benefits of meditation.

Sensory Deprivation

The first scientific evidence does not involve meditation per se, but concerns an experimental situation which has some similarities to meditation practice. This is sensory deprivation, which has been actively studied since 1951. There are two types of sensory deprivation. One reduces sensory input by placing the experimental subject in a totally dark, soundproof room. His hands are encased in soft cotton; the temperature is constant and mild, and he lies on a soft mattress. The other type does not reduce sensory input per se, but does diminish perception. In this latter case the subject wears opaque goggles so that he sees only a diffuse white with no forms or colours. A constant monotonous noise is generated, and no other sounds are heard. Approximately the same results are obtained in either type of experiment. In both kinds the subject lies relatively motionless; he is free to think or sleep as he pleases and may terminate the session if he so desires. Experiments have lasted from four hours to five days.[29]

The lack of practice and lack of any attempt at mental discipline makes sensory deprivation a passive procedure notably different from meditation. However, both meditation and sensory deprivation involve a temporary withdrawal from external stimuli without loss of consciousness, and thus a comparison is warranted.

Perhaps the most characteristic feature of sensory deprivation research to date is the great discrepancies in the findings of different researchers. For example, some studies have shown it to impair learning, while others find that learning is enhanced.[30] Most of the early studies reported that the great majority (in some cases all) of experimental subjects had strong visual and sometimes auditory hallucinations beginning from twenty minutes to seventy hours after entering the experiment. Other researchers, however, reported very few hallucinations. Suggestion is a partial, though not total, explanation for this difference in frequency of hallucinations. One study found that under identical sensory deprivation conditions a group of subjects which was told that hallucinations were frequent and normal had over three times more

29. *Sensory Deprivation,* by Solomon, Kubzansky, Leiderman, Mendelson, Trumbull, and Wexler. Cambridge, Mass.: Harvard University Press, 1961.

30. *Science,* Vol. 123, "Effect of Sensory Deprivation on Learning Rate in Human Beings," by J. Vernon and J. Hoffman. June 15, 1956, pp. 1074–75.

than an identical group which was given no such information.[31] This no doubt explains many of the psychic experiences of those yogi devotees who seek visions while meditating in isolation.

Recent studies have indicated that the emotional atmosphere created by the experimenters plus the subjects' attitudes, knowledge, and expectations may have greater effect on the results of the experiment than do the physical aspects of sensory deprivation.[32] Regarding meditation, this fact suggests the importance of moral, intellectual, and environmental preparation. It also suggests the importance of taking a few moments before meditation to create a wholesome frame of mind.

What is most significant for the purpose of this writing, however, is whether or not sensory deprivation and its accompanying social isolation facilitate awareness of one's inner emotional conflicts and thereby facilitate personality growth. Several studies have indicated that such is the case. Most significant was an experiment conducted on thirty white male psychiatric patients in Richmond, Virginia. The group consisted of approximately equal numbers of neurotics, schizophrenics, and character disorders, and all were subjected to a maximum six hours of sensory deprivation. Each subject was given a battery of psychological tests the day before the experiment, and the same tests were repeated the day after and again one week later. The tests rated the subjects on twenty items such as anxiety, depression, hostility, memory deficit, disorganized thinking, etc. It was found that on each of the twenty items some subjects improved, some worsened, and some revealed no change. However, the desirable changes outnumbered the undesirable ones by a ratio of two to one, and one week after the experiment most of the beneficial changes were found to have persisted while the undesirable ones had mostly subsided. Some subjects showed no desirable changes on any of the twenty items; others revealed as many as thirteen. The average subject improved on four of the twenty items and worsened on two. The experimenters also reported that the subjects displayed "increased awareness of inner conflicts and anxieties, and heightened perception of the fact that

31. *Archives of General Psychiatry,* Vol. 8, "Studies in Sensory Deprivation," by J. Pollard, L. Uhr, and W. Jackson. May, 1963, pp. 435–53.
32. Ibid.

their difficulties stemmed from inner rather than outer factors... A second major change observed was a less rigid utilization of repressive and inhibitory defenses. The reduction of incoming stimulation led to recall and verbalization of previously forgotten experiences in many instances. For some subjects this recall was anxiety-inducing..."[33]

Other studies have supported this finding that short-term sensory deprivation is psychologically beneficial. (Deprivation of a day or more is likely to be detrimental.) However, other carefully conducted investigations have found no such improvements,[34] and therefore further studies are indicated before any definite conclusions can be made about the therapeutic value of sensory deprivation.

Electroencephalographic Analysis of Meditation

In 1963 a fascinating and unique report on Zen meditation was presented by Dr. Akira Kasamatsu and Dr. Tomio Hirai of the Department of Neuro-Psychiatry, Tokyo University. It contained the results of a ten-year study of the brain wave or electroencephalographic (EEG) tracings of Zen masters.[35,36]

The EEG tracings revealed that about ninety seconds after an accomplished Zen practitioner begins meditation a rhythmic slowing in the brain wave pattern known as alpha waves occurs. This slowing occurs *with eyes open* and progresses with meditation, and after thirty minutes one finds rhythmic alpha

---

33. *Archives of General Psychiatry,* Vol. 3, "Therapeutic Changes in Psychiatric Patients Following Partial Sensory Deprivation," by R. Gibby, H. Adams, and R. Carrera. July, 1960, pp. 57/33–66/42.

34. *Archives of General Psychiatry,* Vol. 8, "Therapeutic Effectiveness of Sensory Deprivation," by S. Cleveland, E. Reitman, & C. Bentinck. May, 1963, pp. 455–60.

35. *The Science of Zazen* (a 16 mm. sound motion picture and accompanying pamphlet, both in English), by A. Kasamatsu and T. Hirai. Tokyo University. April, 1963.

36. *Folia Psychiatrica et Neurologica Japonica,* Vol. 20, No. 4, "An Electroencephalographic Study of the Zen Meditation (Zazen)," by A. Kasamatsu and T. Hirai. December, 1966, pp. 315–36.

waves of seven or eight per second. This effect persists for some minutes after meditation. What is most significant is that this EEG pattern is notably different from those of sleep, normal waking consciousness, and hypnotic trance, and is unusual in persons who have not made considerable progress in meditation. In other words, it suggests an unusual mental state; though from the subjective reports of the practitioners, it does not appear to be a unique or highly unusual conscious experience. It was also found that a Zen master's evaluation of the amount of progress another practitioner had made correlated directly with the latter's EEG changes.

Another finding of the same study concerned what is called alpha blocking and habituation. To understand these phenomena let us imagine that a person who is reading quietly is suddenly interrupted by a loud noise. For a few seconds his attention is diverted from the reading to the noise. If the same sound is then repeated a few seconds later his attention will again be diverted, only not so strongly nor for so long a time. If the sound is then repeated at regular intervals, the person will continue reading and become oblivious to the sound. A normal subject with closed eyes produces alpha waves on an EEG tracing. An auditory stimulation, such as a loud noise, normally obliterates alpha waves for seven seconds or more; this is termed alpha blocking. In a Zen master the alpha blocking produced by the first noise lasts only two seconds. If the noise is repeated at 15 second intervals, we find that in the normal subject there is virtually no alpha blocking remaining by the fifth successive noise. This diminution of alpha blocking is termed habituation and persists in normal subjects for as long as the noise continues at regular and frequent intervals. In the Zen master, however, no habituation is seen. His alpha blocking lasts two seconds with the first sound, two seconds with the fifth sound, and two seconds with the twentieth sound. This implies that the Zen master has a greater awareness of his environment as the paradoxical result of meditative concentration. One master described such a state of mind as that of noticing every person he sees on the street but of not looking back with emotional lingering.

The Social Fruits of Meditation

Through science, technology, and social organisation Western man has built a civilisation of unprecedented wealth and grandeur. Yet despite this mastery of his environment, he has given little thought to mastery of himself. In fact, his newly-acquired wealth and leisure have heightened his sensuality and weakened his self-discipline. It becomes increasingly apparent, however, that a stable and prosperous democracy can endure only so long as we have intelligent, self-disciplined, and properly motivated citizens; legislation and education alone will not ensure this. Buddhism presents a technique by which this can be obtained, but the responsibility rests with each individual. No one can cure our neuroses and strengthen our characters except ourselves.

In the Sumbha country in the town of Sedaka the Buddha once said:

> "I shall protect myself," in that way the foundations of mindfulness should be practised. "I shall protect others," in that way the foundations of mindfulness should be practised. Protecting oneself one protects others; protecting others one protects oneself. And how does one, in protecting oneself, protect others? By the repeated and frequent practice of meditation. And how does one, in protecting others, protect oneself? By patience and forbearance, by a non-violent and harmless life, by loving-kindness and compassion. "I shall protect myself," in that way the foundations of mindfulness should be practised. "I shall protect others," in that way the foundations of mindfulness should be practised. Protecting oneself, one protects others; protecting others, one protects oneself. (SN 47:19)

Appendix

Some Observations and Suggestions for Insight Meditation

The preceding was written in 1964 with a few minor revisions and additions made in the latter part of 1965. Now, at the start of 1972 and after six years in Thailand, it seems befitting that I review my own words. For the past years have not only added to my own experience with meditation, they have also brought me into close and prolonged contact (often close friendships) with other meditation practitioners, many of whom are more dedicated, more skilful, and more experienced than I.

One is impressed with the variety of personalities who undertake practice. Some are experimental, critical, and pragmatic; others more devotional, dedicated, and idealistic. Some seem well adjusted and at peace with themselves and the world, while others seem desperate to find happiness and purpose in life. Some adhere literally to every detail of the scriptures, while some instead are dedicated to the interpretations and methods of their respective teachers. Still others attempt to find the ways and means alone by their own individual and unaided efforts. Likewise the techniques and methods which these people have undertaken are also highly varied and divergent.

During this period of personal practise and consultation with others, I have seen what I believe to be some genuine achievements and also some notable failures. The question then is: What is it that succeeds and what is it that does not? And why? Or to state the matter more precisely: One may succeed in one area of meditative development but not in another.

In order to evaluate progress at meditation one must have some criteria or standards against which to judge. Thus we must ask ourselves, What is it that, short of Nibbāna, we expect to find in one who has made genuine progress along the Eightfold Path? Momentary periods of euphoria, altered perceptions, or other transient episodes of unusual states of consciousness are not what we seek. Likewise, we are not in pursuit of occult powers, unusual

EEG patterns, or control of the autonomic nervous system (such as slowing the heart rate or changing body temperature).

With reference to the Four Noble Truths, we note the Buddha's words: "One thing do I teach: suffering (i.e., *dukkha*) and the end of suffering." Thus if one has truly progressed, we would expect that where previously sad and depressed, one is now less so; where previously selfish, one is now more giving; where previously defensive, secretive, and guarded, one is now more open and self-assured. Worry and anxiety should be reduced. Objective humility should replace conceit. Instead of recurrent thoughts of anger and "getting even" one is more forgiving and at peace with the world. It is felt that such attainments have been observed, occurring as the result of properly directed Buddhist practice.

Again with reference to the Four Noble Truths, it is craving or desire which causes our unhappiness and produces our mental defilements. Thus only by attacking the problems of craving, wanting, and desiring can progress be made. I speak now not so much of the crude and obvious desires such as hunger and sex but of the more subtle ones of egotism, emotional dependency, and desires for possession. One may fast for two weeks and yet never once look at the fact that the real reason for fasting is to feed one's ego—to be better, more disciplined, more pious than one's fellow practitioners. Or one may work diligently attempting to win the approval, confidence, and affection of a stern and aloof teacher and never once realise that one is attempting to compensate for the frustration and lack of love from a stern and aloof parent. To really break through these "hang ups" one must focus attention, not on the sensation of breath at the nostrils, but instead focus on the agonising feelings of inadequacy, mediocrity, loneliness, or rejection in one's heart.

When asked, "What have you gained from meditation?" the correct answer should be "nothing." For meditation is not for acquiring but for giving up—a full and complete giving up of the self. Too often people put in a half-hour each day at meditation in the same way that they put in a half-hour studying French. After so many months or years one has a new attribute, a new skill to add to one's already impressive repertoire of virtues, achievements, talents, and abilities. "I can speak French, play the piano, ski, type sixty words a minute, and meditate as well." Such a person is either compensating for strong feelings of inadequacy or else is badly afflicted with narcissism.

Another way in which meditation becomes misdirected, as a result of the very motives which determined it, is the quest for new sensations or experiences, i.e., *lobha.* Many seek from meditation the very same thing they seek from drugs—i.e., an overwhelming ego-immersing experience of sensations, perceptions, colors, emotions, and "transcendental states beyond words."

It is not meant to belittle such experiences and say that they have no significance or no value. But as with taking LSD or seeing a good motion picture, they quickly pass into memory. And once past, in a very short time one's old mood changes, petty jealousies, conceits, and irritations are back just as strong and as frequent as ever. If there has been no true and lasting personality change, then Buddhist meditation has fallen short of its intended goal.

At the opposite extreme are persons whose approaches to Buddhism are excessively dogmatic, literal, orthodox, and moralistic. They strongly resist a pragmatic, eclectic approach to meditation and are hyper-concerned with the nuances and fine points of Buddhist tradition and decorum. From these sources one repeatedly hears such statements as, "To progress at meditation there must be strict moral discipline," or "You cannot expect fast results but must work for years." Now there is truth in both these statements. But in this context they are really symptoms of extreme rigidity and dogmatism, which in principle is no different than the dogmatism of many Christian missionaries or other persons doggedly committed to a given institution. One's commitment to the tradition and to the letter of the teaching is so strong that one is incapable of truly practising that very same teaching which advises one to have no prejudices and to see truth as universal and independent of any institution. I feel that this unfortunate phenomenon accounts for several instances of very diligent and dedicated meditation practitioners who, despite years of intensive practise, reveal little more than chronic, mild depression mixed with plodding determination.

The theme of guilt and self-punishment is one factor (though not the only one) which tends to perpetuate the phenomenon of diligent striving with minimal results. It usually begins with one taking a highly idealistic, moralistic, and sometimes devotional approach to Dhamma. One tries for one-pointed concentration and complete suppression of mental defilements. One fails and tries again; fails and tries again. Blaming oneself for one's failure one comes to feel guilty and tries even harder, again failing. With this the austerity of one's practise comes to take on a self-punitive nature. Angry with oneself, one becomes more severe with oneself.

For those who have some insight into their dilemma, there may be the added problem of feeling guilty about feeling guilty or becoming irritated that one gets irritated. But insight is also the first step to resolution. The second step is to back off and relax a bit. As the Buddha said, the guitar string once too slack has now been wound too tight, and to produce harmony the tension must be relieved. For idealistic, moralistic personalities, letting go and relaxing are the very things that intensify one's guilt. Yet in principle this is much like what the Buddha did when he renounced austere asceticism and took up the middle way. The practitioner must stand back and re-appraise his whole involvement in Buddhism and examine the matter fully without fearing the consequences of his decision.

In evaluating progress at meditation it is important to distinguish between true Buddhist attainment and adaptation. Any human being (or for that matter almost any biological organism) when placed in a new situation goes through the process of adjusting, adapting, and growing accustomed. This is true of human life in general, and it is true of a man who takes the robes of a Buddhist monk. With the passage of time he grows to accept his role, to acclimatise, and to learn to "work the system"; he may become contented and happy by virtue of duration and age alone.

This process of adaptation is especially relevant in the case of intensive meditation practice where one may spend weeks or months confined to a small room, leaving that room only for brief meetings and instructions from the meditation master. In such situations the practitioner may get extreme feelings of peace and happiness, of clarity and alertness of mind such as never before seen, and also he may glimpse what appear to be transcendental states. (However, moments of depression, agitation, sobbing, etc., are also common, depending on the person.) Many who have completed such training have come away greatly impressed and highly praising this technique. However, it appears that all of these impressive subjective experiences vanish as soon as one comes out of cloistered isolation, and then, much like a drug experience, they remain only as memories. Moreover, many people who have "finished the course" appear to manifest the same selfishness and general human shortcomings as found in human beings picked at random. In addition, there is a hazard in that some "graduates" have revealed extreme pride relative to their attainment.

From this it should not be assumed that there is nothing to be gained from such intensive training. On the contrary, I have frequently suggested it to persons seeking competent meditation instruction. However, I do feel that the empirical evidence shows that for many if not most people this technique alone is insufficient. And the very facts of the Eightfold Path and the Buddhist scriptures in general support this thesis. Thus it would be wise to resolve one's mundane problems of social adjustment and other emotional conflicts before attempting more specialised practises.

Quite often a cloister which protects one from all forms of insults, humiliation, irritation, and anxiety may induce a false sense of attainment and lull one into complacency. We can confront and abolish our mental defilements only when they are actively alive in our minds. We cannot do this when they are but hazy memories or intellectually created notions. Consequently many practitioners have found that their progress is enhanced by having true life situations of social interaction and frustration. On the other hand, an excessive exposure to such interactions and frustrations may exceed one's ability for alert mindfulness, and one thereby insidiously becomes involved with the quarrels and fascinations that breed hatred and sorrow. When living in a cloister where no problems arise, one's defensive reactions and dispositions may lie dormant and thus remain hidden. But in ordinary lay life, temptations, sensations, and problems arise so fast that much of the daily routine is little more than a repeating pattern of perceive, react, and solve; perceive, react, and solve; perceive, react, and solve; and so on.

Thus for many practitioners the solution lies in a middle way between these extremes: that is, a situation in which one still has a moderate exposure to chores, annoyances, and social interactions, but this is interspersed with intervals of quietude and meditation. Such intervals may be a duration of hours or a duration of weeks, depending on individual needs and circumstances. Thus by maintaining an optimal amount of involvement with social and sensory arousal, such a one does more than just perceive, react, and solve. With mindfulness he is able to catch the perception and reaction as it arises. He observes it, scrutinises it, and evaluates it. In so doing, it may then be modified, abandoned, or developed as seen fit. He acts with mindfulness instead of on habit or reflex, and thus new responses and solutions may be learned. If (as some psychologists have claimed) one's personality is the sum total of one's perceptions, responses and reactions, then in this way the growth and development of the personality is possible.

The optimum proportion of time that one should spend in isolated meditation as contrasted with the time spent in more mundane pursuits will vary among different individuals. It will also vary according to the method of practice and with different times and stages of development for a given individual.

I state these above conclusions not only from a theoretical position and not just because they seem to be revealed in the life pattern of the Buddha and his disciples as portrayed in the suttas. My own limited observations of persons who appear to have progressed at Buddhist practice also fits this conclusion.

It is against such a background of observations and considerations that I have reviewed my own earlier writing on meditation. In essence these words still appear to be sound, and there are no statements that I would see fit to repudiate. However, I feel one point needs to be more strongly emphasised, and that is that a regular daily practice of meditation alone will not be likely to show results unless one is willing to thoroughly scrutinize his or her entire pattern of living and be prepared to revise or abandon this lifestyle if so indicated. In the same way one who undertakes Buddhist training as either a monk or layman would do well not to set a time limit and should not commit himself too strongly to future plans (such as "I will finish my university training" or "I will return to my homeland to teach the Dhamma"). For such a one has already decided beforehand just what he will become and thereby has limited the amount of change that he will allow himself to make.

Also (and partly as a result of Buddhaghosa's writings, i.e., the *Visuddhimagga*) I think I have emphasised too strongly the amount of breathing and other bodily-directed concentrations called for in beginning practice. I say this with some hesitation because it has become popular in some circles to completely disown concentration as important to Buddhist practice, and I do not agree with this view. But if one focuses exclusively on breathing, walking, or whatever to the point of blocking all thoughts and emotions, one is thereby turning one's attention away from the very mental defilements and neurotic conflicts that must be confronted in order to be overcome. Thus it is probably significant that in the Noble Eightfold Path right concentration follows after right mindfulness.

One meets a fair number of people who have (or at least claim to have) made considerable attainment at one-pointed concentration. Yet, with a few notable exceptions, they appear to be just as prone to selfishness and petty jealousies as any ordinary persons whom one might meet at random. Some in fact have shown themselves to be very unhappy, lonely, and/or insecure. On the other hand, persons who have made only slight progress at sustained concentration have, nevertheless, in the course of Buddhist practice, made considerable progress at diminishing conceit, resentment, depression, and selfishness. (However, the one person in my experience who, after months of close observation, appears to have made the greatest progress towards removing mental defilements of all sorts, is also the only person I know who appears capable of entering the third jhāna at will.)

The same is true of the labelling technique which is especially common in some forms of Burmese intensive training. With this technique one, who in meditation, finds himself daydreaming will simply note this and label it "imagining, imagining" or "fantasy, fantasy" and then return to awareness of breathing, body sensation, or whatever. However, daydreams and fantasies are most often an expression of our desires and emotional conflicts. If one examines the daydream in the frame of mind: "What does it express?" "What desire is it attempting to satisfy?" "What feeling does it carry?" then one can gain insight into his emotional needs and at the same time confront those same mental taints which meditation is supposed to overcome. The labelling technique is, of course, highly useful in dispensing with physical distractions such as itches, pains, and noises; and with certain types of moods (e.g., boredom) and certain kinds of memories. But it must be used judiciously; for if used exclusively it can retard progress.

A general rule of practice which many practitioners have used to advantage is as follows: One starts practise by attempting to quiet and concentrate the mind. But after some minutes of finding that the mind repeatedly wanders from its intended object, the practitioner then stands back as it were and asks: "Just what is my present state of mind at this instant?" "What is it that makes my attention wander from its intended object?" This then is analysed and confronted. In principle this is much like another useful technique which is: One does not choose any given meditation subject but instead simply sits and takes note: "What is my mental state now? What gross feelings? What subtle feelings? What memories and expectations? What intentions or desires?" In actual practice this is done not in the form of verbal thoughts, as expressed in the preceding sentences, but rather as a state of watchful observation with few if any word thoughts present. Quite often at such times one finds a subtle mental defilement which must be examined and discarded. That is the idea: "Now I am meditating and want to have something to show for it. I want something to happen." Or it may be: "I want to confront and overcome my anger, but now that I'm looking for it, it seems to have gone," and with this arises a feeling of frustration. Herein one has set a goal and been thwarted. Thus the desiring of this specific goal and its resultant frustration is the very state of mind that must be dealt with. Successful meditation requires catching the immediate present.

Finally a note about the attainments in meditation: unless one is very advanced, one does not expect or aspire to any new or unusual experience such as are known in ordinary life. Instead the attainments are negative ones and thus only seen in retrospect. For example, one suddenly reflects: "A year ago I was chronically depressed, unhappy, irritable, defensive. That rarely happens now. Such and such a thing used to upset me greatly. Now it happens and I hardly notice."

It may be stating the case too strongly to say that in meditation one seeks to gain nothing. For there is an increase in happiness and peace of mind. But when asked, "What have you gained from meditation?" the answer would be: "It is not what I have gained that is important but rather what I have diminished, namely, greed, hatred, and delusion."

ABOUT PARIYATTI

Pariyatti is dedicated to providing affordable access to authentic teachings of the Buddha about the Dhamma theory (*pariyatti*) and practice (*paṭipatti*) of Vipassana meditation. A 501(c)(3) nonprofit charitable organization since 2002, Pariyatti is sustained by contributions from individuals who appreciate and want to share the incalculable value of the Dhamma teachings. We invite you to visit www.pariyatti.org to learn about our programs, services, and ways to support publishing and other undertakings.

Pariyatti Publishing Imprints

Vipassana Research Publications (focus on Vipassana as taught by S.N. Goenka in the tradition of Sayagyi U Ba Khin)

BPS Pariyatti Editions (selected titles from the Buddhist Publication Society, copublished by Pariyatti)

MPA Pariyatti Editions (selected titles from the Myanmar Pitaka Association, copublished by Pariyatti)

Pariyatti Digital Editions (audio and video titles, including discourses)

Pariyatti Press (classic titles returned to print and inspirational writing by contemporary authors)

Pariyatti enriches the world by

- disseminating the words of the Buddha,
- providing sustenance for the seeker's journey,
- illuminating the meditator's path.

www.ingramcontent.com/pod-product-compliance
Lightning Source LLC
Chambersburg PA
CBHW020347170426
43200CB00005B/82
* 9 7 8 1 6 8 1 7 2 1 4 4 6 *